T0288014

Governor Lady

Missouri Biography Series
William E. Foley, Editor

Governor Lady

THE LIFE AND TIMES OF
Nellie Tayloe Ross

Teva J. Scheer

University of Missouri Press
Columbia

University of Missouri Press, Columbia, Missouri 65211
Printed and bound in the United States of America

First paperback printing, 2018

ISBN 978-0-8262-2180-3 (paperback : alk. paper)

Library of Congress Cataloging-in-Publication Data

Scheer, Teva J., 1950–
Governor lady : the life and times of Nellie Tayloe Ross / Teva J. Scheer.
p. cm. — (Missouri biography series)
Summary: "Story of Nellie Tayloe Ross, native Missourian and governor of Wyoming, vice chairman of the Democratic National Committee, and the first female director of the U.S. Mint"—Provided by publisher.
Includes bibliographical references and index.
ISBN-13: 978-0-8262-1626-7 (hardcover : alk. paper)
ISBN-10: 0-8262-1626-9 (hardcover : alk. paper)
1. Ross, Nellie Tayloe, 1880–1977. 2. Governors—Wyoming—Biography. 3. Women governors—Wyoming—Biography. 4. Democratic National Committee (U.S.)—Biography. 5. United States. Mint—Officials and employees—Biography. 6. Wyoming—Politics and government. I. Title. II. Series.
F765.22.R67S34 2005
978.7'033'092—dc22
2005020367

∞™ This paper meets the requirements of the American National Standard for Permanence of Paper for Printed Library Materials, Z39.48, 1984.

Typefaces: Middleton and Minion

To Kenneth

IN MEMORIAM

Contents

PREFACE

A Century of Change for Women

"DEAR MISS Ross," wrote a Wyoming junior high school student on the celebration of Nellie Tayloe Ross's centenary birthday, "you must be kind of proud of yourself because you've done so much for women's lib and everything."[1]

No doubt Nellie received this letter with her characteristic southern courtesy, but the truth is that she and her young admirer were living in different worlds. "I have no interest in women's lib," she said bluntly when asked about it in the early 1970s. "I've always thought candidates for public office should not be chosen on the basis of sex. Being a woman should not mitigate for or against someone," she told *People Magazine* the year that she turned 100.[2] In truth, Nellie *was* supportive of the advancement of women, but she believed that she could best serve that cause by demonstrating that she was an effective public administrator without specifically drawing attention to the fact that she was a woman.

When Nellie died the following year at the age of 101, the *New York Times* obituary described her as "ever feminine, never a feminist; a woman in politics who had not lost her womanliness."[3] Nellie's image as a dignified lady served her well in the male-dominated political world in which she made her career. Working-class women had always been present in the workforce, but when increasing numbers of upper- and middle-class women began to enter colleges and seek employment during the first decades of the twentieth century, many Americans became deeply concerned that women's emergence from the home would defeminize them. Their exposure to the "immoral" public sphere would render them coarse and mannish and make it difficult if not impossible for these women to lead "normal" lives as wives and mothers.[4]

Nellie's demeanor allayed those fears and helped her to be accepted and respected both by the male politicians who surrounded her and by the hundreds of wives and mothers in local Democratic clubs and organizations across the country who saw her as one of their own. Emily Newell Blair, who preceded Nellie as a vice chairman of the Democratic National Committee, said of her, "Few women have known more women or been beloved by so many. . . . Women recognize in her a woman who, when called on, can meet any and every situation with distinction, yet remain always feminine."[5]

Nellie Davis Tayloe Ross was not just a lady, she was a *southern* lady, born in the aftermath of the Civil War. Perhaps partly because the war destroyed so many other aspects of southern life and culture, the southern lady became a powerful cultural icon. She developed into a regional archetype who espoused similar values, outlooks, and comportment regardless of her state of origin. The ideal was that of a woman carefully self-controlled and discrete, adored by and dedicated to her children, loving and obedient to her husband, sensitive to the needs and desires of others, and pious, hospitable, and ever charming.[6] Underneath her gentle, defenseless demeanor, however, there often resided a will of iron. Southern women knew how to get what they wanted, directly if possible but indirectly if necessary. Nellie's character demonstrated all of these attributes. Nellie never let her devotion to her role as wife and mother, her deference to social propriety, get in the way of something she really wanted to do, but in the main, her comportment was ever faithful to her southern, Victorian upbringing. It is no wonder, then, that she rejected the label of women's libber. However, Nellie may not have recognized the dissonance between her stated devotion to her domestic role and many of her actions and decisions following William's death. Once she entered the public arena, her career and social life became at least as important to her as her family responsibilities.

Nellie Tayloe Ross portrayed herself as a wife and mother who had been thrust by circumstances into a career. And what a career it was! In 1924, following the death of her governor-husband, Nellie became the first woman to be elected state governor in her own right. Her Wyoming election, which was covered in newspapers from coast to coast, made her one of the most famous political women in America during the late 1920s and early 1930s. Following her defeat for reelection in 1926, she embarked on a career of writing and speechmaking on the national Chautauqua circuit. Al Smith appointed her vice chairman of the Democratic National Committee (DNC) in 1928. She was drafted to make one of his nominating speeches at the national convention that same year, and she even received thirty-one votes herself for the position of vice president.[7] She directed the DNC Women's Division for the next four years, and she helped to direct the campaign for the women's vote both in 1928 and 1932. In 1933, Franklin Delano Roosevelt tapped her to become the first woman appointed as director of the U.S. Mint. She was renominated to this post three more times by Roosevelt and Truman. In 1953, after having completed a full federal career of twenty years, she retired at age seventy-six. After retirement, she traveled widely and briefly lived in Spain. She took one grandson around the world when she was in her mid-eighties, and she was still traveling abroad in her late nineties.

Nellie was a tiny woman, just over five feet tall, with stunning blue eyes. In keeping with her ladylike style, she never discussed her age; even her official retirement record from the federal government shows her birth year as "18??." In her later years, Nellie's brown hair turned a striking white, and she had grown quite hard of hearing, but a great-niece remembers that well into her late eighties, she could still exhaust any walking companion on the streets of Washington, D.C. In public, Nellie was always impeccably dressed; but since she was also economical to a fault, she was ever on the lookout for a bargain on her clothes and her hats. Stories of her frugality, both in her personal life and as a government executive, are legion; affectionate anecdotes about Nellie's penny-pinching are a common thread in the stories told by anyone who knew her. But as one talks to her family and surviving friends, one is struck far more by the sense of loyalty, admiration, even awe that she seemed to inspire in all. "There was an up-on-the-pedestal feeling about her to me," noted one lifetime friend.[8] With everyone except perhaps her brothers and her sister-in-law Nelle, Nellie firmly maintained a reserve that may have fostered this sense of veneration; no one ever learned a scintilla more about Nellie's private thoughts or opinions than she intended to share.

Nellie was born into a world that was almost beyond the comprehension of the young Wyoming student who had sent her the birthday greeting. She was born in 1876, one hundred years after the signing of the Declaration of Independence, and she died in 1977 after witnessing the nation's bicentennial celebration. Her long and remarkable life exactly spanned the second century of the United States. She was reared in the Victorian era, when upper- and middle-class women were expected to be domestic, decorative, pious, and submissive, but she died as the woman's liberation movement was creating a multitude of opportunities for young women of the 1970s. She lived through the last years of the Indian wars, the Spanish-American War, World War I, World War II, the Korean War, the Vietnam War, and the Cold War. Her life spanned the administrations of twenty-one presidents. She experienced

Prohibition, the struggle for the women's vote, the Great Depression, and the Red Scare. She witnessed the civil rights movement through the eyes of a southern woman whose mother's family had owned slaves. She remembered life before the automobile, and she was already in her late twenties when Orville and Wilbur Wright flew their plane at Kitty Hawk. She was born the same year that Alexander Graham Bell invented the telephone, yet she was still alive to see the dawn of the information age. She was almost twenty when Guglielmo Marconi transmitted the first radio signal, but she lived to watch Neil Armstrong on television when he walked on the moon.

Given Nellie's extraordinary life and accomplishments, one is left wondering why and how history has neglected her. One historian has observed that the story of the first female governor in the United States "is a strangely forgotten episode in American history. . . . Her memory has virtually disappeared from our national consciousness. . . . The lack of library references to America's first actual woman governor in fact as well as name is appalling." When Ella Grasso was elected in Connecticut in 1974, for example, the national press declared that *she* was the first woman to be elected a state governor. This misconception is still commonly cited in historical reviews of women as governor.[9]

One Wyoming newspaper speculated in the mid-1970s that Nellie's lack of involvement in the women's movement was the reason that she has been ignored by feminists and by the substantial number of outstanding scholars in women's history.[10] It is true that Nellie was not a member of and did not aspire to be in the fascinating and powerful inner circle of feminists from the early FDR era. The two contemporaries of Nellie who left the most documentation concerning Democratic Party women of the 1930s, Eleanor Roosevelt and Mary Dewson, were hardly her fans. Roosevelt's and Dewson's papers have been pivotal to researchers interested in reconstructing the contributions of women to politics. What little Roosevelt and Dewson had to say about Nellie was generally dismissive, so it is easy to understand why she may have been ignored by the influential historians of the 1970s and 1980s who formed the core of the women's history movement.

As we enter the twenty-first century, in a time when American women are more generally accepted as leaders and managers, it is hard to imagine the degree to which Nellie was viewed as an anomaly when she was elected governor of Wyoming in 1924. Her election was a "sensation around the world," recalled a former secretary; press representatives from the nation's leading magazines descended on Cheyenne, and many of them stayed for her entire tenure.[11] The novelty of her electoral accomplishment opened doors for her after her defeat for reelection. Everyone in America, but especially women, wanted to see her and to hear what she had to say. Her gubernatorial status made it possible for her to establish a financially rewarding career for herself as a speaker and writer, and it also resulted in her appointments as vice chairman and Women's Division director at the Democratic National Party. But had she not demonstrated subsequent competence as a bureau director, she would never have been renominated for three more terms at the Mint.

Nellie began her public administration career at the very top of two organizations, both as governor and as director of the Mint, so she was unable to acquire leadership skills in the usual way—through trial and error while advancing through increasing levels of responsibility. Likewise, she lacked any formal education or training in business, government, or the law. She was forced, therefore, to rely on her instincts, intuition, and interpersonal skills to create her personal leadership style. Her management practices were astonishingly enlightened for her times; after all, she lived and worked during the period when Taylorism and the military model—bureaucratic organization, hierarchical structure, and a strict division between management and the worker—were being applied to state and federal governments. Nellie's management style was characterized by close personal relationships with some of her subordinates and an integrated approach to her staff as a whole; she demonstrated that she was concerned about and interested in their personal lives, not just their work production.

Nellie Tayloe Ross was a member of the first generation of female politicians and federal executives, but her background was quite different from that of her peers. The majority of women who were appointed in the 1920s and 1930s to bureau- or cabinet-level appointments had earned baccalaureate degrees or, in some cases, had completed graduate education. Women such as Frances Perkins, secretary of Labor under Franklin Roosevelt, and Mary Van Kleek, Grace Abbott, and Julia Lathrop, the first three women to hold federal bureau directorships, had all gained their early job experience in the settlement houses of large eastern or midwestern cities. Many of Nellie's peers had worked their way up through public and private social service agencies, at least partly because social work was a field that was open to women. Society accepted it as a logical extension of women's traditional concerns for the child, the family, and the community. Nellie's contemporaries were often single-minded in the pursuit of their careers. They chose to forgo marriage and family because it was almost impossible for a woman of their generation to balance a work life with a family. Nellie, on the other hand, was far more representative of the typical middle-class American woman. She lacked a college degree, and she spent almost twenty-five years as a wife and mother in Cheyenne before the death of her husband thrust her onto the political stage. She was clearly conscious that her fame and position had made her a pioneer for women, but she was no crusader, nor was she a workaholic.

Unlike her contemporaries who managed successful careers but neglected other aspects of life to do so, Nellie Tayloe Ross achieved a happy balance between work and home. She may have initially chosen a life of marriage and motherhood, but ironically, she ended up achieving the very modern feminine objective of "having it all"—a happy marriage, children, an active social life, and a distinguished career. One could argue that Nellie was more truly modern—and perhaps a more direct spiritual ancestor—of today's women than were the early social workers or suffragettes. Nellie managed to strike a balance between personal and business success that most American women today are still struggling to pull off themselves. Ever since the 1970s, when the women's movement and the economy drove the majority of American mothers into the marketplace, women have been struggling with how to balance a career with marriage, children, and personal interests. One need only flip through thirty years of *any* women's periodical—popular or academic, home-focused or career-oriented—to gain a perspective on how critical this dilemma is for us. "American women—can-do daughters of their country's optimism—still secretly nourish a poignant hope that there is An Answer to the dilemma of work and family," wrote a columnist in 2002.[12]

How Nellie balanced her role as wife and mother with a demanding career presents useful insights for the many young women who will be starting careers within the next decade. Part of Nellie's success in achieving balance had to do with chance and timing, but another part had to do with her extraordinary longevity. "Well, of *course* she managed to do it all," my husband observed at an early stage in my research. "She lived forever!" He was right. While Nellie did not begin her adult life purposely intending to "do it all," she ended up successfully managing a family, the governorship, lecturing in Chautauqua circuits, a role in national politics, and a Federal career because her life was divided into several distinct periods that allowed her to concentrate on and enjoy each aspect of her life *in turn*. I graduated from college in the early 1970s, and it was unthinkable to my peers and myself that we could not have it all, simultaneously. Looking back, I wonder how much we missed of our children's youth because of our unavailability as well as our sheer exhaustion. Given the long life expectancy of today's college generation and the significant career opportunities that the departure of the baby boomers should open up during the next twenty years, there is no reason that the young graduate of 2006 should not be able to consider Nellie's phased model as she begins to plan her own life.

I recently visited my daughter's college, where I treated her and five of her friends to lunch. With Nellie's life in mind, as well as my own experience as a professional working mother, I wanted to interview these young women about their personal plans and priorities. I learned that when it comes to hopes and dreams, little has changed from my generation to theirs. Each one of them, in her own way, wants it all—yet the prospects are daunting. A recent study of career women concluded that "the tough trade-offs faced by middle-aged women dog the footsteps of today's younger woman." In significant numbers, women who have postponed marriage and childbearing have run up against age-related infertility when they were finally ready to begin their families. The solution, writes the researcher, is that "timing is at the heart of the matter. If a high-achieving woman were to make finding a partner a priority in her twenties or early thirties, attaining both career and children would be a much less daunting proposition."[13] This was Nellie's life pattern.

During Nellie's lifetime, women experienced the greatest advancement in their rights and opportunities that the world had ever seen, and Nellie Tayloe Ross was a pioneering representative of that experience. Nellie's narrative, her environment, her life's circumstances, can be used as an example for exploring the social and cultural context that helped to create the modern American woman—the evolution from an undereducated, sheltered dependent to an individual generally accepted in the public sphere, to whom a universe of opportunities lies open.

"The term 'new woman' does not fall pleasantly upon my ears," wrote Nellie in the late 1920s, "for I do not think the so-called 'new woman' is as new as she seems. She is merely adjusting herself to the changing conditions of a new era. . . . What woman does want[,] and all she wants, I think, is better to meet the responsibilities that are essentially hers as a woman and at the same time to have a chance to develop the faculties with which she as an individual has been endowed."[14]

Acknowledgments

I HAVE BEEN both blessed and humbled by the support and involvement of innumerable family members, friends, and colleagues during my years spent researching and writing this book. At the top of the list are two individuals—my husband and a new friend. Despite the fact that my husband, Jon Scheer, concluded that I was certifiably crazy when I returned to school in my late forties for my Ph.D., his willingness to listen and to provide me feedback on my research hypotheses during the creation of this biography has been a constant comfort. Likewise, early in the process of research, I was extraordinarily lucky to find an old and dear lifetime friend of Nellie's, Kenneth Failor, who became a wonderful bridge to the personal and work lives of Nellie Tayloe Ross. Whether over a stiff scotch in person or just by phone, Kenneth was unfailingly supportive and enthusiastic in answering my unending questions. This biography meant a great deal to him, and I was devastated that he died just a few months before I would have been able to put a final copy in his hands.

I am grateful for the financial support of three grant programs, which helped to defray my travel and research costs: the Franklin Delano Roosevelt Library, the American Heritage Center of the University of Wyoming, and the Lola Homsher grant program.

I would like to thank M. E. Sharpe, Inc., for permission to adapt some of the material from my chapter-length biography of Nellie Tayloe Ross, "Feminine Pioneer: Nellie Tayloe Ross, First Woman Governor," in *Outstanding Women in Public Administration: Leaders, Mentors, and Pioneers,* ed. Claire L. Felbinger and Wendy A. Haynes (Armonk, N.Y.: M. E. Sharpe, 2004).

I would like to thank the many individuals who took the time to read and comment on all or part of the book's draft chapters, in particular Carl Cipra, who faithfully read every chapter twice! His support and his keen eye for editing details were invaluable. I also benefited from the input of Rick Ewig, director of the American Heritage Center, University of Wyoming; Carl Hallberg, reference historian at the Wyoming State Archives; Pat McLear, at Missouri Western State University; Harl Dalstrom, at the University of Nebraska at Omaha; Philip J. Roberts, at the University of Wyoming; and Edward Vela, Jr., Kaye Tayloe Collins, Robinette Ross, and William Bradford Ross III. I am also indebted to my professors at the University of Colorado's Graduate School of Public Affairs—particularly Peter and Linda de Leon and Richard Stillman—for their support and guidance.

Nellie's papers contain almost no references to the years before her 1902 marriage, so I was required to piece together the story of her family, her childhood, and her girlhood using census and court records, historical archives and newspapers from Missouri, Kansas, and Nebraska, and secondary sources. Many individuals helped me to identify and locate background sources or information on these early years, but I would like to thank the following individuals and organizations in particular. In Savannah, Missouri: Patrick Clark and Jean Smith of the Andrew County Museum. In Cloud County, Kansas: Terry N. Ferguson, the Cloud County register of deeds; Marilyn Johnston of the Cloud County Genealogical Society; and Sharon Haist of Miltonvale. In Omaha, Nebraska: Claudia Preddy, great-granddaughter of W. R. Davis and Harriet Green Davis, and Joann Meyer of the Douglas County Historical Society.

One invaluable resource was the collection of letters held by Kaye Tayloe Collins, great-niece of Nellie Tayloe Ross. Kaye shared with me letters that Nellie had written to her brother George, but also letters about Nellie that were written to and from George and his wife, Nelle Kreider Tayloe. She spent hours transcribing letters for me so that I could have access to them. I am very grateful for Kaye's support.

Finally, I would be disgracefully remiss if I failed to recognize the unfailing encouragement and assistance that I received from all of Nellie's direct descendants. In particular, I am grateful to William Bradford Ross III, the family "keeper of the flame." Without his support and his willingness to trust me in my portrayal of his grandmother, this project would have been far more difficult—indeed, perhaps even impossible.

Governor Lady

ONE

Missouri Roots

THE BURNING house, high on its promontory near the Missouri River, was visible for miles. A frightened seven-year-old Nellie Tayloe hugged her little sister Mattie and watched her parents and older brothers frantically toss buckets of water and beat at the flames with wet sacks. Nellie's clear blue eyes solemnly followed the white-hot tongues of flame as they darted upward, silhouetted against the black winter sky. The sparks shot up over her head like tiny fireworks, and the air was filled with the acrid odor of smoke as the fire destroyed her family's home.

In later years, Nellie almost never talked about her childhood, not with her children and friends, and certainly not with the many reporters who interviewed her. Based on the papers and records she left behind, it is almost as if her life began with her 1902 marriage to William Bradford Ross. Her brothers were just as tight-lipped about the early years as their sister. None of their descendants can recall the Tayloe siblings ever discussing their childhood. The memory of the burning house was so traumatic, however, that it was among the few stories of her early years that Nellie ever shared.[1]

Significantly, this pivotal early memory was one of loss. It was yet another terrible blow for Nellie's parents, James Wynns Tayloe and Elizabeth Blair Green. The lives that Nellie's parents had expected to lead had been destroyed by the Civil War and its aftermath. The war obliterated the family's way of life, and her parents' financial setbacks had an indelible impact on Nellie's character. Throughout her life, Nellie was obsessed with a fear of poverty. Even though she achieved relative wealth in her later years, her stocks and real estate failed to provide her with a sense of security. Monetary considerations motivated many of her decisions and remained a theme in her letters until the end of her life.

While the family's tragedies left psychological scars, the hard times also brought the Tayloe family together. Although it took the family a generation to recover from insolvency, the hard times also helped to make Nellie and her brothers resourceful. Their hardships forged some of the most important elements of Nellie's character. All her life, Nellie was intensely loyal to her family, and her devotion to her extended family was a pillar of her personality. "It will be a sweet memory to us always to look back over these past years of our lives—so full of varied experiences—how we shared all our hardships and all our joys—and how we loved each other always," Nellie wrote to her brother George shortly after her marriage.[2] Even though Nellie herself barely appears in this chapter of her family's story, the woman she became cannot be understood outside the context of her grandparents' and parents' experiences.

Nellie Davis Tayloe was born on November 29, 1876, on what was left of the substantial plantation that her maternal grandfather had established in Andrew County, Missouri, just outside St. Joseph. She was the sixth child and the first daughter of James and "Lizzie" Tayloe. Her parents had been struggling to make a living on the farm since their marriage in 1863. Strapped for cash and unable to pay their taxes, they were on the verge of losing their share of the family land when their house burned down. Following the fire, the Tayloes sold their acreage in March 1884, just before a sheriff's sale, and moved the family to Miltonvale, Kansas.[3]

James Tayloe never intended to be a farmer. Born in 1832 in Stewart County, Tennessee, where his grandfather had owned a large plantation and several slaves, James's life took a turn away from farming after his father died when he was five. When his mother remarried a few years later, his new stepfather, William Bailey, moved the family to southern Kentucky, where he worked for the Hillman Iron Works. William proved to be a loving stepfather to James and his two brothers. He treated James and his brothers with kindness and insured that they all graduated from school. After James graduated, William helped him get a job as a clerk in the general store that Daniel Hillman maintained to supply his workers. James later repaid William's kindness by naming his first son Wesley Bailey Tayloe. James spent two years working in Hillman's store before striking out on his own. Then, in the spring of 1854, at age twenty-two, he moved to St. Joseph, on the very edge of the nation's westward expansion, eager to make his fortune.

St. Joseph had been founded barely a quarter-century before James Tayloe's arrival. The city remained relatively small, if prosperous, until 1848, when gold was discovered in California, and fortune seekers began to stream through St. Joseph on their way to the West. It was the largest town on the western frontier, and St. Joseph's location on the Missouri River made it a natural gathering site for the traders, soldiers, settlers, and prospectors who were heading west. It was the spot "where for a generation the nation jumped into the awesome great west."[4] The city's farmers and businesses prospered from their sales of wagons, equipment, and provisions to the pioneers and to the military units that were scattered across the Great Plains.[5]

In St. Joseph, James Tayloe found a raw, bustling, noisy town, teeming with construction and commerce—a perfect place for a relatively well-educated, ambitious young man to build a career and make his fortune. He found work with a general merchandise establishment that supplied the growing population of St. Joseph as well as the pioneers and the army. New construction was going up on every block of St. Joseph as the town fathers, anxious to promote St. Joseph as a city of culture and wealth, engaged European architects to construct impressive commercial blocks, theaters, and other public buildings. Newly enriched bankers, merchants, and speculators built ornate and ostentatious mansions on the hills overlooking the commercial district.[6]

About 1858, James and two partners, J. W. Bailey and Thomas R. Smith, established a dry goods business.[7] Their advertisement in the St. Joseph city directory of 1859–1860 announced, "Bailey, Smith & Co., Jobbers and Retailers in Fancy Dry Goods. Silks, embroideries, white goods, millinery goods, gloves, hosiery, notions, &c., &c." In addition to running their store, the partners became involved in land speculation, both in St. Joseph and across the river in Kansas, and they also underwrote several mortgages during the late 1850s and early 1860s. One parcel of land that James owned was in Andrew County, north of St. Joseph, where he and another partner held eighty acres. Either in connection with this land or in the course of his St. Joseph business, James met Elizabeth Blair Green, called Lizzie, whose family held substantial land just south of his own in Andrew County.

Lizzie Green was the daughter of Amanda Davis Green. Together with her husband, Samuel Ball Green II (who had died by the time James met Lizzie), Amanda had been part of a great wave of immigrants into Missouri from Kentucky that began in the late 1830s and continued unabated for more than three decades. As of 1860, one out of every nine Missouri residents had been born in Kentucky, bringing with them the traditions and beliefs of the Deep South, including a favorable disposition toward slavery.[8] The Greens had arrived in Missouri by 1845, when Samuel purchased his first thirty-nine acres in Andrew County. They were among the earliest settlers in the southern end of Andrew County, whose first white residents had arrived about 1837. They found a fertile land, thick with timber and rich in game—bear, deer, wild turkey, other game birds, squirrel, rabbit, and a great variety of fish in the streams that fed the Missouri River.[9]

The Greens worked hard and prospered in Andrew County. Just one month after his first land purchase, Samuel began to buy up additional acreage two or three times a year, as nearby property became available. By 1850, when Samuel was thirty-five and Amanda twenty-five, they had amassed a small fortune in land and slaves. Their Missouri farm and home were valued at twenty thousand dollars, and Samuel also owned thirty-six slaves that were worth as much as his real estate.[10] Samuel had built a Georgian plantation house, considered to be among the finest homes in the County, on one of his farm's highest ridges.[11] From the house's front steps, one looked out upon Green family fields that stretched down to the Missouri River, a few miles away. Three children had been born to the Greens—Lizzie, born in 1845; Harriet, born in 1847; and Samuel Ball Green III, born in 1850.

The fact that Samuel and Amanda had achieved wealth and position did not mean that Amanda's life was one of ease. The larger the plantation, the harder the planter's wife had to work. Another plantation mistress wrote, "It is a great mistake to suppose that the mistress or master of a large plantation . . . lived in idleness. They were the busiest people I have ever known. How could it be otherwise when they had charge of a hundred or of several hundred human beings, who looked to them for everything?"[12] The plantation mistresses usually kept the plantation's keys and maintained the inventory of household goods. They kept a set of books to track household purchases and expenditures. They supervised the slaughter and dressing of hogs, the preparation of sausage, the milking of the cows, the making of butter and cheese, the preservation of fruits and vegetables, and the production of candles and soap. With the large number of persons living on the farm, the supervision of laundry was a major weekly task. The never-ending housekeeping was a particular challenge due to the ash and smoke from the wood fires in every room, the farmyard dirt that was tracked in constantly, and the daily cleaning and wicking of the kerosene lanterns.

Amanda took charge of the management of the entire farm whenever Samuel was away on business. In her own right, she probably supervised all the work of the slaves except for their fieldwork. Despite the common perception that a white overseer was responsible for managing a plantation's slave workforce, his presence was relatively rare; even on plantations with a hundred or more slaves, only 30 percent of plantation owners employed overseers.[13] Amanda was responsible for the health and welfare of the slaves as well as of her own family. She nursed the slaves when they were sick, she insured that the slaves had adequate clothing for both winter and summer, and she may have helped to sew the women's dresses and their household articles such as bedding. Amanda's labors were relatively pleasant compared to those of the family's slaves—but nevertheless, her work was never ending.[14]

Among Amanda's most important tasks was the educational supervision of any children who were at home, either directly or through a tutor or governess. She was also expected to see that her children received the proper foundation in religious and moral precepts. Child mortality was so high that there was a critical emphasis on their spiritual readiness to be received by God. Likewise, the short life expectancy of women due to illness and childbearing gave the task of insuring their children's salvation through Christian faith an urgency that could not be deferred.[15] In an 1841 treatise on the rearing of children, a female author wrote, "Do you ask, when shall we begin to teach our children religion? As soon as you see them. As soon as they are laid upon your breast. . . . As the infant advances in strength, its religion should be love. . . . Mother, if there is in your grave-yard one grave shorter than your child, hasten to instruct him in religion."[16]

Ironically, while Amanda's life was filled with responsibilities and toil, Lizzie's life until her marriage may have been one of ease and enjoyment. It was rare for the parents of girls in Lizzie's social station to focus on preparing their daughters to become plantation mistresses; instead, they educated their daughters in social graces and the liberal arts.[17] Scarlett O'Hara's carefree existence, depicted so memorably in the early chapters of *Gone with the Wind,* was an accurate portrait of the lives of most planters' daughters. Adolescence, that golden period in which a woman of the Southern plantation society could sleep late, gossip with friends, attend parties, and flirt with potential beaus, was sweet but brief. Most young women of this class married early, as did Lizzie, who married James Tayloe at age seventeen.

Many years later, James wrote in his memoirs, "My wife was educated in Richmond Virginia at a French school and was often at White Sulfur [Sulpher] Springs." The Missouri planter families believed in the value of education for their daughters because it prepared them to be better mothers and because the moral training that they received would improve their communities. A number of female seminaries were opened in Missouri. Although they did not offer the Latin and Greek that male institutions provided, they did offer the girls an opportunity to study English, reading, writing, math, and the sciences.[18] Although many of the female academies in central and western Missouri boarded young girls from the country, Samuel and Amanda chose instead to send their daughter east for her education.

It was not possible to determine the specific name of the "French school" that Lizzie attended in Richmond, for there were several schools of similar characteristics in Richmond during this period. Based on the still-existing Richmond school catalogs that list student names, most of the girls were from Virginia, but a significant minority were from other Southern states; in the years before the Civil War, a few even came from as far away as Canada or the New England states. The courses of study of these female academies were similar and were designed to produce young women of culture: English, modern languages, philosophy, music, drawing, decorative arts such as embroidery and painting, and a smattering of math and the sciences. Most of the boarding schools emphasized the practice of French during meals and leisure hours, hence James Tayloe's description of Lizzie's school as a "French school." The 1858 catalog of the Southern Female Institute, which was contemporary with Lizzie's school period, noted, "*Most particular* attention is given" to modern languages. "Two Parisian ladies, one of whom speaks very little English, reside in the family, and it is their special duty to converse habitually in French with the young ladies."[19]

The moral development of Lizzie and her peers was a priority for the female seminaries. Their purpose, according to an official of the Union Theological Seminary, was to produce "intelligent and useful members of society, and fit [young women] for happiness here and hereafter, . . . under the care of well educated men, whose high intellectual and moral attainments will qualify them to train and fit their interested charges for their responsible stations in future life." The 1858 pamphlet of the Southern Female Institute noted, "The boarders employ a portion of every Sunday in the study of the Bible, its Literature, and the Evidences of Christianity. Under proper restrictions, they attend such churches on Sunday morning as their parents or guardians prefer."[20]

James Tayloe's reference that Lizzie was "often at White Sulfur Springs" speaks volumes about the family's social level and speaks to his pride that he was able to catch this eligible young woman for himself. The "White Sulphur" was the preeminent place for Southern families to meet and socialize during the all-important summer season. Because the members of the Southern planter society were isolated on their rural farms and scattered across several Southern states, a primary purpose of the season at White Sulphur Springs was for the young men and women of this class to meet, court, and engage for marriage. The season was filled with a delightful succession of dances, teas, riding parties, and carriage rides, which provided ample opportunity to meet and assess prospective spouses. An early twentieth-century Southern writer noted,

> The life of the Southerner in the majority of instances was modeled after that of the English aristocracy. . . . The members of the governing families of the South had intermarried and were largely inter-related throughout the Southern country. I would say that the ruling families of the South did not number more than four hundred, and these were bound together in many instances by ties of close relationship, by blood, and by marriage. . . . So, if a member of [one of these families] came from under the shade of the hanging moss of South Carolina, from the cotton fields of middle Georgia, from the hemp lands of Missouri, or the corn and wheat plantations of Virginia, he was not a stranger, but was known and taken in to one or another of the circles of this great resort.[21]

It is unlikely, given the difficulty and lengthy duration of a trip between St. Joseph and western Virginia (now West Virginia), that Amanda or Samuel joined Lizzie at White Sulphur Springs, particularly since its season coincided with the growing season. It was a common practice, however, for parents to arrange for their sons and daughters to attend the White Sulphur Springs season in their absence—properly chaperoned, of course.[22] Lizzie had two uncles, James and Alfred Davis, who owned farms in Greenbrier County and who could supervise her activities at "the Sulphur." During the summer season of 1860, the summer she turned fifteen, Lizzie stayed with her Uncle Alfred's family. Alfred Ward Grayson Davis was a substantial landowner whose holdings were valued at seventy-seven thousand dollars, so there is little doubt that he and his family were welcome at White Sulphur Springs.[23]

While Lizzie was pursuing her education in Virginia, three more sons were born to Samuel and Amanda between 1850 and 1858—George, Alexander, and Alfred Duff. Then, just a few months after Duff's birth, Samuel died in October 1858 at the age of forty-three, leaving Amanda to manage the large farm, a workforce of forty-seven slaves, and six young children. He left his heirs a plantation house and a farm of more than twelve hundred acres as well as the slaves.[24] Samuel's livestock holdings were relatively modest: 5 mules, 15 head of cattle, 20 hogs, and 3 horses. The probate papers also listed five pages of accounts receivable, either for small unsecured loans, averaging about $150 apiece, or for payments due for the hiring out of Samuel's slaves to his neighbors. Samuel's slaves were valued, in total, at $28,200 or more, constituting over half of Samuel's personal property value.[25]

While the institution of slavery was morally reprehensible, one should keep in mind that Samuel and Amanda Green lived in a time and a society of different values and imperatives. The culture in parts of Missouri, including Andrew County, was just as Southern as in states like Maryland or Kentucky. Samuel was a Kentuckian and an enterprising capitalist in the finest American tradition. According to the prevailing Southern thought, to prosper as a large-scale farmer and hemp grower, he required the help of slaves. And at the social level of the Greens, it was expected that the family would maintain a retinue of black house servants.[26] As calls for abolition grew stronger, one of the most difficult problems involved compensation for slaveholders like the Greens, should their slaves, considered valued property, be freed. One Missouri historian has noted that "The destruction of slavery caused considerable loss of property for the ex-masters in Little Dixie. Many felt that they had been 'robbed.' "[27]

In 1860, Claiborne Fox Jackson, a man of strong Southern sympathies, was elected governor of Missouri. In his 1861 inaugural address, he declared that although he hoped the simmering controversy between North and South could be settled peacefully, he was fully prepared to lead the state into secession if the nation split over slavery. Jackson's statement ignored the fact that a majority of Missouri residents had made it clear that they were far more supportive of compromise than secession. As the rail lines began to replace the rivers for transportation of cargo, Southern ties through the port of New Orleans became less important than the Northern railroad routes to markets in the east. Missouri farmers and businessmen stood to suffer badly if Missouri seceded. In addition, Missouri would have been surrounded on three sides by Union territory—Illinois, Iowa, and Kansas—if it chose to secede. Not only was it likely that Missouri would find itself a bloody battlefield, but also its geographic placement would have facilitated the flight of Missouri slaves.[28]

After the Civil War began in earnest in April 1861, Northern and Southern partisans in Missouri formed militias. Governor Jackson appointed Sterling Price to head the Missouri State Guard. The War Department reassigned regular Union troops to the eastern theater of military operations, leaving the Union-supported Missouri State Militia, led by John M. Schofield, to defend the state. Missourians found themselves engulfed by lawless bands of locally mustered home guards who fought, looted, and burned in the name of protecting the Union. The "half-soldier, half-civilian" home guards fell outside the jurisdictional control of the governor; some were established under an 1861 order by General Nathaniel Lyon, commander of the Department of the West, to organize loyal citizens in order to insure the peace. Others were just neighborhood vigilante groups, organized to protect their own homes; these groups answered to no higher authority. The situation was complicated by the strongly pro-Union Kansas Jayhawks, who had been skirmishing with proslavery Missourians since the middle 1850s and who now crossed over the Missouri River to attack the border area, including Andrew County.[29]

By June, Schofield had issued an order that declared, "[All] rebels and rebel sympathizers [will] be held responsible in their property and persons for damages done by the guerrillas." They were fined up to five thousand dollars for every Union soldier or citizen who was killed or wounded, and any sympathizers would be forced to reimburse Union partisans in full for any damage to their property. The effect of the order was to polarize formerly neutral citizens whose sympathies were with the South.[30]

In an attempt to stem the violence, the provosts and military commanders forced thousands to take oaths of loyalty to the United States and, in many cases, to put up substantial performance bonds. The oath affirmed:

> I will bear true allegiance to the United States; . . . I will discourage, discountenance and forever oppose session, rebellion and the disintegration of the Federal union; . . . I disclaim and denounce all faith and fellowship with the so-called Confederate armies, and pledge my honor, my property and my life to the sacred performance of this my solemn oath of allegiance to the Government of the United States of America.[31]

People refusing to take the oath were either arrested or summarily ordered out of their homes and banished. Individuals who were found to have violated their oaths forfeited their bonds. Many had all their property confiscated, and some were shot. One observer recalled that in "many instances," Southern sympathizers were forced out of doors, whereupon their homes, "with the accumulated earnings of a lifetime, were burned before their eyes. . . . I remember having counted twenty-nine blackened chimneys which marked the spot where once stood that number of country homes."[32]

James's business, the partnership of Bailey, Smith and Company, had continued to grow and prosper with St. Joseph. He remembered, "We were doing a fine business until the Civil War, when each army and Jay Hawks were around us all the time and they robbed all the merchants and businessmen." In 1862, James was labeled a Southern sympathizer, banished from St. Joseph, and told that if he returned, he would be shot. James made his way to his mother's home in Kentucky, where he laid low for a year. However, his engagement to Lizzie brought him back by early 1863. "On my return to Missouri without permission I called at the Army headquarters and told the head officer that I had returned and was ready to be shot if he required it. He at once told me that if I took the oath of loyalty there would be no trouble. I took it for I was a loyal man yet sympathized with my people in the South."[33] He and Lizzie were married at Christ Episcopal Church, St. Joseph, on January 15, 1863.

One historian has written that the Civil War was "the sorriest chapter" in the history of St. Joseph.[34] The city had been settled by Southerners, who, at the time of the war, owned more than two thousand slaves worth about $1.5 million; thus, in addition to their heartfelt sympathies with Southern relatives and friends, they clearly had an economic interest in continuing the chattel slavery of black people. On the other hand, the city's mercantile roots had fostered a generally tolerant attitude toward settlers and businessmen from the North. After President Lincoln called for Missouri volunteers to defend the Union, the townspeople were tortured by their contradictory allegiances. When a group of Southern supporters tore down the U.S. flag, the mayor requested federal troops from Fort Leavenworth. Every time the Union troops left the town, rioting and looting by both sides ensued, resulting in the reestablishment of military rule. The result was that nearly every business closed down, employment disappeared, and property values declined precipitously.[35]

An early history of Andrew County recounted,

> During the years 1862–63, and a part of 1864, a reign of terror existed in Andrew County, the like of which the citizens pray may never again be enacted within her borders. Innocent men were shot down by unknown parties, and persons claiming to be Union men, who were really a self-constituted band of outlaws, rode the country at midnight, wreaking vengeance upon all persons suspected of being in sympathy with the Confederacy.[36]

Missouri suffered through the "most widespread, longest-lived, and most destructive guerrilla war in the Civil War." People stayed in their towns or on their farms, afraid to venture out, and many houses were deserted. Crops stood unharvested in the fields as slaves fled westward into Kansas and men joined or were pressed into the militias. Newspapers closed down or were burned out; two papers in Andrew County, the Southern-leaning *Northwest Democrat* and the Union's *Plain Dealer*, were destroyed. Armed men from both sides marched in the streets of St. Joseph and around the Andrew County courthouse square. Bridges and railroad tracks were destroyed. Trains and steamboats were robbed and fired upon. No taxes were collected, so no services were available from the civil governments. Inflation was rampant, but property values were in free fall. Banks suspended specie payment, and money was so scarce that postage stamps were used as currency. As one historian summarized, "Hardly any area remained untouched by the dislocations of war. In the rural regions, one never knew when he might be visited by guerrillas or militiamen with varying demands. Property was no longer sacrosanct, and life became cheap. Pillage and assassination were commonplace. The weekly press reported enough atrocities on private citizens committed by both sides to fill a long book."[37]

During the first two years of the Civil War, the number of runaway slaves increased markedly in Missouri, and Amanda Green, concerned about her investment, sent most of the family's remaining slaves to Mississippi, where she had an older brother. Amanda hoped that the slaves would be less likely to flee if they were moved into the heart of the Confederacy, far away from the tempting borders into Kansas and Iowa. Shortly after Lizzie and James married, Amanda and her oldest son, Samuel, left for Mississippi to check on the slaves. While Amanda was in Mississippi, she put James in charge of the plantation in Andrew County, leaving him to look after a few elderly slaves and her younger children. Lizzie's sister, Harriet, was already an adult, but the three boys were still quite young—George was ten, Alexander nine, and Duff five.

Despite his lack of farm experience, James and his small workforce labored to plant and tend the fields near the house. Of the Greens' one thousand acres, probably only about ten were cultivated in 1863, including seven of tobacco. It was a difficult period, because the Greens were known to be Southern sympathizers, and the Union proponents nearby were well aware that the Green house was always open to Southern soldiers. James did his best to keep a low profile that summer. Notwithstanding the unsettled conditions in Andrew County, the family made it through the growing season, unscathed by the violence and lawlessness that surrounded them. Even though he lacked farming experience, James was proud that he was able to have produced an excellent crop. In late August, the family and remaining slaves harvested the tobacco and looked forward to clearing a substantial sum.

On August 31, 1863, shortly after the crop had been brought in, the plantation was visited by a band of home guards, who had heard that Confederates were inquiring about the location of the Green house. The soldiers were believed to be from the Third Provisional Regiment, Enrolled Missouri Militia, which had been organized early in 1863.[38] By the fall, the regiment's commander, Colonel William Herren of Savannah, had instituted a campaign to rout out any ex-Confederate soldiers and Southern sympathizers. Under Order Number 24, these individuals were placed on the "disloyal list, and were afterward subjected to many abuses by returned Federal soldiers and others who assumed authority to 'suppress the Rebellion in Andrew County.' "[39]

The home guards ordered James and the Green family out of the home. They went through the house, torched the beds, and watched with the family while the house burned to the ground. Along with the clothes, furniture, and carpets, the fire destroyed the photographs, letters, and journals that documented the stories of Amanda's and Lizzie's lives.

Under the headline of "More Houses Burned," the Union-oriented *St. Joseph Morning Herald* noted on September 2,

> The residences of the widow Green and Mr. Speed Wilson, about four miles from this city were burned on Monday evening by a squad of soldiers. . . . These acts of incendiarism are becoming so frequent as to demand the serious attention of the Commander of this District. It is alleged, however, that Wilson and Mrs. Green are rebels, and we have no doubt of the truth of the charge. Wilson is said to have harbored and fed Joe Hart and his outlaws, and if this be true, his house ought to have burned with him in it.
>
> Mrs. Green's residence was one of the finest in the county, and her loss must be considerably over $5,000. The lady, if we mistake not, has not resided upon her farm for more than a year, and the wanton destruction of her property is an outrage which cannot be too severely condemned.[40]

As soon as they left, James fled down the hill to the slave quarters on the banks of a small creek. "At midnight, I heard soldiers coming, and fearing they had come to murder me, I tried to hide behind the cabin. When I heard a hundred guns lock with the command to halt! I had to stop and was told they were friends—had come to get my body, as other vandals had reported they killed me. I hardly know how to express my feelings at this day and hope no one of all my friends will ever have to go through so great trouble. This caused my wife to lose her health, which she never regained until 30 years after."[41]

The next morning, James abandoned the farm, his precious harvest, and the remaining slaves. He fled to St. Joseph, taking with him his new wife, the Green children, and Lizzie's maternal grandmother, Harriet Bragg Davis, who had been living with Samuel and Amanda on the farm. In somewhat of a quandary concerning what to do about the remaining Green slaves, who were reluctant to leave their home, James gave them two teams and wagons as well as food and supplies to last them several months, and convinced them to move to Kansas.

The newlywed husband suddenly found himself responsible for supporting his young wife, her grandmother, and her four younger siblings, but with no idea how to do so. Most of the St. Joseph businesses had closed. Then one day, on the streets of St. Joseph, James met a German immigrant named Andrew Herman, a Southern sympathizer, who was also looking for some way to earn his livelihood. The two men ended up striking a deal. James gave Andrew permission to live on the Andrew County farm, and Andrew agreed to pay James half of whatever he could raise from the farm. A week later, James and a bodyguard returned to the farm to see how Andrew was doing. Andrew had gathered in and sold the apples from the orchard for seven hundred dollars! For the next two to three years, the Tayloes and Greens survived by renting out the Green lands, too fearful to return to Andrew County themselves. Bailey, Lizzie and James's first child, was born in 1864 while the family was still living in St. Joseph.

In April 1865, Lee surrendered the Confederate army at Appomattox. The same year, Amanda Green returned from Mississippi. She had lost the last hope of conserving her investment in the slaves, and there was no longer any reason for her to stay. The wealth and possessions that she and Samuel had worked a lifetime to acquire, the house and household items that she had loved, and the lifestyle she had known as the wife of a Southern planter were all gone. When Amanda joined James and her children at their refuge in St. Joseph, she was a sick woman. James sent for doctors, and her daughters nursed her, but it was of no use; she died ten days after returning to St. Joseph, at the relatively young age of forty-one. Her mother, Harriet Bragg Davis, died the same year. They were likely buried next to Amanda's husband, Samuel, in the small family burial site that overlooked the Green fields, at the edge of Amazonia Road.

Amanda's death closed the door on any hope that James may have had of resuming his mercantile partnership with J. W. Bailey. As the husband of the eldest daughter, James found himself responsible for rearing the younger Green children and dealing with the Green estate. After negotiating with the Republican court, James was able to get himself named executor of the Green estate and guardian of the Green children by posting bond of an almost impossible twenty-five thousand dollars. By 1865, there was little left of the Green estate except for the land and several hundred dollars in debts. James and Lizzie built a frame house near the foundations of the burned-out mansion. While James took up farming, his old partners in the J. W. Bailey Company rebuilt the business into a prosperous dry goods store that operated in St. Joseph at least through the mid-1880s.

By 1867, all the older Green children except for Lizzie began to sell off their shares of the family landholdings whenever they needed to raise money. The farm was shrinking in the same piecemeal way it had grown under their father. Samuel Green was still living with James and Lizzie in 1870, and the two men were together farming the remaining pieces along the southern border of Andrew County. Harriet Green married a first cousin, W. R. Davis, and the two settled on an adjoining piece of land with Harriet's and Lizzie's brother George. However, by 1872, they had apparently decided that they could do better for themselves in town. Harriet and W. R. sold her share of the land and moved into St. Joseph. By 1873, W. R. Davis and Sam Green were partners in Davis and Green, a lumber business, and Sam was boarding at their St. Joseph home.

As the other Green siblings gave up on the farm and moved into St. Joseph, James and Lizzie stayed on. James became the local justice of the peace for Jefferson Township, earning the honorary title of judge, by which he would still be remembered fifty years later.[42] Between 1866 and 1874, four more sons were born to James and Lizzie: William Alexander, Samuel Green, James Wynns Jr., and George Green. In 1876, the year that Nellie was born, an assessment list of personal property estimated the value of the Tayloe family's personal property at only $369.

After the war, Missouri farmers like James Tayloe produced more food than ever before, but the prices they had to pay for seeds, implements, machinery, and any household items the family could not make were higher than ever. Beginning in 1860, American farmers' income began a steady decline that lasted until the 1890s. The federal government had financed the Civil War by issuing approximately a half billion dollars in paper money not backed by coin. In 1866, Congress authorized the gradual retirement of these greenbacks, and in 1873, it demonetized silver. The nation was firmly back on the gold standard. But the same year, a default in railroad bonds resulted in the Panic of 1873 and the subsequent failure of eighteen thousand businesses. While the nation suffered through a decade-long depression, western farmers fought unsuccessfully for a reduction in the high tariff rates and an expansion of the money supply. By 1878, the circulation of greenbacks had dropped by $150 million from Civil War levels. To Missouri debtor families, this meant that their obligations had to be repaid in dollars that were considerably more valuable, as well as harder to come by, than the currency with which they had incurred their debts.[43]

After the Civil War, whites in Missouri and elsewhere in the South gave the Democratic Party their fervent allegiance. The western and southern wings of the party battled the high railroad rates, protective tariffs, and a national monetary policy that penalized farmers and favored eastern financiers. Democrats claimed that the Republican Party's constituency consisted of fabulously rich eastern money interests, who sought to centralize power in the federal government, thereby destroying states' rights and individual freedom.[44] Given Nellie's Southern heritage and her memories of the family's economic troubles on the farm, it was only logical that she remained a Democrat her entire life. The ideal of limited government, which during that period characterized the Southern Democratic Party, remained an important theme for Nellie. A pamphlet she prepared in the late 1920s for the Democratic National Party reflected her belief that these principles should remain the core of the party's philosophy.[45]

Nature also played a role in the tribulations of James Tayloe on the Missouri farm. On August 8, 1874, great clouds of Rocky Mountain grasshoppers invaded Andrew County. The farmers watched in trepidation while the swarms continued to pass overhead for several days. As James and the other farmers pondered how to protect their ripening crops, the grasshoppers passed out of the county. But enough of them had landed in the area to lay millions of eggs. The following April, when the grasshoppers began to hatch, they were so numerous that they covered every inch of ground, a horrible, crawling mass that devoured crops, pastures, and trees. James's crops as well as his apple harvest were decimated. James and his neighbors worked until the Fourth of July, planting corn, millet, and vegetables to replace the lost wheat crop. The weather that summer of 1875 was favorable, and the replacement crops were bountiful—but they were so abundant that prices dropped to the extent that most Andrew County farmers were barely able to break even.[46]

As the pampered daughter of a prosperous planter, Lizzie Tayloe was totally unprepared for the life of a poor farmer's wife. Even if the family had still been prosperous, girls from Lizzie's class usually married too young to have acquired household management skills. "They went to their marriages still firmly identified with the role of daughter. No wonder, then, that they found the new responsibilities of household mistress bewildering."[47] If this was true for a young woman who married into an existing plantation, with black servants who could help her to master the house's routine, it must have been doubly overwhelming for Lizzie, who had to start from scratch, in a new home, with no hired help and no mother or other maternal relatives to help her.

It is unlikely that Lizzie had any hired help during the early years on the farm, although she did have one servant by 1880.[48] Although Lizzie had suffered from poor health ever since the home guards had burned down the plantation house, she nevertheless managed a heavy load of household chores, which probably included tending a kitchen garden, raising chickens, churning butter, making cheese, and drying fruits and vegetables for winter use. With the help of the men and her children, she hauled up to two hundred gallons of water from the well each day for cooking, cleaning, and laundry. The laundry itself, which generally took at least one day for washing and another for ironing, probably consumed almost one-third of Lizzie's work time.[49] Lizzie had the constant task of feeding the fire for cooking and hot water; she prepared three heavy farm meals each day and baked the family's bread. She may have made the family's candles and soap, too, since money was scarce. Many farmwives also sold butter, eggs, and honey to bring in cash for the family. During planting and harvest, they helped out in the fields.[50] And finally, they bore and raised children. Lizzie bore eight in all. In 1873, she also buried two of them, seven-year-old William and two-year-old James. In 1880, Lizzie's second daughter, Hattie Green Tayloe, called Mattie, was born. The family's final baby, Alfred Duff Tayloe, was born in 1882.

Because of the joint efforts necessary to run the farm, Nellie began life in a family where a genuine economic partnership existed between husband and wife. Furthermore, on the nineteenth-century, unmechanized farm, *every* family member above the toddler age had to pitch in and do his or her part to help make the farm a financial success. Although she was too young to be conscious of the fact, in her early years Nellie experienced a true working mother who was substantially contributing to the family enterprise. One anthropologist has pointed out that on farms at this time, the necessity of sharing the work load "overrode the political and economic factors that subordinated women. . . . These wives found a distinct rural reality in which they could define equality on their own terms."[51]

Nellie always idolized her older brothers, who were unfailingly caring and protective of her throughout their entire lives. They helped Nellie's mother teach Nellie to read when she was barely five, and she loved to read with them during her earliest years.[52] In the fall of 1883, when Nellie was six, she started her formal education at the Maxwell School. With her brothers Sam and George, Nellie walked the two miles from the house to school and back. Her teacher at Maxwell, Frank Reno, remembered her as "one of the brightest and sweetest children I ever knew, in or out of the school room. . . . In the many years I taught in [the area], I don't recall any pupil for whom I felt more of a personal attachment than little Nellie Tayloe."[53] Teachers of that period often spent the night in the homes of their students, and Mr. Reno recalled frequently staying the night at the Tayloe home.

During the years that James and Lizzie spent in Andrew County, the family attended the Jimtown Methodist Church, just a few miles from the farm. James Tayloe had been reared a Methodist. His mother was a "devout Christian [who] belonged to the Methodist church [and] raised all her children to observe all the rules of the church."[54]

> Training the young, Methodists agreed, belonged in the private sphere of life. This was a sphere that Methodists, along with other Evangelicals, shaped and sacralized as the realm of heavenly homes, saintly mothers, and impressionable children. Methodist leaders assumed that children would be taught the Bible and Christian attitudes by their parents. The home was to be "a little church" in which children and young people learned the moral values of Christian citizens.[55]

Southern Methodists had broken away from other American Methodists in 1844 over the slavery issue, and the Jimtown church was Southern Methodist.[56] The Southern Methodists had transitioned from an English-style liturgy in their services to informal preaching, lay ministers, and open-air revivals. Unlike the Calvinist Presbyterians and Congregationalists, who believed that an individual's state of grace depended wholly on God's initiative, the Methodists believed that it was an individual's personal responsibility to accept or reject God's offering of grace. Acceptance of grace came through a continuous process of seeking God's forgiveness and demonstrating one's devotion through piety and good works. Also, the Methodists were more accepting of an active role for women than the Calvinists or Episcopalians; Methodist women were given leadership roles in Sunday schools, benevolent associations, and missionary work, and they were even occasionally invited to preach, read sermons, and address revival meetings.[57] This moderate acceptance of a public role for women, as well as the emphasis on personal responsibility that underlay the sermons Nellie heard each Sunday, reinforced the lessons she was learning at home.

By 1877, James Tayloe had fallen behind in his taxes. Taxes were a postwar scourge for cash-poor Southern families. One Louisiana matron wrote,

> [A]t present we are living at as little expense as possible with no perceptible income. We are taxed according to the ante-bellum tax lists—including our slaves and property swept off the earth by the armies. A fine sugar estate, near us on the river, worth two hundred thousand dollars, was sold last week for taxes, which were seven thousand five hundred dollars. The whole estate—land, dwelling, sugar house, stock—brought only four thousand dollars. There could scarcely be completer confiscation than these unrighteous tax-sales under which millions of dollars worth of property are advertised for sale.[58]

James was hopelessly behind on his taxes by 1881, when he was still trying to pay off his 1877 tax bill.[59] The Tayloes carried on until the winter of 1883–1884, when a defective flue caused the disastrous fire that Nellie remembered so clearly as an adult. Several factors probably led them to give up the farm. They may have feared that the unpaid back taxes would cause them to lose the farm. They also had a heavy mortgage on the land, and they may have been having difficulty paying the mortgage notes. Harriet and W. R. Davis had decided to make a new start in Miltonvale, a small Kansas town just being established, and they may have urged the Tayloes to join them. A doctor had advised James to move Lizzie to a different climate for her health. A move to Miltonvale, where Lizzie would no longer bear the heavy responsibilities of a farmwife, would have provided Lizzie a much easier life.

James cleared over $1,500 after paying off the mortgage on his farm. Using the proceeds, James was planning to go back into merchandising. He had visited Miltonvale, assessed the business opportunities, and decided to open a grocery store. Lizzie was comforted by the thought that she would have her sister's family nearby, but she grieved that she was leaving behind the graves of her parents and two little sons.

Before the Tayloes left Andrew County, the neighbors held a farewell reception for Judge Tayloe and his family that was attended by the families from miles around. Forty years later, the Tayloe family was still remembered as "one of the most prominent and highly respected in the Maxwell community."[60]

TWO

Prairie Girlhood

THE TAYLOES arrived in Miltonvale full of hope for a prosperous future, and their optimism was more than matched by the dozens of other new residents who were arriving in town each week. "We know of no other town in the State that has brighter prospects for future success and prosperity than has our own little city," wrote the local newspaper editor the year that the Tayloes arrived.[1]

Miltonvale owed its existence almost entirely to the railroad. As soon as bridges were constructed across the Missouri River, railroad companies began to lay tracks to the west. Milton Tootle, a St. Joseph businessman who owned several acres in north-central Kansas, was eager to maximize his Kansas real estate investment. He proposed to the Kansas Central Railway the establishment of a railroad town on eighty acres of land, and he sweetened the deal by offering the railroad the deed to every other lot in town.[2] As soon as the town was platted in November 1881, Tootle issued ten thousand dollars' worth of railroad bonds to pay for the construction of a narrow-gauge track between Leavenworth and Miltonvale. Only five months later, the first train pulled into the Miltonvale station, whistle blowing, to the cheers of the town's new residents.

Miltonvale was an overnight success. One of the first settlers described the site as "just one lone tree and a water hole," but less than a year later, Miltonvale boasted fifty homes and stores, including a bank, a lumberyard, two drugstores, a hotel, two livery barns, four grocery stores, and a hardware store.[3] Up and down the formerly empty streets, crews were throwing up houses as fast as they could, but not fast enough to meet the demands of the newly arriving settlers. In 1882, the *Miltonvale News* noted that "the hotel is so rushed that a body can hardly find his place at the table," and that "every carpenter and mason and painter in Miltonvale is being driven to his utmost capacity now-a-days." The following spring, the newspaper editor worried, "there is a great need of more buildings . . . Rent is too high. There is not a single residence in the town but is occupied by one or more families. There is not a single room upstairs to let but what is taken as soon as it is completed, and still others are inquiring constantly for houses to live in."[4]

The entire state of Kansas was booming. Between 1870 and 1880, the state's population grew from 364,400 to 996,100, and this pace of increase continued well into the 1880s. Farm families were pouring into the state, attracted by the fertile soil and the reports of ample precipitation. During the late 1880s, rainfall in central Kansas was at or above the mean, and local farmers were harvesting bountiful crops. The railroads and land promoters were promoting a theory that the settling of the prairie and the planting of trees and other vegetation would result in favorable, and permanent, climatic change. In 1881, the year of Miltonvale's founding, Cloud County, Kansas, received over eighteen inches of rain, and the prices for corn and wheat reached their highest point since 1865. In the general mood of contagious optimism, it was easy to forget that crop failures had been widespread just one year earlier, when less than ten inches of rain fell on the area.[5]

The population boom was also supported by the nation's recovery from the Panic of 1873. By 1877, eastern financiers were looking for new investments. The land boom in Kansas seemed like a wonderful opportunity to realize fabulous profits by financing mortgages. Since the mortgage companies were earning high interest rates on their money, they could afford to overlook the security of those loans. The price of lots in prairie towns soared far beyond the province of mere appreciation into the dominion of hopeful illusion. Caught up in dreams of future wealth, farmers as well as townspeople were using borrowed money to buy more land and equipment. Between 1880 and 1887, the mean per capita mortgage debt more than tripled. By 1890, there was an average of one mortgage held in Kansas for every two men, women, and children.[6]

Attracted by the prospect of these seemingly limitless opportunities, James Tayloe and his family arrived in Miltonvale in March 1884 and took up temporary residence with Harriet and W. R. Davis and their two daughters,

Minnie and Grace. W. R. had already opened a bank on the town's principal commercial street, and James had decided to open up a grocery store.[7] By the first week of April, the Tayloe family had settled in, and George and Nellie had enrolled in school. Nellie's first reporting period at the end of the second week showed that she had earned a 97 in reading, a 95 in spelling, but only a 60 in arithmetic.[8]

While Nellie and George were settling in at school, James's two eldest sons—Bailey, nineteen, and Sam, sixteen—were helping their father start his business. On April 18, James purchased property from his brother-in-law at the corner of North First and West First streets and set up his new store, which he named the Red Front Grocery. His first business announcement appeared in the May 15 issue of the *Miltonvale News,* and by July, he had begun to run large display ads in most issues. Both he and W. R. were aggressive advertisers during their early years in Miltonvale. "The election is over, let us have Peace, Prosperity, and Plenty of Trade," proclaimed a Red Front Grocery banner ad on November 27.

Tragedy marred the Tayloe family's first Christmas season in Miltonvale. Little four-year-old Mattie Tayloe had seemed in perfect health on Christmas Day, and she had experienced a wondrous holiday season—she was just old enough to look forward to gifts and holiday festivities, but not too old to have lost her belief in Kris Kringle. Two days after Christmas, Mattie developed a severe case of the croup. Lizzie nursed her around the clock, but there was nothing that could be done. The devastated family gathered around her bed, watching Mattie's little chest heave and listening to her wheezing and gasping for breath. Shortly before five in the afternoon on December 29, she asked for her papa to pick her up, and then she slipped away.[9] It was Nellie's first experience of losing someone close to her.

The Tayloe family may have lived behind or above the store during their first two years in Miltonvale, or perhaps in rooms at the crowded hotel. However, James's business was doing very well; the *Miltonvale News* estimated in May 1887 that the Red Front Grocery had grossed over three thousand dollars during the previous two weeks. In February 1886, James purchased two residential lots at the corner of North First and Church streets, two blocks down from the family store, and began construction on a substantial two-story home of about eight to ten rooms. The house's wraparound veranda led into double parlors, which featured high ceilings and tall Victorian windows. A large dining room completed the public rooms on the first floor. The interior wood trim was decorated in the latest fashion: faux finishes that simulated ash, maple, and other grains. Five bedrooms and another veranda were located on the second floor. The house was completed around January 1887. In March, the Tayloes graded and landscaped their yard, planting tree saplings on the barren land. The same year the Tayloe house was completed, James purchased a team of ponies and a new buggy.[10]

Since there was no Southern Methodist church in Miltonvale, the family began to attend the United Presbyterian Church.[11] On February 18, 1886, James, Lizzie, and Nellie formally joined the Presbyterian Church, along with W. R., Harriet, and Minnie Davis. In March 1888, James was elected a Presbyterian ruling elder, and in May 1889, he was appointed chairman. By August 1889, both James and Bailey were representing the Presbyterians at a local Sunday school convention of all Miltonvale churches. James's civic activities extended beyond his superintendency of the Sunday school; he was elected second vice president of the Miltonvale board of trade in February 1887, and he was elected to the city council in April 1889. In a town that was ferociously Republican, James continued his active support of the Democratic Party; in an 1887 Democratic caucus meeting, he was elected chairman of the delegates to the county convention.[12]

While James was busy establishing his store and participating in civic affairs, Lizzie finally had time to lavish on her children and her lovely new house.[13] James had hired a twenty-year-old female servant to live in with the family shortly after they arrived, and although Lizzie was still actively involved in labor-intensive housekeeping chores, her burdens must have seemed comparatively light after the heavy labor she had endured on the farm.[14] Relieved of the economic partnership that she had shared with James on the farm, Lizzie could concentrate on making her home into that peaceful haven from the world that represented the Victorian ideal. It was the era of "separate spheres," which lasted from approximately 1840 to 1890, during which women of social status generally confined themselves to the private sphere of home and family while their menfolk claimed the public sphere of community affairs, political involvement, and economic activity.[15]

During the long, cold winter nights, the Tayloe family gathered together for warmth and cheer around the coal-burning stove in the kitchen. "Dependent on their own talents and interests for their evening entertainment, people experienced family intimacy later lost in an age of central heating, electric lights and television," wrote one historian of the nineteenth century.[16] The family members likely took turns reading aloud from the

Bible, the local newspaper, and whatever classics the family owned or borrowed from the town's Free Reading Room, while Lizzie and Nellie occupied themselves with the never-ending task of sewing and mending.[17] Lizzie made sure that all her children absorbed a solid grounding in the Bible. Nellie's son would later describe the enduring effect of these amusements: "My uncle George, when he used to come visit, and my mother would vie with each other in quotations from the Bible and Shakespeare, trying to outdo each other reciting quotations. . . . I couldn't give you a quotation if someone asked me now, but they could quote whole passages."[18]

Lizzie also made sure that Nellie learned to play the piano. There was a music teacher in Miltonvale, but it is possible that Lizzie herself taught Nellie to play. Nellie must have enjoyed the piano and practiced diligently, because when the family later moved to Omaha, Nellie became a music teacher. Years later, when she lived in Washington, Nellie still loved to gather her friends and family around the piano to sing carols and other old-fashioned tunes at Christmas.[19]

Miltonvale gave the Tayloe family their happiest years together. Lizzie's health had improved as a result of the move to Kansas, James's business did well during the early years in Miltonvale, and the family had far more time for leisure activities than they had on the farm. The Tayloes were among the social leaders in the town, and on at least two occasions, they hosted large society balls that featured music, dancing, and good food. "The attendance was large and our leading society people participated in the pleasures of the occasion," wrote the newspaper editor. "The best of order prevailed . . . and the management [was] all that fashion or etiquette could demand."[20]

People in Miltonvale before the turn of the century had to make their own fun, and the local paper was full of news about birthday parties, community suppers, songfests, theatricals at the local opera house, picnics, fishing parties, and church activities.[21] Horseback riding parties were popular in Miltonvale. Nellie's brother George owned two horses, and it was in Miltonvale that Nellie developed her love of riding; one article of the *Miltonvale News* mentioned that she had taken a fall while riding across the prairie.[22]

Although she was Presbyterian, Nellie was an active member of the Epworth League, a social group sponsored by the Methodist church. For one program, Nellie played the piano, at another she sang a solo, and at a third, she delivered the opening scripture reading.[23] When a local Sunday school organization formed another group called the Loyal Legion, Nellie was appointed to its program committee.[24]

It was all very well for Nellie's brothers to participate in community organizations, but the family hesitated about the propriety of permitting Nellie the same freedom. Other than in church-sanctioned activities, Nellie's parents were reluctant to allow her to perform in public. Many years later, Nellie told a Girl Scout troop in Wyoming that the family was scandalized when she begged to be allowed to play a horn in the local girls' band. "I remember distinctly what a ripple it caused in our family, and though reluctant consent was given, I always had the feeling that I had strained the proprieties to the very limit in going into that band."[25]

As she reminisced about the band, Nellie emphasized to her young audience how much life had changed for girls since her own Victorian childhood in Miltonvale:

> Even when I was a young girl many of the activities and pleasures, which are now considered most wholesome and proper for girls, were looked upon with a good deal of disapproval. The violent sports, for instance, which bring the ruddy color to your cheeks and the springiness to your steps, would have been scarcely considered lady-like. So-called refinement suggested [a] dependent, clinging vine, delicate type of girl, who has in this generation been completely eclipsed by the rollicking, rosy faced, buoyant spirited girl, whom we all admire. My, aren't you glad you didn't live in that day when any departure from old traditions was likely to shock somebody's sensibilities?[26]

Even though Lizzie Tayloe had been able to discharge the arduous physical tasks of a farmwife for over a decade, her husband remembered her as having suffered from broken health during most of her marriage. Likewise, although Nellie lived to be a vigorous 101 years old, family members remembered her as a sickly child.[27] The actual or perceived poor health of Lizzie and Nellie was part of a much larger trend. By the 1880s, the American upper and middle classes had become increasingly alarmed about the general state of health of the American woman.

Contemporary writers suggest that the late nineteenth-century increase in female fragility and delicacy can be attributed to an unfortunate and dangerous fad: Victorian society had equated poor health and nervous disorders with true femininity. It had become fashionable to be ill. Lizzie's and Nellie's generations also lived during a transitional period; most women of their class had lost their economic role, but few were encouraged or were brave enough to pursue higher education or a career. Many headaches, nervous conditions, and delicate constitutions were probably due to boredom and depression. "Dependence and powerlessness . . . had a physical cost," observes one feminist historian. Illness offered these "angels of the house," who were charged with continually sacrificing their own pursuits and interests for others, a socially sanctioned opportunity to be pampered and indulged, to be the centers of family attention.[28]

Another Southern woman from Lizzie's generation who shared Lizzie's relatively high level of education wrote in her diary after the Civil War, "I feel sometimes such an impatience of my life and its narrow lot as I can scarcely describe. I want to go and see something better than I have ever known. . . . I want to go, to take wings and fly and leave these sordid occupations. . . . I think sometimes it is cruel to cultivate tastes that are never to be gratified in this world."[29] Lizzie could also have decided to give herself up to boredom and inactivity; however, she chose a different path. In addition to her teaching responsibilities at the Presbyterian Sunday school, Lizzie became a founding member of the Miltonvale chapter of the Women's Christian Temperance Union (WCTU) in 1888.[30] Both James and Lizzie, therefore, became role models for Nellie; their examples taught her that she had a responsibility to contribute not just to the well-being of the family, but also to that of the larger society.

Founded in 1874, just two years before Nellie's birth, the WCTU rapidly grew into the largest organization of women in the nineteenth century. The organization was born in the Protestant American churches, where many women had already found a role in missionary societies or, as in Lizzie's case, in Sunday schools. It enjoyed wide support across denominational lines: Methodists, Presbyterians, Baptists, and Lutherans as well as Quakers, Unitarians, Episcopalians, and other, smaller groups. Ninety-four percent of the members had been born in the United States and were of English, Irish, or Scots ancestry.[31] By the 1880s, chapters of the WCTU could be found in thousands of small towns and large cities across the United States and its western territories, and by 1890, it boasted a total membership of almost 150,000 members.[32] Because it had its roots in church activities, which were considered to be an appropriate outlet—or even a duty—for upper- and middle-class women, the WCTU drew thousands of women to take their first steps into the public sphere. The WCTU members have been called "biblical feminists" by some writers. They believed that they had the right to agitate in the moral struggle against the evils of alcohol because the doctrines of their churches, which held them accountable for their deeds and actions, meant that they were equal with men in the eyes of their Lord.[33]

Whereas enlistment in the much smaller suffrage movement required a woman to readjust her conception of her proper place, temperance placed her under no such philosophical burden. "This new activism did not for most [women] result in a . . . new view of the female temperament or women's sphere. They still accepted women's role as one of nurturant domesticity. They wielded power, but their conceptions of what women could do did not immediately change to fit this new-found power. . . . The WCTU was a 'safe' women's movement."[34] It gave purpose and meaning to women who were searching for a larger role than wife and mother.

The WCTU was organized in Kansas as a statewide organization in 1878, just four years after its national founding. In 1880, Kansas became the first state to vote on an amendment to its constitution prohibiting alcohol.[35] In 1881, the state legislature began to write a bill to implement prohibition; the new law, the Benson Act, went into effect on May 1, 1881, just before the town of Miltonvale was platted. When Lizzie's Miltonvale WCTU chapter was founded, it had no need to demonstrate against the public sale of liquor because the new town had no saloons; the chapter was involved, however, in support for women's suffrage. In 1887, the legislature enacted a law that granted Kansas women the right to vote in municipal elections, largely as a result of WCTU lobbying.[36] Following the passage of the suffrage law, the regular WCTU column in the Miltonvale newspaper declared,

> There is nothing but illusion in the expressed fears of some persons that to make voters of women is to unsex them. In all local affairs of a social or religious nature women are the best workers and they are the best planners. . . . Did any woman ever lose the love of her husband, the esteem of the community, or her own self respect by doing work of that kind? Women are just as much interested in good government as men are, and they have quite as clear a conception of what ought and what ought not to exist, in the community or the state, as men have. . . . A woman that is fit to have the care of a family is fit to have a voice in the government of a community.[37]

Although Lizzie's chapter was nominally involved in support for women's suffrage and enforcement of the Benson Act, in the main it appears to have been a social group. Just the same, it did provide leadership opportunities for the prominent women in the city. Following the first municipal election in which Miltonvale women could vote, the newspaper observed, "Among those who voted we noticed the representatives of the best families in the city. . . . Carriages were running all day carrying the ladies to and from the polls."[38]

For her part, Lizzie presided at chapter meetings, she represented her chapter at the 1887 county convention, and she researched and delivered papers, including one on "the Progress of our Cause" and another on the organization of the WCTU.[39] Thus, Nellie had the opportunity to observe a mother who demonstrated leadership for women, but always within the careful bounds of socially accepted activities. She also observed that it was possible for a woman in a leadership position to retain the respect and approval of her husband. "She was a great temperance worker," James proudly remembered.[40] Throughout her later life and career, Nellie adopted her mother's model in reconciling a woman's traditional role with her public responsibilities and leadership opportunities.

On Christmas Day 1888, James presented his wife with an extravagant gift—a pair of $150 diamond earrings.[41] The couple celebrated their twenty-sixth wedding anniversary the following month. It is unlikely that James shared with his wife the fact that the family was living above its means. Either the grocery store was not doing as well as reported in the *Miltonvale News,* or business had dropped precipitously as the Miltonvale economy had begun to falter. Perhaps James himself was ignoring the truth, but just three months before James gave Lizzie her new earrings, the family home had been assigned to the Miltonvale State Bank for $13.17 of unpaid taxes. The family's happy times in Miltonvale were almost over.

One year later, on Christmas Day 1889 and exactly five years after they buried little Mattie, James and his children attended Lizzie's funeral at the Miltonvale Presbyterian Church. The winter dampness had settled in the Miltonvale hollow, and Lizzie had fallen ill early in December. By mid-December, she appeared to have improved, but on December 23, 1889, she succumbed to what her obituary called typho-malaria. At the funeral, the church was overflowing with Lizzie's friends and neighbors. Her Sunday school class of little boys sat together in her honor as the choir sang, "We Shall Meet beyond the River."[42] The family buried Lizzie in the Miltonvale cemetery, on a quiet hill overlooking the town. To her right were two matching gravestones, one for her daughter Mattie and another stone, perhaps only commemorative, for her two little boys who had died years before in Missouri.

In later years, Nellie said that the worst day in her life was the day that her mother died. Even though her mother died when Nellie was barely a teen, she always thought of her mother as the greatest influence in her life. Before she died, Lizzie pulled Nellie close to her and said, "Nellie, never fear. Because after I die, I will always be with you and I will always be your guardian angel." And until her last moments, Nellie was comforted by the sense that her mother was nearby.[43] Lizzie's husband mourned, "Her loving kindness and true love of her children no one could excel. . . . I am rejoiced to say not one of her children have forgotten the Christian teaching of their dear mother."[44] And Nellie, who taught a Bible class in her later years and who faithfully attended her parish church until her death, never did.

Nellie's brothers, whom she adored, did everything they could to protect and support her following the death of their mother.[45] Among the few anecdotes that she shared about her girlhood, Nellie told a story about her teenage years that illustrated Sam's paternal treatment of his younger sister.

> I think of the teenage-age [years] . . . as the time of my life when I knew more than I have ever known since. I was most positive in my opinions, and ever ready to proclaim them, on weighty subjects, from which older and wiser heads might well have backed away. I must have been quite insufferable.
>
> Early in my teens I was vain as a peacock; [I] loved pretty clothes. Even yet I can see myself decked out and feeling very grand one fine Sunday morning in a new blue silk dress, velvet trimmed. . . . My observant grown-up brother, evidently feeling that his motherless little sister needed "taking-down" a bit, proposed that we take a walk. A-walking we went and every step of the way he lectured me roundly, pouring into my ears the theme "pretty is as pretty does." Take me down he did!
>
> As to the strong opinions I used to hold and voice so blithely, time and experience have had a very modifying influence upon them and has tempered the assurance with which I gave expression to them. The years have taught me that almost all of the great questions, vital to us, admit of varying points of view.[46]

Although James's grocery business may have continued to be profitable as late as 1887, Miltonvale had actually begun a long slide into economic depression starting in 1886. The crop yield that year was moderate, but the high average temperature hurt the condition of the grazing fields. Cattle went into the winter, which turned out to be brutal, in less than prime condition. By spring, what was left of the herds was sacrificed to meet the payment demands of insistent creditors. The relentlessly hot weather of 1886 was repeated in 1887, and the harvest was almost a total loss that year and in 1888.

In 1889, local farmers harvested a record crop of corn, but to no avail. James Tayloe recorded, "I have seen corn so abundant that it was used for fuel."[47] The *St. Louis Globe Democrat* of October 20, 1890, noted, "Corn dropped to 20 cents a bushel at [the county seat of] Concordia, Kansas, the corn center of the nation, due to an oversupply of the crop coupled with a shortage of hogs and cattle to eat it. Some farmers didn't even bother to crib the corn." In Miltonvale, about thirty-five miles from Concordia, corn was selling for ten cents a bushel.[48]

Dozens of farmers in the Miltonvale area, burdened with excessive mortgages, either lost their farms outright or were forced to sell them for next to nothing because the bottom had dropped out of the real estate market. The countryside that had once been dotted with farmsteads, two to a mile, began to depopulate, and so did the town. In 1886, at its highest population point in the nineteenth century, Miltonvale had an estimated 770 residents. It shrank to 616 in 1887, and to 419 by 1889.[49] In its misery, Miltonvale had a lot of company. Hundreds of little towns in Kansas and elsewhere in the arid Midwest were decimated by the loss of their residents or were even abandoned totally. In the late 1880s and early 1890s, roads across the prairies were crowded with penniless, hungry families in wagons with "In God we trusted, in Kansas we busted" chalked on the side.[50] Some of them were heading farther west, while others were returning to the more hospitable regions of the eastern farmlands.

Duff Green, Lizzie Tayloe's and Harriet Davis's brother, came to Miltonvale to visit with his wife in July 1890. Duff had established a prosperous real estate and loan business in Omaha, while the family's Miltonvale businesses were both failing. During his visit, the Davis, Green, and Tayloe relatives grappled painfully with plans for the family's future. When the Greens returned to Omaha, Nellie's brother George went with them, since his prospect of working at W. R.'s bank had evaporated.[51] He moved in with his Uncle Duff and his Aunt Margaret and got a job clerking at the Merchant National Bank.[52] Nellie's brother Sam had already left for Texas to read law with his uncle, George Davis Green. W. R. and Harriet moved to Omaha sometime in 1891, where Harriet's brother Duff gave him a job as a loan collector.

After the Davises left, James and his children Bailey, Nellie, and Alfred were the only family members left in Miltonvale. The Tayloes held on until the spring of 1892 so that Nellie could graduate from Miltonvale's high school; the town had shrunk, and the class was so small that only four other girls graduated with her.[53] The Tayloes were still living in their home, but James had failed to redeem the mortgage by paying the tax bill, so in February 1892, the bank sold the home. James lost his business to another tax sale the same year. Even though Nellie could observe that many Miltonvale families were sharing the Tayloes' misfortunes, the loss of the family home and the humiliation of business failure must have stung.

The *Miltonvale News,* which itself went out of business less than a year before the Tayloes left town, delivered the chronicle of the dark times just as it had the prosperous ones. "Several of our citizens expect to emigrate to Oregon in the spring. . . . Take our advice, all ye who are contemplating a change, and 'look before you leap,'" warned the editor. In another issue, while reporting on a particularly busy day, the paper noted wistfully, "Saturday was full of life; crowded streets; busy clerks in stores, and everybody happy reminded us of the good times that were." In 1889, a departing merchant used the *Miltonvale News* to say goodbye to all his friends and customers: "Away out in the Territory of Washington my wife and I shall often revert to the kindness, the generosity, the unselfish consideration experienced at the hands of the good people of Miltonvale."[54]

The Tayloe family returned to the bluffs of the Missouri River. They moved into a neighborhood of modest Victorian bungalows just south of the downtown Omaha area. Their status was respectable, but they were in no position to enter Omaha's social circle. During their ten years in Omaha, they moved frequently from one rental house to another, but they always stayed within a few blocks of the Davises and the Greens. Harriet continued to be closely involved in the rearing of her niece and nephews, particularly Alfred, who was about ten when the family moved to Omaha.[55] When James and his remaining children arrived in Omaha, George, who was working at the Merchant National Bank and living with his aunt and uncle, moved back in with his father and siblings. Bailey got a job as a laborer at the Chicago Lumber Company, and Nellie helped the family finances by hanging out a shingle as a music teacher.[56]

When James left Miltonvale for Omaha, he was sixty years old. Stepping in yet again to help his sisters' families, Duff Green offered James a clerical position in his business where, except for brief ventures into real estate or loans, James continued to work for ten more years. Miltonvale had been his last opportunity to make good in a business, and it had also been the site of his second and third experiences with mortgage default. In his life, James enjoyed the most important of life's blessings: caring parents, a happy marriage, and children who loved him dearly. However, he was never able to achieve sustained success in commerce. Both in postwar Andrew County, Missouri, and in drought-beset Miltonvale, James had endured more than his share of bad timing, but it also seems probable that James simply was not a good businessman.

James and Lizzie Tayloe had moved to center stage in the family history when they took over responsibility for the family farm in 1863. Now it was the turn of Nellie and her siblings. Of the five surviving Tayloe siblings, four went on to become extraordinarily successful. Two, including Nellie, became respected public servants, and Nellie became one of the most celebrated women of her generation. Two others founded a company, achieving the business success that always eluded their father, and became very wealthy men. The last sibling was struck down by disease and was gone within ten years.

As Nellie matured during the Omaha years, so did the nation. With its release of the 1890 census, the Census Bureau announced the closing of the American frontier. Westward and eastward expansion across North America had met in a still thinly populated middle, thereby extinguishing the distinct line of settlement that had formerly characterized the edge of "civilization."[57] When the Tayloes moved from the family farm to the small town of Miltonvale and subsequently to the medium-sized city of Omaha, they were participants in the first wave of an enormous demographic trend in which Americans moved off the farm and into towns and cities. Ever since the nation's founding, the percentage of population that lived in urban areas had steadily increased. In the 1870s, the decade of Nellie's birth, rural areas accounted for 74.3 percent of the nation's population. By 1890, two years before the Tayloes moved to Omaha, the percentage of population in rural areas had dropped to 64.9 percent. In 1850, only one American city boasted a population of five hundred thousand or more, but by 1900, three cities had populations exceeding one million.[58] As thousands of small towns competed for population and commercial investment across the heartland, winners like Omaha began to grow into true urban areas. Between 1880 and 1890, Omaha's population of 31,000 more than tripled to about 102,500.[59]

By the 1890s, the Jeffersonian ideal of a republic of self-sufficient yeoman farmers and independent merchants was being supplanted by the reality of an industrial powerhouse in which an ever-growing proportion of workers was employed in impersonal factories and firms. Historian Mark Sullivan, who was born just two years before Nellie, described the fundamental changes that were taking place in American society, and his description summarized the decline of Miltonvale as well as the failure of James Tayloe's grocery business. The nation, wrote Sullivan, was experiencing a painful process of

> little shops closing down, big factories growing bigger; little one-man businesses giving up, great corporations growing and expanding; rural communities becoming stagnant, big cities pulsing forward; farm districts thinning out, cities growing denser; fewer shopkeepers able to buy where they would, more compelled to take what a monopoly gave them, and at a monopoly's price; fewer craftsmen, more factory operatives; fewer workers known by name to their employers, more carried on big factory payrolls as numbers.[60]

But for the Union Pacific Railroad, the squat, ugly little settlement of Omaha might have gone the same way as Miltonvale during the 1880s. In the late 1850s, it had been just one of many river towns vying for riverboat traffic, and it trailed behind its much larger and more prosperous neighbor, Council Bluffs, Iowa, on the other side of the river. However, the railroad line between Chicago and Council Bluffs, paired with a terrain west of Omaha that was favorable for the laying of the transcontinental railroad, insured the town's future prosperity. Nevertheless, Omaha was hit hard by the drought years despite the presence of the Union Pacific Railroad. Omaha's population stagnated, and it was not until near the end of the decade that Omaha again began to prosper.[61]

Even during the economic slowdown, the contrast between Omaha and Miltonvale was stark. The Miltonvale business district comprised less than four blocks of small businesses, and the store owners knew all their customers personally. Except for Saturdays, when farming families came to town, filling the streets with their wagons and buggies, the shopping district was comparatively quiet. By comparison, in Omaha's bustling and much larger downtown center, most owners and customers were strangers to each other. Along the river, industrial chimneys punctuated the skyline, while to the south, a gritty commercial district sprawled near the Tayloes' neighborhood. South Omaha was home to an enormous railyard and numerous warehouses for wholesalers who used Omaha as a distribution and shipping center. The city had dozens of boardinghouses to serve the transient laborer population as well as significant numbers of gambling dens and houses of prostitution. One historian described nineteenth-century Omaha as "a town neither pretty, nor clean, nor safe, nor well-governed, nor chaste, nor sober, nor particularly honest, nor 'good' in any moral sense."[62]

Omaha gave Nellie her first exposure to the American melting pot. Of the city's estimated 102,500 residents in 1890, about one-third were foreign-born, living in small, ethnic neighborhoods. Rudyard Kipling passed through in 1889 and formed a biased impression of a town "populated entirely by Germans, Poles, Slavs, Hungarians, Croats, Magyars, and all the scum of the Eastern European States." At the national level, fourteen million immigrants, primarily from southern and eastern Europe, flooded the American job market between 1885 and 1910. The Tayloes benefited from this labor source; sometime in the late 1890s, they were able to hire a serving girl who had emigrated from Germany about 1897. The immigrants were good for the economy because they insured a continuous supply of cheap labor, but they were bad for the native American worker because they depressed the value of real wages. Their customs, languages, foods, and clothing, so different from those of the mainstream, made them targets of fear and mistrust.[63]

The Tayloes moved in 1898 to a rowhouse on Mason Street, where James and his sons remained until around 1905. In order to supplement the family income, the Tayloes shared their home with a family of boarders—a traveling salesman named Alfred Sidwell, along with his wife and two children.[64] The Sidwells became friends as well as boarders; Margaret Sidwell, who was sixteen years older than Nellie, helped Nellie and the servant with cleaning and cooking, and she may even have become her confidante and substitute mother. They were among the guests that Nellie invited to her wedding just a few years later.[65]

The Omaha years gave Nellie her first experience in juggling the demands of work and home. Despite the presence of a servant, Nellie was ultimately responsible for the family household management. "The woman who employs one maid-of-all-work, and then demands that she shall be a superior cook, laundress, waitress, parlormaid, and chambermaid, is an impossible mistress to suit," opined one advice book of the 1890s.[66] There was simply too much housework for one young woman to handle alone. Nellie's task of balancing her homemaking responsibilities with finishing her education, teaching private students, and eventually managing a full-time teaching job was different in character, but just as difficult, as that of the twenty-first-century working woman. On one hand, Nellie had a full-time servant; but on the other, she lacked most modern labor-saving devices, and she was housekeeping not for one family, but for two.

While living in Omaha, Nellie reached marriageable age. Since no prospective husbands presented themselves during this period of her life, she began to look around for something to occupy her time. In the 1890s, school districts were actively recruiting women as schoolteachers because the men of moderate educational levels who previously had been attracted to the occupation had turned instead to better-paying jobs in the expanding commercial bureaucracies. Many cities, including Omaha, had established their own programs for training teachers. Omaha started its program in 1891, just one year before Nellie graduated from high school and moved to town.[67] The programs were designed primarily for young women who had completed at least a grammar school education. Some teachers were as young as sixteen, although teachers in cities such as Omaha were generally in their early twenties when first appointed.[68]

Teaching and nursing were the two professions open to women at the turn of the century, even if they were not yet considered to be professions. They were honorable occupations for a woman of Nellie's class, especially since they could be thought of as an extension of a woman's responsibility—nurses cared for the sick, while teachers nurtured children. Also, the nation's continuing preoccupation with morality in both pedagogy and curriculum acted to the benefit of women who were seeking employment as teachers; "school boards adhered to the symbol of woman as the paragon of moral virtue in their preferential recruitment of female teachers."[69]

Omaha and other school districts gave first preference to local residents, so Nellie knew she had an excellent chance of obtaining employment when she finished her two-year course. Teaching salaries were low—and lower for women than for men—but a teaching position nevertheless gave Nellie the opportunity to earn more than teaching the occasional piano student. The average monthly salary for a male schoolteacher in Nebraska in 1895 was $44.18, paid only during the months of the school season. Nebraska's female schoolteachers that same year averaged $38.66—about 15 percent less than the men.[70] Teaching meant that Nellie could contribute a larger sum to the family income, but more importantly to a woman who had been a helpless bystander during the family's economic misfortunes, it gave her a measure of control over her own financial well-being.

In light of the educational and certification requirements to become a teacher in the twenty-first century, it is curious to look back on a time when college training was not yet considered a mandatory prerequisite for schoolteachers. As late as 1910, only 5 percent of teachers throughout the United States had education beyond the high school level. The average length of a young woman's teaching career in the prairie states was estimated in 1905 as less than four years—exactly the length of Nellie's tenure—after which most women married and resigned or were terminated. Therefore, it made little sense for a school district or for the teacher herself to invest substantial sums in her academic preparation. Nevertheless, teaching constituted one of the largest segments of employment for women. About 8.8 percent of all Nebraska women taught during some portion of the 1890s, and teachers constituted over 16 percent of all employed Nebraska women between 1890 and 1895.[71]

A 1901 group photograph of some of Nellie's fellow teachers at a Nebraska summer institute creates a compelling picture of her own character as a turn-of-the century teacher. Sixty serious but pleasant-looking teachers focus on the camera in front of them. The women, almost all of them dressed in long, dark skirts and starched white shirtwaist blouses with tiny neckties, appear strong, proud, and direct. Their hair is uniformly pulled up and back in conservative style. Almost all are very young. More important than their youth, however, is the air they exude of professionalism and enthusiasm. These women and their peers helped to educate the generation that brought up their own children during the Great Depression. Despite the teachers' youth, their lack of academic preparation, and their short tenure, they and their peers did a superb job in educating the citizens of Nebraska. By 1900, the rate of illiteracy in the prairie states of Kansas, Iowa, and Nebraska had dropped below 3 percent, the lowest in the nation.[72]

As far back as the colonial period, the original purpose of community schools was not to create critical thinkers but to insure that American children could read their Bibles.[73] Well into the Victorian era, the religious and moral instruction of children continued to be an essential justification for public education. By the 1880s and 1890s, however, fundamental changes in American demographics and in its social and economic systems had produced a different educational imperative—that of creating literate constituents who were capable of discharging their responsibilities as citizens in a democracy. Public schools could not only speed the assimilation of immigrant groups, but also provide American businesses a supply of educated workers for occupations that required mental proficiency as well as muscle. Public schools also provided a path for upward mobility for the brightest members of the working class, who might otherwise become involved in strikes and labor unrest, so it provided an escape valve to help prevent a future revolution. Leading educators like John Dewey and Horace Mann viewed the classroom as a laboratory in which students could learn and practice democratic principles as they absorbed the value of American patriotism.[74]

At no level of education was this new educational priority more evident than at the kindergarten level, where Nellie earned her four years of teaching experience. Kindergartens first developed in Germany early in the 1840s and 1850s, but they did not catch on in the United States until the 1870s, when they were seized upon as a tool to help acculturate lower-class and immigrant children. Along with lessons on their shapes, colors, and letters, the teachers imparted liberal doses of Anglo-Saxon morality and values to their small charges.[75] Not only would the children's chances of success in primary school increase as a result of the kindergarten experience, but also the children could act as an important Americanizing influence on the adult family members at home. There were only about ninety-five kindergarten classes operating in the United States in 1875, but by 1890, there were approximately five thousand.[76] Given the large influx of immigrants to Omaha, the establishment and support of kindergartens in Omaha schools was a given. Nellie was on the front line of this Americanization initiative, since one of the schools where she taught was in Omaha's Little Italy and another was in the Polish neighborhood.[77]

Nellie's four years of teaching helped her develop skills that were critical to her future career. She experienced, from the inside, how hierarchical organizations work. She reported to a principal, who both established school policies and transmitted school district goals and directives from the superintendent. As she observed how her principals supervised her—the positive and negative aspects of their management styles—she also learned how to supervise and direct her students. She learned how to work as a team member with the other teachers, both the ones she liked and the ones she found difficult. The lesson plans that she developed gave her a foundation for developing work plans later as a governor and bureau director. She began to develop public speaking skills, and she learned how to attract and hold the attention of an audience; after all, if one knows how to keep a room of five-year-olds focused on task and on topic, how much harder could a state legislature possibly be?

Nellie was far too intelligent for these important workplace lessons not to have had their impact on her expertise, so one is left asking why, in later years, she never credited her teaching experience as a foundation of her work skills. It is certainly possible that, for whatever reason, she simply did not consider teaching to be an important ingredient in her success. A more likely possibility, however, is that the portrait of a woman governor whose sole training had been as a wife and companion made a much better story. Nellie's official biography began to be written during the gubernatorial years, but it was honed during her Chautauqua and political periods, when her life story became a marketing tool for her speechmaking and writing career. With the help of her advisors and the Chautauqua promotional machine, as well as reporters (whose primary goal was to create the most compelling story possible), the "official" Nellie Tayloe Ross biography, a careful combination of fact and omission, took on its final shape. Just as the official biography glossed over Nellie's teaching experience, it also emphasized her patrician genealogy and inferred a wealthy Missouri childhood. The formative years in Kansas and Nebraska received barely a mention.[78]

While Nellie was completing her education and starting a teaching career, her brothers George and Alfred were acquiring the commercial expertise they needed to found a company. Both George and Alfred began their careers with a series of positions as clerks, copyists, and bookkeepers. By 1901, George had gone to work at the Carpenter Paper Company as a salesman; Alfred joined him at Carpenter in 1903. By 1904, they had decided to found their own paper company, and they moved to Memphis, where they would not have to compete directly with Carpenter. George, who married a young woman named Nelle Kreider in 1905, stayed home and ran the Memphis office, while Alfred, who did not marry until 1917, went on the road to sell. By around 1906, James Tayloe had followed his sons to Memphis, and he alternated living with George and Nelle in Memphis and Sam and his wife in Texas until his death in 1920. The Tayloe Paper Company struggled during the Depression, but it eventually became enormously successful.[79] The brothers' wealth made it possible for them to help Nellie financially during the periods of her marriage when money was tight.

Nellie's eldest brother, Bailey, was already twenty years old when the family left their Missouri farm. In order to help his father during the difficult years on the farm, it is likely that Bailey had discontinued his education before graduating from high school. He was too old to return to school in Miltonvale, and besides, his father needed him at the store. Although his three younger brothers had attained the education they needed to progress in the business world, Bailey was never able to advance in Omaha beyond positions as laborer and watchman. Of all the Tayloes, James's elder son was the one most harmed by the family's economic misfortunes. Perhaps because of his poor prospects, Bailey never married. Then in 1896, when he was thirty-two years old and still living at home, he contracted a severe case of paralysis, probably polio. Since all the other members of the family were working outside the home, they were unable to provide Bailey the intensive nursing care that his condition required, so they found him a place at the Sisters of Mercy Hospital across the river in Council Bluffs, Iowa. There he remained for two and one-half years until he died in January 1899. On January 23, George made the sad trip back to Miltonvale with Bailey's body to bury him next to his mother and siblings. None of the other family members attended the burial. True to her disinclination to discuss the past, Nellie never mentioned Bailey to any of her grandchildren.[80]

During the Miltonvale years, Nellie had had the opportunity to take several short trips by train. She made a few visits to her relatives near St. Joseph, accompanied by her father or aunt, and she joined her cousin Minnie on a trip to Plattsburg, Missouri. After Sam Tayloe moved to south Texas, George took Nellie down to visit their brother. It is likely that these short excursions merely honed a yearning for travel that had been with Nellie her entire life. Nellie had probably been dreaming of a much bigger trip since she was a little girl. With her love of reading, the more she learned about the great cities and monuments in Europe, the more she longed to see them herself, and she had probably been talking to her family for years about her dream to visit Europe. Sometime around 1896, when she was twenty, her older brothers surprised her with a ticket to Europe by steamship.[81]

With the improvements to sea travel made possible by the introduction of steamships, thousands of Americans each year flocked to the shores of Europe on sight-seeing expeditions during the last decades of the nineteenth century. By 1875, more than one hundred "steam palaces" belonging to Cunard and eleven other lines were shuttling Americans across the Atlantic. As the number of female travelers swelled, the steamship lines introduced innovations and amenities designed to attract this new market. The ships featured beautifully appointed public rooms, ceilings of stained glass, and comfortable chairs finished in silks. Likewise, the private staterooms were decorated with an eye to pleasing a lady. Thomas Cook and other travel agents introduced relatively inexpensive package tours that provided women a quasi-chaperoned experience and gave them a welcome sense of security for their overseas adventures.[82]

Despite her burning desire to see Europe, it must have been a daunting prospect to travel alone across the United States and the Atlantic Ocean, and even more so to manage the logistics of travel—unfamiliar languages, strange lodgings, foreign currencies. Even though more and more American women were venturing to Europe on their own, it took no small courage to do so, because they were pushing the limits of customary female behavior. Many Americans were alarmed at this new expansion of women's freedoms, and their criticism led some women to self-doubt. One of them, a woman who had traveled to Paris to study and write, wondered if "this revolt against security in which I myself was taking part was not a fatal adventure bound to injure the family, the one institution in which I believed more than any other."[83] Clearly, Nellie's family was supportive of her desire to visit Europe, yet the trip nevertheless demonstrates her willingness to risk unconventionality when it came to doing something she deeply desired.

The overland crossing by railroad and the ocean crossing by steamship were in themselves significant adventures for a young woman who had never traveled unaccompanied and had never seen a city larger than Omaha.[84] Nellie was thrilled with the grandeur of the ship—she always loved luxury—and was invigorated by her conversations with her sophisticated fellow travelers. Throughout her life, Nellie demonstrated exceptional skill in charming those around her, so she probably developed a congenial group with whom to pass her time. It is easy to picture her during the Atlantic journey, sitting under a blanket on her deck chair and watching the gray-green waves of the Atlantic as she worked on a letter to the family. Another young woman, overwhelmed with the sights, smells, and sounds of France in 1890, wrote, "By the time I reach Italy, I shall not have an adjective left."[85]

Nellie briefly referred to this first European trip in several of her speeches later in life. Although she did not list the areas she visited, she indicated that she covered several countries. The only specific memories of Nellie's first European trip come from discussions she had with her grandson Robert, who studied abroad during college.[86] When Nellie and Robert compared their impressions, Nellie recalled having toured throughout France, and she especially remembered exploring the Loire Valley by horse and carriage. Nellie loved the Loire châteaux, and her favorite was the 440-room Château de Chambord, surrounded by an enormous forest where François I, who commissioned Chambord, hunted in the early sixteenth century. She was entranced by the castle's fantastic roofline of towers, domes, dormers, and cupolas, the enormous spiral of its grand staircase, and the fierce-looking stone salamanders that adorned many parts of the building. She also remembered walking the streets of the tiny village outside the gates of Chambord. In a speech to a group of young women several decades later, Nellie reminisced,

> While I do not feel so very old, I do feel that my girlhood [was] lived in some other world, so radical have been the changes since reaching womanhood in the customs, conventions, and the viewpoint of the people upon matters relating especially to women. In the matter of dress, for instance. When I was young like you girls, I took a sight-seeing trip of a large part of Europe clad in a high-necked black gown with a long train and a broad-brimmed hat set on the top of my head and anchored with a hat pin (not very securely anchored, either). And I went climbing cathedral towers, holding on to my train with one hand and the hat with the other. Finally in exhaustion, I mutinied and said I would take the rest of them for granted. And never shall I forget my weariness, and I am sure now that it was due to my mode of attire.[87]

In 1882, another young American woman observed, "There is nothing like travel to teach one to appreciate the right of opinion in others and bring one to realize what a mote he really is in the vast shifting sands of the humanity of our great world."[88] Once Nellie left behind the cocoon of her own country, she was changed forever by a new awareness of other cultures and lifestyles. The success of this first solo tour likely gave Nellie a taste of the sophistication and cosmopolitanism for which she had longed, as well as a new level of confidence in her independence and her own grit.

Around 1900, Nellie took another trip, this one to visit relatives of her father in Stewart County, Tennessee. Although this journey lacked the drama of the European adventure, it changed Nellie's destiny and set the course for the rest of her life. While in Tennessee, she met a young lawyer named William Bradford Ross.

THREE

Wife and Mother

HE WAS THE handsomest man she had ever seen. He had dark, wavy hair that never thinned over the years, but instead turned to the distinguished salt-and-pepper combination that graces so many successful politicians. His features were strong, his brow was forceful, and his eyes carried a twinkle. "My beloved handsome, charming, noble husband," Nellie wrote of him.[1] From the moment the couple met—most likely during a trip to Paris, Tennessee, where Nellie would visit her Uncle Thomas and Aunt Sallie Tayloe—Nellie was smitten.[2] "He was a veritable extrovert. He radiated good cheer when he entered a room at a gathering. He was courtly in his manner toward the ladies," Nellie remembered.[3] They were to become one of those rare couples whose mutual affection, respect, and passion grew with each passing year. After his death, Nellie mourned, "Is it presumptuous of me to feel, that few women in the world have been blest with [what I have] lost—for however unworthy I have been, never was woman more loved & admired. . . . The ardor increased with the years rather than diminished. What is more, he had respect for my intellect & depended upon it for assistance to him. He thought I was beautiful and told me so nearly every day that we were married."[4]

William Bradford Ross was twenty-six years old the year the couple met, and Nellie was twenty-four. The two shared a background and an upbringing that made them a perfect match. Nellie's paternal grandfather, John Tayloe, was a lay minister in the Methodist Church who had been born in North Carolina and moved to the western frontier in Stewart County, Tennessee. Likewise, William's paternal grandfather, Samuel, was a Baptist preacher who was born in North Carolina and who moved to Stewart County in 1808 with the earliest settlers. The families shared a common pioneer path, a strong tradition of fundamentalist faith, and the experience of economic ruin as a result of the Civil War. Both William and Nellie experienced hard times growing up. William's father, Ambrose, who was clerk of court in Stewart County, had lost most of his considerable assets after the Civil War because they had been held in Confederate currency.

William—Billy to his family, Will to Nellie—was born on the family farm in December 1873 in Dover, Tennessee, about twelve miles from the birthplace of Nellie's father. He was the sixth of eight children born to Ambrose and Missouri Ross. Just as Nellie had lost her mother at age thirteen, so William had lost his father at age eight. William was born with a hunger for success and advancement, but since he and his two brothers refused to touch what little money that Ambrose had left their mother, he was forced to fund his own education by alternating periods of study with periods of work and borrowing money to make ends meet.[5] He spent one undergraduate year, 1897–1898, at Peabody Normal College, which at that time served as the local liberal arts college for the area surrounding Nashville.[6] William could not afford to stay long enough to earn a degree from Peabody or from the University of Nashville, with which Peabody was then associated.[7] Sometime after his year at Peabody, he may also have attended a term or a summer session at the nearby law school at Cumberland University.[8] However, William received his substantive legal training in the manner that most nineteenth-century legal students, including Nellie's brother Sam, received theirs—by reading law in the office of an experienced attorney. William completed his legal apprenticeship in the offices of Judge J. W. Stout of the Sixth Tennessee division, and he often told Nellie in later years that in his opinion, there were no more able legal practitioners in the nation than in Stewart County.[9] After he was admitted to the Tennessee bar, William spent about a year in nearby Paris, Tennessee, where he practiced law with his brother Smith.[10]

After their brief time together during Nellie's 1900 visit to Stewart County, William and Nellie conducted their courtship largely if not solely through their letters, none of which have survived.[11] As the relationship became serious, the pressure increased on William to make a decision about establishing his permanent law practice so that he could support a wife. William may have suffered from a chronic cough or series of colds that led his family to believe—erroneously—that he suffered from tuberculosis. He decided that his best course was to move west, where the drier air might improve his health.[12]

On September 13, 1901, a brief article in the *Cheyenne Daily Leader* noted that W. B. Ross of Tennessee had arrived in Cheyenne and rented an office in the Mercantile block to set up a law practice.[13] One day later, the banner headline on page one of the paper announced the death of William McKinley, twenty-fifth president of the United States. McKinley had succumbed to an assassin's bullet after several days of hanging on to life. William's law practice was founded the same week that Theodore Roosevelt was sworn in as the nation's first Progressive president.

Progressivism, wrote Richard Hofstadter in *The Age of Reform,* was neither a consistent nor a carefully crafted national program, but a "rather widespread and remarkably good-natured effort of the greater part of society to achieve some not very clearly specified self-reformation."[14] It shared many of the reform goals of the late nineteenth-century Populist Party, whose membership had largely comprised disaffected southern and western farmers; by the turn of the century, the farmers had been joined by small businessmen, professionals, and many civic groups from across the middle-class spectrum. They "took the 'once-radical' populist ideas, clothed them in middle class respectability, and made them acceptable to the average American."[15] The Progressives urged governments at all levels to drop their laissez-faire approach and to take an active role in improving many aspects of the American system, improving governmental operations including civil service reform; providing new social services; enacting legislation to protect workers, women, and children; and forcing big business to acknowledge the significance of the public interest and the primacy of the law over corporate practices.

On their Tennessee farm, William's family had suffered just as much as Nellie's from the nation's fiscal and monetary policies that favored the Eastern establishment, particularly the tight money supply, the unforgiving lending practices, and the monopolistic shipping rates. William arrived in Cheyenne resolved to enter politics as a Progressive advocate for the people. A side-by-side comparison of the 1902 state platforms underscored the difference in philosophies between the two major political parties in Wyoming. The Republicans declared their continuing support for a national tariff to protect American corporations, they endorsed the national policy that excluded Chinese immigrants, and they condemned "all conspiracies . . . intended to restrict business, . . . to limit production, or to control prices." The Democratic platform called for direct election of U.S. senators by the people, compulsory arbitration of labor disputes, municipal ownership of public utilities, and "immediate and effective legislation and the vigorous enforcement of laws to protect the people from the oppressions of trusts and monopolies." They condemned the tariff and "discriminating rates in transportation," both of which brought hardship upon the consumer, farmer, and small businessman. The Democrats also called for the establishment of workman's compensation for employees who were injured on the job; such a bill had been rejected by the most recent, Republican-controlled, state legislature. Finally, they called for tax reform to equalize the taxation burden and to force corporations to contribute a fair share of the revenues needed to support the state's programs and expenditures.[16]

A year after establishing his law practice, William traveled to Omaha to claim his bride. On the evening of September 11, 1902, Nellie and William were married in the Tayloe home under a canopy of trailing green foliage in a parlor filled with yellow and white roses and palms. Nellie was dressed in a gown of white chiffon over satin, which was decorated with ruffles and lace.[17] In the wedding announcement, the *Cheyenne Daily Leader* referred to "the popular young attorney, W. B. Ross," who was "rapidly becoming a leader of the younger Democracy of the state."[18] Hoping to evade any post-marriage shenanigans by his Cheyenne friends, William had put out the word that he and Nellie would not arrive in town until around the first of October. His intentions were defeated when someone sent a telegram to Cheyenne that the newlyweds would be arriving September 12 on the one o'clock train. The couple had left to catch the train directly from their late-evening reception.[19]

When the train pulled into Cheyenne the next morning, the couple looked out of the train's window to see a crowd of William's new friends, waiting to greet them and escort them to the little rental house that William had set up for Nellie. Nellie's first impression of her new town was its imposing depot, a Romanesque monument constructed from huge blocks of Colorado sandstone, complete with a clock tower, that proclaimed to every visitor and resident the power and dominance of the Union Pacific Railroad. Driving away from the depot, Nellie caught a glimpse of the state capitol building eight blocks away, anchoring the other end of Hill Street (now Central Street). As the merry group of young friends drove through downtown Cheyenne, Nellie took note of the small business district—rows of one- and two-story stores fronting unpaved streets, complete with hitching posts. After ten years in the comparatively big city of Omaha, Nellie found herself back in a small frontier town that stirred her memories of Miltonvale. "In some ways this is quite a little city," Nellie wrote her brother George, "but in many ways it bears the ear marks of the country town. We have wooden and gravel sidewalks out our way, & O, how dusty the streets are. It must be destruction on shoes and skirts—and ruinous to complexions."[20]

In this first letter home to her brother George, written about ten days after her marriage, Nellie shared her mixed feelings about her new life: "O, Georgie, I never dreamed how hard this parting was going to be. To think that I am gone from you all for always almost breaks my heart. I would be perfectly happy but for that. And yet we would none of us have it otherwise. Mr. Ross is as kind and good and loving as any man could ever be—and we are so happy and contented—only when I think of this bitter parting from you all whom I love. I wish I could tell you what a good kind husband I have. I know we shall be so happy together. He is the only man in this world for me. If only I could have had you all! I suppose I want too much."[21]

Nellie and William started their married life in a modest five-room bungalow at 713 East Nineteenth Street. Nellie bragged to George how well the first few meals she cooked for her husband had turned out. She was having a wonderful time in her new role as wife, arranging the first house that was truly hers. "I wish you could see our little home—it is so nice," she wrote George. "Of course there is still a great deal to be done before it will be in real good order. . . . The rooms are all a good size. . . . The kitchen is nice and large—a nice large pantry and cellar—and the bathroom is large, with such a nice porcelain tub. Our dining room is such a pretty room. I believe we will enjoy it most of any."[22]

In this letter to George, Nellie also introduced a theme that would continue to appear throughout her life in her correspondence to family and to friends—her preoccupation with money. The early years of financial loss and insecurity haunted her all her life. Nellie wrote her brother about one of William's pending cases and the fee he expected to receive for his work, and then fretted about the cost of living in a town where almost all goods had to be brought in by railroad: "I am just horrified all the time at the prices of things—it is simply appalling. *Every thing* is so high. . . . Mr. Ross says he gets even with them when it comes to charging fees—if he didn't we would starve. . . . I feel as if I were eating gold all the time."[23]

When William and Nellie married, he was still struggling to pay back the money he had borrowed to finance his studies and apprenticeship. "Not a promising start," Nellie later wrote, "for a young pair dependent entirely upon the precarious income of a youthful lawyer's practice." Yet they viewed their financial handicap as a challenge, their new lives as an adventure. "We were happy, hopeful, and ambitious in the Cheyenne of the new century—a cow town in which there still lingered some of the vivid frontier color."[24] Nellie's earliest assessment of William's practice and prospects was positive. She wrote George that she had met the Presbyterian minister, who declared that everyone in Cheyenne respected William and expected great things from him. "Mr. Ross has gotten several hundred dollars [in] collections. . . . When I think that he has only been here one year and how much practice he already has and what a host of good friends he has, I think it is just wonderful. If he can do so well in one year I don't think we need be uneasy about the future."[25] Nellie was happily in love as she settled into her new life as William's wife, confident that he would be able to provide her a secure and prosperous future.

Although it is unlikely that Nellie gave her legal status as a wife a single thought when she agreed to marry William and follow him to Wyoming, she had landed in a state that accorded her more rights and equity with men than any other. Wyoming, the "Equality State," had been the first to grant women full suffrage when it became a territory in 1869. When Wyoming was on the brink of statehood in 1890, female suffrage was a potential threat to the territory's admission to the union. The question was placed before the voters in the draft constitution. Two-thirds of the voters voted affirmatively, demonstrating resounding support for the principle of equal suffrage. The U.S. Congress threatened to withhold statehood if female suffrage was not removed from the state constitution, but the territorial officials replied that they would forgo statehood before they gave in on this issue. When President Benjamin Harrison signed the statehood bill in July 1890, Wyoming's women became the first in the United States to enjoy the voting privilege.

At least as important as the right to vote was Wyoming's early passage of several acts relating to the rights of married women to hold and control their own property. The legal status of women in America derived from English common law, under which a husband and wife were considered to be a single person with inseparable interests. Blackstone's *Commentaries on the Laws of England,* the most important legal authority in the eighteenth century, both in England and its colonies, declared that in the eyes of the law, a wife surrendered her very existence as a separate person upon marrying. Her land and other possessions became the property of her husband, as did any property she acquired after their marriage or any income that she earned. A wife could not be party to a legal suit, make a will, or sign a contract. If an aggrieved woman was able to obtain a divorce, her husband automatically retained custody of the children. If a husband died, the wife could not gain guardianship of her children. The first married women's property acts that began to redress these inequities were passed in the mid-nineteenth century, but as late as 1900, thirty-seven states had still failed to pass legislation to allow women to control their own property. However, in Wyoming, the territorial statutes passed in 1869 gave women the right to own their own property and control their own income and earnings, and they prohibited husbands from mortgaging the family homestead without the wife's freely given signature. It also forbade the pay discrimination against female teachers from which Nellie had suffered in Nebraska. On the other hand, not until 1915 did Wyoming pass specific legislation that accorded wives custody of their children.[26]

Nellie had little time to adjust to her new life as a wife before she became a mother. She was pregnant within the first month. On May 20, 1903, just eight and one-half months after her wedding, Nellie delivered twins, the premature delivery no doubt caused by the multiple births. George Tayloe was named after Nellie's brother, while James Ambrose was named after both Nellie's and William's fathers. The tiny newborns were not strong; in fact, Nellie remembered their condition as "dreadful"—and the two young parents despaired that one or both would not live. It was several weeks before their survival was assured.[27]

Nellie and William adored their babies. Unusually for his generation, William was actively involved in the rearing of his sons. When they woke during the night, William always rose to be with them. As soon as they were able to sit up, William took over the responsibility of bathing them so that Nellie would not have to stoop over the tub. It was William who put the boys to bed and heard their prayers.[28]

A few months after their birth, Nellie wrote George, "Will and I have come to the conclusion that there was never such a pair in the world. And you know if *we* think so it is true. . . . I just wish you could see how smart & cute they are. If you could just see them lying side by side & how they both follow us with their eyes as we move about the room and laugh when we speak to them.

Ambrose especially seems to have some big joke on hand all the time. Sometimes we hear him laughing out loud when he is all alone in the dark." Despite her delight with her perfect babies, the care of the twins sometimes overwhelmed Nellie when Will was not there to help. One day when every attempt to comfort her two colicky babies had failed, she simply threw herself down on the bed to wail alongside the inconsolable twins. She remembered thinking, "though those babies might survive the perils of infancy, their mother would never live to tell the tale."[29]

Two months after the twins' first birthday, Nellie was pregnant again. Alfred Duff Ross, named after Nellie's brother and her uncle in Omaha, was born on April 13, 1905. By September 1905, Nellie felt secure enough in the children's health and her own mothering skills to take a long dreamed-of trip east to show off her three babies. She spent two weeks with her father in Omaha and a few months in Memphis with Alfred, George, and George's new wife, Nelle; then on to Paducah, where she stayed with Will's brother Smith, and finally to Dover, Tennessee, where Will joined them for the holidays. Nellie loved having her babies petted by all the relatives, and she engaged a nurse for part of the trip, so she was able to get her first good rest since the twins were born.[30]

Despite all their worries about the twins' precarious health, it was not George and Ambrose who were touched when disaster struck the family. Sunday, February 18, 1906, was one of those delightful western winter days when the sun shines brightly and promises that spring is coming. Nellie had gone to church on her own, leaving the three boys home with their father. Will tucked baby Alfred into his buggy with pillows and blankets and put him in the backyard to take in the sunshine. He had been inside the house only a few minutes when a neighbor knocked on the door to ask why the baby was not in his buggy. Will tore out of the house to find that the baby's movements had overturned the buggy. Alfred was under his pillows and blankets, where he had smothered.[31] The accident made an already solicitous father even more anxious and protective. When the couple's last son, William Bradford Ross II, was born in 1912, William insisted that they take him everyplace with them for fear that something might happen to him.[32]

About three months after Alfred's death, the couple purchased a lot in Nellie's name at 902 East Seventeenth Street, two blocks from the city park and near the edge of town. The excitement of dreaming about their new home and watching its construction helped to take their minds off the loss of their baby. They both wanted a colonial-style house, and they found the plan of a house in Salem, Massachusetts, that seemed to fit the bill. Economic reality forced them to give up some of the features on their wish list, but Nellie insisted on wood-burning fireplaces in the master bedroom, the dining room, and the living room. When finished, the main floor had a large entry hall, a comfortable living room, a small kitchen, and a grand dining room that was perfect for entertaining. Upstairs were the master bedroom and two bedrooms for the twins. After Bradford was born, Nellie made a nursery for him out of the sunporch that adjoined the master bedroom.

The years in the new house were happy ones. William and Nellie entertained often, but when the family was alone on a winter's night, they took pleasure in the same kind of pastimes that Nellie's family had enjoyed in Miltonvale. They gathered around the living room fireplace and toasted marshmallows or popped corn while William, who was a wonderful storyteller, regaled the boys and their friends with stories from the Bible or tales of his Tennessee boyhood. Nellie would make hot chocolate, and sometimes she would gather everyone around the piano to sing.[33] William and Nellie loved to read aloud to one another, and they worked their way through a small library of the classics. When William came home for lunch, Nellie hurried through her meal so that she could read to him until he had to go back to the office; after they went to bed, they read aloud until both their voices gave out and they could no longer stay awake.[34] When her son Bradford remembered those years, he pictured his mother in the kitchen, feet propped up on the open oven door for warmth, an open book in her lap.[35]

Nellie often had a maid, but during the periods when she could not find one, William always made the boys help their mother. William and the boys made a game of competing to see who could be first to get to Nellie's dining chair to seat her, and William delighted in distracting the boys to make them lose. William was physically affectionate with his sons. "I used to say I thought [the boys] would sit in [William's] lap until they were grown men," Nellie wrote to her grandson. "And yet he was not easy going with them. He was quite exacting. He required unqualified respect from them. Not one of them ever said 'yes' or 'no' to him. When their father told them to do something they moved."[36] As the twins got older, they became quite a handful as they egged one another on—playing hooky, running away, balancing on rooftops, and falling out of trees. They were the pride and the despair of their parents.

The arrival of Bradford, the twins' younger brother, helped to console William for the loss of Alfred. As a child, Bradford gave his parents very little trouble, and he was his father's sweetest joy. Quoting the Bible, William often referred to Bradford as his "beloved son," with whom he was "well pleased."[37]

"Bradford & I fared very well last night," wrote William to Nellie when she had taken the twins to visit family and left Bradford at home. "I read to him, we sang, and had as good a time as we could without you. He seemed to be very happy but I could hardly stand it . . . I love you so much my precious wife, I am very lonesome without you. . . . There is no house without you. I would never take any pleasure or happiness in it if it was not for you—rugs, pictures, beautiful furniture would mean nothing without you."[38]

William used Nellie as a sounding board for his legal work. He loved discussing his work with her, explaining legal points and seeking Nellie's common-sense opinion on his strategies and arguments. Nellie was proud that William sought her counsel, and she unconsciously began to absorb legal principles as she helped him to analyze his cases.[39] With her insecurity about money, she was also vitally interested in the financial details of William's practice. While Nellie and the three boys were on another family visit sometime after 1912, William wrote to her about the status of his cases: "I was to get $100 Monday for the case I tried at Douglas & I will be paid no less than $2500 to take that to the Supreme Court. . . . Then I have three cases to be tried at Cheyenne next week. . . . I will send you some money as soon as I have some to spare." He also promised Nellie that in the future, he hoped to charge his clients enough so that Nellie would have better luck in retaining a servant.[40]

Inevitably, there were stresses in the marriage. William had a mercurial temper, and he was quick to take offense. He had a jealous nature, and he became angry when he imagined that some man had flirted with his wife. "There were times when he would take offense at something I had said or done, when I would have no idea in the world what it was," Nellie told her grandson.[41] From Nellie's viewpoint, William was a man of such ironclad principles that he was far more likely to attract legal work from small businesses and private citizens of limited means than from the large corporations from which he could have earned lucrative fees, but at the risk of compromising his ethics. In addition, his leadership activities in the Wyoming Democratic Party as well as the offices he held over the years limited his legal income, both because of time constraints and potential conflicts of interest. Nellie wanted to associate with Cheyenne's highest social echelon and to live, entertain, and dress as befit the social level to which she aspired. It bothered her that William's political activities limited his money-making ability.[42]

To find herself married to a man who placed the advancement of his political career ahead of the promotion of his potentially lucrative legal practice must have been a bitter shock to Nellie. Yet as a stay-at-home wife and mother, she was helpless; her social position precluded her ability to contribute financially in some way to the family finances, had she even desired to do so. All she could do was worry, and urge William to concentrate on attracting lucrative cases.

Even though she never doubted his love, Nellie later admitted to fretting that "[a]t times he may have disapproved of me."[43] Despite his willingness to confide in and seek counsel from his wife concerning his professional and political life, William may have been somewhat taken aback with some of Nellie's opinions and priorities. The authors of an influential study of marriage in the 1920s have explained that men of William's generation, who were reared as Victorians, were unprepared for the attitudes and behaviors of their wives after marriage. "That the man and his new wife have contradictory ideas of the rôle of the modern wife is an unsuspected fact to both members of the alliance before its consummation. . . . It is the product of social conditions outside the home that have operated upon the woman more than upon the man and made her insistent upon privileges for which her mother and grandmother would not even have dared to ask."[44] Beyond their wives' desire for greater freedoms, there were even more shocks in store for William's peers. The "modern" woman of the early twentieth century expected far more gratification from her marriage than her mother had. Marriage was no longer a mere compact of financial support in return for housekeeping and child-rearing. The new woman expected emotional fulfillment and romantic love, and she even expected physical fulfillment.[45] The new husband of William's generation found himself "utterly unprepared and baffled by the requirement of the modern wife who insists that sex relationships should not be for her a duty, the fulfillment of the legal right of the husband, but a personal satisfaction."[46]

Although her boys were still young, Nellie developed an extremely active social life during the early years in Cheyenne. Her name appeared regularly in the social column of the Cheyenne newspapers. In 1908, when the twins were just five, Nellie listed her social activities for one particularly busy week in a letter to Nelle: "I went to a very pretty luncheon and card party yesterday. . . . The opening meeting of the club this week was quite a 'function.' . . . Then I played cards one night; went to a theater party another; went to a little party at Mrs. Hoels one afternoon, called with Mrs. Bennett at the post another afternoon. Refused an invitation to a dance because my husband wasn't here & am expecting to go to the club dance tonight with him. Don't you think I have done pretty well to do all that?"[47]

The truth is that although Nellie adored her husband and sons, and they her, her domestic responsibilities were simply not enough to satisfy Nellie's energies. The years as a Cheyenne wife and mother, during which Nellie sought supplemental fulfillment in her activities outside the home, set the pattern she would follow the rest of her life. It is unlikely that Nellie was aware of the contradiction between her stated devotion to home and family and the way she actually spent her time. However, the same contradiction was evident when she later proclaimed that her highest value was domesticity while at the same time she was spending almost all of her time on her speaking career, while her last son stayed behind in Wyoming. Yet the restlessness that propelled Nellie into her social life was hardly unique in her generation; as the introduction of labor-saving devices ameliorated the time-consuming burdens of homemaking, many of Nellie's contemporaries were similarly searching for meaning and diversion outside the home.

In a 1910 article in the *Atlantic Monthly* entitled "The Change in the Feminine Ideal," Margaret Deland described the New Woman—not those rare women whose exceptional accomplishments had distinguished them in each generation, but the average wives and mothers of America. Deland's description was marked by more than a little ambivalence about the changes she had observed, and she expressed a fear that the sea change in womens' attitudes would have an unanticipated, possibly dangerous impact on society.

> The feminine ideal has changed, and is still changing. . . . We need only compare the women of to-day with our mothers to realize how great the change is. . . . They did not talk about their "rights"; they fulfilled them—in taking care of their families. . . . [We] have begun to say that the old selflessness—dear and admirable beyond a doubt to those who were made comfortable by it—was often demoralizing to an appalling degree. . . . The young woman of today is supplementing a certain old-fashioned word, *duty*, by two other words, "to myself."[48]

One expression of Deland's New Woman was the enormous growth in the women's club movement; "they are admirable and helpful organizations, but they all express in one way or another the restlessness of growth," wrote Deland.[49] During the first quarter of the twentieth century, the women's club movement represented to Nellie's generation what the temperance movement had been to her mother's—the most popular activity outside the home for middle- and upper-class women in America. By the early 1920s, women's clubs across the country had a combined membership of almost two million. The earliest clubs were founded in the late nineteenth century as societies in which women researched literary and cultural topics and took turns presenting papers to one another. Many of the clubs evolved into substantive public service organizations—a female manifestation of the Progressive movement.

Nellie's membership in the exclusive Cheyenne Woman's Club, to which she was elected in the early years of her marriage, was one of her most valued social connections. The Cheyenne Woman's Club helped to establish Cheyenne's first public reading room, it participated in charities and Red Cross fund-raising, and it pestered the municipal government for years to install lights in the city park. Primarily, however, Nellie's club limited itself to social and literary activities. Two examples of its annual research themes, around which the members' papers were organized, were "France" (1907–1908) and "Modern Literature and Biography" (1914–1915).[50]

Since the club movement drew more American women to pursuits outside the home than any other organized institution, it was viewed with suspicion and with more than a little derision by the male establishment. Literary clubs such as Nellie's, ironically, were considered more dangerous than the social service clubs. Community improvement projects could be justified as an extension of a woman's responsibility to care for her home and family, but a woman's desire to study and improve herself for the pure pleasure of it was shockingly selfish.[51] No less a forum than a national women's magazine, the *Ladies' Home Journal*, frequently warned women of the worthlessness of their club studies and the harm that club involvement could cause them. The magazine's editor derided the ability of club members to research and deliver substantive papers, referring to the study programs as "undigested, superficial knowledge that is worse than no knowledge at all." Catholic Bishop J. Cardinal Gibbons wrote, "I wish I could show [American women] the ultimate results of participating in public life. It has but one end—the abandonment, or at least the neglect, of the home." Two years later, a former president of the United States, Grover Cleveland, warned, "I am persuaded that without exaggeration of statement we may assume that there are woman's clubs whose objects and intents are not only harmful, but harmful in a way that directly menaces the integrity of our homes and the benign disposition and character of our wifehood and motherhood. . . . [T]he best and safest club for a woman to patronize is her home."[52]

Looking back, Nellie justified her club activities for their contribution to her gubernatorial skills as well as for their benefit to her family. "I believed that it was the binding obligation of every wife and mother to avail herself of every means of self-improvement. . . . I know scarcely any person more pitiable than the mother . . . who has failed to keep pace with her husband and children. Mere devotion and provision of their creature comforts is not enough," she wrote. Nellie never achieved her goal to be elected club president, but she did serve for two years on the executive committee and for one term as first vice president. Discounting her years of teaching experience, Nellie later credited the club with what little public speaking experience and leadership skills that she acquired before her gubernatorial election. "To the Cheyenne Woman's Club I am indebted for the development of qualities and capacities that helped me meet the demands of public office. It was something like the training men receive in county boards, municipal councils, and legislative halls. It is an experience that sharpens the wits and develops the gift of expression, particularly of oral expression. . . . It was in that little forum that I received what training in public speaking I carried into the office of Governor."[53]

During the years of their marriage, William was even more involved in outside activities than was Nellie. He served as president of the Kiwanis Club, president of the Young Men's Literary Club, and chairman of the board of trustees of the Young Women's Christian Association. He was a thirty-second-degree Mason and a member of the Anti-Saloon League and the Episcopal Dancing Club. During their earliest years in Cheyenne, the Rosses attended the Presbyterian Church, where William helped to found the Presbyterian Brotherhood and was elected as its first president. After the family members were confirmed at St. Mark's Episcopal Church in 1916, William was elected to the church vestry, on which he served until his death; he also served on the Sunday school and parochial committees.[54] But it was William's political activities that occupied the majority of his time away from his home and that limited the income he could earn from his legal practice.

William began to establish a statewide political reputation when a law was passed in 1904 to abolish licensed gambling halls in the state. The gambling interests denounced the law as an unconstitutional invasion of personal liberty. Aside from his belief in the constitutionality of the new law, gambling offended William's strict moral code. Against the odds, he took on the high-profile case and argued it up to the Wyoming Supreme Court, where he won.[55]

On the strength of favorable publicity generated by the case, he quickly announced his intention to run for county prosecuting attorney against W. R. Stoll, who had taken an unfortunate public stand against the constitutionality of the gambling law before the Supreme Court decision was announced. Upon William's election, even the Republican-leaning *Wyoming Tribune* was complimentary of William. "He is a brilliant young man, honest as the day is long and we believe courageous. He has the makings of a splendid lawyer. The *Tribune*'s advice to Mr. Ross is . . . Don't set out to turn things topsy turvy in a day. Pursue a wise, moderate course, and try to carry the people with you."[56]

The incumbent prosecuting attorney, supported by Cheyenne's gambling establishments, contested William's election. Even though many of his ballots were thrown out during the recount, William was declared the winner and was sworn into office. However, the Republican-controlled Board of County Commissioners refused to approve his bond. Stoll remained in the prosecuting attorney's office for eight more months. When the case was finally decided in William's favor, the judge found that William's opponents had fraudulently attempted to steal the election from him by clumsily altering ballots. During those intervening months, William was prevented from prosecuting or defending cases, and the county refused to release his salary to him. "It was an experience that worked real hardship on the family of a struggling young lawyer, and one not calculated to deepen in his wife a fondness for politics," wrote Nellie. But the incident was a major vindication for William; within three weeks after he finally assumed office, every gambling house in Cheyenne shut down.[57]

William stood for reelection in 1906 but was defeated by Republican Clyde Watts, his former law partner. In 1908, William ran for state senate; after an apparent victory, he lost by six votes following a recount. In 1910, he was defeated in a run for U.S. Congress. At that point, Nellie put her foot down. "He and I had come to an understanding that he would eschew politics for the rest of his life, that is, as a candidate for office. His consideration was partly out of consideration for my desire . . . and . . . I am sure . . . he questioned, as did I, the wisdom of abandoning for even a few years, in the event of his election, a practise that had taken years of effort to build to satisfactory proportions. Our sons were growing up. Two were away at school, and their needs were multiplying daily."[58]

After their twins completed their elementary grades in the Cheyenne schools, William and Nellie sent both of them to boarding schools in the

South. George attended the Webb School in Tennessee while Ambrose attended the Gulfport Military Academy in Mississippi. When Bradford reached high school age, he attended Sherwood Hall in Laramie.[59]

The twins continued to worry their parents as they reached high school and college age. "On the way to town I got caught speeding," wrote Ambrose in one letter from his boarding school in Mississippi. "I went to court and was fined seventeen dollars & sixty cents. . . . I tried to argue out of it, but the judge wouldn't listen to me. I had to get the money [from the headmaster]. Now, I know you haven't any money to pay speed cops, & I know that you don't like it at all, but it can't be helped. . . . I'm just as sorry as I can be." Ambrose, whose ambition was to become a rancher, disliked school and was homesick for Wyoming and his family. "I have just counted the days till I will get home again—sixty-five. I can't hardly wait till I will get there. . . . I love you all so much & wish I were home with you."[60]

Although George eventually earned a Rhodes Scholarship, his grades at the university were mediocre. After the winter term of 1922–1923, during which he dropped one class and earned one A, one C, and three Incompletes, his parents informed him that he needed to take some time off and grow up before they would pay for any more schooling. "Now one reason we want you to stay out of school is because you are not composed; have no poise; go off half-cocked & fly into a passion without any excuse or provocation. Those things are millstones around your neck & are going to block your success unless you get yourself in hand," counseled William.[61]

Just when it appeared that the twins were beginning to mature, thirteen-year-old Bradford entered his own rebellious period. About 1925, Nellie wrote her brother, "You know how much of the time I was in despair about the naughty things George & Ambrose used to do and now Bradford is at a stage that he is ready to try anything and does so many naughty things that I truly fear sometimes that he will turn out to be not even respectable. Then I remember I used to feel the same way about the others & they seem to have improved. But I've never known the kind of child I hear parents speak of as never having given them a minute's worry."[62]

Nellie and William shared their consternation concerning their sons' misdeeds and their general disapproval of the attitudes and behavior of the youth with most parents of their generation. The Ross parents and their peers had developed their ideas, values, and opinions while growing up during the 1870s and 1880s. Their viewpoints struck the boys' generation as obsolete, frequently irrelevant, occasionally amusing, and sometimes even abhorrent. The boys' generation had a multitude of activities and attractions that pulled them from the home and exerted external influence on their behavior—Boy Scouts and other organizations, sports and other school activities, parties, and the movies. The automobile gave them a freedom and a mobility unknown to their parents, and it facilitated dating and sexual experimentation. The standards of proper behavior had changed so much that it was a very confusing time to be a parent.[63] As one mother at that time worried, "You see other people being more lenient and you think perhaps that it is the best way, but you are afraid to do anything very different from what your mother did for fear you may leave out something essential or do something wrong. I would give anything to know what is wisest, but I don't know what to do."[64]

Despite Nellie's adamant desire that William refrain from office-seeking, in 1918 he made an unsuccessful run in a tight primary race for the Democratic gubernatorial nomination. Many believed that he lost the race because U.S. Senator John Kendrick, a leader among Wyoming's Democrats, supported his opponent.[65] Four years later, William's friends encouraged him to try again. A major scandal in the Harding administration, Teapot Dome, had significant reverberations in Wyoming and rendered the Republican Party vulnerable.[66] While his supporters increased the pressure on William, Nellie mounted her own campaign to keep him from running. But on the final filing date, Nellie gave in; William's candidacy was announced in the evening papers.[67] This time, he secured his party's nomination.

On the Republican side, the primary race turned into a nasty war of words between the incumbent governor, Robert Carey, and challenger John Hay. On the Democratic side, the race was complicated by the involvement of an organization called the Association for Progressive Political Action. The PPA declared that William was too conservative to carry the Progressive banner. At a July conference of the PPA, the organization endorsed George E. Kendler, a farmer and former member of the state legislature, for governor, and John Kendrick for U.S. senator. While the PPA's platform clearly was more radical than William's campaign pledges, his proposals nevertheless were progressive. He called for a tax cut for individuals, for economy provisions for state government, and for measures designed to aid farmers, ranchers, and the working man. He also campaigned against the "miserable failure" of President Harding, whom he called "a tool of designing politicians and a catspaw for Financial Greed." The *Wyoming State Ledger* refused to take sides in the primary race, declaring that both men were honorable and able candidates.[68] Despite the lack of support from the radical wing of the party, William won the primary election.

In a surprising upset in the November general election, William was elected governor by a majority of fewer than 1,000 votes of the approximately 62,000 cast. "The dazed electorate of the Equality state is holding a post-mortem on the most amazing political upset in its history," wrote one newspaper editor.[69] William was the only Democrat to be elected to a state government position without the support of the PPA. He was helped by the Harding scandals, but also by the fact that Wyoming was deep in a depression caused by postwar deflation; crop and livestock values had dropped, and the railroad had cut wages. William may also have been helped by the bitter Republican primary, which sent some Republican voters to the Democratic camp.

In his inaugural address, William called upon the Republican-controlled state legislature to work with him in a spirit of cooperation, and he pledged to consult with them in partnership. In the light of the Wyoming depression and the fact that the state government had been carrying a deficit for several years, he called for elimination of all unnecessary expenses, abolishment or consolidation of public departments, and deferral of new government initiatives. He pointed out that Wyoming was blessed, as no other state in the union, with an abundance of coal, oil, and other natural resources; how could it be that so many of its citizens were suffering economically? The answer, he suggested, was that such a high percentage of the state's wealth was in the hands of large corporations, which, as nonresidents, were not required to pay Wyoming tax. The tax burden, therefore, fell disproportionately on the private citizen. He pledged to seek legislation that would require corporations to help support the state from which they derived their wealth. Finally, he dealt with the topic of prohibition. He recognized the considerable contingent who personally opposed prohibition and who flaunted their noncompliance with the law. But the law was the law, William declared; failure to enforce prohibition would lead to an alarming public disregard for other statutes, endangering our rule of law. He pledged to enforce prohibition until that day, if ever, when it might be repealed.[70] William's address received uniformly positive reviews from the state's newspapers. The *Douglas Budget* declared that his program represented what the people wanted and deserved. As for his proposal to tax the corporations, the *Budget* editor wrote that William had struck a "responsive chord. No one should desire that corporate wealth be penalized, but there has arisen a strong demand that corporate wealth should pay a just proportion of the taxes, and there is little doubt that this has not been the case in the past."[71]

William expanded on his inaugural themes when he presented his state of the state message containing his specific legislative proposals. In addition, he proposed two labor law initiatives, one to prohibit the employment of children under the age of fourteen and the other to establish an unemployment compensation program; he was unsuccessful in promoting these progressive measures in the Republican legislature. When his proposal to extend provisions of the Farm Loan Act to help ranchers and farmers through the depression failed to pass in the regular session, he called the legislature into special session in 1923, during which the Farm Loan Act of 1921 was amended as William requested. At his urging, the state legislature passed a proposed constitutional amendment to establish a severance tax to provide the state revenue based on the value of oil, coal, and minerals extracted from Wyoming land.[72] He was also successful in achieving an increase of more than 20 percent in the state's royalty in Standard Oil's Salt Creek fields, a victory that one historian called "no mean achievement in a time when corporate power was plundering the American West of its mineral resources and driving from office those politicians who tried to check its march."[73] One is left wondering how much more William might have been able to achieve, had he lived to serve out his entire term.

Nellie loved her new life as Wyoming's First Lady. Her days were filled with the luncheons, teas, and receptions that she so enjoyed, and her evenings were filled with entertaining legislators, Wyoming citizens, and out-of-state officials. William continued to use his wife as a sounding board, discussing with her his policies, legislative politics, and the personalities with whom he worked. The first summer William was in office, Nellie wrote Nelle a long letter about the wonderful trip that she and William had taken all over the state, a narrative filled with details of the parties, receptions, and lovely homes where they had been entertained. The same month, President Harding succumbed to illness and exhaustion while he was on a trip to the West Coast. When Harding died, William was asked to deliver a memorial address in Sheridan the day of Harding's burial; lacking staff or references on the road, William worked on the speech with Nellie until late in the night. "The truth is I finished it, at four o'clock in the morning," wrote Nellie to Nelle.[74]

The only downside to her exciting new life was the terrible expense of entertaining constantly and dressing herself appropriately on a governor's salary. Once William became governor and his practice ceased to generate new income, Nellie's only recourse was to throw herself body and soul into supporting her husband's political career, in the hope that his performance, reputation, and high-level contacts would eventually pay off financially. Nellie confided to Nelle that William was frequently mentioned as a future candidate for the Senate, but she simply did not see how they could afford for him to run. "It truly is hard for people as poor as us to fill this position with any dignity," she wrote Nelle.[75] A month later, she wrote to her son George, who was working as a park ranger in Yellowstone, and the letter was filled with money worries. After advising him of the importance of his starting a nest egg for himself, she told him that William's creditors were pressing him hard to repay his outstanding loans.[76] In February 1924, she received help from an unexpected quarter. Nellie's uncle, Duff Green of Omaha, had left her five thousand dollars when he died in 1908, and Nellie's brothers had given her very favorable terms to invest in the Tayloe Paper Company when they set it up.[77] Their 1923 profit had been much larger than expected. "To have my indebtedness reduced that much is too good to be true," she wrote George. "Your having let me have that stock, giving me a sense of having something to fall back on in case of need, I verily believe has lengthened my life. I doubt if many people have suffered more anxiety than I have in my life—over keeping the wolf away."[78]

The summer of 1924, the Democrats prepared for their presidential nominating convention, to be held at Madison Square Garden in June. James M. Cox was the candidate of the party's conservative wing, while Alfred E. Smith, governor of New York, represented the urban East. To the western mind, Smith was associated with machine politics, immigrants, Catholics, and the anti-prohibition movement—all that was wrong and dangerous in the party. William Gibbs McAdoo, son-in-law of Woodrow Wilson, hoped to combine the support of southern and western delegates to defeat Smith, but in order to make his strategy work, he was forced to accept the support of the Ku Klux Klan. William, who was already committed to McAdoo, represented Wyoming. Writing Nellie that McAdoo had invited him to a private breakfast, he told her that he doubted McAdoo could win the nomination. The feeling over the Klan issue was just too strong. As one historian described it, "[i]n the circuslike atmosphere of Madison Square Garden, . . . Catholic fought Protestant, wets fought dries, and urbanites fought farmers in an embarrassingly public display of the fundamental divisions within the party."[79] What made matters worse was that the convention was one of the first to be covered live on the radio, so millions of Americans were able to sit in on the slugfest. McAdoo and Smith ended up battling through 103 rounds of balloting until finally the convention settled on a third candidate, John W. Davis. William returned from New York disgusted with the proceedings but proudly declaring that he had not cast a single vote for Smith. He simply could not support Smith's "wet" position on prohibition.

In late September, William took to the road to promote his proposed constitutional amendment to introduce a severance tax. On Tuesday, September 23, Nellie accompanied William to Laramie, where he was scheduled to speak on the tax to the university assembly during the day and a Council of Industry dinner that evening. William was in excellent spirits as he and Nellie mingled with the dinner crowd before his speech. Sometime during the night, after returning home, William began to experience extreme discomfort from what he concluded was indigestion. The next morning, however, he was so ill that he could not go to the office. Finally, his severe abdominal distress forced him to call a doctor. After one look at William's distended abdomen, his doctor was so alarmed that he called for a surgeon from Denver and insisted that William move to Memorial Hospital. At one o'clock Wednesday afternoon, the doctors decided that they could not wait for the surgeon to arrive, and they operated. They found that William's appendix was destroyed.[80]

Nellie wrote George an optimistic letter on Friday; the abdominal distention had not yet subsided, but the doctors were hopeful. By Monday the twenty-ninth, however, William's condition had deteriorated, and another specialist from Denver arrived to consult with the Cheyenne doctors. William's condition was grave; he was beginning to slip away. William's brother arrived, and Nellie's brothers offered to come as well, but Nellie told them to wait.

As the letters and telegrams of concern and support poured in from across Wyoming and the nation, Nellie maintained her vigil at the hospital, where she was only permitted to see William for a few minutes at a time. She was too shocked and overwhelmed to break down. When it became clear that William might not survive, George traveled from Memphis to support his sister. He arrived by train in Denver around noon on Thursday, October 2, where he was met by Wyoming's adjutant general, who drove him to Cheyenne. But he was too late. William died around 3:15 that morning at Cheyenne's Memorial Hospital. The death certificate recorded his cause of death as "thrombophlebitis—septic, caused by appendicitis."[81]

When William's body was placed in the capitol's rotunda for a few hours before the funeral, hundreds of mourners filed by to pay their last respects. So many floral arrangements were sent to the family and to the state that two trucks were required to move them. William's funeral was held at St. Mark's Episcopal Church, where four ministers presided during last rites. The church overflowed with mourners, and dozens stood in respect outside the church. In Cheyenne, businesses remained closed, flags flew at half-mast, and the streets were lined with mourning standards. An honor guard, composed of the University of Wyoming's Reserve Officers' Training Corps, escorted the body to Lakeview Cemetery. The corps stood at attention while William's casket was lowered into the ground. There in the Ross family burial plot, William rejoined his little son Alfred, who had gone before him so many years before.

James Wynns Tayloe, father of Nellie Tayloe Ross, ca. 1870. *American Heritage Center, University of Wyoming*

Elizabeth Blair Green Tayloe, mother of Nellie Tayloe Ross, ca. 1870. *American Heritage Center, University of Wyoming*

Nellie Davis Tayloe, ca. 1886. *American Heritage Center, University of Wyoming*

Main Street of Miltonvale, Kansas, ca. 1895. *Cloud County, Kansas, Historical Society Museum*

Cheyenne, Wyoming, taken from the top of the Union Pacific Railway Depot, ca. 1890. Note the state legislature at the end of the street. *Wyoming State Archives, Dept. of State Parks and Cultural Resources*

Nellie Tayloe Ross and her twins, *left to right,* Ambrose and George. *American Heritage Center, University of Wyoming*

FOUR

Governor

NELLIE WAS devastated. She had been able to maintain an appearance of composure during William's sickness and hospitalization, but when her brother George arrived—her most intimate confidant besides William—she gave in to her loss and despair. She could not stop dwelling on William, but she also could not talk about her happy married years without breaking down. "When she gets on the past it is terrible for her and I assure you hard on the listeners," George wrote Nelle.[1]

With George to lean on, she gradually began to regain her composure and to deal with the funeral arrangements and the many other decisions that demanded her attention. Then, the afternoon of William's funeral, Nellie was presented with a significant issue to distract her from her grief. Dr. J. R. Hylton, chairman of the state Democratic Committee, called on her at the Executive Mansion to urge her to accept a nomination to complete her husband's term of office. The decision to offer Nellie the nomination was likely motivated by the fact that William died just one month before Wyoming's biennial elections. Since William's term still had two years to run, there were simply no other Democratic candidates who had established the public name recognition they would need to win a campaign. The Democrats had nothing to lose by gambling on Nellie's candidacy.[2]

Nellie turned to George for guidance on this astonishing proposal, and the two spent hours considering the idea from every aspect, as friends and advisors also weighed in on the idea.[3] On one hand, it seemed likely that Nellie could never win the election. Even though the independent-minded Wyoming electorate tended to vote for the person, not the party, it tended to favor the more conservative Republican Party. It was also to be expected that Nellie's sex would work against her, despite Wyoming's pride in its motto, "the Equality State." The governorship was a man's job. George was concerned that the blow of defeat would be more than Nellie could handle at that point in her life. Also, Nellie herself was uncertain whether she had the physical stamina to handle the stress of the position. On the other hand, Nellie's financial situation was desperate. William had left many debts, and he had borrowed against his life insurance policy. After all the debts were paid and the family car was sold, George estimated that Nellie's assets would consist of little more than the family home, which George dismissed as a "white elephant" worth little more than five thousand dollars.[4] If she won the gubernatorial election, her salary would be six thousand dollars per year.[5] Nellie needed the money, and she was too proud to accept a charitable annuity or a sympathetic appointment to a position such as state librarian—both were options that state officials and others had suggested to help her. For his part, George worried that if Nellie ran and lost, she would squander public sympathy. A new Republican administration would be unlikely to offer her any assistance, and she would be penniless. He urged her not to risk losing a pension or a position by running for office.[6]

When Nellie later told the story of her decision to run, she ascribed her primary motivation to an unselfish desire to finish her husband's unfinished gubernatorial agenda.[7] While this factor undoubtedly played a part in her deliberations, Nellie neglected to include another consideration in the story's official version that was probably just as important: She was personally ambitious, and she wanted the job.

"Nellie is as keen a politician as any of them," George wrote Nelle after observing Nellie handle meeting after meeting on the nomination question. "She wants to run and the Democrats want her but there is a great question as to her winning. . . . My recommendation to her today is not to run. Think she will probably run. She will certainly take a chance if she finally thinks she could probably win. No one ever wanted it more."[8] But Nellie remained true to her upbringing as a southern woman. It was considered unwomanly to admit to personal ambition, and more particularly it was unseemly to aspire to such a groundbreaking public position. As the natural politician that George watched Nellie rapidly become, Nellie kept her less attractive motivations to herself. To the world, she emphasized her unselfish desire to accede to the public call and surrender her privacy on behalf of her husband's memory and in the interest of public service. Her self-sacrifice would garner sympathy and would sell well at the polls.

George had a business appointment in Chicago on Monday, October 13. He had planned to leave on Saturday morning, spend the weekend with his Aunt Harriet in Omaha, and leave for Chicago Monday morning in time for his meeting.[9] As his Saturday departure approached, however, Nellie again fell apart. She pleaded with George to stay until she decided what to do and the nominating committee had announced its selection. George promised her that he would stay until Monday morning, but he could not wait until the nominating process was completed. The state statutes had no nomination provisions to cover circumstances such as William's death, so there had been a delay in proceeding until a ruling of the state's attorney general. When the attorney general ruled that the gubernatorial candidates must be nominated by party convention, both the Democrats and Republicans had scheduled nominating conventions for the Tuesday after George's departure. As George bid Nellie goodbye, he told her that she had his support no matter what she decided to do about the nomination.[10]

On Tuesday, October 14, the Republican state convention nominated Eugene J. Sullivan, a Casper attorney, and the Democratic state convention nominated Nellie. After the roll call of counties, George W. Patterson of Laramie formally placed her name before the Democratic convention. Patrick O'Connor of Casper was the only other candidate nominated. When it became obvious that the nomination would overwhelmingly go to Nellie, O'Connor requested that his name be withdrawn from consideration. The delegates enthusiastically adopted a motion to make Nellie's nomination unanimous. Because of the legal uncertainty of the nominating process, a state committee of Democrats took the precaution of also nominating Nellie as their candidate.[11] Following the two nomination processes, a committee of delegates came to the Executive Mansion with the news of her unanimous nomination and the members' personal pledges of loyalty and confidence. After Nellie formally accepted the nomination, the party filed her name as their candidate just forty-five minutes before the deadline. Nellie's platform was simple: to promote the policies of William's administration and to complete his legislative agenda.

Sullivan campaigned hard for the three weeks leading up to election day, but Nellie did not. Vigorous campaign appearances might belie the image of the sympathetic bereaved widow, and in truth, the image was accurate. Now that the distracting excitement of the nomination process had passed, Nellie was again consumed with her loss. She wrote to George's wife and begged that she come to Cheyenne to support her; if Nelle could not leave her family, then perhaps Alfred's wife, Sara, could come. "I do long for a woman of my family. O, Nelle, I wouldn't have you know what this grief is. To know that William has gone out of my life, that I'll never in this world see him again or hear his dear voice—you couldn't dream what it means."[12]

While Nellie declined to campaign on her own behalf, her supporters actively supported her candidacy through speeches, letters, and tasteful newspaper advertisements. Joseph C. O'Mahoney, a Cheyenne attorney who had been a political associate of William's and who was to become Nellie's principal advisor, made several speeches on her behalf around the state.[13] Senator Kendrick, the state's most important Democrat, declared his public support for Nellie even though he had failed to support her husband. He pointed out to voters how fitting it was that the Equality State be first to elect a woman as governor, and he praised Nellie's intelligence, honesty, and common sense. As the chief advisor to her husband, Nellie deserved recognition for her contribution to her husband's accomplishments as governor. Only Nellie could complete the work that William had begun, wrote Senator Kendrick.[14]

From the moment she was nominated, Nellie was astonished to find herself besieged by reporters and writers from across the country. She was disgusted and embarrassed to find the personal details of her private life reported to the world.[15] In the melodramatic writing style of the times, writers exaggerated the dramatic and tragic aspects of Nellie's life. For example, in writing of Nellie's courtship, one reporter from the *Kansas City Star* wrote of the "young lawyer [who] fell violently in love with the dark-eyed daughter of southern aristocracy."[16] Another reporter fabricated a touching scene of Nellie bravely accepting her party's nomination, flanked by her three sons, when in fact none of the boys was present. But far worse than the dramatic embellishments were the insistent reporters, looking for the public interest angle, who pressured Nellie to stage quirky photographs or to provide information she considered indecorous and irrelevant.[17] Although Nellie refused the request of one motion picture operator to wield a broom or a rolling pin, Miriam Ferguson, who was running for governor in Texas at the same time, was not so astute in managing her own image. She agreed to pose for undignified photographs of herself in her bonnet, feeding her chickens and canning peaches. What is worse, Mrs. Ferguson left a few unforgettable quotes, the most notable of which is, "English was good enough for Jesus Christ and it's good enough for the children of Texas!"[18]

Despite her capacity for misspeaking, Miriam Amanda Wallace Ferguson was not an uneducated woman. Born one year earlier than Nellie, she was a college graduate, having attended Salado College and Baylor Female College in Belton, Texas.[19] In 1899, she married James Edward Ferguson, who was elected governor of Texas in 1914. After her husband was impeached during his second term and thereby rendered ineligible for reelection, Miriam entered the race for governor. Her initials, M. A., led the press to give her a nickname she despised, "Ma" Ferguson. The campaign bumper stickers proclaimed, "Me for Ma, and I ain't got a dern thing against Pa." Although she insisted that she and not her husband would govern the state, she was quoted as stating that a vote for her was also a vote of confidence for her husband. Miriam was elected the same day as Nellie, but she was not inaugurated until fifteen days later. Her first term was stained by her failure to fulfill a campaign pledge to reduce expenditures, irregularities in the granting of pardons and paroles, and accusations that she and "Pa" had accepted bribes. She lost a battle for renomination, but she came back to win another term in the 1932 elections. She made one last, unsuccessful bid for the governorship in 1940. Like Nellie, Miriam Ferguson portrayed herself as fundamentally a wife and mother. Unlike Nellie, she played along with inappropriate demands from reporters, who parlayed Miriam's role as a farmwife into a folksy image that may have helped her to win her first election. However, Miriam's behavior also brings into stark relief the wisdom of Nellie's refusal to pander to the press and to guard her image as a dignified lady. Ma Ferguson is remembered, but she is remembered for her colorful personality, not for any accomplishments as governor.[20]

The day before the Wyoming election, the Democratic State Committee ran a newspaper advertisement consisting of two letters, one from Nellie and one from a supporter, Edna Bartlett. To women voters of Wyoming, Nellie wrote, "You may give assurance to those who desire to cast their votes for me, that they may do so in confidence that in the event of my election, I shall do all that is in my power to reflect credit upon womanhood and upon the fair name my husband has left me as a precious heritage." Bartlett's letter attacked all the stereotypes that might lead voters not to elect a woman. Concerning the objection that a woman might not be strong enough, she pointed out that mental strength, not physical strength, was the quality needed in a governor. Bartlett played on the common belief that women were superior to men in goodness, moral courage, and Christian faith. And to counter the prejudice that women were too emotional, Bartlett insisted that Nellie's predominant emotion, love for her husband, would be her greatest asset. "The noble emotion of love will keep her clear-headed and steady, as she thinks solely of her husband's honor and the accomplishment of his plans."[21]

Nellie spent election day at home in the Executive Mansion, receiving political supporters and friends.[22] The garage of the Executive Mansion had been designated a polling place, so from time to time, Nellie looked out to watch the voters come and go, mindful that they held her fate in their hands.[23] Around two o'clock in the afternoon, she walked out to the garage to vote herself, accompanied by her twenty-one-year-old twins, who were voting in their first election.[24] She spent the evening at home with her three sons. When the first precinct reported in, Joseph O'Mahoney called her with the news that the precinct, a Republican enclave, had split down the middle; it meant, O'Mahoney assured her, that she was sure to carry the state.[25] O'Mahoney was right. By the next morning, the returns placed Nellie about 7,000 votes ahead of Sullivan. She ended up winning the race by more than 8,000 out of almost 79,000 total votes cast; of Wyoming's twenty-three counties, Nellie carried twenty. Her telegram to her Memphis family announced with more than a little pride, "Principal Republican newspaper has conceded my election. . . . Am only successful Democratic state candidate."[26]

Not only was Nellie the sole Democratic candidate in Wyoming to win a statewide election, she also won by the largest margin of any state-level candidate. Sullivan's association with the oil business cost him votes, since the Teapot Dome scandal was still fresh in the minds of the Wyoming voters, but undoubtedly sympathy played a deciding role in Nellie's election. Nellie was not the first Democrat to achieve an upset in Republican Wyoming; both her husband and John Kendrick had achieved similar victories. In O'Mahoney's assessment, Wyoming voters had once again demonstrated their tendency to vote for the person, not the party.

Newspapers around the country struggled to assess the import of two women being elected their states' chief executives.[27] Opinions ranged from positive endorsements that were supportive of women's abilities to scandalized predictions of imminent failure. The *Milwaukee Journal* noted that because of the executive leadership skills required as governor, the success of Nellie or Mrs. Ferguson would "immeasurably [advance] the cause of American women in politics." The *Birmingham News* supportively concluded that since women were "natural-born housekeepers," the "infinite detail of a Governor's office" should interest any woman. The *New York Times* rejected such stereotypes when it noted that if the two women proved to be successful governors, "it will be not because they are women, but because they have sense, intelligence and character." But the *Cincinnati Enquirer* sniffed that neither woman had ever "executed anything more constructive probably than baking a pie or making a bed. . . . Texas and Wyoming taxpayers reasonably may be expected to learn that the maudlin ineptitude they have exhibited is extremely unprofitable."[28]

Within Wyoming, the press coverage was unequivocally positive. Even the Republican papers expressed support for Nellie's election and pride in Wyoming's distinction as the first state to elect a woman governor. The *Wyoming State Tribune* reminded readers that several of the state agencies were directed by ex-officio boards comprised of the five individuals elected to statewide offices, and pointed out the substantial influence that women would have on those boards. For the first time, women would comprise 40 percent of board membership at agencies, including the board of pardons and the state land board. In addition, Nellie would serve as commander-in-chief of the National Guard of Wyoming, chairman of the State Game and Fish Commission, and the State Farm Loan Board. "The nation, the world, will watch that experiment [of a woman's leadership] with keen interest, with critical interest," the *Wyoming State Tribune* editor concluded.[29]

A core group of advisors began to form around Nellie as soon as she was elected, including Joseph O'Mahoney, State Examiner Byron S. Huie,[30] Attorney General David J. Howell, and S. G. Hopkins, Wyoming's interstate water commissioner. Two days after the election, Huie warned Nellie how important it was to quickly prepare letters of gratitude to her key supporters around the state, several of whom were Republicans. He also reminded Nellie of the critical and difficult tasks immediately ahead of her—preparation of the state budget and the governor's annual message to the legislature. William had been fortunate enough to have substantial assistance on his budget from the outgoing governor, but even so, he and Huie had worked for almost two weeks full-time to complete the final draft. Despite the urgency of the tasks facing her, Nellie had decided that she simply had to retreat to the care and solicitude of her family. Nellie telegraphed George and Alfred of her intention to leave for Memphis within the week. "Ask family not to inform friends my approach, need quiet rest," she wrote.[31] Huie offered his assistance to Nellie to prepare her own budget as soon as she returned to Wyoming.[32] Nellie returned to Cheyenne around the first of December and immediately immersed herself in the preparation of her inaugural address, the budget, and the state of the state message. "For days and days all my waking thoughts were devoted to it, and even in my dreams I phrased statements on taxation, farm loans, local budgets, and banking reform," she remembered. Nellie's crash course in Wyoming's politics and economy consumed her until her inauguration day.[33]

Nellie assumed gubernatorial office in one of the bleakest economic periods ever experienced in Wyoming. Two events occurred in 1919, triggering a depression in the early 1920s that did not lift until the onset of World War II. The first was the conclusion of World War I, which substantially reduced foreign demand for American foodstuffs and resulted in a drop in crop prices. The second was the summertime drought of 1919, exacerbated by a hard winter that came six weeks early; by October, snow blanketed the state. Wyoming farmers harvested less than half a normal-size crop that fall. The lack of adequate grass forced ranchers to ship at least one-third of their sheep and cattle out of the state before winter began, and it sent the price of hay and grain to support the remaining livestock over the winter sky-high. Then, in April 1920, a fierce snowstorm killed off the second third of the ranchers' stock. Wyoming ranchers, who had owned more than a million cattle worth nearly $74 million in 1919, saw their herds and valuations drop to about 800,000 head worth just $23 million in 1925.[34] The sheep ranchers fared no better; wool dropped from 80 to 25 cents, sheep from $18 to $6, and lambs from $8–12 to $3.[35]

The agricultural prosperity of the wartime years had encouraged prospective new farmers to file new land claims, and existing farmers and ranchers to expand their holdings.[36] Between 1916 and 1919, inclusively, there were 29,888 new land filings under the 1916 Homestead Act, of which 8,990 were filed in 1919 alone. In the wake of the postwar deflation and depression, farmers and ranchers struggled under an increasing burden of debt, which totaled $15 million in 1920, or almost 30 percent of total property value.[37] Inevitably, Wyoming's bank industry was affected as bankers and ranchers defaulted on their real estate and livestock loans. In the three years beginning in 1919, deposits fell by 30 percent to less than $20 million.[38] Between 1920 and 1924, inclusively, sixty-eight state and national banks failed in the state, over half of which closed their doors in 1924 alone.[39] Fingers were pointed in every direction—the agricultural depression; faulty loan practices, including making large loans to bank officers and stockholders; inadequate oversight by bank directors; and a lack of competence on the part of the state and national bank examiners.[40]

Wyoming's extractive industries also suffered in the 1920s. Although oil production rose from 13 million barrels in 1918 to 44 million in 1923, in 1924 it began a slump that lasted until 1933, because the bulk of Wyoming's remaining oil was believed to be heavy black crude, which lacked the demand of the more desirable light oil. To offset lower prices for their oil, Wyoming producers had substantially increased production in 1923—from 26.7 to 44.8 million barrels—but their profits dropped nevertheless. On average, Wyoming black crude yielded 40 percent less than light crude, and the cost of transporting the oil to buyers further reduced profits. The market for Wyoming gas during the 1920s was even worse than that for oil. Gas output remained depressed until the installation of pipelines to western and midwestern states during the 1930s, and oil output did not surpass the 1923 total until the 1950s.[41]

Beginning in 1920, Wyoming's coal producers coped with the economic vagaries of an unstable market, which lasted until the onset of World War II. Living standards for the coal miners and their families were far worse than for the farming families and even the oil workers, on account of the hardscrabble conditions in coal-company towns and the dangers of working the mines. Poor ventilation caused drowsiness, which increased the risk of accidents; coal dust caused black-lung disease and even tuberculosis; and accidents disabled and sometimes killed miners. Wyoming's worst mining disaster occurred in 1903 at the Hanna Number 1 Mine, where an explosion killed 169 miners. Wyoming's mines were unionized, and the miners' leaders had negotiated for mine safety laws and safer working conditions. Wyoming had provided for mine inspectors and ventilation standards; however, actual compliance with the safety statutes was low. In the two years leading up to Nellie's election, two explosions in mines owned by the Kemmerer Coal Company resulted in the deaths of 138 men.[42] In sum, Nellie faced challenges in her first term that would have severely tasked any new governor, no matter how experienced in business or government.

The morning of January 5, 1925, Nellie dressed herself all in black, which she covered with a protective veil that fell to her waist. She set out for the capitol with a supportive circle of family members; her brother Sam had traveled from Texas, Nelle had arrived from Memphis, and her sons George and Bradford were by her side. Again she regretted that Ambrose had not traveled back to Wyoming for her inauguration, but her concern that Ambrose get settled into his new job in Mississippi had kept her from insisting. Nellie experienced a sharp sense of déjà vu as her little group worked its way through the throng that spilled out of the senate chamber and filled the stairways and the great hall under the capitol dome; she reflected sadly that she was tracing the same path she had taken so proudly just two years earlier for William's inauguration.[43] When she reached the little room behind the Senate dais, she was greeted by Justice Charles N. Potter of the Wyoming Supreme Court, who was to administer the oath of office. It was a fitting coincidence that Potter had served in the 1889 constitutional convention, which had passed Wyoming's female suffrage clause. They were joined by acting governor Frank Lucas and by Nathaniel Thomas, bishop of the Episcopal diocese of Wyoming. Justice Potter opened the door to the packed room, and over his shoulder Nellie could see the crowd of legislators, friends, and reporters, complete with a camera rolling to record the historic event. Sam gave her an encouraging smile and offered her his arm, and they followed Bishop Thomas into the senate chamber.

Bishop Thomas opened the ceremony with a brief invocation. "Oh Lord, . . . look down from Heaven . . . upon this Thy servant to whom the Governorship of this State has been committed. . . . Strengthen her with thy might [and] stimulate her with Thy wisdom." After Frank Lucas pledged to Nellie the future cooperation of himself and all the other members of the state administration, Nellie rose from her seat and walked alone to the podium. She looked across the audience and, in a voice so low that her audience strained forward to catch her words, delivered her first public speech, a brief, five-paragraph statement. First, she thanked Secretary of State Lucas for his service as acting governor. Then she restated her intention to continue the program and policies of her husband. She told her audience that she assumed the governorship "with a profound sense of the high obligation it imposes upon me. . . . [My election] calls forth in this solemn hour my deepest gratitude, and challenges me to rise to the opportunities for service thus made possible, and to dedicate to the task before me every faculty of mind and body with which I may be endowed, . . . relying upon Divine help for strength and guidance."[44]

As she concluded, Justice Potter took her arm to help her down the stairs to the floor of the chamber, where he administered the oath. "I do solemnly swear that I will support, obey and defend the constitution of the United States, and the constitution of this state, and that I will discharge the duties of my office with fidelity," she repeated after Justice Thomas. "The impressiveness and solemnity of those vows sank deep into my soul," wrote Nellie; she would find herself reflecting on the words in the vow many times over the next two years.[45] The swearing-in concluded, Justice Potter announced, "I have the honor of introducing to you Governor Nellie Tayloe Ross," and the spectators rushed forward to offer their congratulations.[46] Then, in a bittersweet scene that marked the gubernatorial transition from William's administration to her own, Nellie signed her oath of office, seated at William's desk and surrounded by her family.[47]

When Nellie assumed the Wyoming governorship, public expectations of governors and the breadth of their roles and responsibilities were in the early stages of radical change. They were metamorphosing from their traditional, ceremonial, and public-relations role to that of modern chief executives with substantive administrative responsibilities. American governors could trace their roots back to the colonial governors, who were representatives of the British crown. The events leading up to the Revolutionary War had bred a considerable wariness of executive powers, so it was to be expected that when the independent states wrote their constitutions after the war, they created weak governors whose tenures were severely limited and whose principal function was to carry out the policies dictated by their legislatures.[48] As additional states joined the union, they tended to copy the constitutions of their sister states, so the weakness of the governor's position was perpetuated across the nation, including in Wyoming.[49] As late as 1917, a delegate to a Massachusetts legislative convention declared, "Our present conception is to elect a figure-head Governor, a man who has important ceremonial functions, some power of supervision, some minor duties, but who is not the administrative head of the State."[50]

The problem with this philosophy, however, was that the increasing complexity of the nation's economy and the plethora of technological innovations around the turn of the twentieth century had intensified both the need for improved public administration as well as the public's taste for government services.[51] State expenditures ballooned as a result of new public works projects, most notably the construction of public highways to accommodate the proliferation of automobiles. Road maintenance had heretofore been a county responsibility, but the need to link local roadways for an increasingly mobile public, as well as the enormous cost of grading and paving state roads, required the states to step in. In general, the legislatures responded to the demand for increased government by creating a plethora of commissions and boards that reported directly to them rather than to the governors. Yet the more agencies that the legislatures created, the less control and oversight they were able to exercise. Around the nation, progressive governors—among them Robert LaFollette in Wisconsin, Hiram W. Johnson in California, Charles

Evans Hughes in New York, and many less well-known governors such as William Ross in Wyoming—began to wrest the lead policy-making role from the hands of their legislatures. In the East, the power of progressive governors was enhanced by the disclosures of the muckraking press, which assisted the governors in curbing the powers of political machines such as Tammany Hall.

Starting with the establishment of the Interstate Commerce Commission in 1887, the federal government had experienced the same pattern of ad hoc growth as the state governments. In 1910, President Taft established a Commission on Economy and Efficiency to study how the increasingly unwieldy government might be better managed. The focus of the commission's 1912 report was on the utilization of a budgetary system to control and direct government operations. In lieu of the ad hoc system of individual, poorly coordinated agency appropriations bills, the commission recommended that the executive establish overall policies and priorities and then communicate these recommended policies in the form of a unified budget for the consideration of Congress. Spurred on by the Taft commission's recommendations, many states appointed similar commissions to examine their operations and recommend improvements and reorganizations. Some of the most prevalent state reform proposals included establishment of an executive budget, a consolidation of state agencies under the supervision of the governor, an increase in the gubernatorial term of office from two years to four, establishment of a centralized planning authority to aid the governor in policy creation and execution, and a transition to a "short ballot." The short ballot reduced the number of statewide officials elected independent of the governor's authority, thereby increasing the governor's control over the entire state government.[52]

Under the Wyoming constitution, the governor's term of office has always been four years. Conversely, the state legislature has declined to establish a short ballot; the Wyoming governor continues to share power with four other elected officials, each of whom enjoys independent authority under the constitution—the secretary of state, the auditor, the treasurer, and the superintendent of public instruction. Many Wyoming state agencies are headed by a board comprising these five individuals. Other than the agencies governed by the five-member commission, Nellie did have broad appointive authority for the heads of other state agencies, subject in most cases to confirmation by the state senate. She had the authority to remove any officials appointed during her term or by prior governors, although she was required to file a justifying statement for her removal with the secretary of state.

During Nellie's tenure, the immediate staff of the governor was limited to an executive secretary, who acted as an administrative and legislative aide, and a private secretary. Among Nellie's first acts as governor were her reappointments of her husband's administrative team: Ruth Harrington as her stenographer and Edward B. Almon as her executive secretary.[53] Nellie had no formal planning staff, so Almon assumed a limited planning advisory role in addition to his other duties. Wyoming had instituted an executive budget system in 1919, providing Nellie with a powerful tool in dealing with the state legislature. The budget statute made Nellie the state's chief budget officer, charged with developing an overall financial plan and presenting it every two years to the state legislature. In August 1925, Nellie supplemented her technical staff by appointing Roy Seney, a Sheridan man with business management and bookkeeping experience, as her assistant budget officer. Nellie also counted herself fortunate that Wyoming was one of only two states in which the attorney general was appointed by the governor, not elected, so that she could count on the loyalty of Attorney General Howell.[54]

The general assessment of the governors in Wyoming has been that their effectiveness has largely depended on their personal skills rather than their formal constitutional authorities. Their power and influence, both during Nellie's term and in the present, are neither particularly strong nor weak when compared to those of other states. "While governors are obviously important, they are seldom as powerful as people think," notes one analysis. "At best, Wyoming governors are persuasive, influential leaders. They are not political 'bosses.' "[55]

"The way laid out for me was not exactly a bed of roses," Nellie wryly remembered. In addition to the urgent need to grapple with the statewide depression, Nellie faced a Republican majority in both houses, and she was the sole Democratic member of the many boards that were composed of the state's five elected officials. She was a political neophyte and was considered a lightweight because of her gender. It seemed a perfect opportunity for the legislature to strengthen its political power at the expense of the governor. From the moment she was inaugurated, the courtly treatment that Nellie had received from the state's Republican leaders evaporated, and she was plunged into partisan politics. There would be times over the next two years when she would look up from her desk and gaze upon the portraits of former governors, taking strength from their supportive presence; it comforted her to know that all of them, including her beloved William, had faced their own crises, but somehow each had survived.[56]

Even though the Republican-controlled Eighteenth Legislature entered the political duel with many advantages on its side, the outcome was by no means a foregone conclusion. Republicans may have held majorities in both the upper and lower houses, but they lacked the two-thirds majority in both houses that they needed to override a gubernatorial veto. Besides, Wyoming's constitution was as jealous in curbing the power of the legislature as it was in limiting that of the executive. In the 1920s, the Wyoming legislative session by law could not exceed forty days every two years. Most of the legislators were ranchers, farmers, or held full-time jobs, so they were not interested in extending the legislative term. Lacking the support of personal or committee legislative staffs that could have broadened the oversight and involvement of the legislature in agency affairs, the Wyoming legislators were true citizen-representatives who spent the majority of their time on their own affairs, in their home districts. They had neither the time nor the inclination to scrutinize the affairs of the big corporations or to devise new programs or services that would have resulted in additional taxation. This arrangement amply suited Wyoming's chief financial interests—the ranchers, the oil and coal companies, and the railroad—which were in a position to exercise substantial influence over individual legislative members. The real political battles in Wyoming were as likely to be among powerful lobbies such as the Stock Growers Association, the Farm Bureau Federation, and the Union Pacific Railroad as between Republicans and Democrats in the statehouse.[57] In fact, one political observer went so far as to describe the legislators as wearing the "brass collar" of the Union Pacific.[58]

The weekend after Nellie's inauguration, Cheyenne's quiet streets started to bustle as the members of the Eighteenth Legislature gathered from the far-flung farms, ranches, and little towns of Wyoming. Across the street from the railroad depot, the lobby of the Plains Hotel was filled with the excited children and proud wives of the legislators, who had accompanied their fathers and husbands to Cheyenne to witness their January 13 swearing-in ceremony. The occasion took on the semblance of a friendly high school reunion; in a state as thinly populated as Wyoming, there were few strangers among the crowd.

The lobby's air was blue with smoke as small groups of legislators began the process of angling for leadership roles and choice committee assignments. Eager lobbyists were there, too, hoping to pick up information about potential bills and keen to promote their organizations' positions. The women were wearing their best dresses and hats while most of the men, Stetsons in hand, sported the standard uniform of western businessmen: conventional suits spiced up with cowboy boots, string ties, and the occasional silver belt buckle. The legislators had strong western faces, lined and weathered from years of exposure to the sun and wind; they gazed directly at one another—most had blue eyes—and they extended sociable greetings in gruff but friendly voices. They shook hands that were calloused from hard physical labor. These were the representatives of Wyoming, ready to act for their neighbors and do their best.[59] Nellie knew most of these men. She had entertained them in her home and visited them on their ranches, and she counted many of them, Republicans as well as Democrats, among her friends. But in her role as governor, some of her old friends had become her political adversaries. She later described her experience with the Eighteenth Legislature as "forty days of sustained tension."[60]

Two days after the legislature convened, Nellie looked down on a statehouse chamber that was packed with legislators from both houses, the judiciary, state officers, and their families. In front of her was a microphone that had been set up for the first time in the legislature's history so that her voice, unaccustomed to speechmaking projection, could be heard by all.[61] "[This] occasion is one to inspire all with the loftiest motives of patriotism. . . . Not to serve special or personal interests, not to be the spokesmen of any particular class or party, have we been entrusted with the task before us, but to labor as best we may, with unselfish devotion to the great cause of popular government, for the advancement of the common interests of all the people," she began.[62]

Nellie then reviewed the past two years' accomplishments during William's administration, and it was clear from her choice of words that she strongly believed herself to be speaking for him as much as for herself. When William assumed office, she noted, the two most critical issues facing the state were the need to institute a program of strict economy to address the state's continuing deficit and the imperative to address the financial difficulties facing ranchers and farmers due to depressed crop and stock prices. Working with the legislature, William had been able to hold state spending to a minimum, secure an increase in the taxes assessed the railroad, and extend a loan program that had been set up to help farmers and ranchers. Despite his efforts, the state deficit had not yet been liquidated, for a variety of reasons that Nellie explained in her message. She was unwilling, however, to call for higher state taxes; the deficit would have to be dealt with by continued reductions in state expenditures because the tax burden on the Wyoming citizen was simply too high.

Nellie outlined eleven areas of proposed legislation, only three of which—

the need for strict state economy, the extension of a loan program for farmers, and the determined enforcement of prohibition—derived directly from her husband's own legislative program. Concerning prohibition, she pledged to continue William's program of aggressive enforcement. She noted that under existing law, it was illegal to sell but not to purchase alcohol, and she urged passage of a bill that would close this loophole. Finally, Nellie followed William's lead in asking the legislature to help the state's agricultural and livestock sectors by making permanent the existing farm loan program.

The remaining eight of Nellie's legislative proposals were her own, although they were faithful to the spirit of William's progressive philosophy. Her proposals focused on the plight of the state's industries and workers as well as the critical need to fund state activities in light of reduced tax receipts. First, Nellie pointed out that although the state had done everything it could to hold down taxes, the average citizen's tax burden had not gone down because cities, counties, and school districts had increased assessments at their levels. She called for legislation requiring these local taxing bodies to adopt the same system of executive budget that had proven such a valuable tool at the state level. Second, Nellie declared that the topic of most concern to Wyoming's citizens after tax reduction was the high number of bank failures, and she endorsed legislation to strengthen the bank examination program as well as to safeguard the accounts of individual depositors. Third, Nellie reminded the legislators that the state's light-oil fields were almost depleted, and she suggested that they establish a commission to explore how the state could market its less desirable stock of black oil to provide the state additional royalty income. Fourth, Nellie referred to a recent state constitutional amendment that had authorized the legislature to enact a bill to dedicate one-third of mineral royalties to the support of public schools; she promoted passage of such a bill, since it would reduce the pressure for higher local taxes to meet school needs. Nellie also urged the legislature to increase its financial support of the state university, which she proposed to pay for by reducing other state expenditures. Her sixth and seventh proposals related to passage of additional mine health and safety provisions and protective legislation to support female employees in industry. Her final recommendation was that the legislature ratify a pending federal constitutional amendment designed to curb the use of children in the labor force.[63]

The legislature handed Nellie her first legislative defeat less than one week into the legislative season when the senate declined to ratify the child labor amendment. While the vote tally did not fall along strict party lines, it was nevertheless a loss for Nellie's progressive agenda. Her opponents based their disagreement with the amendment on the issue of states' rights and the power of the farming and ranching lobbies. Legislators on both sides of the aisle were concerned that the amendment would interfere with the right of Wyoming parents to enlist the help of their sons and daughters on family spreads, and they believed that Wyoming's legislators, not those in Washington, should decide what legal protections were best for the state's children. The federal government, in their view, had already assumed far too much power over Wyoming lands and commerce. Besides, declared one senator, "Labor in God's open sunshine can't hurt any child. . . . It's not work but idleness that I'm afraid of."[64]

From this first defeat, Nellie learned firsthand the necessity of insuring that her own party members were firmly united behind her agenda as well as conducting behind-the-scenes negotiations with her opponents. Nellie later admitted that she entered office harboring the negative stereotypes about politicians that are still prevalent today, but she left office with a profound sense of respect for the men in her party. She found them willing to advise her when she asked, respectful of her decisions even when she chose not to act in accord with their counsel, and never condescending to her because she was a woman. In her chronicle of the gubernatorial years, she stoutly defended politicians and politics in general. "I resent the injustices that [prejudice against politicians] puts upon some of the most unselfish and patriotic persons I have known. . . . We should never forget that some of the greatest and most sublime characters in history, whom all the world now delights to honor, were politicians."[65]

"During every hour of the day I was engaged in interviews with members of the assembly, friendly and unfriendly, trying to advance my own program or to prevent the enactment of laws I disapproved." She remembered in particular one battle over the bill to reform the state banking system, an initiative that she particularly supported. When it became clear to the banking interests that some kind of bill would pass, they were able to insert language stipulating that the governor would appoint the members of the Banking Commission from individuals submitted by the Bankers' Association; in addition, the Banking Commission would have the authority to appoint all bank inspectors. In Nellie's view, the bill would have stripped the governor of appointive control and emasculate the program of bank examination. Nevertheless, she was in a difficult position; if she vetoed a program that she had promoted, she would open herself to charges of inconsistency. Nellie invited the bill's chief sponsor to her office, where the two politely but pointedly exchanged threats of veto and veto override. The senator saw that Nellie meant business, concluded that he could not make good his override threat, and removed the offending language from the draft bill before it reached her desk.[66]

The banking reform incident was a textbook case for how the veto tool can be used effectively in the give-and-take of legislative politics. Ideally, vetoes and veto overrides should be thought of as bargaining chips rather than a suitable resolution to policy disagreements. "This power [should be] used as a last resort," notes one political scientist. "In normal circumstances the governor does not have to use his veto, for the legislature generally is willing to adapt legislation so that it can be passed without the risk of a veto." However, despite her effective handling of the veto to resolve the banking reform issue, Nellie was not so fortunate in her subsequent political maneuvers. By the end of the legislative session, she had vetoed eight bills, or about 5.4 percent of the bills made law; none of her vetoes, however, were overridden. Her vetoes were more an indication of her firm stance on issues rather than a failure to negotiate successfully, particularly given the antagonistic posture of the Eighteenth Legislature. Her veto percentage was about average for all governors, and William's veto record with the Seventeenth Legislature, at 7.8 percent, was higher than hers. Her Republican successor did not formally veto any bills, but if one considers the bills that became law without his approval, then his percentage was 4.4 percent.[67]

Among her vetoes were two bills that she considered incursions of executive authority. The first was of Enrolled Act 19, which would have limited gubernatorial appointment of water division superintendents to candidates proposed by the state engineer.[68] The second was of Enrolled Act 47, which transferred the control and supervision over interstate water negotiations from the governor's authority to that of the state engineer.[69] Several of her vetoes were to become issues during her reelection campaign. When she vetoed a special levy to pay the state's overdraft because of her desire to hold the line on new expenditures, Republicans blamed her for financial ineptitude and irresponsibility. Perhaps even more politically sensitive was Nellie's veto of a bill to hold a special election in the case of a senatorial vacancy. Nellie was convinced that the real purpose of the bill was to prevent a Democratic governor from appointing a new senator, should Wyoming's elderly Senator Warren, a Republican, die in office. Her stated reason for the veto was to save Wyoming voters from the heavy expense of a special election. The Republicans, however, held that Nellie had vetoed the bill in the hope that she would then be able to step in if Warren died or was incapacitated during her second term. Nellie would later conclude that the Republican allegation about her true motives swayed enough voters that she lost the election.[70]

At one o'clock the morning of Sunday, February 22, the Eighteenth Legislature adjourned, having stopped the clock at midnight in order to wrap up its business within the forty-day constitutional limitation. During its term, the legislature had acted favorably on only five of her eleven legislative proposals, and even with these five, she did not achieve all she had requested. The legislature failed to authorize the use of mineral royalties to support public schools, and it declined to act on her proposal to explore the commercial possibilities of black oil. It did establish fines and a term of imprisonment for the manufacture and sale of alcohol, but it did not criminalize its purchase as Nellie had requested. It passed several statutes concerning mine health and safety, but it did not address legislation for the protection of women workers. It did nothing with Nellie's proposal to require local government budgetary systems, and it did not increase its financial support of the state university.

In an editorial postmortem of the legislative accomplishments, the *Casper Tribune* called the legislators incompetent and concluded that the session would go down in history as one of the least productive in Wyoming's history. Even the consistently pro-Republican *Wyoming State Tribune* concluded that the legislature's "most conspicuously outstanding service was negative, expressed not through enacted legislation but through refusal to enact proposed legislation."[71]

Nellie still had twenty months in office before she would need to stand for reelection, but her opportunity to effect state policy through legislative action was over. In the end, Nellie's duel with the legislature concluded in a draw. Nellie was successful in her goal of preventing an erosion of gubernatorial power, and although she was generally unsuccessful in achieving her legislative agenda, she was not less successful than the obstructionist legislature itself, which failed to enact a more substantive register of bills. Perhaps Nellie's legislative program was simply too ambitious. "Decide early what two or three things you want to accomplish [and] develop a sound public information program to let people know," one governor advised his successor.[72] One is left wondering how much more of her legislative agenda she might have been able to accomplish if, with her reelection, she could have embarked on a second legislative session armed with experience, a public relations plan, familiarity with her Republican opponents, and more seasoned political relationships with her Democratic allies.

FIVE

Wyoming Statesman

"THE GOVERNOR IS the most visible state official," noted one political scientist in the 1960s. "He is much . . . sought after for television, radio, and public appearances. As a consequence, he is able to focus public attention on issues which he deems important. There is little assurance that he will always be able to influence public opinion but there is little doubt that he has ample opportunity to be heard."[1] For Nellie, the first woman governor and therefore something of a national celebrity, this statement was doubly true. Through her words and her acts, and for better or worse, she had the opportunity to cast more national attention on Wyoming politics than it had ever received.

The first invitation to step onto the national scene arrived less than two weeks after Nellie's inauguration, and it came through her social connections. Her friend Eula Kendrick, wife of Senator John Kendrick, wrote to urge Nellie to attend the upcoming Coolidge presidential inauguration as Eula's guest and, while in Washington, to deliver a speech at a dinner sponsored by the Woman's National Democratic Club; the officers of the club were offering to pay for Nellie's railroad ticket to Washington. The purpose of the dinner was to begin laying the groundwork for the next presidential campaign. Delivering a keynote address to an assemblage of national Democratic leaders might be "a little appalling at first thought, I know, . . . [but] I am sure you could make a wonderful success of it." Mrs. Kendrick inferred that this first speech might well lead to greater things in the future, and she counseled Nellie, "Don't forget that you belong to the whole world now, not only Wyoming."[2]

Nellie took her time in accepting Mrs. Kendrick's invitation. She was absorbed in legislative politics, Nellie responded, and she was concerned that she might not be able to conclude her consideration of last-minute legislative bills in time to attend the inauguration. The letters traveled back and forth, even after the club officers agreed to postpone their banquet until March 7 if Nellie would only agree to speak. The matter was still open the second week of February when Nellie wrote to Nelle, who had recently returned to Memphis after her Cheyenne visit to attend Nellie's inauguration. "I told Mrs. Kendrick, if I went, perhaps you would be with me. . . . I haven't said yet that I would go but that I would if possible. How I can get time to prepare an address I can't see yet." Nellie was feeling the stress of her responsibilities. "It's the same concentration every day," she wrote Nelle. "Interviews all day long; as one walks out, another walks in—except when I've been at Board meetings & that is a tension sure enough. I'm well though, & that is all I ask, just to be well." Nellie closed her letter by asking about Ambrose, who had just quit his job in Mississippi. "Where is my Ambrose, do you know? . . . I wonder if he is returning to Memphis [before heading back to Wyoming]. The dear boy, he is feeling sick at heart I can tell, going out from the home nest, on his own responsibility. How sorry I feel for him," Nellie fretted.[3]

By mid-February, Nellie had decided to accept Mrs. Kendrick's invitation. Nelle would join Nellie en route and serve as her traveling companion. The two women arrived at Washington's Union Station on March 3, where Mrs. Kendrick and a special reception committee waited to welcome them to the city. Nellie's new political sponsor guided the two women through a dizzying succession of receptions, luncheons, and theater parties, many of which were in Nellie's honor. Nellie quickly became the toast of the town. The *Washington Post* described the sensation that Nellie created during the inaugural parade, dressed in mourning garb of black velour, and declared that "the honors in the procession went without doubt to Governor Nellie Ross of Wyoming. . . . [She] received applause all along the line. . . . Guests in all the special seats rose to pay homage to the first woman governor to ride in an inaugural parade."[4]

The evening of March 7, more than three hundred persons gathered in the ballroom of the Mayflower Hotel at the annual banquet of the Woman's National Democratic Club. The list of the evening's contributing patrons ran six column inches in the *Washington Star* and read like a who's who of the Democratic Party, including Franklin Roosevelt, Bernard Baruch, James Cox, Mrs. Woodrow Wilson, Mrs. William Jennings Bryan, and Mrs. Cordell Hull. In her speech, Nellie lauded Wyoming as a pioneer in female suffrage and office-holding, and she shared some of her early impressions and experiences as governor. The next day, the *Star* declared the dinner a brilliant affair. Nellie was launched as a national figure in the Democratic Party, and both she and the party would benefit. "Dear Mrs. Ross, the good that you did us and the charm that you radiated while here in Washington would be cheap to us at one thousand dollars," wrote one of the banquet's sponsors, Florence Harriman.[5]

Sometime during or after her Washington trip, Nellie drafted several handwritten pages concerning her experiences and impressions. The narrative creates a striking portrait of a woman who is straddling two worlds. As the only female governor at the inaugural festivities, Nellie had not joined the masculine camaraderie of deal making and cigars, but she no longer belonged solely with the political wives. Her account was filled with the social aspects of her trip—the luncheons and parties, the women she had met, and descriptions of their homes, clothes, and jewelry. Her only reference to the political is her wistful observation that if William had been alive to attend the inauguration with her, he would have had the knowledge she lacked of the political: "The distinguished men on the floor of the Senate—the company at the dinners & receptions, he would have known about them all. The things each Senator stood for . . . & the great speeches they had made."[6]

Nellie was left to find her own accommodation between the two worlds. On one detail she was clear: she was determined to preserve her feminine image as a dignified lady. "I had not realized that the people over the country were so interested in me or the situation in which destiny has placed me. . . . But really it would be hard to exaggerate it. Millionaires, Ambassadors, Judges, & women, bless their hearts, of every station, pouring in to my ears praise & tribute, . . . and all with one accord, expressing pleasure that I . . . do not represent the over-powering, masculine, militant type of 'politician' that violates their sense of what the Lord intended a woman should be."[7]

After returning from the excitement of Washington, Nellie's days fell into the predictable if frenetic pattern experienced by all governors. Most mornings, she left the Governor's Mansion between nine and ten o'clock for her short walk to the capitol building, and she tried to leave by around six each evening so that she could spend her evenings with Bradford or quietly socializing with friends. Her official work hours, therefore, were not long, but inevitably, she often spent her evenings devoted to the reading and staff work that she could not get done between office appointments. There was barely enough time in the office in between engagements to read—let alone draft—correspondence and speeches.[8] Every day, the office was inundated with invitations from Wyoming and the rest of the nation to make speeches, attend conventions, and participate in ceremonies and ribbon-cuttings. Nellie's crowded office bustled with the noise of constant visitors, and she found herself scheduled for back-to-back meetings and interviews. The first week of every month, Nellie devoted most of her time to meetings of the many boards and commissions of which she was president; since she was the only Democrat, she was reluctant to miss any of the monthly meetings, and she almost declined to attend Coolidge's inauguration because it would require her to miss some of them.[9] Her diligent, businesslike performance earned her a positive early assessment from a neighboring state. After she had held office for three months, the *Denver Post* observed, "One of the surprising and edifying circumstances of her governorship has been the fact that she has conducted her office not like a gentle-faced, soft-voiced appealing woman in the mourning of a widow, but as an intelligent, tactful, resourceful individual."[10]

When Nellie returned from Washington, she found a letter waiting for her from a Chicago friend, Joyce Clark. Joyce urged her to accept an invitation to participate in the Woman's World Fair, which was to be held in Chicago in April. "Really Nellie, I believe for you to give these women a chance to meet and know you for a few hours is an honor and a pleasure that you owe them. . . . And you owe it to yourself as well. Show the women what an excellent example you are!"[11] The purpose of the fair was to showcase the accomplishments of women, so of course the organizers were keen to get Nellie involved; they hoped that Nellie's participation would help to increase the convention's attendance.

Frugal Nellie might have declined their invitation if she or the state of Wyoming had been required to fund the trip, but the organizers offered to pay all her expenses. When she arrived in Chicago, she learned that the fair's sponsors were Republicans and that the convention's proceeds would go to Republican women's clubs. After that, as her secretary humorously noted in a letter to Nellie's son, she and Nellie cheerfully ran up their hotel service bill and considered it to be their personal contribution to the Democratic cause![12]

The fair's sponsors had been right about Nellie being an excellent drawing card; 750 women signed up to attend the Luncheon for Famous Women, and 1,200 more were turned away. Nellie was the second speaker, and she "charmed everyone," according to her secretary. In her remarks, Nellie complimented the organizers on how well the fair had showcased the "progress of women in every line of endeavor." Women's accomplishments made her proud of her sex and grateful to have lived in a time when so many avenues were open to them. She may have been thinking of her mother when she noted that "they of the last generation approached the borders of the promised land which we their daughters have walked in triumphantly to possess—exemplifying that 'One shall sow and another reap.'" In earlier generations, she noted, the only place where women could command respect was within the home; any activities outside this sphere carried with them a certain stigma. "[But] in this day [woman] can and does enter, without impairing her self-respect or that of others, . . . any avenue of service she desires. . . . I believe the time has passed when reasonable people contend that to best serve the welfare . . . of her family a woman must limit her interest and activities to four narrow walls." Nellie reminded her listeners of the awesome responsibility that had fallen upon women when they achieved suffrage, and she closed by hoping that as full citizens, women might become a substantive force for good, perhaps even leading "the nations of the earth into paths of permanent peace."[13]

During the summer of 1925, Nellie represented Wyoming as a participant at the national Governors' Conference in Poland Springs, Maine. Nellie took Bradford on this trip, and the two of them had a wonderful time. Nellie continued to straddle the disparate worlds of male politicians and their wives as she made new friends among the governors and received many invitations to visit their homes after the conference. After her initial shock that she had become an object of popular curiosity, Nellie had grown to love the attention and the many perquisites that she received as a public figure. "O, if you could have seen the enthusiasm, the kindness with which I have been received and treated everywhere!" she wrote Nelle. "At Bar Harbor I met many millionaires, and you should have seen them clamoring for introductions & attention from the first woman Governor. . . . (I'm almost afraid to put this on paper for fear other eyes outside the family might fall on it)."[14]

During the conference, Nellie offered to host the 1926 meeting in Cheyenne; upon returning from Maine, Nellie urged the Cheyenne Chamber of Commerce to support her bid. Nellie was successful in securing the conference, which was held in conjunction with Cheyenne's annual Frontier Days celebration. Twenty-five governors traveled to Wyoming to participate in the meeting, again earning Wyoming public attention and praise.

The first annual Governors' Conference had taken place in 1908, when thirty-nine governors met in Washington at the request of Theodore Roosevelt to examine the management of the nation's national resources. The conference was established during the period when governors were beginning to assume substantive policy and managerial responsibilities. It provided governors a useful forum in which they could explore common issues and learn from one another's experiences, as well as focus public attention on issues important to many states.[15] Nevertheless, one political scientist has concluded that the Governors' Conferences during Nellie's era were primarily social affairs that lacked substantive results. "With due respect to those who worked hard on the Governors' Conference . . . through the years, there was not very much to show for the effort. Barely half the membership ever showed at the annual meetings . . . until after World War II. . . . The records contain many heated discussions about Social Security, deficit spending, and states' rights, but the hot air was the most notable product of it all."[16]

Despite its apparent limitations as an influential body during the 1920s, the Governors' Conference further enhanced Nellie's reputation and brought positive recognition to Wyoming. At the Poland Springs session, Nellie was invited to deliver the governors' response to the address of welcome from Governor Ralph Owen Brewster of Maine. Her remarks and demeanor earned high marks from the eastern press. She was the "most gracious and lovely character in American life today" and was "a Wyoming booster in every way," according to the *Lewiston (Maine) Daily Sun.* The *New York World* wrote that "she was versed in all the subjects that came up, alert in all of them. The banner of Wyoming she brought east floated high." It is impossible to determine whether her fellow governors were as impressed with her performance and contributions as the newspaper reports suggested, or whether they actually treated her with patronizing courtesy and excluded her from their backroom discussions while she socialized with their wives.[17]

Nellie and the other women who were elected to public office in the 1920s generally were treated kindly by their male peers, but seldom were they treated as true equals. The men who distributed rewards and positions rarely offered women substantive assignments, and most newly elected women lacked the skills and personal power necessary to take such positions for themselves. In the division of committee assignments, female elected officials often found themselves named to "women's interests." For example, Hannah Kempfer, a farmer who was elected to the Minnesota legislature, was an unsuccessful candidate for chair of the Conservation, Game, and Fish Committee. Her loss was explained by the fact that "man has always assumed that the privilege of hunting and fishing is his; to the women belongs the honor of cooking the food when it is captured." Meanwhile, one of Kempfer's female colleagues was tapped to chair the Public Welfare and Social Legislation Committee.[18]

Figuring out how to deal with their new peers bewildered many male politicians. Elected women did not fit in the clearly defined female categories with which they were familiar—mother, wife, or sister. Many political women learned that the most effective way to get along with both male officials and male voters was to conform to the feminine roles that men already knew. Nellie was a master at playing the feminine part, but many other successful female politicians in their middle years did the same. Belle Moskowitz, a powerful advisor to Al Smith during his campaign for the presidency, never gave him advice in front of other people, she never sought a position or recognition for herself, and she neutralized the threat of her presence during meetings of Smith's inner circle by sitting in the background and knitting. Molly Dewson, Nellie's successor at the DNC Women's Division, "decided early on that the best way for a woman to function in politics was to get men to think of her as an aunt or mother." Frances Perkins, whom Franklin Roosevelt appointed to his Industrial Commission when he was governor of New York, reminisced in her oral history about a New York state senator who revealed his feelings and thoughts to her in a way she knew he never would with a man. She concluded it was because she was a woman.

> I was a woman, and one he thought of as a good woman who would not make fun of him. . . . I learned from this that the way men take women in political life is to associate them with motherhood. They know and respect their mothers—ninety-nine percent of them do. It's a primitive and primary attitude. I said to myself, "That's the way to get things done. So behave, so dress and so comport yourself that you remind them subconsciously of their mothers."[19]

The womanly image was a double-edged sword. Female politicians had been as steeped in feminine stereotypes as the men of their generation. Their acculturation as nurturing, noncompetitive, nonassertive, and accommodating meant that they were often unequipped to engage with men in political battles.[20] Women, who had gained their political experience working together cooperatively in settlement houses and in the temperance and suffrage campaigns, were dismayed by the cutthroat nature of male politics. "They look like gladiators. We find them fighting animals," wrote Emily Newell Blair.[21] Since it appeared that men were in politics as much for the blood sport as for the cause, women were even less inclined to jump in to the fray.

One of the ways that male politicians and voters dealt with their bafflement about women in office was to ridicule or belittle them. Asking Texas governor Miriam Ferguson to peel peaches for the camera was one example. In another, Jeannette Rankin, the first woman elected to the U.S. Congress, was described by a Chicago reporter as a "'Montana suffragist—right out of the cattle country' packing a .44 six-shooter and trimming her skirts with chaps fur." When the deeply pacifist Rankin followed her conscience and voted with a tiny minority against the U.S. entry into World War I, most newspapers carried stories of her weeping at the failure to stop the declaration of war. Rankin later called the "weeping stories . . . a form of ridicule, . . . the only effective weapon the militarists could use."[22]

Inevitably, women politicians could expect the press to report on their personal appearance and attire. Nellie's mourning attire spared her a lengthy discussion of her outfit the day she was inaugurated, although one reporter commented on how her lip trembled as the outgoing acting governor paid tribute to her husband. However, a subsequent analysis of her role in the Colorado River Compact included a gratuitous description of her dress and demeanor: "She is an attractive woman with cameo-like features and a face that lights up when she talks; she wears feminine clothes and speaks with a soft southern slur." In a similar example, a *New York Times* reporter described the entrance of the new secretary of state, Florence Knapp, to the assembly chamber: "She wore a peach colored velvet dress and was a picture of loveliness. . . . Her clear, musical voice carried plainly to all parts of the chamber. She plainly won the hearts of the spectators almost instantly." For her part, Mrs. Knapp declared simply that all she asked was the opportunity to do a good job in her new position.[23]

Women candidates could anticipate substantial hurdles in winning nomination to office; they could assume that many of the nominations they *did* receive would likely be to elections the party chairman had already decided could not be won; and, once elected, they could anticipate that their reelection campaigns would be difficult. Women officeholders could also expect to be grilled by reporters about how they were managing their family responsibilities. Any suggestion that a woman had neglected her family was likely to affect her reelection chances.[24] The voters, both men and women, generally considered that a woman's most important job was her responsibility to her husband and children; women politicians neglected this aspect of their public image at their peril. Likewise, it was not ladylike to own up to personal ambition. Nellie admitted her ambition to her brother, but she claimed publicly that she had accepted her party's nomination draft reluctantly, solely to carry out her husband's policies. One is left wondering about the possible psychological costs women like Nellie paid in the conflict between their public and private positions. When Emily Newell Blair looked back on her decision to accept the draft as a DNC national committeeman, she wrote,

> With the better knowledge of myself the years have given me, I realize that I did really want to do it. But so much was I held by my Victorian training that women did not do things just because they wanted to, that, feminist though I had become, the thought of doing anything for self-realization had to be well padded by rationalization.[25]

The character of a gubernatorial administration is shaped to a large extent by a governor's personal preferences and interests. Nellie loved to travel, she loved to meet people, and over time, she began to enjoy giving speeches. The Republicans seized on her out-of-state trips as an opportunity to gain political advantage; they roundly criticized her for her frequent absences from Wyoming. After she attended the Governors' Conference in Maine, a particularly nasty letter printed in the *Kemmerer Gazette* suggested that "it behooves Wyoming to have a good man as secretary of state. Frank Lucas has been acting governor of Wyoming so much while the governor attends pink teas up in Maine and other cooler states that he doesn't know when he gets up in the morning whether he is secretary of state or governor." The *Wyoming Eagle*, a Democratic paper, quickly rose to Nellie's defense, pointing out that "it was perfectly proper for Governor Robert D. Carey to attend the governors' conference, but, of course, Governor Carey was both a man and a Republican."[26] Nellie's out-of-state travel made good campaign fodder for the Republicans, but in fact, she was absent from the state only thirty-four days during her two years in office.[27]

Within Wyoming, Nellie considered her travel to be an important responsibility. "The people naturally want to see and know their Governor, and I regarded it my obligation, and a privilege as well, to acquaint myself by personal contact with their needs and desires in every part of the state," she wrote. Her fondness for travel showed in her colorful, almost poetic description of her Wyoming travels. "In every little town and settlement, in the lonely homestead as well as in the large ranch, in the tang of the sage-brush even, and in the brilliance of the Indian paintbrush—Wyoming's state flower—I found delight. . . . Often, at a turn in the road, there would suddenly burst upon my view long stretches of beautiful and fertile valleys. Checkered with fields of varied crops, they looked like cross-patch quilts, and I was as proud of their productivity as if I had cultivated every patch with my own hands."[28]

Nellie was equally lyric in her description of Wyoming's people:

> I naturally like people—all kinds and patterns—and often in the most isolated sections of our state I have found exceptionally vivid and captivating personalities; men whose bearing and ability would mark them for attention in any environment; women whose charm and distinction would grace any drawing room. And why not? It was the sons and daughters of the older sections [of the country] who made of this, that was once a trackless desert, the great empire it now is, and the very nature of the life in a new country has developed in them to a high degree the same qualities which characterized their fathers before them. One thing I have learned, and that is that the heart of the great world is fundamentally kind.[29]

In August 1925, Nellie spent two days in Denver, where she was elected presiding officer of a meeting attended by the governors, senators, congressmen, and state engineers of Colorado, Wyoming, and Utah. The purpose of the meeting was to discuss how best to protect the water rights of the four states that contain the upper basin of the Colorado River.[30] For several years, the three states at the lower end of the basin had been promoting construction of the Boulder Dam, both to insure water storage and to protect against flooding. At the August meeting, the upper-basin participants issued a statement that they were willing to support construction of the dam, but only if their states were insured an equitable distribution of the water as provided for in the draft Colorado River compact. In October, Nellie accompanied Wyoming's interstate streams commissioner and attorney general to Washington, where the three represented the state's interests at a hearing convened by the Federal Power Commission. While some press reports may have exaggerated her leadership role in the water rights dispute because she served as the presiding officer at the Denver meeting, it seems likely that she was an active player in the process, which eventually led to a favorable ruling by the commission.[31]

In late August 1925, Nellie wrote her brother George a long letter in which she confided her concerns and opinions with the frankness that she always reserved for her family. She wrote George of her recent, "painful" decisions to remove two of William's appointees. In April, Nellie had charged the Game Commissioner, Frank Smith, with frequent intoxication, abusive language in a letter to a Wyoming citizen, and poor handling of the fishing license program; after threatening to fight the charges in a public hearing, Smith resigned. In August, she had forced the resignation of the Law Enforcement Commissioner, M. S. Wachtel, after an investigation found that he had failed to enforce the prohibition law, that he had himself been intoxicated on the job, and that he had accepted protection money. "It means repudiating William's appointees & men who helped elect him & me. The line of least resistance would be to let things drift along. But I can not betray my great trust. . . . Knowing as you do how high-strung & nervous I have always been I think you could hardly believe how cool I have been able to keep *so far* in the face of such serious responsibilities. Something entirely new seems to have been given me," she told George.[32] The firings not only violated Nellie's deeply held sense of loyalty, but they also signified that she had transcended her self-conception as a nonassertive woman who avoided conflict and relied on charm to manage her relationships. While her actions would not have been particularly noteworthy if taken by a seasoned administrator, to Nellie they were a breakthrough and a source of great pride. She referred to the firings in her biographical account under the heading, "The Matter of Loyalty":

> I may say that never for a moment did I doubt what the Governor before me would have done in the same circumstances. In his own high courage I had a stimulating example. In any event the responsibility now was mine. In those few instances where it was necessary, after a thorough investigation, I made changes.[33]

During Nellie's two years as governor, her youngest son, Bradford, was still home with her at the Governor's Mansion. He turned twelve the month before his mother was elected. During her many trips away from Cheyenne, Bradford was cared for by mansion staff members, at least some of whom had been with the family since William's election. Bradford gave his mother little worry, and he was a comfort. Likewise, George had matured during his year working as a ranger at Yellowstone, to which he had retreated when he failed to win a Rhodes scholarship. The superintendent at Yellowstone sent Nellie an excellent report on George: "No finer, cleaner and more upright man ever served the National Park Service. . . . I assure you that we shall always have a place for him." George returned to school in Laramie in 1925, changed his major to law, and was successful in his second application for the Rhodes—aided by his mother's influence, according to some press reports. He left for Oxford in 1926.[34]

Ambrose, however, could not seem to find his way. He had finally realized that his hopes of becoming a rancher were unrealistic. He disliked school and had left the University of Wyoming because he thought it robbed him of ambition. Although he believed he preferred living in the South, he could not get settled there, either. In November 1924, he wrote his mother that he was unhappy in his new job in a store in Itta Bena, Mississippi. Three weeks later, he wrote her about a new job possibility in Greenwood.[35] In February 1925, he was back in Cheyenne. "I have been home for three days now & have been trying to figure out things," he wrote to his Uncle George. "When you and I thought that I had more friends here than in the south, we were mistaken. I am sure I never would be contented here. . . . I wonder after this letter just what you think of me. Probably a little disgusted. I am with myself." By April 1925, he was back in the South, working for his uncles at the Tayloe Paper Company in Memphis, where Nellie wrote him a cheery but concerned letter. "I do hope you are finding your niche. I have so much sympathy for you and yet I realize that the time has come that you *must* settle down to serious business."[36] Yet Ambrose gave up on this new opportunity as he had all the others. Despite his stated dislike of the West and of higher education, he returned to Wyoming and to the University in Laramie in the fall of 1925.

In the early summer of 1926, as the fall election approached, Nellie wrote to Nelle, "The political pot is boiling. The Democrats expect me to enter the race and you may be sure there is going to be a terrible fight." Nellie explained that she had just finished a public-appearance sweep through northern Wyoming, with another being planned for western Wyoming. Later, after her defeat, Nellie would maintain that she had lost her reelection bid in part because she chose to concentrate on her duties in Cheyenne rather than on running a lengthy campaign. However, although Nellie did schedule her campaign trips around her board meeting responsibilities, in truth she had already hit the campaign trail by the beginning of June. Her advisors wanted to make sure that she started her rounds of the state as early as possible. "You should just see how they 'put me through,'" she told Nelle. "It never seems to occur to my good friends that I might need an hour's rest. They almost follow me into my bedroom and I made eight speeches in seven days."[37]

The Republicans held their nominating convention in Casper the week of June 7; their goal was to select a candidate acceptable to all party factions so that they could enter the gubernatorial race unified behind a single candidate. Many of the delegates pushed to tap the popular former governor Robert D. Carey, but he told them that he would not accept their nomination. The

Republicans passed over Secretary of State Frank Lucas and Dr. H. R. Lathrop of Casper, both of whom had filed for office. Instead, they selected Frank C. Emerson, who for several years had served as state engineer. Emerson was given a unanimous endorsement after five rounds of balloting.[38]

The Democratic slate, finalized about July 15, included Nellie for governor and Wilson S. Kimball, a Casper businessman, for secretary of state.[39] In her platform statement, Nellie promised voters that she entered the campaign unfettered by any promise or obligation to corporate or personal interests. She challenged Wyoming voters to name a single act of hers where she had failed because of her sex. She expected no special consideration because she was a woman; rather, she asked that her administration be judged solely on its merits. She summarized her future program of economic conservatism and social progressivism: "Vigilance in the enforcement of law, economy and efficiency in government; the development of all the resources in the state; a sympathetic consideration of the welfare of labor and opposition to special privilege of every kind and character."[40]

The Republicans immediately went on the attack. The *Wyoming State Tribune* criticized Nellie's lengthy platform statement while it praised Frank Emerson's succinct twelve-point program. It pointed out that in her statement, Nellie had used "I" sixty-nine times and "my" thirty-eight times, compared to four uses of "our" and one of "we." It also accused Nellie of taking credit for accomplishments that actually belonged to the legislature or to the five-member state boards.[41] P. C. Spencer, chairman of the Republican state committee, set out to organize a significant assault on Nellie and her administration. He prepared fact sheets that Emerson and the Republican press could use to refute each of Nellie's stated accomplishments. For example, one fact sheet, Memorandum No. 65, entitled "How Governor Ross Has Decreased Taxes for the Farmer and Rancher???" included a county-by-county refutation of Nellie's claim to have reduced the state tax levy. Another discussed seven state debits, totaling $140,000, which the fact sheet claimed Nellie had failed to address in her executive budget. Also included in the Republican campaign files was a listing of influential women across the state, which the campaign organizers hoped could be enlisted to influence women against voting for Nellie.[42]

The Republican press, fed its information by the Republican campaign organization, obligingly produced one negative story after another. In addition to stories criticizing her vetoes, accusing her of fiscal incompetence, and alleging that her travel was excessive, the press printed a letter from one woman, Mrs. C. Watt Brandon, whose husband was publisher of several Republican newspapers. Mrs. Brandon alleged that Nellie had failed to appoint a single woman to an office previously held by men. Nellie's defender, the *Wyoming Eagle,* vigorously refuted each of the charges, but there is little doubt that the negative press had its impact on her reelection chances.

Nellie had refused to play the women's rights card, asking instead that voters judge her solely on her accomplishments. Other party members were not so circumspect. In late September, Thomas Taliaferro, an attorney from Rock Springs, wrote an open letter to the women of Sweetwater County in which he warned his readers that failure to reelect Nellie would permanently injure the ability of women to be elected to other high offices. Republican women quickly published scathing rebuttals. Therese A. Jenkins, a "pioneer suffragist who has been a Wyoming resident for over 50 years," retorted that Nellie did not deserve women's vote because she had never done anything for female rights and suffrage. A Mrs. H. C. Chappell from Natrona County, wrote that "I, as a woman, resent the allegation [that a vote against Nellie is a vote against women]. I am not against a woman for governor, but I am against a woman who is not fitted for the office. . . . We have had two years of passive do-nothing administration. Do we want four more years of it?"[43]

Nellie also faced Republican allegations that she had been nothing but a figurehead governor and that all the substantive decisions during her administration had been made by her advisors. It was logical that Nellie, who lacked personal political and administrative experience, would turn to men she trusted for guidance. She freely admitted to seeking counsel from several advisors "so that I might go into battle armed with knowledge of the legal questions involved and with an understanding of the extent of my own authority and its limitations."[44] To a large extent, Nellie was in a no-win situation as a result of sex stereotyping. No one had questioned the executive authority of William or any other male governor who sought advice from friends and allies. If Nellie had not accepted counsel from experienced voices, she would have been just as likely to attract criticism for arrogance and political naïveté.

In comparison to the aggressive, well-organized and -financed Republican campaign, there is no evidence that Nellie's mentors in the Democratic party developed any specific strategy beyond printing campaign ads and newspaper articles that praised Nellie's performance as governor. Lacking the knowledge of any other way to approach her reelection, Nellie used the skill she had developed so well—her public speaking. She threw herself into an intensive campaign tour; for the last seven weeks leading to the election, Nellie crisscrossed the state in a big Hudson driven by W. S. Kimball, the Democratic candidate for secretary of state.

It was a rare day that Nellie failed to participate in at least three events; some days, she was scheduled for as many as seven. She often started her appearances by nine in the morning and finished her last speech at ten in the evening, speaking at community centers, schools, churches, and even private homes. She began in the Republican-leaning northern counties and worked her way down the state to spend the critical last few campaign weeks in the "southern tier of 'Union Pacific' counties, where the labor unions were strong [and] the ranching interests weak"; in the south, the Democrats held a substantial majority of about five to one over Republicans.[45] Wherever she went, Nellie was greeted by record crowds. No matter what the political preferences might be of her audiences, it was clear that they held Nellie herself in high esteem.[46] "Have just returned from the biggest meeting I ever addressed," she wrote George and Alfred from Casper in late October. "People standing like sardines in the rear & hundreds turned away. . . . So it is every night—crowds packed to the doors. . . . If I'm defeated it will be with the most wonderful prospects [with which] any one went forward to meet defeat. . . . [The Republicans] are making a vicious attack on me, here, and all over the state."[47]

Nellie did everything she could to prevent her campaign from stooping to muckraking and mudslinging. In response to Republican attacks, she simply campaigned harder. She was determined to stay focused on the issues rather than responding to or indulging in personal attacks. "No story has been too wild for the opponents of Governor Ross to put into circulation," declared the editor of the *Wyoming Eagle.* He suggested that reports of Nellie's success on the campaign trail had made her opponents desperate, and he confidently predicted her reelection. Nellie herself was not so sure of victory. "People are betting large odds on my election & yet I don't feel sure of it," she wrote her brothers.[48]

Her concern may have finally led her, in the last month of the campaign, to play the "female" card despite her initial declaration that she desired to be judged solely on her accomplishments. At a rally in early October, she told her audience, "If I am defeated the whole nation will say that your first woman governor has been a failure. I appeal to you to do me justice, not to place me in a false light before the nation." In a statement quoted on November 3, she said, "I am not asking you to vote for me because I am a woman, but because I am a woman I do not think you will repudiate the first woman governor."[49]

On election day, the Republicans achieved a clean sweep of statewide offices. Nellie's race was by far the closest; of the 70,000 votes cast for governor, Nellie lost by fewer than 1,400. In comparison, the vote margin for secretary of state was 7,000 votes, state treasurer 5,000, state auditor 8,000, and superintendent of public instruction 16,000, which suggests that she was successful in attracting crossover Republican voters despite the negative campaign publicity.

Many factors contributed to Nellie's loss. She had lost significant support in two counties where she had pushed for removal of county officers for cause; the voters resented her intrusion into county affairs.[50] The editor of the *Wyoming Eagle*, Tracy McCracken, concluded that the lack of effective campaign organizing by the Democrats at the county and precinct levels was as responsible for Emerson's victory as were the negative allegations of the Republicans. "[The Republicans] do one thing honestly which we did not do and which we should have done," McCracken wrote Nellie's brothers. "They saw to it that all of their own people were registered and that all of their own people actually voted. We should have done this, but lack of organization and lack of funds prevented." Finally, McCracken estimated that about two to four thousand voters voted against Nellie simply because she was a woman—not a large number, but more than enough to make a difference in such a tight election.[51]

"Of course I'm stung by defeat but by no means crushed," Nellie wrote her brothers. "It may be best. Perhaps four more years of the strain would have been too much for my good. Anyhow I have no choice. I've no idea where to turn or what I'll do." It seemed to Nellie that in defeat, she had lost William all over again. Any grief that she had postponed due to the demands of the governorship would now have to be dealt with. In addition, she was losing her home of four years, which forced her to make some speedy decisions about where she would move and what she would do to earn a living. She told her brothers that she was not interested in being tied to an apartment, especially since she expected her new life might involve extensive travel. She was considering placing Bradford at Sherwood Hall, an Episcopal preparatory school in Laramie. "The truth is," she concluded, "the more I think, the less I know what I'm going to do."[52]

The ever-supportive *Wyoming Eagle* told its readers that it would be many years before another Wyoming governor would bring greater honor and recognition to the state. "We venture the prediction that the career of this illustrious woman has only begun. Her state and nation need the continued benefit of her talents and noble character."[53] From outside the state, the comments of the *Boston Herald* reflected the national assessment: "Few will mourn the passing of Mrs. Ferguson [of Texas] from office. But Mrs. Ross will go out with the respect of her own community and her own state and with the good will of the country."

Contemporary opinions concerning how effective Nellie was as a governor covered the spectrum from extraordinarily accomplished to inconsequential. No one, not even her Republican opponents in Wyoming, labeled her incompetent. Almost all assessments agreed that she had worked hard and had discharged her responsibilities with dignity. The question that remained was whether she had simply functioned as a sympathetic figurehead. In the opinion of the *Wyoming Eagle* and of many out-of-state newspapers, Nellie was among the best governors of her time. On the other hand, even her personal secretary, when later asked to list Nellie's accomplishments, was unable to name any specific examples.[54] Among the less-enthusiastic press appraisals of Nellie's performance was that of the *Snake River (Wyo.) Sentinel:*

> Mrs. Ross seemed to be just as short on any items of outstanding achievement as her record is short of items of scandal which is all fair enough. There has been little doing in a positive way in the state during the past year. . . . Just a plain case of a gentlewoman going ahead with her unique office supported by a sympathetic electorate composed of loyal Democrats and chivalrous Republicans. . . . She exploits her position in a social way both within and without the state and has probably done more visiting and made more addresses than any governor we have had in many years.[55]

Now that more than seventy-five years have passed and the partisan passions of Wyoming's 1926 election have long been extinguished, how should history evaluate the nation's first woman governor? It may be helpful to classify a governor's responsibilities into three distinct, if overlapping, categories—policy formulation, administration, and public relations—and then to assess Nellie's performance in each of those areas. Governors' policy programs primarily consist of their legislative proposals, their success in securing their proposals' passage through the legislature, and their subsequent implementation of those policies through the state agencies. Their administrative responsibilities are expressed through their powers of appointment and removal as well as their supervision of the state agencies under their direct management. Their public relations programs, which include their public pronouncements, ceremonial appearances, press contacts, and speechmaking, serve both to promote their policies within the state as well as to advance their state's interests elsewhere.[56]

With regard to her policy-development responsibilities, Nellie's performance was respectable, if not spectacular. During an arduous burst of work, study, and consultation, Nellie was able to craft a coherent set of legislative proposals in the brief period between her election and the beginning of the legislative session. She had the help of her husband's former advisors, but she also proved to be a quick study. Despite Nellie's statements that she served merely as caretaker for William's policies, an analysis of her legislative proposals demonstrates that the majority of her proposals were actually her own. William borrowed at least as much from the policies of his progressive Republican predecessor, Robert D. Carey, as Nellie did from William.[57] When it came to passage of her legislative policy proposals, Nellie was handicapped by the adversarial nature of her Democratic administration's relationship with the Republican legislature. However, her performance was no less effective than that of the Eighteenth Legislature, which is primarily remembered for its failure to get anything done. While she was not able to overcome the legislature's rejection of her proposals, she did avert Republican attempts to erode Wyoming's gubernatorial authority and prerogatives.

Nellie believed that her familiarity with William's policies and political experience had equipped her with the knowledge and skills she needed to perform as governor. However, there is a significant difference between exposure from the sidelines and substantive political skill based on personal performance. A study of the background of governors holding office between 1870 and 1950 found that almost every incumbent had held some political office before being elected governor. Nationally, prior experience in the state legislature was by far the most common denominator among governors; in Wyoming, over half of the governors had served in the legislature.[58] As Al Smith wrote concerning the experience he gained in the New York State legislature before being elected governor, "No man knows law and the reasons for it, what made it possible and the forces opposing it, better than the member of the legislature who gives his work study and proper attention. . . . [The legislature] gave me a breadth of vision that I could obtain in no other way."[59] Nellie was able to function far more effectively as a policy formulator than her lack of experience would have predicted, thanks to her intelligence, her hard work, and her interpersonal skills. However, if she had been able to acquire political experience in the legislature or another political office before her election as governor, she might indeed have become one of Wyoming's most outstanding governors.

Nellie's lack of experience likewise affected her performance in the administrative area. However, she was fortunate that the management aspects of her position were not nearly as important in the 1920s as the other two components of her gubernatorial responsibilities. If Nellie had been elected fifteen years later, her lack of prior administrative experience would have been a much greater handicap. She served as governor during the period when the position was in transition from a mere figurehead role, generally limited to public relations responsibilities, to a substantive one, a modern chief executive, responsible for directing large, complex bureaucracies and for administering substantial executive budgets.

One of Nellie's most important management roles was as state budget officer, and her performance in that area became a point of campaign controversy as Republicans and Democrats traded accusations concerning the failure to reduce the state's overdraft. It is impossible to determine which party's position was correct; both sides interpreted the sequence of budgetary events to its own advantage. Nevertheless, the controversy itself is a blemish on an administration that declared fiscal economy and solvency to be among its highest policy priorities.

In her own subsequent account of the gubernatorial years, the only reference that Nellie made to her management responsibilities—that is, the staffing and supervision of state agencies—was her removal of two state officials. Since Nellie shared supervisory responsibility with the four other executives elected statewide, she cannot be held solely accountable for the management of those boards and commissions. But for those agencies for which she had sole executive responsibility, it appears that Nellie provided little or no leadership; her agency heads were left to manage their own affairs. There is no record that Nellie made any effort to study the performance or the organization of her agencies with an eye to improving the efficiency or effectiveness of her administration. Given the steep learning curve required by all aspects of her position and the inevitable daily issues that demanded her immediate attention, Nellie had little time to learn about and master the tools of management—the briefings, reviews, and special studies that would have helped her to identify areas of improvement, develop expectations for her agency heads, and hold them accountable for performance.

Nellie excelled in the third component of her position, public relations, which was a far more important factor in gubernatorial performance during the 1920s than it would be today. Public relations rely much more on "people skills" and communication expertise than they do on prior experience, and in these areas Nellie was superbly talented. The opening wedge of Nellie's public relations success may have been her unique status as the first female governor; however, one should not discount her excellent public relations performance simply because she took advantage of her unique status. The "female governor" angle, poorly played, could just have easily worked against her; it certainly did for Miriam Ferguson. Nellie was able to bring considerable attention and acclaim to the state of Wyoming, and her public relations skills made her extraordinarily popular with Wyoming's citizens, despite her re-election defeat. Through her, Wyoming exercised leadership relating to interstate water rights and a broad range of issues important to the Governors' Conference. Because of her, Wyoming attracted more attention, all positive, than it had ever received during its history as a state; thanks to Nellie, Wyoming enhanced its reputation as a bastion of equal rights and progressivism.

Nellie Tayloe Ross is not numbered among the Wyoming governors whose administrations left behind substantive legacies in the areas of policy formulation or administration. However, it is likely that no other Wyoming governor has been able to bring the state more beneficial national attention and acclaim than Nellie. Nellie brought dignity to the office of governor, and her personal skills were a good match for the era in which she served Wyoming. Just as important as her service to her state, her successful performance helped to pave the way for aspiring female politicians who came after her.

SIX

Chautauqua Speaker

"HOW GOOD of you to write so sweetly to the sister who for the first time in her life walks out into the world homeless," Nellie wrote to Nelle a few weeks after her defeat.[1] Nellie had just turned fifty, and she had no idea what to do with the rest of her life. She had no husband, no income, no job, no formal education beyond her decades-old teacher training, no savings, and a family to support. For a woman who had always worried about financial security, it must have been a frightening moment. She immediately began to explore how she could capitalize on her fame as the nation's first woman governor. While still in office, Nellie had already accepted reimbursement for at least two articles, but after her defeat, Nellie sought the services of an agent to help her market her work. Nellie engaged Eula McClary, the owner of a photo, news, and feature service, to seek bids for an article that she planned to write about her marriage and her gubernatorial years.[2]

When her old advisor, Joseph O'Mahoney, became aware of her arrangements with McClary, he warned her that in her eagerness to market her fame, she was endangering the very reputation that made her so admired by the public. Her ability to make a living as a writer and speaker depended on that reputation. "I wired [McClary] the suggestion that she abandon all attempts to get in touch with editors on your behalf. I have the feeling very definitely that it would be neither dignified nor helpful," he wrote Nellie. By intervening, he assumed the responsibility for guiding Nellie financially—a role that he would continue to play for two decades or more.[3] On O'Mahoney's advice, Nellie accepted an offer of twenty-five hundred dollars from *Good Housekeeping* to write three articles, which were published in a three-month series entitled "The Governor Lady" in the fall of 1927.[4] She would supplement these articles the following year with an account of her first year on the Chautauqua circuit.[5] The four articles were the closest that Nellie came during her lifetime to writing an autobiography. Ignoring, as always, her difficult early years, Nellie began the account of her life in "Governor Lady" with her marriage to William.

One feminist scholar who reexamined Nellie's autobiographical account in 2000 has suggested that Nellie's references to her domestic priorities were "carefully contextualized for rhetorical effect." In the presentation of her life and her career, Nellie had to achieve a careful balance; she had to present herself as a competent politician while reducing the threat she represented to a public unaccustomed to powerful women. She did so by emphasizing the paramount value she placed on her roles as wife and mother. Nellie's underlying message was that she was no radical, but merely a typical American woman who rose to the challenge of her circumstances. The author concluded by taking note of Nellie's widespread fame in her time, suggesting that "if Ross's public had not perceived that she accepted the cultural values of her time, she would not have gained the public voice that she had."[6]

The editor of the autobiography of Emily Newell Blair, who preceded Nellie as vice chairman of the Democratic National Committee, observed that Blair was unwilling "to admit her active role in promoting her own career and in seeking power and influence. It was, she claimed, . . . her husband who would have been unhappy if she had confined her activities to domestic duties."[7] It was unseemly for a lady to admit to personal ambition. Nellie had denied her own personal ambition when she decided to run for governor, and in her autobiographical writings, she continued to deny her ambition because she was clearly conscious of the feminine image upon which she would make a career. One wonders how aware Nellie actually was that her private actions were sometimes in conflict with her stated ideals and values.

Early in December 1926, while still in office, Nellie went to Washington to attend her last meeting of the executive committee of the National Governors' Conference. From Washington, she took a train to Philadelphia, where she had accepted an invitation to dedicate a fine new building to house the Gimbel Brothers' department store. Waiting to greet her at the railroad station were Philadelphia's mayor and his wife, accompanied by many of Philadelphia's leading citizens. Her procession through the streets of Philadelphia included a platoon of mounted police, the police band, a police motorcycle corps, a cavalry company of the national guard, and the Gimbel Color Guard of 180 flags. She wrote her family, "Thousands of people had gathered at the station to greet my arrival & all through the streets, crowds lined the sidewalk almost as they did at the president's inauguration. Flags & Wyoming banners hung high." She warned George and Nelle not to share the letter outside the family circle, lest she appear to other readers to be bragging about her fame.[8]

After the Philadelphia stop, she journeyed on to Syracuse, where she spoke at the annual national meeting of the League of Women Voters.[9] A reporter in attendance wrote enthusiastically that the speech left "many women wondering whether they had been listening to the 1928 Democratic vice-presidential candidate. The league's nonpartisan flag was nailed to the mast and therefore there was not the slightest whisper of Governor Ross as a possible candidate in the convention sessions. The undercurrent of discussion, however, . . . was that the time is ripe for a woman candidate and that Governor Ross would be acceptable in many quarters. The impression gained ground from a letter sent to the convention by Gov. Alfred E. Smith in which he referred to her as 'typifying the woman citizen at her best.' "[10] It was not the first time that Nellie had been mentioned as a vice-presidential candidate; a Consolidated Press Association reporter had written a syndicated article on Nellie's possible candidacy as early as July 1926.[11]

By the end of December, Nellie had firmed up her plans for 1927. To tide herself over the holiday, she had rented rooms in the home of a Cheyenne friend for herself and Bradford, whom she had indeed enrolled at Sherwood Hall for the spring term. She was anticipating a subdued Christmas, spending most of her time packing and moving out of the Governor's Mansion. In January, she would travel to Memphis to spend about three weeks with George and Nelle. After a brief rest with family, she would journey on to Tallahassee, where she had been invited to stay with the governor of Florida and his wife. Then she would launch her new career as a speaker and writer.

Despite her insecurity about her lack of a reliable income, Nellie quickly learned how very marketable she was. She was besieged with dozens of invitations to speak at meetings and conventions. Their sheer number forced her to decline most of them, although she did accept several speaking engagements on the East Coast beginning in late March. The prestigious League for Political Education in New York City, whose directors included Al Smith and Henry Taft, had engaged her for a thousand dollars to be their keynote speaker at an upcoming meeting. She had agreed to speak at the Woman's City Club of Albany, where Governor Smith had invited her to be his guest.

She had also signed a contract to join the summer tour of the Swarthmore Chautauqua Circuit. The ten-week Chautauqua tour alone would earn her substantially more income than her entire 1926 salary; the *Wyoming Eagle* speculated that her 1927 earnings would most likely exceed a full four years of gubernatorial salary.[12]

Although Nellie was relieved to have resolved, at least temporarily, her worries about financial solvency, she was still unsettled emotionally. She warned Nelle that her Memphis stop would be short; she needed to hurry back to Wyoming to begin preparing her speeches and articles. "If I'm to meet the engagements I have credibly, I must get back & settle down & prepare. Back to where? Indeed I do not know yet. I am not able to figure it out—how or where I can live in peace of mind. But it must be in Cheyenne. It must not be said of me that, aggrieved, I have shaken the dust of Wyoming off my feet."[13]

Between her spring speaking engagements, Nellie spent long hours perfecting the basic speech she would deliver while on the Chautauqua circuit. Over the years that Nellie contracted with Chautauqua, she developed several versions of her speech material, but the primary topics were her gubernatorial experiences ("The Governor Speaks on Politics and Politicians") and the new political responsibilities of postsuffrage American women ("Progress and the Eternal Feminine").

A few years later, Nellie was infuriated when a nationally syndicated columnist speculated about who had written Nellie's speeches for her. Nellie never employed a ghostwriter; even as a newly elected governor, she had written her own speeches. Ruth Harrington Loomis, who served as private stenographer to both William and Nellie, recalled that while William expected her to draft his final letters and speeches from quick dictation, Nellie was more particular: "She crossed her t's and dotted her i's. She had a great command of the English language, and knew what she wanted to say and how she [wanted to say] it." Decades later, in a speech to the Wyoming Press Woman's Association, her first secretary from the Mint talked about Nellie's extraordinary vocabulary. "I used to wonder, in the years with her, about that vocabulary. It was so unique. I never heard anyone else use the type of words that Mrs. Ross would use in her dictation and her speeches. And then one day she explained it to me, that as a young married woman, here in Cheyenne, and through the years when her children were small and growing up, she and her husband read aloud to each other on every occasion they had . . . [from the Bible and the classics]. So I think that that was where she acquired that very unusual vocabulary."[14]

Early drafts of Nellie's articles and speeches that have survived contain paragraph after paragraph of heavily edited lines, documenting her meticulous attention to flow, order, and word choice. One stenographer who helped her while she was drafting a Chautauqua speech noted that she went over and over her dictation, striking and rewording until he was almost driven to distraction.[15] Once when her Mint secretary asked her why she labored so long over each word, Nellie told her that Justice Holmes had labored a full year on only one paragraph, so she felt that she was entitled to take a few extra days to do an entire speech![16]

Nellie wrote that she considered her first summer on the Chautauqua circuit "among the distinct privileges of my life."[17] Most twenty-first century Americans would be hard-pressed to define Chautauqua, but to their early twentieth-century ancestors who hailed from the farm or from small country towns, Chautauqua was a major phenomenon. For many, it was the eagerly awaited highlight of their entire summer. Both Chautauqua and the related lyceum movement sprang from a thirst in nineteenth-century small towns for education and enlightenment.[18] Chautauqua took its name from the New York village where the movement was founded in 1874. It began as a summer camp to instruct Sunday school teachers on the Bible and other religious topics, but the courses quickly expanded into an extensive liberal arts curriculum. In response to Chautauqua's growing popularity, in 1878 its founder set up a correspondence program with a full four-year course of study. In 1883, the Chautauqua University was granted the authority to grant degrees; by 1891, enrollment had swelled to 180,000 participants—housewives, farmers, merchants, and ambitious shopgirls or clerks who hoped to advance their careers or enrich their lives. Chautauqua was a peculiarly American movement; it was embraced by quintessential, upwardly mobile Americans, can-do individuals with a desire for self-improvement. Chautauqua flourished because most American colleges of the era were unwilling to accommodate nontraditional students such as working adults, and many colleges still refused to admit women. One early promoter of Chautauqua wrote that it was "the first great popular campaign to prevent education from becoming a privilege for the favored few."[19]

Small-town citizens out on the great midwestern plains were just as eager for intellectual stimulation as their peers in New England, where most of the permanent community Chautauquas and lyceums were located. Cut off from the yeasty ferment of new ideas and multicultural contacts found in American cities, rural Americans spent their lives in self-contained little worlds. Few traveled farther than the county seat or closest market town. For intellectual stimulation, they were limited to the local daily or weekly newspaper and the traditional exchange of gossip with the same old group of neighbors. Many towns still lacked libraries in the early 1900s, relatively few towns had cinemas until the late 1910s, and radio broadcasting was not widespread until the 1920s.[20] "Weary of mud-road isolation, they thirsted for knowledge, for the exposition of new ideas not accessible to them," wrote Harry P. Harrison, the famous Chautauqua promoter who would sign Nellie to his bureau immediately after her inaugural summer. "Above all, they were hungry for escape from their own flat horizons into the fascinating world that lay beyond. . . . Lecturers who 'had been there' could evoke these exotic scenes."[21]

In 1904, a promoter named Keith Vawter came up with the idea of "circuit Chautuaqua," which enabled him to reach this eager audience. That year, the leaders of fifteen small Iowa towns signed engagement contracts guaranteeing the sale of season tickets for an entertainment program of seven days; thus Vawter could afford to engage nationally known speakers and entertainers for his program. These tent-based, portable Chautauquas would eventually crisscross the prairies, visiting one small town after another following a carefully planned schedule. From 1920 to 1924, more than ten thousand communities a year hosted tent Chautauquas; in 1924, when circuit Chautauqua reached its zenith, more than forty million Americans attended Chautauqua events.

For one week every summer, the atmosphere in each hamlet was electric with excitement as families flocked to the tents to listen to luminaries such as William Jennings Bryan, Theodore Roosevelt, Jane Addams, and Susan B. Anthony. The cosmopolitan speakers dazzled their audiences with talks on literature, history, travel, religion, and politics. Into towns where most people shared the Protestant faith and the Republican Party came Catholic, Democratic, and even foreign speakers, who introduced their audiences to new ideas about democracy, society, and citizenship. As one Chautauqua performer reminisced, "More often than not it was the lecturer under the canvas at a muddy crossroad who first introduced the pros and cons of high or low tariff, prohibition, juvenile courts, votes for women. Parents heard talk of supervised playgrounds, school lunches, free milk for babies, warnings that the little red schoolhouse no longer was good enough."[22] But Chautauqua introduced small-town Americans to more than just lecturers. It gave many of them their first exposure to nationally renowned professional musicians—soloists and ensembles who played both classical and popular works. Audiences were also entranced by magicians, impersonators, dancers, dramatic readings, plays, and even animal acts.[23]

It took more than fame to make a successful Chautauqua speaker. First of all, it required great stamina to survive the constant travel, the vagaries of small-town lodging and restaurants, and the daily strain to one's public speaking voice. Second, it took considerable public speaking talent to render one's subject, no matter how potentially interesting, into a forty-five-minute speech riveting enough to hold the interest of the thousand men, women, and children who were packed onto hard wooden bleachers in a suffocatingly hot tent. Many famous people washed out after just one season on the circuit, but Nellie continued to participate until the end of the Chautauqua era.

Nellie used her laborious speech-drafting process as her basic preparation for the delivery itself. Since she was delivering her Chautauqua speeches to sizable audiences under very poor acoustical conditions, she became expert in the arts of voice projection and elocution. Her diction was crisp, and her measured delivery was characterized by studied timing and intonation. Nellie paused frequently, both to emphasize her points and to enhance her listeners' comprehension. One could identify the impact of her early years as a teacher; at times, her delivery almost sounded as if she were still patiently lecturing to a group of willing but uninstructed students. Her accent betrayed her Missouri roots—it was not strongly southern; rather, it was an interesting and pleasant blend of southern and midwestern, with a studied incorporation of British pronunciation. The overall effect was one of cultured intelligence.[24]

Nellie loved the Chautauqua circuit. She enjoyed the adulation of her audiences and the special attention showered on her by local dignitaries. She took to the travel, the arduous schedule, and the crowds of people with gusto. Even so, her description of the physical demands is evocative:

> A contract for a lecture engagement, every single night except Sunday for eleven continuous weeks, in a different town each time, necessitating daily motor trips averaging perhaps sixty miles, and sometimes amounting to two hundred and more at a stretch; the ever-present consciousness of an obligation to offer to an intelligent, if long-suffering, public a

> speech constructive in character, and to "put it over" every single night in a manner acceptable enough to hold the audience even though the rains descend, the floods come, and the winds beat upon the tent—a tent *not* founded on a rock[!][25]

After her summer with the Swarthmore Chautauqua organization, Nellie was approached by the Redpath Bureau, the most famous Chautauqua bureau of them all; would Nellie be willing to deliver a series of lectures during the 1927 winter lyceum season? Joseph O'Mahoney stepped in to negotiate on Nellie's behalf. "I have no doubt that the Governor did not mention the fact to you, but it is a fact, that there is a considerable sentiment in some of these Western States for offering her name at the next Democratic National Convention for the Vice-Presidency," O'Mahoney wrote the Redpath manager, Harry P. Harrison. "While of course, nothing may come of that suggestion, nevertheless the mere association of her name with such a position . . . might offer the opportunity of securing larger fees both to the profit of the Bureau and the Governor."[26]

As Harrison and O'Mahoney began to negotiate the possibility of a summer 1928 contract for Nellie, Harrison used Nellie's lyceum speeches to assess her effectiveness and marketability as a speaker. His discrete inquiries yielded positive assessments of her performance. One sponsor wrote him, "I will take this opportunity to tell you how thoroughly delighted everyone was with Mrs. Ross. . . . The word[s] I have heard used in commenting on her part in the program are: 'taste, discrimination, sound common-sense.' We felt that she demonstrated in just the way that we hoped she might the contribution that a woman of her abilities and character can make in public service. Her voice carried perfectly to the remotest members of her audience and there was none of the irritation that sometimes occurs with woman speakers who cannot be easily heard."[27]

Before her top-billed evening lecture, Nellie's audience would be entertained by a musical act; in 1929, Nellie's leading act was Edna White's Trumpeters.[28] After the crowd spent itself in a rousing response to the trumpeters' musical fireworks, it was ready to settle in and listen with respectful attention to the famous Governor Lady. Dressed in an evening gown, Nellie walked out onto the platform, hung her black handbag on the back of a carefully placed chair, and turned to her audience to deliver yet another rendition of "The Governor Speaks." Each night, as she gauged the reaction of the individual audience to her remarks, she presented a unique version of her basic remarks, in part to make the repetitive nature of her task more interesting for herself.[29]

She often began her speech with one of her favorite icebreakers: "I am hoping somewhere about the rafters, the shade of Dr. Samuel Johnson might be lurking, and filled with remorse, over that contemptuous remark he made about women speaking in public—. . . 'It is like a dog walking on his hind legs. Not well done, but you are surprised that it is done at all.' "[30]

Since what interested people about Nellie was her unique experience as a female chief executive, Nellie's speech text gave particular attention to the political roles and responsibilities of American women. She pointed out to her audience that women had begun to enter every occupation formerly closed to them, including the clergy. Their expanding opportunities had made many people intensely uneasy, fearing that the new equality might endanger the fundamental structure of society. Nevertheless, she declared, now that women had ventured into the business world, America would never be able to step back to the past. But one field of endeavor remained largely closed to women, and that was politics; most men were simply unwilling to share true power with female aspirants. Nellie was careful to declare her belief that mothers of young children should forgo public service in order to concentrate on their maternal responsibilities; for other women, however, the time had come when female candidates for office should be judged on their political capabilities, not their sex.

"[There] is the conviction deep in the minds of many men, and sad to say of women too here and there, that women haven't the mental capacity that men have to grapple successfully with the profound problems of government," Nellie declared. But "it is not just to discriminate against a woman because she is a woman, nor can she justly receive immunity from the stern judgment of the public because she is a woman if she has failed in office." Even those women who were not interested in seeking office for themselves bore a special responsibility to become educated about and involved in political issues. They owed this responsibility not just to their country, but more specifically to their families. "Upon the day that the mother kisses her little son good-bye and sends him off to school she commits him to the care of the government. . . . The ballot has placed in the hands of woman the power tremendously to influence, if not actually to determine, the conditions under which her children shall be reared," she declared.[31]

In her speech, Nellie managed to blend a call for equal opportunity and a belief in the capabilities of women to achieve in any field with a deference to the traditional role of the wife and mother. Her message was perfectly pitched to small-town America; she demonstrated respect and understanding for her core audience of wives and mothers while justifying a call for her listeners to embrace the responsibilities that became theirs with the passage of the Nineteenth Amendment. Nellie rejected the label of "feminist" her entire life, but if one defines feminism as a belief in equal opportunity and selection based on merit, then a feminist she was.

In 1925, just one year after Chautauqua attendance hit its all-time high, not a single one of the fifteen major booking bureaus made money on their Chautauqua tours; by 1926, more than half had gone out of business. Nellie joined the circuit the following year, yet despite her fame and that of the other performers, Redpath was unable to sustain a profit. "It is disappointing to know that you lost money on your contract with me this last week," she wrote Harrison. "I am wondering if we included the Springfield Ill. engagements in this series, with the understanding that I take no fees for them, whether that would offset your loss on me for this week. I would be very glad to do that or anything more you can suggest to bring your profit up to what you expected."[32]

The truth was that Chautauqua was about finished. By the late 1920s, few people were interested in sitting in a hot tent and listening to a long lecture on a serious topic when even the smallest town had new and exciting leisure activities available, just a short drive away in the family automobile. As their audiences drifted away, the seasons of the surviving companies became shorter and their programs dropped from a week to three or four days. "[Chautauqua] died in 1932," wrote one historian, "under the hit-and-run wheels of a Model-A Ford on its way to the movies on a newly paved road. Radio swept it into the ditch, and the Wall Street crash and the subsequent depression gave it the *coup de grâce*."[33]

Indeed, why should an American family in the late 1920s put up with the crowds and the uncomfortable wooden bleachers to go see someone famous when they could sit in the comfort of their living rooms, cool drinks in hand, with their choice of famous people, dramas, or music just a twist of the radio dial away? It is impossible to overstate the impact radio's magic had on the American way of life—radio was more transformative than either television or the Internet in their respective times. With radio, the nation had become a single transcontinental village in which time zones and distances were irrelevant and in which, for the first time, Americans heard the same songs, laughed at the same jokes, and learned the same news at the same moment. As people across the nation tuned in each night to chuckle at the latest adventures of *Fibber McGee and Molly,* to sing along with zippy commercials for the latest brands and products, and to listen to riveting news stories like Lindbergh's transatlantic crossing, they were absorbing the common knowledge, attitudes, and values that transformed them into modern Americans.

A 1924 article entitled "How Radio Is Remaking Our World" proclaimed that radio's twenty million listeners had already purchased almost three million radio sets in order to listen to the nation's almost six hundred commercial broadcasting stations. The article predicted that radio would eradicate the sense of rural isolation that had led to the steady migration from the farm to the cities. Radio would do more than all other modern inventions—the print media, the telephone, the phonograph, even the automobile—to make farming families feel like part of the national community.[34]

Radio transformed American politics, as well. The most famous historical example of radio's political impact was Franklin Roosevelt's fireside chats, but he was far from the first politician to take advantage of the medium. The 1920 presidential election was the first to be covered live on radio. By 1928, Al Smith, the Democratic presidential candidate, believed that radio "played probably the most important rôle in the national campaign." He pointed out that a candidate who broadcast a political speech over the radio could reach millions of citizens in an evening, whereas a New York State politician who depended exclusively on live speaking engagements could speak every night to a thousand people for an entire month, and still only reach about 1 percent of his electorate.[35]

Radio became an important ingredient in a candidate's political success. At the 1928 Democratic convention,

> For the first time in history the keynote speech of a national political convention was timed at Houston last night to suit the convenience of the great radio audience—a skillful strategic move to make it possible for this vast assemblage, practically the entire country, to hear their most powerful keynoter sound the Democratic battle cry. How the Democrats outsmarted the Republicans . . . may be realized when it is remembered that [the keynote speaker at the earlier Republican convention] began his speech at 12:25 o'clock in the afternoon. . . . Not so with the Democrats. They gave everyone a chance to get a good dinner beforehand and to become comfortably settled in plenty of time for the convention's real opening.[36]

Radio played a part in Nellie's fame, as well. Just as the radio expanded by the thousands the number of voters who heard Al Smith speak during the 1928 campaign, so it gave Nellie a national exposure that she could never have achieved behind the speaker's podium alone. Nellie's first radio address was in June 1925, when she and the Colorado governor jointly shared the microphone at Denver radio station KOA.[37] Nellie's speeches at the Woman's National Democratic Club in Washington and the Woman's World Fair were both broadcast, as was her nomination speech for Al Smith at the 1928 Democratic National Convention. By the time Nellie was campaigning for Franklin Roosevelt in 1932, her radio broadcasts were so frequent that they barely received mention in the press.

❧

While Nellie was almost constantly on the road with her political and Chautauqua commitments, she stayed in contact with her three sons and her brothers through frequent, lengthy, and affectionate letters. George was still in England, studying at Oxford. Nellie had hoped to visit him the summer of 1928, but she regretfully decided that she could not take precious weeks off in the middle of the Chautauqua and campaign seasons. Bradford, who turned sixteen in the fall of 1928, was still at boarding school in Laramie; in the absence of his mother, he spent vacations at the Wyoming ranches and at the homes of family friends.

Ambrose remained Nellie's greatest family worry. He and Thelma Hinds, a young Laramie student whose father was a clerk in a local grocery store, were expecting a baby. On September 22, 1927, the couple slipped down to Fort Collins, Colorado, where they were quietly married at St. Luke's Episcopal Church. It does not appear that relatives from either of the newlyweds' families were invited to attend. Ambrose took a job as a traveling salesman for Ralston Purina, and Thelma apparently accompanied him on his selling trips across Arizona, New Mexico, and the Texas panhandle. Their baby was born about March 1928 in Arizona.[38]

Nellie wrote her brother George about the same time the baby was born that she had sent several letters to Ambrose, but she had not heard back from him for weeks. "I do wonder what ha[s] developed with them—where his wife is & whether she is having the care she needs. You know, culpable as he is, he is my child & I have a measure of responsibility for what he is. I want to do my full duty if only I can see [it]. I don't want him to ever feel that his mother gave him a stone in place of bread. What can I do for him and what should I do[?]" It must have been particularly painful to watch Ambrose struggle because, of her three sons, Ambrose tugged hardest on her heartstrings; she confided to her Mint secretary on at least one occasion that Ambrose had been her favorite. To Ambrose she wrote, "I love you, my Ambrose. I'd go hungry & cold for you if it could put the qualities in you that you will have to develop for yourself. . . . You can not be really helped until you get down to something & stick to it long enough to get a foothold. . . . I suppose this $150.00 I've lately sent you will see you through with the scheming & economizing that you & Thelma should, in your condition, do. Little do you know how much of it your father & I had to do."[39]

On Friday evening, December 28, 1928, Ambrose and a friend from college were driving along a highway outside Saratoga, Wyoming. As a sleet storm obliterated their visibility and turned the roadway into a sheet of ice, Ambrose attempted to pass a hayrack and lost control of his automobile, which skidded off the road and crashed. His friend was thrown from the car and received a few bruises, but Ambrose was trapped beneath the car, his neck broken; he had died instantly. "Of engaging personality, bright, energetic and lovable, he was just at the age where those splendid characteristics were being developed," the editor of the *Wyoming Eagle* wrote sadly. Another obituary remembered him as "of a rugged type—taking to outdoor life and the hardier amusements that mark this type of man—but he was held in high esteem by those who knew him best."[40]

As condolences from the nation's governors, other public figures, and the general public poured in from all over the country, Thelma Ross traveled to Rawlins, Wyoming, with her mother to accompany Ambrose's body to Cheyenne. On Monday morning, December 31, Nellie endured her third family funeral at St. Mark's Episcopal Church in Cheyenne—first little Alfred, then William, and now one of her firstborn, George's twin. With Bradford hovering protectively nearby, Nellie suffered in dignified agony as her son's fraternity brothers and college friends carried Ambrose's casket out of the church. Her automobile slowly followed the hearse to Lakeview Cemetery, where she laid Ambrose to rest next to his father.

Ambrose's death was the last straw. Nellie had been on the road almost constantly since completing her term in office. Whenever Nellie felt particularly stressed, she was likely to become ill. Nellie consulted her doctors, who told her that she needed to take a period of extended rest. She decided that it was time to take the trip to Europe that she had postponed the prior summer. Remembering how much she had enjoyed her own youthful jaunt to Europe, she decided to take Bradford with her. By the end of February, she had pulled Bradford out of school for two months and had booked passage for the two of them on the SS *America*. As she prepared to sail from New York on March

2, Nellie wrote Harry Harrison, "As a result of your interest . . . and that of other friends, Bradford and I find ourselves ensconced in the finest suite on the ship at minimum price. This you know is a profound secret. . . . Truly I am treated with kindness beyond my deserts."[41] Nellie was carrying letters of introduction from Vice President Charles Dawes and Secretary of State Frank Kellogg; with these, she would meet such luminaries as Prime Minister Ramsey MacDonald of Great Britain; the U.S. ambassadors to Great Britain, Germany, and France; the Lady Lindsay; and the Vicomtesse de Salignac Fénelon.

Bradford spent the first twenty-four hours of their voyage excitedly exploring the ship while his mother dealt with a bout of seasickness and kept to her cabin. After Nellie recovered, the two of them enjoyed a pleasant crossing. Nellie engaged in her favorite pastimes of people-watching and conversation, but her recent tragedy was never far from her mind. "Half the little remnant of family left to me was by my side in the person of my last born . . . setting sail with me to join the other half, his big brother at school on the other side," she wrote in her trip journal. Indeed, when Nellie and Bradford stepped off the train in Oxford to greet George and a friend, she could barely contain her tears. "The joy of meeting them was mixed [with] the sense of overwhelming affliction we had suffered in the loss of precious Ambrose."[42]

Nellie's status as a former governor, as well as her letters of introduction, opened many doors. She had tea with the prime minister, and she met several times with Lady Astor, who hosted a dinner and a reception in Nellie's honor. Nancy, Viscountess Astor, was a Virginian who had moved to England following her divorce from her first husband. In 1906, she had married Waldorf Astor, who served as a member of Parliament. When her husband succeeded to the peerage, Lady Astor was elected to his seat. She was the first woman to take a seat in Parliament, and she served from 1919 until her retirement in 1945. Nellie must have attended Lady Astor's swearing-in at Parliament, following a 1929 election. She later wrote how impressed she had been by a twenty-four-year-old Scottish woman, Jennie Lee, whom she had watched take the oath of office as a member of Parliament. "A little school teacher was she, who looked more like a school girl—the daughter of a miner who had no social prestige to advance her interest, but one who by sheer force of brains and character had won for herself that distinguished recognition. She received it, too, 'mid an ovation that fairly made the rafters ring." Nellie was particularly struck that almost 20 percent of the sixty-eight women who ran for seats in Parliament in that election had been successful—all the more surprising because women had had the vote such a short time in Great Britain.[43]

Although Nellie and Bradford spent most of their time in London, Paris, and Oxford, where they visited George, they did make time to visit the battlefields in France and Belgium. Nellie noted how much more fervently the English talked about international relations, and their hopes for a continuing peace, than did Americans. When she mentioned this impression to her son, a surprisingly mature Bradford responded, "But don't you know there wasn't a home in all this country that wasn't touched by the [Great] War?"[44] Then, when they passed through French and Belgian towns that had been laid to waste, and when they gazed upon row after row of crosses in the war cemeteries of Château Thierry and Belleau Woods, Nellie began to comprehend the import of world war and to appreciate how little most of her countrymen knew or understood about its carnage, loss, and destruction. For the first time, she bore witness to the desolation that her grandparents and parents had experienced during the American Civil War. If her father or mother had ever talked to her of those desperate times, the scarred earth and ruined towns of Europe may have given her an empathy for their tribulations that one can only gain through personal observation.

"The trip I feel has been of great benefit to me physically—and I hope in other ways too," wrote Nellie to her Redpath manager. She returned to the United States ready to face a new Chautauqua season; her opening date for the 1929 season was set for May 3 or 4 in Columbus, Georgia. Nellie was eager to work her European experiences and observations into her speech material. "I was much impressed that the women of [Great Britain] are more keen about their political privileges than those of our country. . . . I was impressed too that they have a more profound understanding of public questions than the women of our country generally have," she wrote in a subsequent speech script.[45] Nellie's speeches almost always contained a reference to the obligations of women to assume their rights and responsibilities as enfranchised Americans, and she used her observations of Great Britain to remind American women that they, too, could aspire to public office. However, her sobering visits to the European battlefields introduced an entirely new topic to Nellie's basic Chautauqua presentations. Nellie had added a lengthy plea for support of the peace movement:

> In my opinion, before [world peace] is realized, the whole attitude of the public mind toward war must be changed through education. It must be changed so that we shall not always be planning for war, but for peace. The whole record of civilization as set down in history, song and story, has tended to glorify war. . . . The school books feature the conquering hero but they do not dwell upon the little homes laid waste in his track,

> the wife left desolate and unprotected with little children upon her hands to feed and clothe and provide with education if she can.
>
> . . . Time was when we women could only weep over the tragedy of war but now the day has arrived when we have a responsibility equally with men for the solution of that problem. . . . It may yet be the hand of woman that will lead the world into the path of permanent peace. . . . Mere material growth and prosperity is not the sole end of government and it is through fostering conditions that conserve life and promote the spiritual development that there lies woman's greatest opportunity as a new citizen, to serve her country.[46]

Prior to the stock market crash of October 1929, Nellie ironically was enjoying the most prosperous period of her life. For the first time, she could afford to save and invest, and she was determined to build a nest egg to insure her financial security in future lean times.[47] In the late 1920s, most people with any cash to spare were as eager as Nellie was to benefit from the stock appreciation that seemed to have no ceiling. They had never known a more affluent period; wages and spending power were high, business was booming, employment opportunities were abundant, and taxes were low. But the nation's prosperity was by no means widespread. Many working-class Americans were little more than one paycheck away from eviction or mortgage default, and the federal government had not yet adopted a system of unemployment insurance.[48] In 1929, 21 percent of American families reported incomes of less than $1,000 on their tax returns, and 71 percent reported incomes of less than $2,500, which was the amount that the Bureau of Labor Statistics estimated a family of four needed to achieve an adequate standard of living. Together, the 36,000 richest families in America earned as much as the poorest 11.7 *million* families.[49] Americans at every income level had also become addicted to credit; one-sixth of the national income was dedicated to installment purchases of cars, radios, furniture, and all the other material goods that Madison Avenue had convinced them were necessary to their happiness.[50] The credit spree extended itself to the purchase of stocks; after all, speculators reasoned, a margin loan could always be repaid after the inevitable appreciation of stock prices.

As a result of the speculative fever, about 40 percent of stocks were trading at prices that exceeded their fundamental values by the time the stock market reached its peak in September 1929. On October 15, 1929, savvy investors began to quietly unload their stock; by October 24, the first wave of panic occurred, and on that "Black Thursday" almost 13 million shares were sold. The following Tuesday, the panic selling resumed. Over 16 million shares were traded, leading brokers to call in their margin accounts. Investor equity totaling $15 billion, or about 15 percent of the Gross National Product, simply evaporated. Over a period of ten weeks, stocks on the New York Stock Exchange had lost half their value, and by June 1930, they had dropped to about 20 percent of their value before the crash.

The vast majority of Americans who owned no equities were at first untouched by the stock market crash. However, as the cash-strapped banks began to close their doors, thrifty Americans lost their life savings. By 1933, about 45 percent of the nation's banks had failed. Hunger marches and riots occurred across the country. The Depression became a vicious circle: Businesses that produced goods laid off their employees because their products were not selling, but laid-off workers had no money with which to purchase goods. By the time that World War II spurred production and employment again, twenty thousand businesses had gone bankrupt and twelve million Americans had lost their jobs.

The scope of the economic impact was unparalleled in a nation that had survived many depressions during the nineteenth and twentieth centuries. President Hoover, an exceptionally able administrator, had no precedent to guide him through the crisis. He fervently believed that it was the responsibility of the individual citizen to take care of himself, and that it was not the role of the federal government to become involved in public assistance. After all, he reasoned, he himself had overcome poverty and adversity through hard work and perseverance. It was beyond his conception that there were structural issues in the economy whose scale simply overwhelmed individual grit. Unlike the earlier depressions, this time the nation was unable to work itself out of the downturn. As people lost their farms and homes and experienced real hunger, they began to turn to the federal government in desperation, demanding that Hoover intervene in the economy. The stage had been set for a shift in policy within the Democratic Party during the 1932 election—a shift to an activist social-economic role for the national government—to the horror of the party's conservative wing.

By the time the stock market crashed, Nellie had a steady income as the director of the Women's Division at the Democratic National Committee as well as her income from speeches and articles, so she was little touched by the economic calamity that slowly enveloped the nation. Those lucky individuals who had secure jobs were able to weather the 1930s by merely tightening their belts. Although her son Bradford remembered the abandoned stores and the breadlines on the streets of Laramie and Cheyenne, the Depression left barely a ripple in Nellie's letters and speeches.[51] In March 1930, she demonstrated no understanding of the growing crisis when she wrote Harry Harrison at the Redpath Bureau that she was thinking of writing a new speech for the 1930 season. Instead of her experiences as governor, which she pointed out had become somewhat stale and dated, "I am wondering if the public would like better something more up to the minute, for instance, a discussion of economic problems like the control of water power, the public utilities problem, tariff, etc. . . . Or do you think they would like a discussion of personalities now prominent in Washington?"[52]

In the same letter, she asked for a personal favor. "I do want to ask you whether you think there would be any place in the Chautauqua organization where Bradford would be acceptable. I am confronted with the problem of where to place him with confidence that he will be safe. . . . He has grown to be a big boy now, taller and heavier than when you saw him, and is cool of nerve and absolutely trustworthy, unless I am badly deceived. Do you suppose that he could qualify for a driver and would such a place be available? I [would] even consider having [him] travel upon expense with me if necessary rather than to have him away from me unsatisfactorily situated, though I can ill afford such an expense as that."[53] Harrison wrote back to assure Nellie that he would be happy to employ Bradford as a driver. The result was that Bradford spent his seventeenth summer traveling with his mother. Nellie's engagements that year took her all over the Midwest, as far north as South Dakota and Minnesota and as far south as Oklahoma.

At some point, their itinerary took them through northwestern Missouri, and Nellie, who probably had not returned to Andrew County since her family's move to Miltonvale more than forty-five years earlier, took her son to the family farm. She directed him to drive down the old Amazonia Road until he brought the car to a stop by a small cemetery, surrounded by a fence of iron grillwork. The two walked over to the family grave site, dominated by Samuel Green's tall burial monument. Nellie and Brad looked down over the farm that Samuel and Amanda Green had created from Missouri wilderness, and Nellie told him about the fine house that the home guards had burned down in 1863. She spoke of her mother, describing Lizzie's strong influence over her, and told how much she still missed her.[54] As Nellie contemplated her earliest years, one wonders whether she thought about how different her life might have been. If her mother's family had been able to keep the land and her father had been a successful farmer, Nellie would have grown up surrounded by the extended family she so cherished, perhaps to marry a neighboring farmer or a St. Joseph businessman. Instead, out of her family's setbacks, Nellie had reaped an unexpected lifetime harvest of fame and fortune.

SEVEN

National Campaigner

IN MAY 1928, Redpath Chautauqua's manager wrote to Joseph O'Mahoney, "We have had one or two dates that we have had to cancel on account of [Nellie's] article regarding Al Smith, which, of course, is ridiculous, but it simply shows the narrowness of some people."[1] That same month, Nellie had published an article in *Scribner's* entitled "Progress, Prohibition, and the Democratic Party," in which she attempted to reason with "dry" Democrats who might consider abandoning the party if the 1928 convention failed to nominate an antiprohibition candidate. Nellie was laying the groundwork for the nomination of Al Smith, for whom she had begun to campaign in early 1927.

For the Democratic Party, the election of 1920 ushered in a long, dry stretch of banishment. The party had inherited the mantle of progressivism from Wilson's administration, but the American public had made it clear by electing Harding that it no longer wanted an activist government. The Democrats spent the next twelve years engaged in a bitter struggle over their party's basic values and policies, searching for the voter formula that would put them back in the White House. For more than seventy-five years, Democrats had championed the urban working class and had protected them from the attacks of anti-immigrant organizations such as the American Protection Association, but paradoxically, they had also represented conservative, native-born western and southern farmers. It was no longer possible to ignore the fundamental schisms within the party. One historian has described the Democrats in the 1920s as an uneasy coalition of "immigrants and Klansmen, Catholics and Protestant fundamentalists, rednecks and shanty Irish, bosses and antibosses, wets and dries."[2]

The "wets and dries" were especially troublesome for party unity; by 1922, the prohibition issue threatened not only to split the Democratic Party, but also to redraw the nation's structure of political alliances. It had become such a defining issue that voters were classifying politicians in both parties primarily by their stances on prohibition. In a national poll conducted that year, over 300,000 people opted for strict prohibition enforcement, while 500,000 other voters were split between two alternative proposals to reform or repeal the Eighteenth Amendment. The principal support for prohibition came from farms and small towns and from the West and South, while its opponents were more likely to be city dwellers from the Northeast.[3] Not only did prohibition foster dissension between regions, it also drew attention to divisions of class, religion, and ethnicity—the rich and sophisticated upper class versus the moral and virtuous middle class, and the largely Catholic immigrants from Ireland, Germany, Italy, and eastern Europe, clustered primarily in the cities, versus the American native stock. The urban immigrants found allies among the Americans who worked beside them on the shop and factory floors; together they developed a "'vibrant alternative culture' in which the saloon and the enjoyment of strong drink figured prominently as symbols of community and autonomy."[4] Prohibition was "the rearguard action of a still dominant, overwhelmingly rural, white Anglo-Saxon Protestant establishment, aware that its privileges and natural right to rule were being increasingly threatened by the massive arrival of largely despised (and feared) beer-swilling, wine-drinking new American immigrants."[5]

In the late nineteenth century, Lizzie Tayloe and her generational peers from small-town America, who made the Women's Christian Temperance Union the largest women's organization in the country, had declared prohibition the single most important issue for American women. As long as women remained solidly behind it, politicians dared not challenge the issue for fear of its impact on their reelections. By the 1920s, however, women no longer presented a solid front on the issue. Elite socialites such as Irene duPont, wife of the wealthy industrialist Pierre duPont, became involved in the Association Against the Prohibition Amendment (AAPA), founded in 1919. Mrs. duPont and other female proponents of prohibition repeal challenged the right of the WCTU to speak for all women on the prohibition issue. Opponents claimed that prohibition cases were clogging the courts and the jailhouses, that prohibition was unconstitutional because it was an unreasonable intrusion into the individual American's privacy and freedoms, and that the widespread flaunting of the Eighteenth Amendment was breeding a general disrespect for the law.[6]

As governor, one of Nellie's legislative priorities had been the aggressive enforcement of prohibition in Wyoming, and she had removed her law enforcement commissioner when he failed to act in this area. Nellie's strongly prohibitionist history suggests that she should have remained an avid supporter of prohibition to the bitter end. Her mother had steeped her in the morality of temperance; she was a white Protestant; and she was a rural southerner who had transplanted herself to a rural western state.

"The record of my private and official life entitles me to classify myself as a 'dry,'" Nellie wrote in the *Scribner's* article. She argued that to insist on prohibition as the primary selection criterion for a presidential nominee would neither preserve prohibition nor promote party interests. It would split the Democratic vote and deny the party the Republican crossover votes they would need to win the election. She reminded her readers that there were domestic and international issues far more critical to the nation than a candidate's position on the Eighteenth Amendment. Should the nation allow itself to be sidetracked by the prohibition issue, "the result most certainly would be severe loss to the progressive cause, for the history of special privilege teaches us that it never thrives better than when the public eye is turned in some other direction."[7]

Privately, however, Nellie warned Smith that his position on prohibition could cost him dearly at the polls. In March 1928, she telegraphed him,

> REPORT YOU WILL DEMAND PARTY DECLARE ITSELF IN PLATFORM MODIFICATION. PROHIBITION LAW CAUSES APPREHENSION AMONG SINCERE DRY DEMOCRATS. IF YOU . . . DEMAND CHANGE YOU . . . SEPARATE YOURSELF FROM THE SUPPORT OF SINCERE PROHIBITIONISTS WHO WANT TO WORK FOR YOUR NOMINATION BECAUSE THEY BELIEVE IN YOUR QUALIFICATIONS.[8]

Nellie's 1928 article and speeches on prohibition earned her the censure of "drys" around the country, particularly from WCTU chapters.[9] But she had incited even more controversy a year earlier when she had declared that she would like to see the country elect a Catholic president, a pointed reference to Smith's religion. In a speech to the Woman's National Democratic Club in Washington, Nellie denounced religious prejudice as unworthy of "the precious heritage of American citizenship." It was time, she declared, for the nation to prove that the United States was indeed a republic,

> and not in name only. . . . I hope that the democratic women of this country will not be found wanting, but that they will fearlessly proclaim . . . that they will sanction no policy that deprives any person in the

> United States of the full rights and privileges of citizenship because of religious affiliation. I believe that the sin of intolerance is the greatest sin of the age. It is amazing that those who call themselves Christians can harbor and encourage in others a sentiment so inconsistent with the teachings of Christ.[10]

Whenever Nellie espoused a decisive position on a controversial issue, she ran the risk of alienating part of the public that adored her; the Chautauqua cancellations were merely the most visible proof that she was endangering her own popularity as well as her income from speechmaking. Nellie must be given credit for her mettle. She was too astute a judge of human nature to have taken these steps without a clear understanding of the implications. Even if she had unintentionally blundered into controversial waters, her ever-present advisor, Joseph O'Mahoney, would have warned her of the risk she was running the first time the press quoted one of her public statements about prohibition or religion. Therefore, Nellie chose to take a calculated risk that her bold support of Smith would pay off for her. If Smith won the nomination, as it appeared he would, and if she had publicly supported him from the first, then she could possibly win big—perhaps even the vice-presidential slot on the Democratic ticket. On the other hand, if Smith lost, she might find herself shut out of politics forever, having simultaneously endangered her income by alienating a large segment of her adoring female audience.

As Nellie prepared to travel to California in March 1928 to campaign for Smith in the presidential primary, O'Mahoney wrote Smith's close advisor, Belle Moskowitz. After addressing the logistics of Nellie's itinerary, he added, "It occurs to me to suggest that, in view of the repeated attacks to which Mrs. Ross has been subjected since her declaration against religious prejudice before the Democratic Woman's Club . . . and which have been redoubled since her specific declaration for Governor Smith, it would be a tactful thing for the Governor to express appreciation." Moskowitz responded, "We have been reading Governor Ross's speeches most carefully, and, in fact intend reprinting at least one for circulation in various quarters. You may be sure that all of us deeply appreciate what she is doing and know what her help means to us." Nellie's California appearances indeed drew vocal opposition from WCTU members and others opposed to Smith's candidacy. The *Los Angeles Examiner*, however, reported on the huge turnouts all over the state to hear Nellie speak: "California women, like those of not a few other places in the country, hold her in such esteem . . . that they mention her as a most likely vice-presidential possibility . . . Smith and Ross. Al and Nellie."[11]

There were no critical issues of national security or economy resting on the outcome of the 1928 election. Ignoring the growing signs of impending economic disaster, America was busy enjoying itself in a bubble of peace, prosperity, and isolation from world affairs; the stock market crash was still a year away. The election would come down to the personalities and qualifications of the two candidates, Al Smith and Herbert Hoover, who were both considered outstanding.[12] Smith and Hoover each offered a sterling record of accomplishments and public service. But although both men were certainly qualified, in personality, they could not have been more different.

Herbert Hoover, a reserved, intensely private man, was born on a midwestern farm and was orphaned at age nine. A Quaker, Hoover overcame the poverty of his childhood to graduate with an engineering degree from Stanford and earned a fortune before he retired at age forty. Turning to public service, he made a name for himself managing the food relief program during World War I, and then he served as secretary of Commerce. The first election of his life was the 1928 presidential election.

Al Smith, in contrast, had been involved in politics since he had allied himself with the political machine of Tammany Hall as a teenager. Smith was an Irish Catholic, born on New York's Lower East Side, who dropped out after grammar school to support his mother and siblings in a series of menial positions following his father's death. When Tammany procured for him a position as county process server, he began his rise—court clerk, state representative, speaker of the state assembly, sheriff of Manhattan, and president of the New York City Board of Aldermen, culminating in his election as governor in 1918. He came to the 1928 election with four terms of experience as the widely respected progressive governor of New York. Always at his best with an audience, he favored cigars and fancy clothes, he sported a derby hat, and his style was loud and flamboyant. Most of all, he was a lightning rod for the two issues that defined the 1928 election: religion and prohibition.[13]

Smith's viewpoint on women in politics was complicated. He was a deeply conservative man who, despite his flashy image, was devoted to his religion, his family, and his retiring wife. In 1917, when a delegation of women approached him in the state legislature to ask for his support for women's suffrage, he reportedly "shot a stream of tobacco juice at a spittoon and told them that as far as he was concerned a woman's place was at home." On the other hand, one of his closest and most powerful advisors was a woman, Belle

Moskowitz. She played to Smith's ambivalence about political women by always remaining in the background; she never advised Smith or discussed strategy with him in front of others, so he never had to feel that he was deferring to a woman's opinion.[14]

Smith may have been ambivalent about women in politics, but nevertheless, he was a consummately practical politician. When women obtained the vote in New York State shortly after his first election as governor in 1918, he responded by appointing a well-qualified woman, Frances Perkins, as a board member on the Industrial Commission. When she asked him why he wanted to appoint her, he told her it was based on her solid credentials in public health and safety. He knew a lot of Democratic women, he said, but most of them were there because they were related to male politicians. It would be an insult to women to select one simply because she had a famous male relative. Yet a few years later, when Franklin Roosevelt succeeded Smith as governor and told Smith that he was thinking about promoting Perkins from board member to agency head of the Industrial Commission, Smith advised against it. Smith warned Roosevelt that Perkins's male subordinates would object to working directly for a woman.[15]

Smith's opinion of Nellie herself was probably as complicated as his overall attitude toward women. He appreciated her campaign work on his behalf; he recognized the respect she commanded among women constituents; but he disliked female politicians who had achieved their positions through their husbands or fathers. In her biography, Eleanor Roosevelt related an anecdote about one of Nellie's visits to Albany when she and Smith were both governors:

> Since Governor Smith did not really feel that a woman should be the governor of a state, he gloated over the fact that he had asked [Nellie] some questions which from his point of view required exact figures for a proper answer. Mrs. Ross could not give them to him, and told him . . . that she would have the figures sent to him after she went back to her home state. . . . To Governor Smith, who could reel off every figure that had to do with the government of the State of New York, this seemed sacrilege, and he was surer than ever that no woman could really be a good governor.[16]

While Smith may not have approved of Nellie's position as governor, if he had concluded that Nellie would have been his strongest asset as running mate, there is little doubt that he would have tapped her. But when asked a month before the Democratic convention if he had a specific running mate in mind, he responded to a reporter, "That is something those boys will have to work out down there [at the Houston convention]. Collective judgment is always best."[17] Largely assured of his own nomination, he could afford to sit back and let the selection process play itself out.

By June 26, Houston was transformed from a sleepy, muggy backwater into a raucous, crowded, contentious maelstrom as enthusiastic delegates poured into town and filled the streets and hotels. Fruit carts, ice cream vendors, and brass bands jostled for elbow room on the streets with clusters of energized Democratic men and women. The women were the most noteworthy presence, for 152 women attended the 1928 Democratic National Convention, the highest number at any convention since 1900, when a lone female delegate had been granted the honor of seconding the nomination of William Jennings Bryan.[18] Will Rogers was there, "dry" wit ready, to report on the convention. "The whole talk here is wet and dry," he told his readers. "The delegates just can't wait till the next bottle is opened to discuss it. Prohibition is running about a quart to the argument here and now. The South say they are dry and by golly if the bootleggers don't rush on some more mighty quick they will be."[19]

Rogers's irony aside, the "dry" women delegates were deadly serious in their goal to stop Smith's nomination. One hundred of them convened a solemn parade down a sultry street to promote their cause. The WCTU and the National Women's Democratic Law Enforcement League members claimed that they controlled over four hundred votes that would block the nomination of Smith or any other "wet" candidate. But opposing them were the members of the National Women's Committee for Repeal of the Eighteenth Amendment, who were planning to introduce a repeal plank to the resolutions committee.

The Associated Press reporter who was covering women's issues noted that the subject of prohibition was even affecting the candidacy for the national committee vice chairmanships. She quoted the state committeewoman from Georgia, who declared that "the choice of [vice chairwomen] will have a tremendous influence on the women's vote in the South in November. The Southern women will not follow a woman they don't admire, and the dry issue is very important to them." Among the five women that the reporter listed as the female delegates' favorites for the vice chairman slots, the first two were Eleanor Roosevelt of New York and Florence Farley of Kansas. Perhaps because of her controversial stand on prohibition, Nellie was not listed among the likely selectees.[20]

The male delegates were equally emotional and just as split on the prohibition issue as their female peers. "Wets" and "drys" were divided into numerous splinter groups. It was clear that the final prohibition plank in the Democratic platform would be a compromise that would leave everyone at the convention dissatisfied with the party's official policy statement.[21]

Despite the threats and maneuvers of his opponents, despite the many favorite-son candidates, Al Smith's nomination was never in jeopardy. He simply commanded too many votes. When it was time for the presidential nominations, Franklin Roosevelt laboriously took the few steps from his seat to the podium, triumphing over his polio-induced handicap with the aid of a cane and leg braces and accompanied by waves and supportive cheers from the multitude in Sam Houston Hall. "I come for the third time to urge upon a convention of my party the nomination of the Governor of the State of New York," he told his listeners. After reviewing Smith's impressive qualifications and accomplishments, he took a jab at what he considered were the pro-business, anti-people policies of the Republican administration:

> In an era of the ready-made we must not accept ready-made government; in a day of high-powered advertising we must not fall for the false statements of the most highly organized propaganda ever developed by the owners of the Republican Party. We do not want to change these United Sovereign States of America into the "United States, Incorporated," with a limited and self-perpetuating board of directors and no voting power in the common stock holders . . .
>
> . . . [We need] a leader who grasps and understands not only large affairs of business and government, but in an equal degree the aspirations and the needs of the individual, the farmer, the wage earner—the great mass of average citizens who make up the backbone of our nation. America needs not only an administrator but a leader. . . . We offer one who has the will to win—who not only deserves success but commands it. Victory is his habit—the happy warrior—Alfred E. Smith.[22]

Then it was Nellie's turn. As one of three women chosen to deliver seconding speeches for Smith, Nellie approached the microphones arrayed in front of the speaker's podium. She reminded her audience of Smith's powerful qualifications and qualities and his distinguished record of public service. She was confident, she told the delegates, that by election day,

> legions of people who until now have listened only to Governor Smith's enemies, will have informed themselves of the progressive reforms he has

> effected on behalf of all his constituents, rich and poor alike. . . . They will have learned of his defense of the rights of women [and] of labor. . . . To such a one the people may with safety commit the most serious public problems. They may and must now turn to him and his party as the only instrumentality through which they can see reestablished in the national government those high principles for which our forefathers freely spent their life blood, and that constitute to us so priceless a heritage; the principles that dominated the administrations of Jefferson, Jackson and Woodrow Wilson.
>
> . . . Therefore, I embrace the privilege accorded me, and in the name of the progressive Democrats of Wyoming I second the nomination of him who richly deserves the highest honor at the hands of his party, and of the nation—the Honorable Alfred Emanuel Smith, governor of the state of New York.[23]

As soon as he secured the nomination, Al Smith wasted no time in proving how accurate Nellie had been in her nominating speech when she told the delegates that Smith was "known to say what he means and mean what he says." In his acceptance telegram, Smith horrified the "drys" when he informed them that he believed fundamental changes to the prohibition law were needed. If elected, he would seek to lead the country toward a "sane, sensible" solution to the prohibition problem. He inferred that he would seek a rescission of the Eighteenth Amendment, restoring the issue of temperance to the states.[24]

With Smith's nomination and acceptance completed, the convention reached that moment that Nellie may have hoped would be hers—the nomination of Smith's running mate. Mrs. T. S. Toliver of Wyoming rose to the microphone to place the name of Nellie Tayloe Ross in nomination for vice president:

> For four years, as much as any one person, she has been in the eyes of the nation. . . . The nomination of a woman to the office of Vice-President would be in complete harmony with the spirit of Democracy. It is a fact worthy of the attention of every woman in this nation that the Democratic Party has taken the lead in giving recognition to women. . . . [When she was governor,] her administration was marked by honesty, sincerity and courage. I present to you a name in every way fitted to stand with that of Alfred E. Smith; I nominate for Vice-President Nellie Tayloe Ross, former governor of Wyoming.[25]

Nellie's nomination was seconded by a male delegate from Idaho, W. R. Chapman. "I am not here to second the nomination of any man for the vice-presidency, as we have learned in recent history that the vice-presidency is not necessarily a man's job," he declared. "I am here, however, to second the nomination of a most unusual woman, a woman of inestimable charm, of unusual experience, the successful administrator of that most glorious of all institutions, the American home, and the first of her sex in this country to become the chief executive of an American state." Delegates from ten states would award Nellie 31 votes for vice president on the first ballot—but Senator Joseph Robinson of Arkansas received 914 votes. Following this first ballot, Nellie gracefully rose to address the chairman and threw her voting support to Senator Robinson, to the applause of her fellow delegates.[26]

Despite the press speculation that accompanied Nellie on her speaking tours, she probably never had a serious shot at the vice-presidential slot. To counteract the visceral antipathy that Smith engendered among nonurban Democrats, the Democrats knew that they would have to select a vice-presidential nominee who was from the West or the South and who was a card-carrying "dry." Nellie could claim both the southern and western regions, but she had sacrificed her reputation as a "dry" when she began her aggressive campaigning for Smith. When the Democratic power brokers got down to the serious business of choosing a vice-presidential candidate, Nellie was relegated to the list of also-rans, which "was crowded with governors, senators and a variety of prominent personages of the party." More significantly, the nation simply was not ready to position a woman one heartbeat away from the presidency; in fact, neither of the major parties would tap a woman for the second spot for fifty-six more years.[27] Nevertheless, Smith repaid her for her loyal campaigning. He tapped her to make his seconding speech, and he was about to make sure that she received a position of high honor within the DNC.

On July 6, shortly after the convention adjourned, Smith wrote Nellie that he had listened to her nominating address on the radio and had "thought to myself how feeble I was in my ability to thank you. When the campaign gets under way, I will have the men in charge see that you are given an opportunity to continue the good work that was so effective at Houston."[28] Smith had made it clear to the male leadership of the national committee that he wanted Nellie selected as vice chairman.[29] On July 11, shortly after the convention adjourned, the male committeemen from each state were convened to elect Smith's choices for the chairman and vice chairmen of the DNC. The male members of the national committee ratified all of Smith's choices, including John J. Raskob as chairman. For the two female vice chairmen, they selected Nellie Tayloe Ross and Florence Farley. On July 28, Raskob appointed Nellie to the additional position of national director of women's activities.[30]

Since 1920, the DNC had been composed of equal numbers of men and women—one male and one female from each state and territory. Thus the unilateral election of officers by the male committeemen was a humiliating blow for the women who were theoretically equal partners in Democratic decision making. The DNC women were livid. Elizabeth Marbury, who had represented New York at every national convention since 1920, angrily wrote Smith, "The method of selecting women to office without giving those who are to serve under their leadership any opportunity of approval or of disapproval is engendering discontent and discouragement." Eleanor Roosevelt, herself passed over for vice chairman, complained to her husband that it would have "been so easy for the men" to have included the female members of the DNC. "I can't understand why they prefer to stir up this current of discontent!"[31]

Eleanor may have felt cheated, but she was hardly surprised; by 1928, she was an old political hand, and she had had ample opportunity to observe male politicians at work. Just a few months before the 1928 convention, Eleanor had published a bitter article in a woman's magazine entitled "Women Must Learn to Play the Game as Men Do." After ten years of suffrage, she wrote, American women were merely going through the motions of political participation and equality. They voted, they were treated solicitously by male politicians, but they had no real power. With the exception of women whose entrée to politics was through a famous male relative, women who had tried to enter politics had been marginalized—by local political committees, at the state level, and in the national organizations. In a prophetic statement, she wrote, "Before national elections they will be told to organize women throughout the United States, and asked to help in minor ways in raising funds. But when it comes to those grave councils at which possible candidates are discussed, as well as party policies, they are rarely invited in." The only solution, Eleanor advised her readers, was for women to organize; to select two or three women in each state whom the women would all agree to support. Women would have to prove to their male counterparts that they were unified and that they commanded votes; only then would men begin to listen to their demands and accord them respect.[32]

Eleanor had learned politics from men the hard way, and over a long period of time. In 1920, following his nomination as the Democratic vice-presidential nominee, Franklin Roosevelt had asked his wife to join him on the campaign trail. Although Eleanor's role during this first campaign was strictly limited to being the candidate's wife, she quickly began to carve out a substantive role for herself, both in grassroots political organizing in Dutchess

County and as finance chairman for the Women's Division of the New York Democratic Party. By 1922, she was actively involved in her own right as a campaigner for Al Smith's gubernatorial run. Her role at both the state and the national level of the Democratic Party continued to grow throughout the 1920s. Eleanor had witnessed firsthand how women were bypassed and discounted in politics, and it had taught her how to play hardball within the party. Nellie, on the other hand, had entered politics from the top. While Eleanor had learned campaign strategy in the county trenches, Nellie's only campaign experience had been her unsuccessful reelection bid. Eleanor had learned that a crucial part of the campaign was the unromantic work of writing campaign literature and licking envelopes, while Nellie's political experience had taught her that campaigning was about getting out on the road, creating alliances, and making speeches.

Nellie and Eleanor together possessed a diverse mixture of similarities and differences. Eleanor was from one of the oldest and most respected New York families, which had immigrated to America in the 1600s. Nellie, who was deeply proud of her own pedigree, was a southerner whose American antecedents were just as old. Eleanor was reared in great wealth, while Nellie's immediate family had struggled financially. Nellie loved the public limelight and was an exceptional public speaker; conversely, painfully shy Eleanor preferred to work behind the scenes. Fate had been materially generous to Eleanor, but perhaps it had not been so emotionally kind. Nellie's nurturing relationship with her parents and extended family had helped her to grow into a remarkably secure and self-confident individual, but Eleanor's family relationships had left wounds from which she never recovered. Eleanor wholeheartedly adored her irresponsible and mostly absent father, whose family banished him because of his mental instability and alcoholism, and she always believed that her glamorous society mother, who died when she was eight, had favored her handsome younger brothers. For a vulnerable, sensitive child like Eleanor, the inevitable result was insecurity.[33]

While Nellie was never involved in causes outside the Democratic Party, Eleanor's political work had quickly expanded to include a variety of other activities and organizations, including teaching, Red Cross work, the League of Women Voters, and the Women's Trade Union League. After her husband irrevocably wounded their marriage through an extramarital relationship, Eleanor sought self-fulfillment in her career, and she created for herself a circle of intimate female friends who were just as dedicated as she to political participation and public service. For the six years leading up to the 1928 campaign, Eleanor and her close friends from the Women's Division of the New

York Democratic Party, including Elinor Morgenthau and Caroline O'Day, had spent many weeks each year touring through New York, where they lobbied for a panoply of causes, including public housing, unemployment insurance, workman's compensation, occupational safety, and protections for women and children in the workplace.[34]

For Eleanor, politics was almost a sacred calling because she believed it was the means to a better society. She believed that "women and men enter politics for different reasons: Men enter politics to pursue their own careers; women are motivated by a desire to change society, to improve the daily conditions of life."[35] In contrast, Nellie never gave her heart and soul to her political career—not as governor, nor at the DNC, nor later at the Mint. She worked hard, she took pride in doing a good job, but she always had a rich life that was separate from her work. She certainly had no desire to change society. Her family, friends, social life, and personal interests were at least as important to her, and probably more so, than her career. While the correspondence of Eleanor and her friends intertwined personal and political matters, Nellie's private correspondence with her family was almost completely devoid of the topics of work and politics. A modern observer might admire Nellie's ability to balance her work with a private life, but Eleanor may well have examined the same behavior and judged Nellie to be self-serving and superficial.

Both Nellie and Eleanor were capable of deep affection and loyalty to their intimates. When it came to their enemies or opponents, however, the two were polar opposites. Perhaps because she had always felt securely loved, Nellie did not seem to take political slights to heart. She did not take her political battles as governor personally; she simply saw them as part of the job. Her personal papers show no evidence of her ever writing a nasty word about Eleanor nor anyone else, nor does it appear that she ever plotted for revenge or payback. At the end of her long public career, she claimed that she had always been treated with kindness and consideration. Nellie was too astute not to have discerned when she had been ill-treated politically, but she simply refused to acknowledge it; perhaps it was her southern cultural upbringing. Eleanor, on the other hand, could be jealous and unforgiving when she was crossed. Eleanor played the political game in deadly earnest, so Smith's elevation of Nellie to a position that Eleanor possibly considered to be rightfully hers may have earned Nellie an implacable, if covert, enemy. Arthur M. Schlesinger Jr. wrote of Eleanor that her "air of artlessness was one of her most deadly weapons; no one could slice off a head with more benign innocence."[36] One of her biographers was even more direct in her analysis:

> One of the myths that ER seemed actively to encourage was that she was naïve politically. Not insignificantly, several people who harbored that illusion were actually victims of ER's political intrigue and opposition. The fact that they saw her as a "dim bulb" rather than as their enemy is probably the greatest testimony to her political style and maneuvering. ER's gracious manner often obscured intense emotions, including disapproval and dislike. She tended to avoid confrontations and occasionally walked away from angry words, but never from the battle. She did not play politics transcendentally—somewhere above the fray. She walked hard edges, made tough decisions, and followed her principles wherever they led.[37]

If Eleanor was angry about Nellie's selection, she had reason. According to Eleanor's memoir, Smith's back-office advisor, Belle Moskowitz, had asked her in the spring to "organize the women's end of the office for the national campaign."[38] After three or four months of dedicated work, she found herself reporting, at least on paper, to Nellie, who was the official chairman of the women's activities committee; the committee's two members, besides Nellie, were Eleanor and Caroline O'Day of New York, a close friend of Eleanor's. Nellie's role as Eleanor's director during the campaign is generally overlooked; many contemporary sources stated that Eleanor was in charge, and Eleanor herself neglected to mention Nellie's role in her autobiography.[39] However, Eleanor's private report of her 1928 campaign activities begins with a recognition that she was working under Nellie's supervision, and the official DNC organization chart for 1928 also shows Eleanor reporting to Nellie as the committee chairman.[40]

Just as Nellie carried two titles at the DNC, Eleanor also served in a dual capacity; in addition to her women's committee responsibilities, she was a member of the DNC advisory committee. The byzantine DNC organizational chart was a tangle of fifty-four boxes and myriad connecting lines, in which many individuals served in multiple capacities. The true decision-making power, however, was held by an executive committee consisting of seven individuals, including John J. Raskob as chairman, Franklin Roosevelt, George Van Namee, and Belle Moskowitz as the sole woman. Even within the small executive committee, some of the members were frozen out of real influence. Franklin Roosevelt wrote that Raskob and Moskowitz had treated him "as though I was one of those pieces of window-dressing that had to be borne with because of a certain political value in non–New York City areas." He was so annoyed that he left the campaign headquarters after completing his assigned tasks and returned to his retreat in Warm Springs, Georgia.[41]

Following her selection as chairman of women's activities, Nellie immediately made arrangements for Ruth Harrington, who had been her private stenographer in the governor's office, to join her for the duration of the campaign as her traveling companion and assistant. She appointed Joseph O'Mahoney's wife, Agnes, as her secretary and as her "eyes and ears" in the New York City convention headquarters. Less than a week after her appointment as chairman of women's activities, Nellie sent out a letter to the entire national mailing list of politically active Democratic women. She told her readers how honored she was to have been tapped to work with the committeewomen and other female Democratic leaders throughout the states, adding that

> the broad policy that will underlie all women's activities, which I am designated to direct, will be utmost cooperation with the men of the party, with the expectation that women will have adequate representation in the regular organization, in all its branches. . . . There is unquestionably a distinct service that only women, in groups and individually, can perform, and that is to disseminate such information respecting the party and its candidates as will satisfy inquiring feminine minds. . . .
>
> My headquarters will be in New York during the campaign. It will not be possible, however, for me to be there constantly and Mrs. Franklin D. Roosevelt, a resident of New York, during my absences, will be in charge, which will insure careful consideration to all communications relative to campaign matters.[42]

On July 14, Franklin Roosevelt wrote his mother that Caroline O'Day had spent that Sunday with the Roosevelts at Hyde Park; also visiting was "Mrs. Ross, lately Governor of Wyoming, very nice and she is to have charge of the Women's Division in the campaign."[43] A note that Eleanor sent her close friend and neighbor, Elinor Morgenthau, about Nellie's first visit to the convention headquarters was less charitable. "Governor Ross arrived yesterday. I think she finds it hard to understand the way we have to function but she will see Mr. Raskob this morning—I doubt if she will know much more when she is through! She will be much better in the long [run] as V. Ch. than in the campaign for she is like you in one way. She wants perfection and it tries her to see what *could* be done and is not done. However, my dear, that is your only point of similarity!"[44]

It took Nellie and Eleanor little time to work out their respective roles.

Nellie enjoyed traveling, speaking, and networking with women in the state organizations and Democratic clubs, while Eleanor preferred to work behind the scenes. In fact, their division of responsibilities represents the most common arrangement between directors, who typically function as the public figure who handles the "outside" functions, and assistant directors, who run the office. "Speaking was still something of an ordeal for me, so it was always understood that my part of the work involved simply organizing the office," wrote Eleanor.[45] Eleanor put together a tight, harmonious group of workers at headquarters, many of whom she drew from her former coworkers at the Women's Division of the New York State Democratic committee. The fact that Eleanor made the day-to-day decisions gave her substantial importance in the women's end of the campaign, but it did not necessarily signify that Nellie was simply a figurehead. Eleanor's letter to Elinor Morgenthau suggests that Nellie had asked Eleanor questions about office procedures, budget, publicity, or campaign strategies, and that she had apparently annoyed Eleanor when Nellie found the arrangements not to her satisfaction. The surviving campaign files from 1928 give little indication exactly how the two women reached decisions or how they shared their authority. However, it does seem likely that neither woman enjoyed true influence outside the women's campaign; the only woman who did was Belle Moskowitz. Molly Dewson later wrote that Belle "had been Al Smith's tutor and mentor to an extraordinary degree. . . . Mrs. Moskowitz was Al Smith's tent pole."[46]

Nellie was greatly in demand as a speaker. Because she was on the podium at least once a day and often more frequently, she periodically wore out. The head of the Women's Speakers' Bureau in the campaign organization wrote her in September, "I hope that you are feeling better now and that you will be able to fill your speaking schedules throughout the campaign, for I do assure you the demand and the need are both great. There are few women speakers of the first magnitude, and practically nobody can do what you can do." The speakers' bureau was hard-pressed to refuse requests for Nellie; women's groups refused to take no for an answer and would go over the head of the speakers' bureau director to Belle Moskowitz if a request for Nellie was denied. An alarmed Agnes O'Mahoney did her best to protect her boss; she telegraphed Nellie, "WHEN YOU COLLAPSED AT NORFOLK, WIRE SENT TO KENTUCKY YOU COULD SPEAK BUT ONCE A DAY. . . . [YOU MUST] ABSOLUTELY REFUSE TO SPEAK MORE THAN [THAT]."[47]

In her autobiography, Eleanor related an anecdote about the demands placed on Nellie:

> I remember one day I had [a staff member] scurrying everywhere to find Mrs. Ross while a tea party waited to greet her. She finally was found completely exhausted, lying on the floor of our diminutive rest room, trying to regain enough energy to face shaking hands with several hundred people. We often were quite inhuman in the schedules that we planned for her, expecting her to make a speech, and write the next one while on the train between engagements. Finally she told me that that was not the way in which she could do her best work and that her schedule would have to be revised.[48]

With Nellie on the road most of the time, part of Eleanor's job was to identify and put out fires in the field organization. One such fire sparked at the women's midwestern campaign headquarters in St. Louis. Eleanor dispatched Mary Dewson—Molly to her friends—to deal with the situation. Eleanor had met her years before at the New York Women's City Club, when Eleanor was the club's vice president and Molly was its secretary in charge of welfare work. A Boston native and Wellesley graduate who had made a career for herself in social welfare and reform, the now middle-aged Molly "favor[ed] tailored suits, . . . sensible low shoes, no makeup, and pince-nez perched precariously on her nose."[49] Molly was a forceful, hardworking woman of exceptional organizational ability and with an equally exceptional ego. Her voluminous scrapbooks and her two-volume unpublished autobiography are critical primary sources for historians of the period. Inevitably, therefore, her attitudes about people and events of the 1920s and 1930s, as well as her own version of her role in those events, has had a significant impact on the historical narrative of her times. Molly's relationship with Nellie would prove to be cordial but distant. Like many in her feminist circle, she had little use and less respect for women who had entered politics as a result of their political husbands—Eleanor Roosevelt excepted. Molly wrote in her autobiography that any rewards or recognition most political women of the late 1920s received were likely to be based more on "their looks, their money, or their late husband's service to the party" rather than their own ability or accomplishments.[50] In contrast, Emily Newell Blair, herself married, was far more understanding and insightful when she wrote,

> These women who come into politics by way of their husbands have been made the subject of scorn by those feminists who want women to stand on their own feet. And yet, from the political viewpoint, they more nearly enter politics and secure nominations by the method and the sys-

> tem through which men win nominations than those feminists who seek to break in from the outside.[51]

After Molly assessed the situation in the St. Louis office, she reported back to Eleanor that it was wracked by in-fighting between two factions; one of the factions was headed by Florence Farley, the other woman whom Smith had placed on the Democratic National Committee with Nellie. Molly dismissed Farley, whose "mental capacity is just nil," as a "flighty flapper," and she labeled the other woman as a terrible schemer; she resolved the issue by sending both women out on the road as speakers. Eleanor was so pleased with Molly's adroit handling of the situation that "we knew that no future campaign should be conducted without her."[52]

Despite the Democratic organization's best efforts, when Election Day rolled around in November 1928, 60 percent of the twenty-one million voters selected Herbert Hoover. Although Smith earned 40 percent of the popular vote, his support translated to only eight states and 16 percent of the electoral votes. Smith's religion and his big-city roots, as well as his stand on prohibition, were his downfall. Overall, the nation's newspapers were kind to Smith in their election postmortems. The *Dallas News,* then a Democratic paper, wrote that "Governor Smith made a gallant campaign under handicaps which probably no man could have overcome and he discussed such subjects as the contest involved with a candor and courage that have never been excelled." The Republican-leaning *Chicago Tribune* concluded that America's Protestant majority chose to select one of its own over Catholic Smith, but that "both parties presented candidates of admirable character, proved ability, and great promise." A Democratic paper from Omaha observed that "it was a campaign of one magnificent man with a divided party behind him against a magnificent party organization disciplined and united." A bitter *Charleston News and Courier* complained that Hoover's election could be attributed to a "deep-seated hallucination of the American people of a subtle connection between the Republican Party and prosperity."[53] Finally, New York newspaper editor Walter Lippman opined that the country simply was not ready to surrender its cherished image of the sturdy yeoman farmer as the quintessential American; Smith's loss was "inspired by the feeling that the clamorous life of the city should not be acknowledged as the American ideal."[54]

The 1928 election defeat inevitably led to Democratic soul-searching and an analysis of what steps the party should take to improve its readiness for the 1932 campaign. The defeat also fanned the party's factional flames, as those Democrats who had opposed Smith's candidacy from the first held him personally responsible for the dismal election results and began to cast about for more promising candidates for future elections. One of those potential candidates was Franklin Roosevelt, who had won the 1928 election to succeed Al Smith as governor in New York. By the end of November, Roosevelt had written dozens of letters to party leaders across the country to solicit their opinions concerning the steps that should be taken to revive Democratic fortunes. "I am of course convinced that had we kept our national organization going between elections we should have done better, and I hope that steps will be taken to have this carried out during the next three years. This is no time to discuss candidates but it is time for putting into effect a permanent working organization. I hope you will write me your views."[55]

From Wyoming, Joseph O'Mahoney sent Roosevelt a lengthy response to his letter in which he heartily endorsed Roosevelt's goal of establishing a permanent DNC organization. O'Mahoney may well have been looking out for Nellie's interests when he included among his numerous suggestions to Roosevelt the idea of establishing "a real woman's department. . . . The importance of the woman vote has been wholly overlooked. . . . There should be a special fund raised for the women and they should have complete control over its expenditures." He also warned Roosevelt that Smith's stand on prohibition presented a continuing danger to party unity and viability. "All efforts to reorganize as the Democratic party will be fruitless, if the impression goes abroad that Mr. Raskob is going to try to make it a wet party. He should make it clear to the country that he has no intention of trying to impose his views upon this subject on the party, and that his only object now will be to help organize [a unified] party."[56]

Nellie followed up O'Mahoney's letter to Roosevelt with one of her own to express her desire to help create a permanent DNC headquarters. "Of course all of us who were active in the campaign knew of the great waste of effort and money because the organization was not in functioning order until the campaign was far spent." Although she was eager to start the task, "I have not had a word from Mr. Raskob and feel I can not relinquish my present engagements until some official action is taken by the Committee." Roosevelt responded early in 1929; he opened his letter with his deepest sympathy for the loss of her son Ambrose, after which he expressed his agreement with the points that she and O'Mahoney had made in their letters. He expressed the hope that Raskob would set aside "contentious issues" and would concentrate on reducing the party's debt and building up the Democratic organization in every state. "The women's end of it is, in many ways, more important than that of the men. I know that you will do everything you can to help." He urged her to confer with him the next time she was in New York.[57] Nellie took him at his word; a few days later, she paid Roosevelt a pleasant visit at his New York City home as she passed through on her way to her European trip. She noted in her journal, "I came away with deepened conviction that the Democratic Party has in him an able leader, so sane & sensible were the views he expressed on party problems. It looks as if our hope for victory four years hence lies in him."[58]

Governor William Bradford Ross, ca. 1924. *Wyoming State Archives, Dept. of State Parks and Cultural Resources*

Nellie signs the oath of office on January 5, 1925; *left to right:* Judge Sam Tayloe, Nellie's brother; George Tayloe Ross, one of Nellie's twins; Nellie (seated at her husband, William's, desk); Nelle Kreider Tayloe, Nellie's sister-in-law; William Bradford Ross, her youngest son; and Chief Justice Charles T. Potter, who administered the oath. *American Heritage Center, University of Wyoming*

Nellie and Edness Kimball Wilkins *(left)*, her longtime secretary at the Mint, 1934. *Wyoming State Archives, Dept. of State Parks and Cultural Resources*

Nellie presents a commemorative coin to President Franklin Delano Roosevelt, ca. 1935. *American Heritage Center, University of Wyoming*

Chief Clerk Bergfeld of the Treasury Department administers the oath of office for Nellie's third term, 1943. Standing to the left is Secretary of the Treasury Henry Morgenthau Jr. *American Heritage Center, University of Wyoming*

A weekend at La Trappe, Nellie's Maryland farm, ca. 1937. Nellie is in the center, flanked by her two young friends, Russell Rowell *(far left)* and Kenneth Failor *(far right)*. The two women are unidentified. *Courtesy of Kenneth Failor*

Nellie and her grandson David Ross in Egypt during their trip around the world, 1961. *American Heritage Center, University of Wyoming*

Nellie in front of her portrait, Washington, D.C., ca. 1976. *Photo by Stan Jennings; American Heritage Center, University of Wyoming*

EIGHT

DNC Women's Director

ROOSEVELT was not alone in pushing the idea of a permanent DNC organization. Some party officials, including Emily Newell Blair, Nellie's predecessor at the DNC, had been promoting the idea since the early 1920s. After losing the election, Smith concluded that the lack of an established headquarters had contributed to his defeat, noting that "it has been the habit of the Democratic party to function only six months in every four years."[1] Smith's selection as DNC chairman, John J. Raskob, was a business executive, not a politician, but he knew how to raise money, and he knew how to set up effective organizations. He would end up spending a million dollars of his own money to help liquidate the party's campaign debt and to place the organization on a firm financial footing.[2] By April 1929, Raskob had appointed Jouett Shouse as chairman of the DNC's executive committee and had given him the task of setting up a permanent office and staff in Washington, D.C.

Raskob issued an invitation to more than three hundred of the party's leaders to attend a June 10 dinner in honor of Jouett Shouse; Raskob and Shouse planned to use the dinner to present their plans for invigorating the DNC. But instead of unifying the party organization, the dinner almost destroyed it; the southern Democrats announced that they would boycott the event. They were deeply suspicious of Raskob because he was so clearly a Smith partisan, and they were still angry about Smith's 1928 candidacy. After furious behind-the-scenes maneuvering, most of the southern Democrats agreed to attend the dinner and to support Raskob's efforts. At the dinner, Raskob announced that Nellie would receive a permanent position at the new DNC headquarters in Washington. Emphasizing the need for party unity, Shouse acknowledged that some Democratic candidates had already begun to organize for the 1932 campaign, but he promised that the new Democratic organization would remain impartial, dedicating itself to working for the good of the party in general.[3]

From the middle of June until the end of August, letters traveled back and forth between Nellie, Raskob, and Shouse as they negotiated the terms of her new, salaried position as director of the DNC Women's Division. To Nellie, Shouse wrote, "I think your mind and mine are running a good deal along the same lines, and I am certain when you come to Washington this fall we shall be able to map out some plans that will prove constructive and valuable." To Raskob, Shouse privately raised his concerns about Nellie's extensive outside speaking engagements and her past practice of billing the traveling expenses of her personal companion to the DNC.[4] Once Shouse and Raskob agreed on a formal salary offer, he wrote to Nellie, offering her a generous $7,500 per annum. For her staff, Nellie would be able to hire an executive secretary and a stenographer. Shouse made it clear that he would not continue to reimburse Nellie for the expenses of a traveling companion. He asked her to report to her new Washington post by October 1 rather than the end of October, as Nellie had requested. Finally, he raised one other, delicate issue.

> There is just one other matter concerning which we should have a definite and clear understanding in order that there may be no possibility of future misunderstanding. That is the question of your speaking engagements before non-political assemblies. How much time do you contemplate this will require? Everybody connected with the headquarters is giving his or her entire time to the work of the headquarters. Certainly there is enough work here to require the most continuous and exacting devotion. It might be that you would be in such demand as a paid speaker before different groups that it would interfere rather seriously with your work of the headquarters. I should like to have, therefore, a full and frank expression from you in this connection.[5]

Nellie had no intention of giving up her outside speaking. She had been juggling her Democratic commitments with her Chautauqua engagements for more than two years, and while she was pleased with the prospect of a full-time salary, she was loathe to lose her substantial income from the Redpath Chautauqua Bureau. She may well have raised Shouse's admonition to Raskob and to Al Smith himself. On September 10, Smith wrote Nellie, "I am in receipt of your letter enclosing copies of letters to Mr. Raskob and his reply to you. I am returning them to you as requested. I am sure we will be able to make a satisfactory settlement of the matter. I have talked to Mr. Raskob already and I intend to meet him tomorrow at noon."[6] Nellie got her way. Her speaking engagements continued without a break—and she did not arrive in Washington until the end of October, despite Shouse's request for an earlier start date.

During her Chautauqua years, Nellie had led a transient existence, living out of a suitcase and continually moving from city to city. As soon as she was confirmed in her DNC position, she was determined to establish a home again. Since she would continue to spend so much time on the road, it did not make sense to purchase a house, so in November 1929, she took an apartment at the very center of Washington's social swirl—the Mayflower Hotel. The opulent Mayflower, located in the elegant shopping district along Connecticut Avenue, had opened in February 1925. The Mayflower was a community to itself; in addition to its thousand transient hotel rooms, it also encompassed 112 permanent apartments of up to nine rooms. Many of Washington's elite called it home, including President Hoover's vice president. So many senators and congressmen kept Mayflower apartments that they were called the Mayflower Bloc. The Mayflower offered its residents their own private street entrance, a beauty shop, dress shop, flower shop, drugstore, health clinic with resident doctor, laundry, and maid service. Their apartments featured antiques, period furniture, oriental rugs, window dressings of silk and satin, and silver-plated fixtures in the bath. Even though the residents enjoyed the Mayflower's catering service, their apartments all included fully appointed kitchens, complete with fine china.[7]

Once settled at the Mayflower, Nellie urged Bradford to come east and move in with her to finish high school, but he declined. He was concerned about changing schools in the middle of the year, and at any rate, he was due to graduate from Sherwood Hall the spring of 1930. The two had generally spent at least a few weeks together every summer in Wyoming, but Nellie's travel schedule was so demanding that they had seldom been able to spend the Thanksgiving and Christmas holidays with one another. They kept in touch with sometimes frequent, sometimes intermittent, but always affectionate letters, with most of Nellie's being dashed off on hotel stationery.

Nellie was too caught up with juggling her political work and preparing for the summer Chautauqua season to travel to Wyoming for Bradford's 1930 graduation ceremony, but he was as understanding as always. His greatest concern was for her health. He had run into Ambrose's widow, Thelma, who told him that Nellie had been ill. "Why don't you tell me when you are sick?" he scolded.

> I haven't heard from you for some time and I worry about you a good deal. . . . If you don't take a rest [this] summer, I will refuse to go to school next winter. You know you don't have to work so hard to put me through college. I can get a job and put myself through. . . . If you don't value your health you should think of me. If anything should happen to you I wouldn't have any desire to live.[8]

After traveling with Nellie as her Chautauqua driver in the summer of 1930, Bradford followed Nellie east and enrolled as a freshman at the University of Virginia. He found the transition between prep school and university-level work much more difficult than he had expected; in fact, he was placed on academic probation after his first term. By the following fall, however, he wrote his mother cheerfully that his grades were "well above passing."[9]

It was not uncommon for women of Nellie's generation who had demanding, high-profile careers to spend weeks or months separated from their children. Nellie's predecessor at the DNC, Emily Newell Blair, was also away from her children for long periods, and she also lived a dual life; she was a Democratic politician when at the national or Missouri state headquarters and a traditional mother and wife during the periods she was at home in Joplin, Missouri (although she also maintained a writing career there). Florence Kelley, a social reformer who became general secretary of the National Consumers League, boarded her children with the family of a male reformer during her years at Hull House in Chicago. Mary Heaton Vorse dispersed her children to boarding schools and various relatives from 1915 to 1922 so that she could pursue her career as a national labor journalist.[10]

The difference between Nellie and these other women is that they did not set themselves up as standard bearers for the traditional domestic woman. Nevertheless, most famous women of that generation had to make painful choices, as historians have noted. Susan Ware wrote that "women who lived the kind of public life deemed worthy of historical treatment almost inevitably had to make decisions and sacrifices that had potentially profound effects on their personal lives," and Alice Wexler observed that these women were forced to construct an "often self-contradictory identity." The children of these famous women differed in their attitudes about their mothers' careers. Florence Kelley's son later wrote that he had been "blessed with the best bringing-up and educating of anybody that I have known of my time."

Conversely, the three children of Lucy Sprague Mitchell, a pioneer in the progressive education movement, bitterly blamed the neglect they had felt in childhood on their mother's career.[11] As for Nellie's sons, other than expressing their concern about the stresses of Nellie's career, they never stated or even inferred in their voluminous correspondence with her that they were resentful about her absences. If they had done so, Nellie's balancing of her career and her role as mother would have been much more painful.

Nellie's predecessor at the Women's Division, Emily Newell Blair, was a Democratic committeewoman from Missouri who had become active in the party around 1920. By 1922, she had been tapped to direct women's activities from the DNC Washington headquarters. Emily started her new position, as Nellie would six years later, without the benefit of any files or records from her predecessor, Elizabeth Bass. Since the DNC gave up most of its office space and barely functioned between elections, there was no place to retain the organizational information that would have been so useful both to Emily and later to Nellie. Emily began her tenure by organizing a network of Democratic women's clubs across the country. "I thought of the clubs . . . as a proving ground for the development of woman leadership," wrote Emily in her autobiography.[12] It was clear to Emily, based on her correspondence with the men in state and local Democratic organizations, as well as the reports she received from women, that women were being frozen out of the actual party structure. The clubs would give women a focus and political experience, and possibly their combined numbers would earn them a voice in party affairs. Emily and her assistants ended up organizing almost three thousand clubs nationwide. Emily became president of the Woman's National Democratic Club after Nellie replaced her at the DNC, but eventually she became disillusioned with the club organization. She later wrote,

> The weakness of my women's organization was that it had to operate through state and local organizations headed by men. My clubs, for example, though stimulated from our headquarters, were told to put themselves at the disposal of their regularly constituted official leaders. Much of my time and effort was directed toward persuading these local organization leaders to accept the help of these clubs. . . . It was a fallacy, I discovered, to think that men in politics always want an effective organization. . . . Men did not want women organized if they were not organized by them.[13]

"When Nellie Tayloe Ross took [the directorship,] the Women's Division was a mere skeleton," wrote the author of one study of the women's campaign in 1928.[14] Not only did Nellie find herself without any files that would have allowed her to build on the institutional memories of Elizabeth Bass and Emily Newell Blair, but she also started with no field structure other than the women's clubs—and she was determined not to depend on them. While she maintained good relationships with the club leaders and she always accommodated their requests for speakers and informational support, she recognized that they were outside the formal party structure, and therefore potentially unreliable in implementing national strategy. She also recognized that many of the clubs were as much about socializing and social position as they were about substantive politics.[15] Therefore, Nellie wrote, "women were urged to seek representation in the regular organization of the party where control rested—that is, in national, state, county and precinct committees—in order that their energies and voices might count in the shaping of party affairs."[16] Nellie blanketed the national organization with letters, information, and publicity, and she used her extensive traveling to establish personal connections with Democratic women and to become familiar with the status of their participation in state, county, and precinct organizations. Within two years, Nellie and her two assistants had succeeded in creating a network that touched 2,600 out of the nation's 3,000 counties. Given their extremely limited staffing and budget, they were only able to scratch the surface of the organizing work that was needed in the two years before the 1932 election, but they made an excellent start.[17]

One Wyoming connection that Nellie maintained at the DNC was her longtime secretary from the gubernatorial years, Ruth Harrington. For her other employee, she had engaged Sue Shelton White as her executive assistant. Sue, an attorney from Tennessee, had been actively involved in the 1928 campaign, and Nellie had met her during a sweep through the South. When Sue dropped by the DNC office in Washington in 1930, Nellie gauged her intelligence, common sense, and campaign experience, and decided that she was perfect for her vacant position.

Shortly after Nellie appointed Sue, she received a warning letter from Eleanor Roosevelt. Eleanor's network had informed her that Sue was an activist for the National Woman's Party. "My recollection [from the 1928 campaign] is that Miss Sue White is a good Democratic worker, but if what they say is true, . . . you would have to watch her extremely carefully. I do not know how you feel about the Woman's Party but I have always been very much opposed to their program."[18]

Women were no more unified concerning their proper place in society and how to advance their status in the 1930s than they are at the beginning of the twenty-first century. Eleanor Roosevelt was a dedicated member of a general grouping called the Domestic or Social Feminists. Domestic Feminists, who included settlement workers such as Jane Addams, Frances Perkins, and Grace Abbott, were progressives who were dedicated to ameliorating societal problems such as the ill treatment of immigrants and laborers, poor sanitation and nutrition, and inadequate education. A more militant group, represented by the National Woman's Party, had split off from the more moderate women's groups, such as the National American Woman's Suffrage Association (NAWSA), over the best tactics to win women the vote. "From the day of its birth, . . . the battle lines between the new Woman's party and the social feminists . . . were clearly drawn," wrote one historian.[19]

After the passage of the suffrage amendment, the "bitter rift among women's organizations" continued over the best way to further the advancement of women.[20] Believing that women and children deserved the protection of society, Domestic Feminists from groups such as the League of Women Voters (formerly NAWSA) and supported by the federal Women's Bureau, pushed for legislation that would limit working hours and set up special protections for women and child workers.[21] The National Woman's Party, conversely, supported total equality, and in 1923 it proposed an Equal Rights Amendment to the Constitution. The Equal Rights Amendment would have eliminated the special protective measures for women that the Domestic Feminists had worked so hard to achieve.[22] One historian wrote,

> For decades, the amendment embroiled the woman's movement in bitter strife and as much as anything else prevented the development of a united feminist appeal. . . . [T]he dispute reflected the different goals sought by various participants in the woman's movement. Female activists could be divided into two groups, . . . the "social feminists" who viewed suffrage as a lever for social-welfare reforms and "hard core feminists" who perceived the vote as only an intermediate step on the road to full sexual equality. The basic division . . . here described as that between reformers and feminists emerged explicitly in the period after 1920 and dominated the relationships between the various women's organizations.[23]

Although Nellie believed in progressive government, she was never an energetic participant in the social-work activities so critical to the Domestic Feminists. Nellie would have rejected any label that tied her to an organized women's movement. Women, she believed, could best advance their status not through feminist organizations, but by doing the best job possible in the workplace and within their families. Her rejection of the women's movement may have contributed to Eleanor Roosevelt's distant treatment of her.

Sue Shelton White was able to straddle the political divide that separated Nellie from the women in the New York State organization. Sue had met Molly Dewson during the 1928 campaign, and the two had become good friends. Despite Eleanor's initial distrust of her, Sue would eventually become part of the circle of Democratic feminists surrounding Dewson and Eleanor Roosevelt, a circle that never included Nellie. Sue and Molly led parallel private lives that were quite different from Nellie's. As was often the case for career women of their generation, each had chosen to establish a long-term committed relationship with another woman rather than to marry a man.[24] However, Sue's feminist leanings and her friendship with Molly did not seem to interfere with her relationship with Nellie. Sue and Nellie became close during their years together, and Sue served Nellie loyally as long as Nellie remained with the Democratic National Committee.[25] After Sue's death, Nellie told Sue's partner, Dr. Florence Armstrong, that she considered Sue to be one of the best friends she had ever had.[26]

"The Boss is in Tennessee," wrote Sue to Molly in June 1931. "She is 'making' Johnson City, Knoxville and Chattanooga this week and goes to Nashville for a conference Saturday. . . . It is rather like stepping into a pool of crocodiles—with the mess things are in there—but she is very tactful and I don't believe anybody will bite her toes off." She fretted to Molly that many of the female county vice chairmen did not know their business and did not seem particularly interested in learning. She was trying to stay calm despite her growing frustration with the slow progress, she wrote, but "let us be thankful we are philosophers and humorists, as well as feminists."[27]

Just as Nellie began her first full-time position in politics, Eleanor Roosevelt was stepping back from her visible role as a leader in the state and national Democratic organizations. Once her husband was elected as governor, she reluctantly concluded that she should steer clear of potentially controversial activities that could cause trouble for her husband's administration. She resigned as editor of the New York State *Women's Democratic News*, but she stayed involved and abreast of activities behind the scenes.[28] Her papers contain several letters from Nellie, as director of the Women's Division, requesting reports or information from the New York State Women's Division, and it is clear that Eleanor was personally involved in drafting or approving all correspondence back to the national DNC. In response to one of Nellie's requests, Eleanor outlined a proposed response for Nancy Cook, executive secretary of the Women's Division in New York State, told Cook that she would like to review the completed report before it was sent to Nellie, and added in one letter to Cook that "I do not think it wise to say any more than is absolutely necessary."[29] The letters between Eleanor and Nellie are invariably polite and formal, and they present a striking contrast to the affectionate notes that Eleanor sent to members of her circle, including Molly Dewson, Elinor Morgenthau, Nancy Cook, and Marion Dickerman.

On November 24, 1929, Wyoming's senior Republican, Francis E. Warren, died in office after serving in the U.S. Senate for almost forty years. Immediately, the national press began to speculate that Wyoming Democrats would tap Nellie to run in the special election to finish out Warren's term. The *Boston Herald* wrote that "the United States Senate, one of the few remaining masculine citadels against the surge of women in politics, may be compelled to capitulate much sooner than anticipated. Mrs. Nellie Tayloe Ross . . . is now very much in the limelight as a prospective candidate for the vacancy. . . . Mrs. Ross . . . steadfastly declines to discuss the subject until the Warren obsequies are concluded, but even if she should be personally reluctant to make the race, it is believed that Democratic leaders will induce her to run."[30]

The *Herald* was correct; that same day, O'Mahoney wrote Nellie a long, private letter to tell her that she was, indeed, the party's choice:

> I am sending you a clipping from last night's *Tribune* wherein you will see that, on the Democratic side, your name leads and mine falls into second place. . . . As I told you yesterday, I do not intend to be a candidate. My own judgment tells me that the force of the anti-Catholic wave has not yet sufficiently spent itself, to make it possible for me to win. . . .
>
> If it seems wise for you to run, it would give me unalloyed pleasure to see you successful and to do everything in my power to advance your cause. . . . I believe you would be much stronger than I as a candidate. You would start out with a wider acquaintance and in a short campaign such as we are likely to have that would be a tremendous advantage. The question is whether it would be sufficient, for in a short campaign, the Republicans would have an even greater advantage over any candidate. . . .
>
> Doubtless there are many voters who regard you more or less as an apostate because of your support of Smith and who would vote against you to punish you. Then, too, there are others who believe that "the

> Senate is no place for a woman." . . . But even after all disadvantages are canvassed, everybody agrees that you are without doubt the strongest candidate we could possibly name.[31]

O'Mahoney warned Nellie that should she decide to accept the draft to run, she should know that most of the state leaders did not believe a Democrat could win the special election. As it turned out, Nellie did not have to make a decision about running. Nellie's Republican successor, Governor Frank Emerson, appointed an interim successor, Republican rancher and oilman Patrick J. Sullivan, pending a special election. Since Sullivan had no political ambitions, many observers believed that Emerson was positioning himself to win the special election. Wyoming Democrats, therefore, attacked the plans for a special election as an unreasonable expense; they wanted a delay until the 1930 elections in November. Wyoming law was amended to remove the requirement for a special election as long as a vacancy occurred within a year of any general election.[32]

By November, Nellie's moment had passed. The Democrats nominated H. H. Schwartz, state chairman of the Democratic Party, who lost the senatorial election to Republican Robert D. Carey. Nellie never again ran for public office, and Emerson, who died in gubernatorial office in 1931, never had a chance to be a senator. When Wyoming's Democratic senator, John B. Kendrick, died in office in 1933, the then-Democratic governor appointed O'Mahoney to Kendrick's seat. O'Mahoney would go on to serve as Wyoming's Democratic senator until 1953, the same year that Nellie retired from public life.[33]

With the 1930 midterm election approaching, Nellie hit the trail to campaign for Democrats across the nation. As a result of the stock market crash and the steadily worsening economy, Republicans were vulnerable, and Nellie sought to capitalize on the financial distress of potential crossover voters. On the stump for Democratic candidates for governor, senator, and U.S. representatives in Nebraska, she told an Omaha audience that "if I were a farmer, or a farmer's wife, and had pinned my faith all the days of my life to the republican party, I'd be ready now for a change." She reminded her listeners of all the progressive legislation passed by Democrats between the years 1910 and 1923, including the Federal Reserve Act and the federal farm loan system. After the stock market crash, Hoover had declared that the federal reserve system had saved the country's finances—but the federal reserve was a system introduced by the Democrats. She recited a list of Hoover's broken promises—"uninterrupted prosperity, banishment of poverty, the end of the poor house"—and then she reminded her audience about "the bread lines, the soup kitchens in the cities, and the widespread unemployment."[34]

Disgruntled Americans across the nation listened to Nellie and her peers. As a result of the 1930 election, Republicans lost about forty seats in the House of Representatives, and the control of the House passed to the Democrats. Republicans still held one more Senate seat than the Democrats, but the Democrats were able to control the Senate thanks to a coalition with a bloc of discontented midwestern Republicans.

In New York, Eleanor marshaled the forces of the state Women's Division for the 1930 campaign to reelect Franklin as governor. Nancy Cook headed up the office, while Eleanor and Caroline O'Day worked on strategy behind the scenes. Eleanor also brought over Molly Dewson from the Consumers League of New York to help draft correspondence and answer letters. Although the women's organization performed effectively as usual, their contributions were not critical to the outcome; Franklin trounced his opponent, garnering the largest majority ever received by a gubernatorial candidate in New York.

It was becoming increasingly apparent that the Democrats might win the 1932 presidential race no matter whom they nominated, and Franklin's victory placed him at the forefront of potential candidates. His campaign managers, James Farley and Louis Howe, formed a presidential campaign organization immediately after the 1930 election. By the spring of 1931, the Friends of Roosevelt offices were up and running in New York City.

Farley recognized the valuable contribution that the women's campaign activities had made in the 1928 and 1930 elections, so he established the same kind of structure for the Friends of Roosevelt organization. Molly would "front" for Eleanor since, as New York's First Lady and wife of the candidate, it was inappropriate for her to openly run the women's campaign.[35] In July, Eleanor wrote to Molly at her home in Maine,

> Franklin has asked me to get busy on this organization work and I have written the enclosed letter which is to go to all women whose names are sent into us from different states. . . . I am sending you this suggested draft and will be glad to have you return it with any suggestions you have, as I am going to ask you if you will be willing to sign it. They will all be done in New York and then sent to you to sign as will any other letter which I dictate. . . . Much love to you always, Affectionately, Eleanor R.[36]

In March 1931, the simmering antagonisms between the Roosevelt and Smith camps were aired in front of the national press at a meeting of the Democratic National Committee. Chairman Raskob, one of Smith's most important supporters, sent out a letter before the meeting to state that he planned to include a plank in the 1932 platform to call for repeal of prohibition. It was a direct challenge to Roosevelt's potential leadership. The Roosevelt strategists immediately began marshaling committee members from around the country to come in for the session and to help in calling Raskob's hand. At the meeting, Raskob's proposal was tabled when it became clear that his supporters were outnumbered two to one. James Farley wrote that "away down deep was the common knowledge that a titanic struggle was going to take place over the presidential nomination and that without publicly saying so, Chairman Raskob and his allies intended to use the all-important machinery of the national committee to stop Roosevelt if they could."[37]

Back at the DNC Women's Division, Nellie and her small staff found themselves in a difficult position. They reported to a chairman who was Smith's strongest supporter, yet whose official office policy was to remain neutral. Nellie's secretary remembered that "we had to be pretty careful then because most of the office was for . . . Roosevelt. But we had to restrain ourselves a bit because we knew the powers . . . now Governor Ross was not part of this New York group." Nellie had decided after meeting with Roosevelt in 1929 that he was the best candidate; however, she had no choice but to keep her opinion to herself.[38] Her inability to voice her support for Roosevelt undoubtedly further strained her already distant relationship with Eleanor, who shared the Roosevelt organization's distrust of the DNC headquarters staff.[39]

The Democrats convened their nominating convention on June 27 in Chicago. The first struggle between the Smith and Roosevelt camps came with the election of the convention chairman. Raskob was furious that the Roosevelt camp had endorsed Senator Walsh of Montana for the post after the committee on arrangements had already endorsed Jouett Shouse; after extended debate, the Roosevelt forces prevailed, and Walsh was elected permanent chairman. In the first ballot for the presidential nomination, Roosevelt garnered 666.25 votes to Smith's 201.75; the voting stretched on for an emotional two hours as each side worked the convention floor. Two more rounds of balloting followed the next day, as Smith held his own delegates but Roosevelt picked up delegates from other candidates. Finally, on the fourth ballot, Roosevelt prevailed when favorite son John Nance Garner gave him his Texas and California delegates—earning himself, incidentally, the vice-presidential nomination. An embittered Smith, who fundamentally disagreed with the direction that Roosevelt planned to take the party and who believed that he was owed the nomination for his long service during the Democrats' years in the wilderness, left Chicago the next day. Roosevelt's campaign manager, James Farley, was elected the new chairman of the DNC on July 3. That night at a meeting of the DNC, Roosevelt thanked Raskob and Shouse for their service to the party, but neither man was there to hear Roosevelt's remarks.[40]

As soon as the convention was over, the Friends of Roosevelt organization swung into action to set up an election strategy. James Farley had no intention of using the DNC organization for campaign purposes; it was too tainted by its Smith and Raskob connections to be trusted. On the women's side, Molly Dewson was named head of the Women's Division in the New York campaign headquarters. Molly was, as usual, spending the summer months at the Maine house she shared with her life partner, Polly Porter, but she and Eleanor wrote back and forth constantly. On July 16, Eleanor wrote Molly a three-page letter on the tentative setup of the Women's Division in New York. A skeleton staff would be maintained in Washington during the campaign, but no regular work would be done there until after the election. Eleanor had been passed over in favor of Nellie in the 1928 campaign; now it was Eleanor's turn to return the favor. Nellie's assistant, Sue White, would be pulled off Nellie's staff and given to Molly. "We will keep in touch with Governor Ross and use her for field work and possibly speeches where we feel her valuable," Eleanor wrote Molly.[41]

A few days later, Eleanor wrote Molly, "I saw Sue White today with Governor Ross and it is going to be a bit difficult to keep Governor Ross where she is supposed to stay, but I think it can be managed." Nellie was trying hard to assume the substantive campaign role that she believed she should play as director of the DNC Women's Division. Sometime in July, she traveled to Maine to visit Molly in an attempt to build a bridge between the DNC and the campaign directors. "I shall long remember with pleasure my little visit with you & your interesting friends at your summer paradise," she wrote Molly. She also shared information about the organizing stop she had made on the way to talk with Democratic women leaders in Boston. One of Molly's staff warned her toward the end of July that "Mrs. Ross is very much concerned indeed over the fact that she feels she is being ignored in the present campaign plans. . . . It is going to take a great deal of tact to handle the Nellie Ross situation."[42]

Sue Shelton White did what she could to bring Nellie and Molly together. She advised Molly that "There is much information of value . . . that my chief could give you. She has been in 40 states during the past two years & has met the party leaders of all factions, both men & women personally, & has their confidence. . . . She is the one for you to talk with, & when I say that, I mean *talk*. . . . I want you to look to *her* rather than to me. . . . I know that she wants to cooperate in every way as her heart has been with you all along."[43]

In the end, Nellie was named to head an "advisory committee" and was dispatched out to the campaign trail. Molly headed the seven-member staff of the Women's Division, which did not report to the advisory committee. Eleanor, who was not officially part of the Women's Division, spent the campaign working at a desk that backed up to Molly's. She advised Molly, worked on correspondence, and acted as liaison with Franklin, Louis Howe, and James Farley.[44]

Farley, with the competent support of the women, engineered an inspired campaign. The Democrats had pledged to repeal the Eighteenth Amendment, but prohibition was no longer an issue; the election was all about the economy. Roosevelt toured the country and, to each group except for organized labor, he promised to deliver what they most wanted—full production for businesses, agricultural programs for farmers, construction projects and other employment opportunities for laid-off workers, and reform of Wall Street for the investors. The only way to lift the nation out of despair and back to secure prosperity was for the federal government to assume an active stewardship over the economy and the social structure of society. In response, President Hoover warned Americans that "[the Democrats] are proposing changes and so-called new deals which would destroy the very foundations of the American system of life. . . . [Their proposals] would crack the timbers of the Constitution. You cannot extend the mastery of government over the daily life of a people without somewhere making it master of people's souls and thoughts. This election is not a mere shift from the ins to the outs. It means determining the course our nation will take for over a century to come."[45] But the weary and desperate electorate had given up on Hoover. On Election Day, Roosevelt received almost 23 million popular votes to Hoover's 15.7 million, and he carried all but six states in the electoral college.

Nellie demonstrated her characteristic trait of loyalty that evening when she penned a kind note to the former DNC chairman, John J. Raskob. "In the first moment of relaxation while awaiting returns I want to express to you my tribute of admiration for your fine sportsmanship & generosity during the campaign. Be assured there is a vast multitude of Democrats thinking gratefully of your monumental service to our party."[46] This gesture belies the notion apparently held by some in the Friends of Roosevelt organization that Nellie's political activities were calculated solely to benefit Nellie herself: The forgotten Raskob was in no position to grant any further favors. The question was whether the Roosevelt organization would now choose to recognize the loyalty and service that Nellie herself had given the Democratic Party since 1924.

With the election over, the Roosevelt campaign office was closed. Officially, Molly's work was done, and Nellie's office resumed leadership of Democratic women. Yet there were signs that Nellie's time as director of the Women's Division was over. Nellie wrote her son Bradford in October that she had failed to receive a salary check for the previous month.[47] Then, early in December, Nellie wrote Molly,

> Sister, are you and I crossing wires or are we not? Letters coming in to me speak of wanting to "co-operate with both you & Miss Dewson" & "Shall I send organization records to both you & Miss D.?" One Vice Chairman consulting me about club programs says "Miss Dewson writes that she is outlining a program for study clubs." . . .
>
> Do you know when my right hand [Sue] is coming [back to Washington]? It seems a year since she left. . . .
>
> [Regarding the proposed study program for women's clubs], I assumed that it was your idea to submit it to me at the Washington Headquarters if my understanding is correct that Mr. Farley expects me to continue functioning here as he said he did, & if I was correct in understanding from you that you were winding up there. I remember our brief discussion about the possibility of a development that would make a change here in the Woman's Division. Perhaps Mr. F. & others close to the Pres.-elect have some new plan in mind. (How fine it would be for you to be here if that is where your interest most lies!) So long though as I do remain I am sure that you will agree that any new proposals relating to women should first come here.[48]

Molly responded blandly a few days later: No, there was no intention on her part to bypass Nellie. No, she had not talked with Farley or Howe; when she was able to see them, she would let Nellie know what they said. No, she did not think it wise to send Sue back to Washington just yet; she might be needed to help clean up the campaign committee's work. She concluded, "You may be sure that no definite action of any kind will be taken by me as I consider myself out of the picture. . . . Cordially yours, Miss Mary W. Dewson."[49]

Molly may have been sincere about her intention to resume her private life with Polly in New York City and Maine. However, it is more likely, albeit undocumented, that Eleanor had already intimated to her that Franklin intended to offer her Nellie's position as director of the Women's Division as soon as Nellie was appropriately rewarded with a patronage post. Her biographer wrote that "after a winter back at her old job at the Consumers League, Molly Dewson was itching to get back into politics, whatever Roosevelt's plans: she had too much unfinished business on her agenda."[50]

The primary piece of unfinished business was patronage. Democrats had been out of office for twelve years; hundreds of people had worked for this victory, and hundreds more were hoping to obtain a federal position. No sooner was the ink dry on the newspapers' election headlines than the press began to speculate publicly on Roosevelt's cabinet selections. Molly Dewson was determined that women should get a goodly share of the spoils, and at the top of her list was the selection of Frances Perkins as secretary of Labor. "One of the most diverting Roosevelt cabinet suggestions," wrote one reporter the first week after the election, "is the belief that he would be the first President to give a woman a departmental portfolio. In this interesting speculative connection the name of Miss Frances Perkins, well known industrial commissioner of New York State, is honorably mentioned. Some authorities think that if any Democratic woman is to be given cabinet rank she should be former Gov. Nellie Tayloe Ross of Wyoming, now vice chairman of the National Committee."[51]

Immediately after the election, Molly had engineered a letter-writing campaign from persons and organizations across the country to convince Roosevelt to appoint Frances.[52] Her efforts occasionally backfired. An officer of the Insurance Institute of America responded to Molly that "I am not going to do it [i.e., write Roosevelt]; not because of any lack of respect for Miss Perkins, but if the President-elect, after having been associated for so many years with this most estimable woman, is in any doubt as to her appointment, it ought not be resolved for him by letters from the outside. . . . The simple fact that it is deemed necessary by Miss Perkins' friends to suggest writing letters does not make a very good impression."[53]

Nellie's supporters, with her full knowledge, were also mounting a letter-writing campaign on her behalf.[54] Sue Shelton White, friend and executive secretary to both Nellie and Molly, felt caught in the middle. She shared a letter with Molly that she had received from a male observer, who wrote, "of course some of the women are divided as to what woman should get the Cabinet position, but the majority of women have whole-heartedly endorsed

Governor Ross, and I think she is the logical one for it, but she will not get it, however deserving, unless there is some work done in the next couple of months." The correspondent inferred that infighting among the women might derail Nellie's selection. Sue assured him that this was not the case; "Women are good sports," she wrote him. To her friend, however, she wrote, "Are they, Molly?"[55]

Sue, of course, was right. If it was politically risky for Roosevelt to appoint one woman to the cabinet, it was downright unthinkable that he would appoint two. Nellie's selection would spell failure for Frances Perkins, and Frances was part of the New York feminist circle. Emily Newell Blair was supportive of the Perkins campaign, but she was aware of the equally spirited effort on Nellie's behalf. She wrote to Molly, "Do you think it would do any good to talk to the Governor [Roosevelt] about intimating to Governor Ross that she would certainly be given something worthy of her and to Ruth Owen the same with the idea of calling off letters from them about the Cabinet. It is not that these letters will do any good for Governor Ross or Ruth Owen but they may divert support from F.P." Two days later, she wrote Molly again about the many women she had heard from who had been asked to write on Nellie's behalf; perhaps, she ventured, Roosevelt might actually prefer to name Nellie rather than Frances? If Roosevelt decided to appoint Henry Morgenthau Jr., a New Yorker, as secretary of Agriculture, then surely he would not be able to name a second New Yorker—Frances—to his cabinet.[56]

Indeed, by the end of December, Roosevelt had received almost seventy endorsements for Nellie as secretary of the Interior.[57] Most were from the Democratic clubs and other women's organizations, but a few were from such disparate sources as the *Sioux City Tribune,* the Bankers Trust Company of Gary, Indiana, and the Terminal Railroad Association of St. Louis. The national committeewoman from Maine wrote to warn Roosevelt that

> [t]he discussion of the appointment of a woman to the Department of Labor is apparently arousing much opposition and labor antagonism, whereas, the fact that politicians generally concede that if a woman is placed in the Department of the Interior there will be less jealousy among the men, and a minimum of opposition within our own party, leads me to present my personal opinion of Governor Nellie Tayloe Ross.
>
> Frankly, I have taken my cue from her in many political difficulties. She is willing to reveal her state of mind and lend ready assistance, but at the same time she is scrupulously ethical, discreet, and highly honorable. . . . She is religiously fair-minded and liberal, she has a knowledge of the general territory of the Country, and a thorough understanding of the peculiar conditions and needs of the various states. She has the power to

think clearly, and to judge accurately. Bitter personal experience has made her conciliatory and sympathetic.

The recognition of her ability by placing her as Secretary of the Interior will have the acclaim of the women of the Nation.[58]

The committeewoman was correct in her assessment that organized labor was opposed to Frances. Labor leaders were concerned that the department, which already had two female bureau chiefs—Mary Anderson at the Women's Bureau and Grace Abbott at the Children's Bureau—would be unacceptably "feminized" by the Perkins appointment. After all, they argued, about 80 percent of the American labor force was masculine. In early February, the *Washington Post* detailed rumors that the president of the American Federation of Labor, William Green, had been offered the Labor post. The backers of Frances Perkins had reportedly agreed to accept Green in lieu of a much less palatable choice—Daniel J. Tobin, president of the Teamsters Union.[59] Either Green turned down the appointment offer, or the *Washington Post* had been wrong. James Farley insisted on February 15 that Roosevelt had not yet made final decisions about the cabinet selections, and soon afterward the *New York Times* speculated that Roosevelt intended to appoint Perkins. The Perkins rumors grew stronger and stronger until on February 23, her name appeared on what proved to be an accurate slate of incoming cabinet officers, except for the position of attorney general.[60]

If James Farley was correct in his later assessment of Roosevelt's intentions, being the secretary of the Interior was probably never an option for Nellie. Roosevelt had decided that the position should be offered to a progressive Republican, in recognition of the support those voters had given him in the election. When Senator Cutting of New Mexico declined the post, it was offered to Harold L. Ickes of Illinois, who had worked on behalf of the Roosevelt Progressive League. Farley also wrote in his memoir that Frances was always Roosevelt's personal choice for Labor. Frances had sterling credentials—a master's degree in sociology and economics from Columbia, years of experience in settlement houses and other social welfare organizations, and several years as head of Governor Roosevelt's State Industrial Commission. It may have been enough for male appointees like Ickes to qualify based on their political service, but it certainly was not enough for the first female cabinet secretary. Thus was introduced a long tradition that lasted at least until the 1970s—and some would say much later—that a woman had to be at least twice as impressive as the male candidates if she was to be selected for one of the federal government's top executive positions.

Something still had to be done for Nellie. Nellie was apparently considered for several posts, including federal power commissioner and assistant secretary of the Interior. Late in March, newspapers reported that Nellie would definitely be appointed U.S. treasurer.[61] Molly Dewson wrote Eleanor a note that suggests Molly first learned of Nellie's appointment in the morning paper, despite her subsequent claim that she deserved credit for Nellie's placement: "I am enchanted at Nellie Ross—Treasurer of the U.S.!! Perfect!"[62] But it was not to be. After James Farley had already offered Nellie the position, Roosevelt's new secretary of the Treasury, William H. Woodin, objected to the appointment of a woman to the post. Farley and Roosevelt deferred to Woodin, and the *New York Times* reported that she would instead be named to the Civil Service Commission.[63]

Woodin's decision, to say nothing of Farley's and Roosevelt's concurrence, was a slap in the face to all the Democratic women who considered Nellie their leader. Even Emily Newell Blair, who had backed Frances Perkins rather than Nellie for a cabinet position, objected. She complained to Molly that "I know all about the Treasurership & Woodin. But I do think pressure ought to be brought on the dear soul to appoint Gov. Ross to it." The women who had worked hard in Nellie's organization expected their efforts, and hers, to be recognized and rewarded. If the party failed to give Nellie an important position, it would anger and demoralize the Women's Division network, which could harm the organization and hinder future recruiting of women to the party. Nellie was known nationwide as a Democratic campaign leader who had paid her dues, while Frances's experience was limited to New York. Blair concluded, "To my mind the appointment to the Civil Service Commission does not 'fill the bill.' In first place she succeeds a woman who is not a regular Democrat. It does not open a new place to women & so give Nellie a chance to appear as a pioneer for women."[64]

It is unlikely that either Molly or Eleanor intervened on behalf of Nellie, but perhaps Joseph O'Mahoney, soon to be Farley's first assistant postmaster general, did. On April 26, the Roosevelt administration announced that Nellie Tayloe Ross would be appointed to a first for women—director of the Mint. Ironically, she would report briefly to the same secretary who had objected to her appointment as treasurer. As events evolved, it became clear that of the positions for which Nellie was considered, the Mint directorship was by far the best. It was the first bureau-level appointment of a woman outside of the "female" appointments at the Women's Bureau and the Children's

Bureau. More importantly, by the end of her first year, Roosevelt's new monetary policies and an increased demand for coins would transform the Mint directorship into a position of real responsibility.

Nellie would stay at the Mint for the next twenty years, as she gradually faded from the public memory. If she harbored some bitterness concerning the political machinations that had landed her at the Mint instead of Interior, she certainly had adequate justification. However, for a woman who was strongly motivated by financial security, the Mint provided her a lengthy appointment that she could never have achieved as Interior secretary. The Mint position allowed her to balance her private life and her career in a way that would have been impossible as a cabinet secretary. Finally, the Mint position allowed her to function without the close critical scrutiny that Frances Perkins endured as the first woman cabinet secretary. Despite her excellent preparation, hard work, and dedication, Frances lacked Nellie's finesse with people; she would suffer through twelve agonizing years as secretary due to her poor relations with Congress, the press, and her employees.[65]

Now that Nellie had been placed, Eleanor Roosevelt acted to push her gently but irrevocably out of the way so that Molly Dewson could assume the directorship of the Women's Division. Although her friend Molly officially held no position in the Democratic Party after the 1932 election, all through the winter and spring she had continued to use the stationery of the now-defunct Democratic campaign organization and to consult with Eleanor on patronage appointments for women. After Nellie's appointment, Eleanor set up a meeting between herself, Molly, and Nellie, in which they worked out future arrangements. Nellie would have to give up her political post as the director of the Women's Division, although she would continue to be vice chairman of the DNC. Following the meeting, Eleanor sent James Farley two draft letters, one to Nellie and one to Sue White, which she told him that she thought he should send rather than she. The letters documented the decisions reached in the women's meeting. The letter to Nellie read, "As I understand it, this [enclosed letter to Sue Shelton White] carried out the plan which Miss Dewson and Mrs. Roosevelt worked out with you and I also understand that you have agreed to be kind enough to occasionally consult with Miss White [if] you have any ideas and that as vice chairman of the National Committee any new policies are to be brought to your attention before the final carrying out."[66]

Thereafter, Eleanor simply forged ahead with issues relating to women. In May, for example, she wrote to explain to Nellie why she had been bypassed in the deliberations about female candidates for a vacancy at the Civil Service

Commission. She blamed the decision not to consult with Nellie on the men. Nellie was a personal friend of another candidate, but "Mr. Farley and my husband were very anxious to give Mrs. McMillan the place. . . . They knew it would put you in a very difficult position to have to say that you had been consulted and therefore I urged them not to write to you before hand. I hope you will forgive me and understand the motive."[67]

In October 1933, Molly Dewson was formally appointed as the new director of the DNC Women's Division. Nellie honored Dewson's appointment at the DNC by hosting a tea and reception in her honor at the Mayflower Hotel in January 1934.[68] Molly ended up serving as director only until August 1934, when she resigned pleading ill health; in truth, the job had strained her personal relationship with Polly Porter. Thereafter, she invented a title for herself as chairman of a nonexistent advisory committee to the Women's Division, which allowed her to stay involved in politics on her own terms.[69]

Dewson is remembered as a far more effective Women's Division director than Nellie, and indeed, she was a dedicated and skillful political strategist. However, she also had two important factors working in her favor that Nellie lacked. First, her close friendship with Eleanor Roosevelt gave her an ear in the White House that Nellie had lacked, which enhanced Molly's influence and accomplishments. Conversely, Nellie served during a period when the Democrats were both out of power and experiencing an internal battle over control of the party and its policies. Second, Molly was able to build on the organizational network that Nellie had created, while Nellie started with nothing. However, Molly's autobiography gave Nellie no credit for her successful organization of a field structure; in fact, she barely mentioned Nellie in her autobiography other than to describe her speaking ability.[70] The person most familiar with Nellie's skills and contributions to the Women's Division, Sue Shelton White, clearly viewed Nellie's expertise in a positive light, but she was unable to "sell" Nellie to the power brokers in Eleanor Roosevelt's circle.

Molly discounted Nellie because she entered politics as the widow of a governor, and she failed to respond to Nellie's attempts to develop a friendship or a closer working relationship, through which she might have come to respect Nellie's contributions. It is possible that her opinion of Nellie was colored by the fact that Nellie preceded her as director. Frequently, there exists distrust and antipathy between two individuals who follow one another in an organization; the predecessor believes that the successor has destroyed the good work left behind, while the successor believes that a large part of his or her accomplishment has been to clean up the mistakes and inadequacies of the predecessor. In the end, Molly was the one who left behind a body of documentation for historians about her activities, while Nellie did not.

In 1934, President Roosevelt instituted a policy that members of his administration could not hold concurrent posts within the Democratic National Committee. Nellie was among the first DNC committee members to be forced out. In reporting her resignation as vice chairman, the *New York Herald Tribune* stated that "Mrs. Ross was known in the Democratic national organization as a holdover from the Smith-Raskob regime. . . . It has been known for some time that she had not worked well with Postmaster General James A. Farley."[71] Nellie clearly did not want to go, but she was gracious until the very last. She wrote Farley,

> I do not know how I could, even if I chose to do so, relate my connection with the Democratic National Committee to the Mint-service in such a way as to serve my own advantage [or] that of any other person. In order, however, to avoid even an appearance of conflicting interests where there are concerned my public service and my identity with the organization of my party, I tender to you my resignation. . . . Permit me, my dear Mr. Chairman, in retiring, to express the pleasure I have found in association with you and the other members of the Committee. Particularly do I desire to pay my tribute to your able and unselfish leadership.[72]

One is left wondering whether Nellie considered herself discarded or ill-used by the Roosevelt camp, particularly by Eleanor and Molly. If so, she chose to keep her own counsel. But a few years later, Leland Howard, who was to become her assistant director at the Mint, escorted her to a reception at the White House. Eleanor Roosevelt crossed the floor to chat with them, and Nellie greeted her politely. After a few brief words, Nellie told Eleanor that she had other people she needed to see. Nellie thereupon turned heel and departed, leaving a shocked Leland Howard alone with the First Lady to watch as Nellie walked away.[73]

NINE

Bureau Chief

NELLIE MAY WELL have owed her position at the Mint, at least in part, to sexism. Clearly her appointment was a landmark advance for women, but it also seemed a safe way to reward Nellie's political labors.[1] As a result of the Depression, Mint operations in 1933 were at an all-time low, so the patronage dispensers may have believed, as a later reporter speculated, that "a woman could easily handle the job."[2] The assumption that Nellie's position was nothing but a sinecure would be proved wrong on two fundamental counts. First, the job turned out to be far more challenging than anyone could have imagined in April 1933; during her twenty-year tenure, Nellie ended up directing the largest expansion in production, staffing, and facilities in the Mint's history. Second, Nellie would demonstrate by the end of her Mint career that she was a far more able administrator than her detractors could have guessed.

On Saturday, March 4, 1933, Franklin Roosevelt was sworn in as the thirty-second president of a troubled nation. "The only thing we have to fear is fear itself," he reassured his listeners. He promised them that things would soon get better. During his first one hundred days, Congress granted him almost unlimited power to experiment with the nation's laws and its very social fabric. Among the many areas affected by new legislation, Congress and the president enacted a Twenty-First Amendment to end the divisive national debate over prohibition, but more importantly, they passed several measures designed to provide employment and stimulate the economy: creation of a federal employment service, the establishment of the Civilian Conservation Corps to employ young men, a grant program to assist states in support of the unemployed and needy, a Farm Credit Act to refinance farmers' mortgages, an overall reduction in government spending, and a Public Works Administration—an employment program that would build a significant portion of the nation's infrastructure of bridges, dams, highways, and military facilities.[3]

Roosevelt had assumed the presidency of a nation whose banking system was on its knees. A credit and currency crisis overseas had resulted in an outflow of the United States' gold reserves as European nations sought to shore up their own gold balances. Since the United States was still on the gold standard, the depletion of gold precipitated a loss of confidence in the dollar. Private American citizens began to hoard their gold; so did banks, reducing their capacity to make loans or advance credit to businesses and the public. As the banks increasingly turned to the Federal Reserve for loans to cover their obligations and their depositors' growing demands, the Federal Reserve Board, its member institutions themselves almost out of gold, begged President Hoover on March 2 to declare a national banking holiday. Hoover was reluctant to take such an action just two days before the end of his term, and his attempts to gain the cooperation or concurrence of Roosevelt were unsuccessful. In the face of national inaction, all forty-eight states had declared bank holidays by Inauguration Day. One of President Roosevelt's first acts was to issue a declaration suspending all banking transactions in the states and territories of the United States.[4]

Banks began to reopen on Monday, March 13, following enactment of the Emergency Banking Act, but Roosevelt knew he would have to take permanent, drastic actions to end the hoarding of gold. On April 5, he signed Executive Order 6102, which nationalized the nation's gold supply and required all individuals to turn in to the Federal Reserve any gold bullion, gold certificates, or gold coin with an aggregate value greater than one hundred dollars.[5] In December 1933, Roosevelt followed up his gold restrictions with an order that nationalized the country's silver supply.[6]

Following enactment of the gold and silver legislation, the Mint director was delegated responsibility for administering that portion of the statutes that related to the industrial use of gold and the purchase of newly mined domestic silver at rates higher than open-market prices. The Mint was also charged with housing and safeguarding the nation's supplies of gold and silver, but its storage facilities for the incoming gold and silver were totally inadequate. Nellie arranged to deposit the bullion in leased space while she instituted a major construction initiative. By 1935, new vaults in Philadelphia, a new wing in Denver, and a brand new mint in San Francisco were in progress, and by 1936, work on a gold bullion depository at Fort Knox, Kentucky, had begun. The West Point depository for silver bullion was opened in 1938.[7]

In addition to overseeing the largest facilities expansion in Mint history, Nellie soon found herself responsible for meeting a huge increase in coin demand. By the end of 1934, a gradual improvement in economic conditions had shocked the sleepy atmosphere at the Mint into production that strained the capacity of the out-of-date facilities; for a significant portion of the year, the Mints were forced to run two or even three daily shifts. In her 1934 annual report, Nellie reported that 65.7 million coins were minted that year, an increase of more than 72 percent over 1933 totals—yet Mint staffing had only increased from 538 to 607, or less than 13 percent.[8]

Nellie's appointment at the Mint was truly groundbreaking, and not just because she was the first woman to head the Mint. She was the first woman to head *any* federal bureau outside the female enclaves at the Women's Bureau and the Children's Bureau. The only other executive position held by women in the federal government prior to Franklin Roosevelt's appointments was Civil Service Commissioner, to which two women had been appointed. In a nation unaccustomed to females with executive power, those selections had been relatively "safe" because both female commissioners had shared decision-making responsibility with two male peers.[9] Urged on by his wife and Molly Dewson, however, Roosevelt ended up naming about fifty women to top- and mid-level appointive positions, the most important of which were Ruth Bryan Owen as minister to Denmark, Josephine Roche as assistant secretary of the Treasury, and Marion Banister as assistant treasurer of the United States.[10]

The lack of federal female executives was mirrored in a generally low level of women throughout the federal civil service. As of 1930, women made up about 22 percent of the nation's civilian labor force, but only 15 percent of the federal workforce.[11] Federal employment opportunities for women tended to expand and contract as economic conditions changed. Women were encouraged to apply in times of tight labor markets, particularly during wartime when men were called to military service, but they were turned away or even discharged when the male unemployment rate rose. In fact, Section 213 of the Economy Act of June 30, 1932, while not specifically singling out females, resulted in the dismissal of three times as many women as men. Section 213 provided that if agencies ran reductions in force, they must first dismiss any employees whose spouses also held federal appointment; it also forbade the appointment of any persons whose spouse was already a federal employee. Section 213 remained in force until 1937.[12]

While the federal government may have been a less-than-welcoming employer of women overall, the Mint, ironically enough, had been a pioneer in their appointment. Other than the occupations of postmistress and lighthouse keeper, which provided jobs for a few fortunate women out in the hinterlands, the semiskilled and nonskilled positions at the Mint were among the first occupations opened to women. The nation's first mint was established by act of Congress in 1792 in Philadelphia, and some time before 1800, women joined its workforce.[13] In Nellie's era, the Mint was certainly no leader in employment of women, but the Treasury Department, overall, was; as of 1939, it had the highest percentage of women in its workforce—36.3 percent—of any department.[14] However, these women were clustered in the lower-level and clerical positions. Nellie expressed pride late during her tenure in the progress women had made at the Mint; by 1948, Nellie's personnel officer was a woman, and another woman held the top civil service post at the Philadelphia mint.[15]

Given the minority position of female federal employees overall, and their almost total absence at the executive level, it is not surprising that Nellie encountered overt discrimination after her appointment. On paper, Nellie reported to William H. Woodin, the Treasury secretary who had objected to her tentative selection as U.S. treasurer on the grounds of her sex. After Woodin left the federal service in December 1933, Roosevelt appointed his old friend and neighbor, Henry Morgenthau Jr., in Woodin's place. Morgenthau, who served as Treasury secretary during the majority of Nellie's tenure, was a competent administrator who worked closely with President Roosevelt on the economic aspects of the New Deal. To those subordinates whom he selected, he delegated considerable authority and was generous with his support and recognition. However, he was also insecure personally, noted for his mercurial temper, and deeply distrusted those Treasury bureau directors who were not "his" men.[16] Nellie preceded him to Treasury, she had a political power base that insulated her from Morgenthau, and—perhaps worst of all—she was a woman.[17]

Morgenthau did his best to patronize Nellie. In fact, he was more than dismissive; at times he was petty and cruel. He generally excluded her from any decision or issue affecting the Mint in which he had personal interest. He dealt directly with Nellie only when he could not avoid it; most of her contacts with the department were with his assistants. In more than nine hundred voluminous diaries, Morgenthau documented the entire eleven years of his tenure at the Treasury, including all his meetings, phone conversations, and official documents; these contain only about a dozen references to Nellie Tayloe Ross.[18]

Each morning, Morgenthau conducted lively informal meetings with his departmental cadre of executive assistants and assistant secretaries. It was in these meetings that most decisions on issues Morgenthau considered critical were made or announced. The meeting transcripts read like sessions of an old boys' club. On rare occasions, Morgenthau and his staff discussed the Mint issues that he considered to be important; examples were adequacy of the coinage supply, mint security arrangements, and mint construction or capital improvements. There was no indication that either Morgenthau or the various assistant secretaries responsible for Mint oversight felt the need to consult with or advise Nellie concerning these deliberations. Morgenthau made his dislike and disapproval of Nellie perfectly clear in these discussions, and the staff was encouraged to guffaw at her expense whenever her name came up. In one example from 1937, one of his assistants told Morgenthau that Nellie had been trying to schedule a meeting to discuss the location of a proposed new mint installation, most likely the silver bullion depository that opened the following year in Roosevelt's and Morgenthau's home state. After joking about Nellie, Morgenthau declared, "This is a little game that, if anybody is smart, they'd keep out, because it's between the President of the United States and myself. . . . [T]ell her she's welcome to go and see the president [without me]."[19] He knew full well that Nellie would not dare to bypass him on this issue.

In contrast to his daily meetings with his immediate staff, Morgenthau's weekly all-hands meetings of bureau directors tended to be staged events in which he conducted a series of one-on-one interchanges, in turn, with each of his bureau directors. The artificiality of the meetings was partly a result of Morgenthau's directive personality, but also because the Treasury Department in the 1930s was a conglomeration of many disparate organizations, so that the bureau chiefs shared few common issues or initiatives. There were the high-status law enforcement bureaus: the Secret Service, the Customs Service, the Coast Guard, and the Bureau of Internal Revenue. There was the Public Health Service, headed by the Surgeon General, with its national network of hospitals. And there was the U.S. Treasury. There were two organizations with government-wide responsibilities, which would eventually become independent agencies—the Budget Bureau, which evolved into the Office of Management and Budget, and the Public Buildings Service, later the General Services Administration. Finally, there were two relatively low-status bureaus whose missions related to production and distribution operations: the Bureau of Engraving and Printing and the Bureau of the Mint. Nellie took no part in the occasional repartee between Morgenthau and the higher-status bureau chiefs. She kept her head low during the weekly meetings, and her involvement was generally limited to reading her one-page weekly briefing.[20]

With the exception of the position of U.S. treasurer—the other Treasury post that had been offered to Nellie—all of the other bureau chief positions in Treasury carried higher salaries than the Mint's, as did most of the assistant secretary and special assistant positions. After five years in office, Nellie must have complained to her mentor, because in 1938, Joseph O'Mahoney—by then the senior Senator from Wyoming—dropped by the departmental offices to suggest it was time to give Nellie a raise. The topic came up in Morgenthau's daily meeting with his immediate staff, provoking yet another round of bantering at Nellie's expense. First, Morgenthau inquired whether he could give Nellie's assistant an increase and bypass Nellie; his staff informed him that regulations made that impossible. The conversation then proceeded:

Morgenthau: Can you give Nellie 250 [more per year]? [Morgenthau wants to limit her raise to $250.]

William McReynolds [Morgenthau's administrative assistant]: No, only five hundred. [The minimum allowable raise is $500.]

Morgenthau: 499?

McReynolds: No.

Morgenthau: Five hundred. All right. She's been here five years. . . . Don't you think that [John W.] Hanes [an assistant secretary] ought to have the Bureau of the Mint and Nellie Tayloe Ross? [He is suggesting transferring the Mint to a different assistant secretary.]

McReynolds: I'm perfectly willing to give it to him. I think Wayne [Taylor] would be perfectly willing.

Taylor: Fine with me.

Morgenthau: Mac, you draw up a Treasury order transferring the Bureau of the Mint to Hanes, effective today.

McReynolds: Is Hanes here?

Hanes: What's this?

Morgenthau: Effective today, we're transferring the Bureau of the Mint and Nellie Tayloe Ross to you.

McReynolds: Don't consent to it.

Hanes: I'll have to think that over.

Morgenthau: Well now, Wayne's pushing me very hard, and so's . . .

Taylor: No, I wasn't pushing you. I said it was fine with me, but . . .
McReynolds: I should think Wayne—he isn't pushing because he never sees her.
Taylor: Oh yes, I do.
McReynolds: I didn't know you ever saw her.

At this point, Morgenthau's secretary, Henrietta Klotz, the only woman present, admonished the assemblage, "You're all very unkind to the lady." Then, McReynolds pointed out that O'Mahoney would consider the raise to be a personal favor and that it would place him under obligation to Morgenthau. Finally Morgenthau begrudgingly agreed: "Keep O'Mahoney happy. Give her five hundred because she earned it a thousand times."[21]

While Nellie's relationship with Morgenthau may have been unpleasant, the reality was that the department exercised little supervision over the Mint's internal affairs. Like most executive bureaus, the Mint enjoyed substantial independence from its department. In 1939, a comprehensive analysis of departmental administration concluded that "the relative absence of central managerial organs, together with the heterogeneous content of the departments, has made the bureaus often so autonomous that they have almost seemed the real departments."[22] One political scientist wryly observed several years after Nellie's appointment that "in too many instances the relationship between the bureaus and the secretary's office resemble[s] the figurative tail wagging the dog."[23] Other than those few issues that interested Morgenthau, Nellie was free to manage her bureau as she saw fit. While technically she functioned under the general direction of the secretary, the fact that she was appointed by and served at the pleasure of the president gave her considerable freedom.[24] One of her subordinates remembered, "Mrs. Ross ran the Mint pretty much on her own. . . . She was governed by a set of statutes that Congress had passed. And as long as she followed these statutes and did not run afoul of the General Accounting Office, there wasn't any . . . need for anybody to supervise her."[25] Ironically, the superintendents of the mints and assay offices enjoyed the same independence from the bureau director, by virtue of their own presidential appointments, as Nellie did from the Treasury secretary. The autonomy of the field superintendents would eventually result in a dramatic—and quite possibly the only—substantive challenge to her authority from within the bureau.

As Nellie prepared to assume her new office, she followed the precedent she set at the DNC when she had turned to her Wyoming contacts to find a personal secretary whom she could trust to be loyal and discrete. She had heard that an old acquaintance, Edness Kimball Wilkins, was in Washington for the burial of her husband, a captain in the U.S. Army, at Arlington National Cemetery. During Nellie's gubernatorial reelection campaign, Edness's father, W. S. Kimball, had been the Democratic candidate for secretary of state; Edness's father and stepmother had spent weeks driving Nellie across Wyoming as she and Kimball campaigned for office. Nellie knew that Edness had excellent qualifications; she had served as secretary to Wyoming's state auditor and later had been promoted to chief clerk in the auditor's office. The untimely death of her husband had devastated Edness and left her with a young son and no plans for the future. Nellie invited Edness to a luncheon with herself and Joseph O'Mahoney's wife, Agnes, Nellie's secretary at the DNC, for what proved to be a job interview. The next day, she called Edness to her office and offered her the position. Edness documented the meeting in a note to her files: "I accepted the offer today. Mrs. Ross has explained that, because of the pressure of the work facing her, she thinks it will be better if I have nothing to distract my attention, and suggests that while I am at home [in Wyoming] I make arrangements to leave my young son, Charles, with my sister Ruth in Wyoming . . ."[26]

Edness's ellipsis suggests the shock and resentment that she did not dare to voice regarding the sacrifice Nellie was asking of her. The incident so rankled her that she was still incorporating the story in speeches in the 1960s and 1970s.[27] It seems out of character that Nellie, who was known for her sensitivity to others, and who had herself suffered through the bereavement of widowhood, would ask a young mother in the first stages of mourning to give up her child. The story uncovers a fundamental conflict within Nellie's beliefs, of which she was probably unaware. Nellie maintained her entire life that the most important role that any woman could play was that of wife and mother, yet she herself had left her young son behind in Wyoming to pursue a career in politics and speechmaking. While there is no doubt that Nellie held motherhood in high esteem, the incident suggests that Nellie valued her career just as highly as she did her domestic responsibilities.

Despite this rocky start, Edness and Nellie quickly formed a close, affectionate working relationship. Edness accepted Nellie's suggestion about her son, and she would serve as Nellie's secretary until 1947, when she returned to Wyoming to care for her elderly father. With Nellie's heavy travel schedule to visit Mint installations, deliver speeches, and campaign for Roosevelt or

Democratic friends in Wyoming, there were sustained periods of time in which she wrote Edness daily. Nellie used Edness as a personal assistant and confidante as much as she did an official secretary, so their correspondence serves as a comprehensive record of Nellie's Mint years.[28]

A cryptic note in Edness's historical files establishes that Nellie was suspicious of the Mint staff in place when she first arrived.[29] Perhaps her recent experience working with Eleanor Roosevelt and Molly Dewson had predisposed her to question the motives and trustworthiness of untested subordinates and associates. It is likely that the distrust was mutual. With the exception of Nellie's immediate predecessor, Robert John Grant, a mining engineer who had prior experience as superintendent of the Denver Mint, every other Mint director dating back to the beginning of the twentieth century had been a patronage selectee who, like Nellie, had no prior knowledge of Mint operations.[30] Distrust has almost always characterized the initial relationships between political appointees and their career subordinates. Political appointees tend to question the competence of their inherited staff and assume that the entrenched employees will attempt to resist or sabotage the policies of the new administration, while the career employees expect that their new bosses will be ignorant political hacks who know little and care less about the programs to which their subordinates have devoted their entire careers. More often than not, however, when new political appointees are interested in learning about the agency and willing to accept the counsel of their career employees, they come to respect and trust their new staffs.[31] Such was the case with Nellie.

Possibly no one was more resentful about her new boss than the Mint's assistant director. Mary Margaret O'Reilly was a tiny, white-haired maiden lady in her late sixties whose grandmotherly appearance belied a will of steel; in fact, Edness characterized her as ruthless.[32] It is likely that O'Reilly started her career as a low-level clerk, and it must have required an almost unprecedented combination of drive and intelligence for her to have climbed so far up through the organization in her male-dominated work environment. When Nellie was appointed, O'Reilly had already been working at the Treasury Department for over twenty-five years, and she had been serving as the Mint's assistant director since the Wilson administration. O'Reilly was a detail-oriented technocrat, and she knew the Mint operations inside and out; she was famous for going up to the Hill to testify in appropriations hearings, armed with a single sheet of figures.[33] Her competence had earned her the deep respect of the department and Congress.[34]

As assistant director, O'Reilly had watched at least three politically appointed directors come and go while she quietly continued to run the bureau. She was undoubtedly proud of her outstanding success as a career woman, and she probably nursed a secret ambition to become director herself, so it would be understandable if she considered Nellie a free-riding political interloper who would steal some of her own thunder as a female executive. Likewise, a woman lacking Nellie's self-confidence might well have been intimidated by O'Reilly's contacts and knowledge. However, Nellie had never been threatened by the expertise of her subordinates. Just as she had taken full advantage of her advisors as governor and Sue Shelton White's talents at the DNC, she was pleased to have such a competent assistant as O'Reilly. In the final analysis, it is irrelevant whether certain decisions and actions were taken by Nellie or by one of her subordinates; as governor or director, she was ultimately accountable. Just as she would have received the blame for any problems that occurred during her tenure, so she must also be given the credit for any accomplishments; that is the essence of managerial delegation.

Nellie's son Bradford captured this aspect of Nellie's personality in an interview after Nellie's death:

> I think she had a great deal of confidence. But she never hesitated to get advice if she wanted it. She recognized people who had great ability. I mean she probably knew some of them had more ability than she had. She tried to surround herself with people that were capable so she could do a good job.[35]

After a brief period of sizing up one another, Nellie gave O'Reilly her trust and support, and O'Reilly gave Nellie her loyalty and even her affection. O'Reilly seemed to fall quickly under the spell of her boss's charm and warmth, if her many surviving letters to Nellie are to be believed. In October 1933, she wrote Nellie, who was out visiting the mints, that "I am so anxious to have your mind at ease about the office here that I have resorted to rather frequent telegrams. They are so much more direct and up to date than letters." After giving Nellie a rundown on the high-priority issues, she closed her letter, "My love to you and every good wish for the success of your visits to our beloved mint institutions." Her loyalty to Nellie was demonstrated in a 1934 letter in which she provided Nellie nuggets of nuanced advice, which she could easily have withheld, but which undoubtedly helped Nellie to make good decisions and come across in public discussions as well informed: "It is probable that the increased facilities at [the San Francisco mint will be] required to handle [the] increase of silver deposits, but it is highly important that no reference be made to that fact. . . . If any curiosity is aroused by the purchase of equipment, speak of it as necessary to expedite gold melting." She also let Nellie know that she was being well received by employees in the mints: "Mr. O. told me Miss D. sent a very nice report about you, that you were a 100% person."[36]

Nellie and O'Reilly soon fell into the traditional pattern of directors and assistant directors, in which the former handles public contacts and makes final decisions while the latter handles the day-to-day operation. As she had with Eleanor Roosevelt and Sue Shelton White, Nellie left O'Reilly to run the office end of affairs while Nellie headed out to the Mint installations to establish relationships with her employees and to learn about Mint operations and issues firsthand. She carried a little notebook, and she created detailed records on the buildings, the people, the problems—whatever seemed important.[37]

During a 1939 visit to one of the bullion depositories, Nellie wrote Edness, "I am having a very interesting stay . . . and feel as always, the importance of these visits. It is impossible to sit in the office and sense all the conditions of which I should know."[38] She was known by the employees in the Mint installations for her keen powers of observation. On one such visit, she was inspecting the new addition to the Denver Mint with one of the technicians, who related the story to Edness:

> They had inspected the inside, and were looking it over from the outside; walking in an alleyway, back of the building. Governor Ross stopped suddenly, and exclaimed, "Mr. White, what is that I see?" He too, looked upward, toward a tall window [but] did not notice anything unusual. Governor Ross said, "I see the door of a vault from this point!" She immediately ordered the window bricked up. Mr. White said he and many other employees, guards, inspectors, contractors—had passed there day after day, studied the building from every angle, but not one of them had realized that there was a vault door that could be seen from the outside; that any criminal could stand out there and study its location, type, and figure out how it might be opened.[39]

As she dealt with the department and made operational decisions back in Washington, O'Reilly would have found Nellie's letters from the field to be valuable information tools. A 1935 letter from Nellie to Edness illustrates the characteristics of their partnership, as well as Nellie's growing impact and knowledge of Mint operations:

> Tell Miss O'Reilly I talked with Mr. Clark from Phila. about the crowded condition of the vaults there. They have bags of bronze stacked in the same vaults with gold coin. The place [is] just crowded everywhere. Mr. Clark promised to try to hurry the silver vault. I also pointed out to him that if one of the generators should suddenly give out that operations over there would stop, which would be pretty serious now. A few months ago when I urged the same risk Mr. Clark thought it far-fetched apparently but yesterday he admitted that the 24 hour operation was a severe strain to the generators & suggested that Mr. Morgenthau might be willing to release the ten or fifteen thousand a new one would cost. . . . I called [Assistant Secretary] Robert, . . . thinking he might propose it to the Secretary.[40]

Gold and silver were pouring in to the Mint institutions. In her 1934 annual report, Nellie reported that the value of the precious metals received that year totaled over $1 billion—more than twice as much as the previous year's total of $487 million. More critical than the storage problem was the security threat that the enormous cache of precious metals presented. Nellie found that the guard force consisted of men from the production line who were approaching retirement age, many of whom were disabled or feeble; in Denver, several were tubercular. Some were found to have criminal records, and others were so unfamiliar with weapons that their hands shook when they were asked to demonstrate their expertise. Nellie secured the agreement of the Civil Service Commission to allow the Mint to establish its own, more rigorous, physical and experience qualifications. She instituted a new training program, modeled on that of the armed forces, and she equipped all of them with more powerful and up-to-date weapons.[41]

Early in 1934, Nellie requested that Secretary Morgenthau ask the Secret Service to evaluate each mint's security arrangements. Nellie's suggestion earned her a rare compliment from Morgenthau, who wrote one of his assistants that he thought Nellie's request was a good idea. After an initial round of assessments, the bureau continued to use the Secret Service for subsequent security reviews. By the time the Secret Service reviewed the Denver Mint in 1938, the vaults in Denver held gold bullion worth $4 billion; the review generally approved of the improved guard force, the time-locking steel doors on the vaults, the procedures for securing and opening the vaults, and the alarm system that Nellie and the Denver superintendent had put in place.[42]

When Mary Margaret O'Reilly turned seventy in 1935, she faced mandatory retirement, but neither she nor Nellie was ready for her to go. That year, Nellie sent President Roosevelt the first of three annual requests that he grant

O'Reilly an exception to the retirement rule. When he approved the 1938 request, President Roosevelt let Nellie know that he would not approve another extension for the following year. In October 1938, Mary Margaret O'Reilly retired, hailed by the *New York Times* as the "Sweetheart of Treasury."[43] Thanks to the counsel and support of O'Reilly, Nellie benefited from a five-year learning curve, shielded from errors she might otherwise have made due to inexperience. By the time O'Reilly left, Nellie had mastered Mint operations and had developed a set of techniques for managing a large-scale organization.

Nellie had succeeded as governor due to her innate political instincts, her intelligence, and her public relations skills—but not her management practices, which she had no opportunity to develop. At the Mint, she grew into a strong and popular administrator. Lacking business experience and management training, she based her leadership style on the organizational structure that she knew best, the family—she always referred to her workforce as "the Mint Family." Nellie was able to create a working environment in which her employees felt valued as individuals, although only a selected few of them were ever invited beyond the cordial veil that Nellie maintained between her personal and private lives. She combined an almost maternal empathy and warmth with the reserved authority of a respected father figure. One of her young employees, who became the Mint's assistant director about seven years after Nellie's retirement, observed that "she was a leader [revered as if she were] the Queen of England."[44]

Nellie, unusually for her times, did not maintain a strict line between her private and public lives. Those few employees whom she admitted to her private life regularly accompanied Nellie on weekend jaunts to the countryside, and they also shared Christmas and Thanksgiving celebrations at her table. She sometimes turned to her personal contacts to fill Mint vacancies. When she needed a staff member with expertise in accounting and economics, she asked her son Bradford if he could recommend someone, and he suggested Leland Howard, who had taught Bradford's accounting class at the University of Virginia while Leland was completing his Ph.D. Leland, nicknamed "Bennie" by Nellie's intimate circle of friends, would go on to become Nellie's assistant director following the 1938 retirement of Mary Margaret O'Reilly. He served as assistant director until Nellie's retirement, in the same kind of collegial partnership that she had enjoyed with O'Reilly. Another employee who became a personal friend was Dorothy Tomlinson, sister-in-law to her son

George; she both worked at the Mint and shared Nellie's home for several years.

In 1936, Kenneth Failor, a young man whom she had met through one of Bradford's friends, accepted Nellie's offer of employment and ended up spending the rest of his career at the Mint. After Bradford finished school and left Washington, Ken moved into his room and boarded with Nellie until his marriage. When Ken was called to service during World War II, Nellie wrote him fondly, "I cannot tell you how much I miss you. I hope you look upon the years you spent in my home with the same satisfaction that I do. . . . It was like having a son go out from my home when you left."[45]

In reflecting on Nellie's interpersonal skills, Ken observed,

> [Nellie] had great success in the Mint, because she had everybody behind her. . . . The first few days I was there, she asked me if I'd drive her to church for a funeral of one of the employees. She had a habit of burrowing in and getting a little information about each employee's family, so that she had something to talk about. And she knew each employee. That gave her a personal part of their lives. . . . When something happened, she was right on hand at the hospital, or at the home, helping them out, doing things.[46]

Over the years that Nellie was with the Mint, she came to know substantially all the employees, both at headquarters and in the field installations, from the top managers to the employees out on the floor. When it came time for promotions, Nellie knew of her employees' relative qualifications, and she had strong opinions concerning their relative fitness for more advanced positions.[47] However, while Nellie "was very good at giving people special recognition, . . . she wasn't overly generous on promoting people." She was as frugal with Mint appropriations as she was with her own money. One day, she and Ken were watching as thousands of coins passed by the women who were conducting a final quality review. "I said to Mrs. Ross, 'Gee whiz, just think of the tons of metal that's going over the . . .' [She interrupted, exclaiming], 'Kenneth, forget about it! . . . If you [say anything], they're going to want a raise when they realize how many tons they're processing!'"[48]

Nellie chose not to hold regular staff meetings—a decision that would thrill most employees who despise the waste of time these meetings entail. Instead, she convened meetings only when there was a specific issue that needed attention, and she limited attendance to only those involved. She insured that all her supervisors kept up to date on bureau happenings by having a file sent every day to the heads of the divisions in the bureau of all the letters she'd signed the previous day.[49] Frequently, she would open a meeting and then move from the conference table back to her desk, where she would listen in while signing letters. She left the key personnel involved in an issue to handle their meetings on their own.

Ken Failor remembered one time when he was still young and learning organizational rules, and he was conducting a meeting with the presidents of smelting and refining companies. As Ken attempted to explain that the Mint believed they were delivering foreign silver in lieu of the required percentage of domestic metal, an exasperated president asked Ken, "Do you think I'm a crook?" Ken responded, "No, I don't think *you* are. But I think your company is!" He remembered that Nellie's head snapped upwards immediately from the letter she was reading, and she shot a look at Ken, but she did not say a word. After the meeting, Ken learned that the presidents had gone straight over to the Republican headquarters and demanded that he and Nellie be the first to be fired when the Republicans won the next election. Nevertheless, Nellie backed up Ken's judgment, and the Mint prevailed. The companies settled. Nellie never said a word to Ken about his handling of the meeting; perhaps for that very reason, he never forgot what he learned that day about handling delicate situations as well as the importance of managerial support.[50]

In another incident, the Treasury Department's general counsel had questioned Ken's view on a procedural matter on which Ken had Nellie's support. The Mint had proposed that before it denied a gold license, the company involved should be given the right to be heard and to reply to the charges. One day, Nellie called Ken into her office and announced that they were going over to meet with the undersecretary to resolve the issue.

> We went in to the undersecretary's office, . . . and she said, "Mr. Secretary, . . . the General Counsel's office has criticized a member of my staff, and when they do that, they're criticizing me." And she said, "If he's right, I'll apologize, but if he's wrong, I want an apology from [the General Counsel]." And she got it from him that day.[51]

The greatest challenge to Nellie's authority occurred in about 1938. During her first five years, Nellie had introduced a number of innovations to modernize and improve the production processes used in the field installations, but she had encountered resistance from the superintendent of the Denver Mint, Mark Skinner. Skinner objected to Nellie's initiatives as a waste of time and money. During the first day of a meeting of the mint superintendents that she had convened in Washington, she learned that Skinner had been criticizing her behind her back, attempting to foment opposition to her leadership among the other superintendents. Nellie recessed the meeting early that day. She spent the evening considering what she should do about Skinner's actions, and she consulted with her son Bradford, who by then had completed his legal training and had been admitted to the bar. The next morning she convened the session, confronted Skinner in front of his peers, and then dismissed him from the room, declaring that there was nothing useful he could contribute to the meeting. "Reeder," she called to her messenger in the outer office as Skinner was collecting his papers, "Give [Mr. Skinner] his hat." Skinner left, muttering under his breath, as word of Nellie's action spread like wildfire through the Washington staff. Skinner would continue as Denver superintendent until 1942, but he never again seriously disputed Nellie's authority.[52]

Within the culture of any organization, the people who are always in the best position to judge the leadership skills of an individual are those below her—those who either enjoy her management style or who feel subjected by it on a daily basis. Many managers are successful in "managing upwards"; they insure that their superiors are kept well informed and that their boss's priorities are regularly met. But some managers achieve these objectives only at great cost to their subordinates. They tend to side with the boss rather than supporting the decisions of subordinates, and they fail to communicate employee concerns or needs upward if they know those issues are unpopular in the front office. These individuals can be successful for a few years, but inevitably, they will be sabotaged by poor morale and employee antipathy if they do not move on. Nellie's core value of loyalty to those close to her resulted in the creation of a very different dynamic. Her employees felt appreciated, protected, and empowered, and they respected Nellie's authority. Nellie created a happy organization.

Instinctively, because of her temperament and her interest in people, Nellie espoused a management style that was on the cutting edge of human resources management for her time. Nellie focused on the big picture, and she left the details to her subordinates. However, she also found a method that worked for her to learn about and keep track of the status of work processes and issues. Nellie was exceptionally effective in balancing the demands of the work processes and the needs of her employees, and the result was high morale, innovation, and high production. Nellie convinced people that she cared about them as individuals. She demonstrated to her managers that she would empower them and stand behind their acts and decisions. She was able, despite the growth in Mint operations and numerous changes in process over which she presided, to create a stable environment in which people felt safe and knew what their responsibilities were. She was not threatened by subordinates who knew more or who were smarter than she. Rather, she used them in a way that gave them authority and ownership and permitted them to do their best work.

Nellie's five-year appointment to the Mint was due to expire in 1938, the same year Mary Margaret O'Reilly was forced to retire. Although she may have worried whether she would be reappointed, she had, as always, the firm support of her mentor, Joseph O'Mahoney. In a lukewarm recommendation, Secretary Morgenthau wrote to President Roosevelt, "Mrs. Ross' five year term of office will expire on May 2, 1938. Her services have been satisfactory to the Treasury and she is endorsed for reappointment by Senator O'Mahoney. I am transmitting herewith a nomination in case you approve Mrs. Ross' reappointment." When Nellie's nomination reached the Senate floor, the reaction was brief but far more supportive. "As a recognition of the exceptional ability and accomplishments of Governor Ross in the administration of the Mint, I move that the President be immediately notified of the confirmation of the nomination," declared Senator O'Mahoney. With no discussion, O'Mahoney's motion passed and Nellie was confirmed unanimously.[53] Nellie was ecstatic, and she immediately wrote to express her appreciation to President Roosevelt:

> I am struggling for words in which to say to you something of the gratitude that is in my heart for your consideration of me in extending my tenure as Director of the Mint. . . . Many times I have wished I could convey to you the real joy and satisfaction I have found in this position which, through your grace, I fill. I feel that there is not a niche in the Government I should like better. The augmentation of work and of functions, incidental to your change in monetary policies, have almost remade the Mint. . . . I gladly report to you the superb spirit and efficiency with which the personnel in the Bureau and in the field institutions, have carried out your policies in so far as they relate to Mint responsibilities.[54]

On the eve of America's entry in World War II, Nellie looked back on an almost unbroken string of coinage production records, beginning with her first full year as director. By September 1941, when she released her annual report for the fiscal year ending June 30, 1941, she reported a domestic coin production of 1.6 billion pieces—the highest total in the history of the U.S. Mint. Her workforce had grown to almost twenty-five hundred employees, or more than 350 percent of the 1934 total.[55] She had presided over a revolutionary expansion in Mint installations and capacity, and she had begun to introduce modernized Mint production methods and security procedures.

The war years were to prove even more challenging. Coinage demand and production continued to achieve record levels each year through 1945. In addition to the heavy domestic demand for coinage, the disruption of mint operations in foreign countries resulted in the assumption of coinage production for other governments. Out of the 4 billion coins produced in 1945, 1.5 billion were produced for other nations.[56]

The war resulted in shortages of three critical elements needed to produce the necessary coins: capital improvements to increase production capacity, qualified employees, and precious metals. Concerning the facilities and equipment, the Mint's plans for additional expansion, which had already been approved by Congress, were shelved when the United States diverted the necessary funding and materials to support the war effort in Europe. Nellie waited until the end of the war, when she warned the director of the government's War Production Board of the crowded and unsafe conditions in Mint installations, informing him that these could only be corrected by immediate expansion.[57] Concerning her staffing, many of the skilled craftsmen she needed to run the work processes and maintain the production lines had been called up for service; many other experienced employees had left, attracted by the higher wages that wartime factories were paying.[58] Concerning the metals, the Mint found itself in direct competition with the War Production Board for tin, nickel, and copper. The Mint metallurgists desperately struggled to develop new alloys for the nation's various coins that would permit the agency to meet demand.[59] In the main, they were successful, but their resolution of the penny shortage was a public relations disaster.

In November 1942, Nellie appeared in a hearing sponsored by the Senate Committee on Banking and Currency, which was considering a bill that authorized the substitution of other materials for the strategic metals then in extremely short supply. She reported that the Mint had effectively depleted its entire stock of copper and that it had not received any additional allocations since May.[60] Nellie had mounted a well-publicized campaign, in newspapers and on the radio, to urge the public to return their loose change collections to circulation, and she had curtailed penny production by 50 percent, but the situation had become critical.[61] Nellie asked the Senate for the legislative authority to substitute pennies made of zinc-coated steel; she told the committee that the War Production Board had promised adequate allocations of these metals. The required legislation passed, and the Mint began to issue the substitute coins, but the public simply hated the new pennies. They looked so much like dimes that consumers were constantly confused and businesses lost substantial sums through careless change-making.

In September 1943, President Roosevelt himself sent a humorous complaint to Secretary Morgenthau: "I . . . tried to use a one-cent piece in a ten-cent slot machine and I was arrested, but let off by the Judge under suspended sentence. FDR." That was the last straw for Morgenthau, who had himself received thousands of complaints. He picked up the phone and made a terse call to Nellie. "Look, Mrs. Ross, we've got to stop making those new pennies. I have finally gotten a complaint from the President and I can't take any more complaints about them." Nellie attempted to explain the War Production Board limitations under which she was operating, but Morgenthau was not interested in hearing what she had to say. The minute he hung up, he called his undersecretary, Daniel W. Bell. "I was stupid enough to call up your pal, Nellie Tayloe Ross," he spluttered. Bell proceeded to share with him exactly the same facts that Nellie had attempted to tell him; coming from Bell, Morgenthau was willing to accept them. The call ended when Bell promised to call the War Production Board and plead for more copper.[62]

One month later, the Mint announced that it would resume production of pennies using a copper alloy. The War Production Board had agreed to make expended copper cartridge shells available to the Mint.[63] In an editorial titled "End of a Bad Penny," the *New York Times* declared that "everyone who has offered one of the new steel pennies for a dime, or even worse, received one in a similar exchange, will rejoice that these pesky things are on their way out."[64] No one was happier than Nellie. In later years, she reminisced, "That awful 'war penny' almost ruined our reputation, but nobody disliked it more than we did at the mint."[65]

On April 12, 1945, less than a month before Germany surrendered, Franklin Roosevelt died of a massive cerebral hemorrhage. President Truman wasted no time in replacing Roosevelt's staff with his own men. Morgenthau keenly hoped he could stay on in his Treasury post, and Truman had vaguely assured him that if he decided to appoint someone else, he would personally inform Morgenthau in advance of any public announcement. Despite Truman's promise, Morgenthau was humiliated to learn through the grapevine that he was to be replaced by Frederick Moore Vinson; Morgenthau subsequently submitted his resignation in July 1945.[66] Vinson only served one year before Truman nominated him to be Chief Justice of the Supreme Court. For the remainder of her Mint years, Nellie would report to Secretary John W. Snyder, a banker who had also spent several years in Washington and in the field as an executive with the Comptroller of the Currency and the Reconstruction Finance Corporation. Snyder had been a close friend of President Truman for twenty-five years, and he shared his Missouri background with both Truman and Nellie. In stark contrast to Morgenthau, Snyder was a calm, straightforward man who was easy to get along with. He respected Nellie as the competent administrator she had become, and the two remained friends the rest of her life.[67]

In April 1950, Nellie sent Secretary Snyder a memorandum to express her appreciation for his testimony before the House Appropriations Committee, in which he praised the innovations Nellie had introduced to the Mint's operating practices.[68] As one example, Nellie had instituted a series of procedures to recover the dust and particles of precious metals that were released during the manufacture of coins. In each mint, workmen were issued spats, aprons, and gloves, which they were required to use while working and which they stored each night at the mint; as their clothing wore out, it was burned to permit the recovery of the dust and particles of precious metals. Before leaving each night, workmen were required to shower, and the water was also processed to recover any metallics. The sweeps from the factory floors and even the fumes and air coming out of the production rooms were filtered for metals, and even the buildings themselves, when renovated or replaced, were chipped down to permit metal recovery. Nellie estimated that the reclamation procedures saved the Mint up to $100,000 annually.[69]

During the late 1940s, Nellie implemented a bureau-wide Management Improvement Program, which anticipated the introduction of the Quality Circles movement in United States businesses by almost forty years. Groups of employees and managers from each mint were encouraged to form groups in order to study their work processes and to identify improvements. One feature of the Management Improvement Program was a gain-sharing cash awards system that encouraged employee participation. In 1952, for example, cash awards of $4,100 were paid to ten workers for twenty-five innovations yielding annual savings of $720,000.[70] Among the most notable accomplishments arising from the Management Improvement Program were the mechanization of the melting and rolling processes in Denver, resulting in a 30 percent productivity increase; introduction of a new water-cooled mold in

Philadelphia, which reduced melting costs by 23 percent; and installation of more powerful motors on the rolling mills in San Francisco, which resulted in a 100 to 300 percent productivity increase in the manufacture of coin blanks.[71]

As Mint director, Nellie proved to be as frugal as she was in her personal life. Nellie took pride in being able to return dollars unspent. For the fiscal year ending in June 1950, Nellie returned one million dollars to the Treasury—more than one-quarter of the bureau's annual appropriation, but still less than the two million dollars she returned in 1948. All told, she returned sizable excess funds four years running, beginning in 1947.[72] One should keep in mind that there had been many years in which she had had to request supplemental appropriations to cover her rapidly expanding operations; nevertheless, Nellie gained a reputation on the Hill for careful shepherding of her share of the government budget. As one syndicated columnist observed in a reference to Nellie's astonishing budgetary record, "No other bureaucrat in memory of the oldest man ever had returned any part of any appropriation, even if he had to sit up nights figuring out new ways to spend it."[73]

As Nellie neared the end of her fourth term as Mint director in 1953, she was seventy-six years old and ready to retire. "Twenty years is a long time," she told reporters, and besides, "I am kind of glad it's over because circumstances have a tendency to make the Director's job anything but a political prize."[74] By the end of her Mint career, Nellie may have been largely forgotten by the American public, but her competence as an administrator was nevertheless recognized by those who mattered. Within her bureau, her employees respected and admired her. On the occasion of her second renomination as Mint director, one employee in San Francisco wrote her that "I really do not know where could be found a more efficient and capable leader and a more respected and loved Director than yourself." From the New York Assay Office, another employee told her that "the work accomplished by this Office as well as at the mints at Philadelphia, Denver and San Francisco could never have been done without your kind counsel and advice. You have . . . helped toward making us one great big family."[75]

At the department, Secretary Snyder considered her "a very capable, very attractive lady."[76] When she mentioned to Snyder that she was nearing the end of her third term, he told her, "We are *not* going to change the Director of the Mint; that is one agency that gives me no worry whatever." A few days later at the White House, President Truman also praised her performance and asked her to stay on for one more term.[77]

As Nellie wrapped up her Fiscal Year 1951 testimony at the House Appropriations Committee with a summary of the Mint's management achievement program, Representative J. Vaughan Gary of Virginia thanked her for an excellent presentation. Referring to the fact that the Mint had returned, unspent, almost a million dollars to the Treasury from the Mint's 1950 appropriations, Representative Gary observed, "it . . . demonstrates that if you give Governor Ross the money she will not spend it unless she needs it." Representative Otto Ernest Passman of Louisiana commended her for submitting a 1951 budget request that was smaller than that for the prior fiscal year, and then he concluded, "Governor Ross, I should like to join the other members of the committee in offering praise for the wonderful work you are doing as Director of the Mint."[78]

TEN

The Washington Years

NELLIE HAD grown up with the nation. While America was still overwhelmingly rural, Nellie was born and spent her early childhood on a Missouri farm. While America moved west and populated the vast prairies, Nellie was passing her teenage years in a homesteading town in Kansas. While America was becoming a nation of city-dwellers, Nellie moved first to the melting pot of Omaha and then to a western state capital. And while America was transforming itself into the leader of the free world, Nellie accepted a position in national politics and moved to the nation's capital, where she would spend the rest of her life.

In Washington, the pace of change before the Roosevelt years might have been termed "glacial" if it had not been for the heat. It was a muggy, slow-moving city that had been deliberately constructed on top of a swamp. With air conditioning still a rare commodity in the early 1930s, many officials in Washington, including Nellie, escaped to the hinterlands each summer. The city's permanent residents passed the sultry evenings on the front stoops of their row homes and boarding houses, gossiping with neighbors and longing for a breeze. Downtown Washington was a hodgepodge of unremarkable office buildings, some dating back to the Civil War. World War I–era monstrosities cluttered the western end of the national mall, and of the classical monuments that now make up the Federal Triangle, only the Commerce Building was already under construction when Roosevelt assumed office. The enormous Center Market, where Washingtonians traveled by streetcar to purchase their groceries, anchored the city's principal commercial thoroughfare, Seventh Street, at Pennsylvania Avenue.[1]

During Roosevelt's first two years in office, men idled by the Depression went back to work to finish the imposing government buildings of the Federal Triangle, including the National Archives building, which rose on the site of the old Center Market. A magnificent Supreme Court building was constructed on Capitol Hill, while the Department of Agriculture's South Building took shape near the Tidal Basin. The entire city felt the energizing effects of the Roosevelt administration's public works projects. The thousands of new workers who descended upon Washington to take part in the New Deal and, later, the World War II effort, created a real estate boom, not just in northwest Washington but out in the Maryland and Virginia suburbs.[2] By the late 1930s and continuing throughout her Mint years, Nellie would invest much of her hard-earned savings in real estate—rental houses in the suburbs and even three farms out in the counties. Nellie increased her wealth by putting the minimum down for purchase, renting her properties, and pocketing the appreciation when she sold; sometimes when she found a particularly attractive opportunity, she would even borrow to cover the down payment.[3]

When Nellie established a home at the Mayflower Hotel following her appointment at the DNC, she had come home to the South. Washington was a fiercely segregated city. One-third of the city's residents were black, and they lived in separate neighborhoods, went to separate schools, worshipped at separate churches, read separate newspapers, and attended separate theaters. They even had their own downtown shopping area, centered on U Street between Seventh and Sixteenth Streets, Northwest. City newspapers listed sale and rental advertisements under separate headings for "White" and "Colored." Blacks could spend their money in white-owned stores down Seventh Street, but they could not eat in the same restaurants or sleep in the same hotels. Many poor blacks lived in crowded, dilapidated alley dwellings; Eleanor Roosevelt found the conditions so shocking that she made their demolition a priority of her husband's administration. Employment opportunities for middle-class black Washingtonians were limited. The relatively few black professionals served their own community. Eighty-five percent of black women worked as domestics, laundresses, and waitresses; one-third of black men worked as laborers, and another third worked as janitors, servants, messengers, and waiters.[4]

Official Washington was single-mindedly focused on politics and the entertaining that facilitated it. People were judged based on the importance of the invitations they received, and their influence and power were functions of their relationships and liaisons. "'Social circles' is no mere figure of speech here," wrote a Washington newspaperwoman of the times. "Society really runs on a planetary system. The White House is the social sun around which revolve the greater planets and lesser planets and moons. Hospitality is handed out in widening and descending rounds—exclusive dinners, less exclusive luncheons, least exclusive teas and 'at homes,' mob-scene receptions."[5]

Nellie quickly immersed herself in the Washington social scene. She loved parties and entertaining, and her interpersonal skills and her political position made her a popular invitee. She was important enough socially that she regularly received invitations to receptions and dinners at the White House, even though she and Mrs. Roosevelt were not close. Nellie observed in a speech that Washington was "the one place where conversation has not become a lost art [due to the many] interesting and attractive men and women one is sure to meet." She treasured her invitations to the political salon of Mrs. J. Borden Harriman, where senators, congressmen, ambassadors, journalists, and fascinating people from all fields gathered for the "most spirited, intelligent and free-for-all discussion of our current public affairs that can be imagined."[6]

Nellie hosted her first big dinner at the Mayflower in March 1930 in honor of her sister-in-law Nelle, who was visiting from Memphis. Among her guests were Mrs. J. Borden Harriman, Senator Thomas J. Walsh from Montana, and Senator John B. Kendrick and his wife, Eula, from Wyoming. From this relatively modest start, Nellie became a regular hostess to Washington's most glittering social stars. Her guests at a tea and reception she hosted at the Mayflower in February 1935 included the ambassador of Russia and his wife; the ministers and their wives from Czechoslovakia, China, and Siam; Justice and Mrs. Owen J. Roberts; several members of the Senate and the House, including the Speaker; and the secretaries of the Interior, Agriculture, and the Navy, with their spouses. Conspicuously not invited were Treasury secretary Henry Morgenthau Jr. and his wife, Elinor. When Nellie hosted her last major social event as Mint director, her more than two hundred guests included the vice president, four cabinet secretaries, four ambassadors, two Supreme Court justices, five senators, four U.S. representatives, and several agency heads and assistant secretaries.[7]

By 1936, Nellie was tired of living in the Mayflower Hotel; her career seemed relatively secure, and she wanted to establish more of a home for herself and Bradford. She decided to rent a spacious, nine-room apartment on the top floor of the Dresden, a grand apartment house overlooking Rock Creek Park; with its four bedrooms, two baths, maid's quarters, and separate living and dining rooms, the apartment was larger than most houses. The rent was thirty-five dollars more than her monthly rent at the Mayflower, but Nellie expected to economize by eating most meals at home rather than in restaurants. Nellie and Bradford retrieved their furniture and household goods, which were still in storage in Cheyenne, and had a wonderful time opening the boxes together and reminiscing about the Wyoming years. Nellie began to frequent the auction houses in Washington, looking for bargains on fine antiques and carpets to finish off her new home. When she went out on the road, she left Bradford in charge of the apartment arrangements. "I told Bradford to keep an itemized account of every cent spent," she wrote Edness from Ohio during a campaign trip. "I want to know how much this buying of furniture & moving is costing me. And I want to make it cost as little as possible. I'm so anxious to get rid of that [loan] note at the bank."[8]

After her appointment at the Mint, Nellie remained as involved in politics as time and regulations allowed.[9] Both President Roosevelt and Secretary Morgenthau had issued policies that limited the partisan political activities of presidential appointees. However, Morgenthau had agreed that the Treasury appointees would be permitted to participate in the 1934 midterm campaign as long as they limited their activities to their home states and they did not use official time.[10] In Wyoming, Senator O'Mahoney was facing a tough re-election campaign in 1934, and Nellie was worried about his political survival. By late October, Nellie wrapped up a trip to the San Francisco Mint and the Seattle Assay Office and headed for Wyoming, where she threw herself into the campaign. "To tell you the truth I'm quite apprehensive about the result," she wrote Mary Margaret O'Reilly. "That's probably because I care so much. He is so fine, so smart & useful to the state. And then as I've told you I personally owe him more than anyone else besides my brothers. I would be crushed if he were defeated."[11] But he was not; with Nellie's help, O'Mahoney was elected to his first full term in the Senate.

As the 1936 general election approached, Roosevelt loyalists worried that Roosevelt would be turned out of office. The nation's Republicans, and indeed many conservative Democrats, were horrified at the extent to which the government had become involved in tinkering with the economy and had insinuated itself into the daily lives of Americans, and the Democratic campaign organizers feared a backlash at the polls. In February 1936, Mrs. James H. Wolfe, Mary Dewson's successor as director of the DNC Women's Division, asked Nellie to join a small group of women to discuss plans for the convention and the campaign. Dewson herself, who was back in her old post as vice chairman of the Women's Division in the New York campaign headquarters, wrote Nellie that she was delighted to have her back on the campaign; Dewson may not have considered Nellie a personal friend, but she clearly recognized Nellie's campaign contributions as a public speaker. Nellie planned to take a leave of absence from the Mint by the middle of August to start campaigning; she wrote Mrs. Wolfe, "I find it unsatisfactory to combine official trips and speaking, and therefore am planning to dispose, as much as possible, of important Mint problems before the campaign, and arrange my affairs so that I shall be free to respond to such requests as you shall make."[12]

Although Nellie believed in filling Mint vacancies with the most competent people she could find, she saw nothing wrong with considering an applicant's political affiliation as part of her overall evaluation of qualifications. She took special pains to place qualified referrals from the president's office or from Democratic congressmen. When Molly Dewson wrote her that the San Francisco Mint superintendent had appointed nine Republicans out of twelve recent selectees, Nellie responded in shock. "Is it possible that right in the bosom of my own Mint family has happened this very thing I have deplored in other government units—the subordination of deserving, capable, Democratic supporters, to Republicans, in dispensing jobs." She promised Molly that she would look into the appointments; in a show of support for her subordinate superintendent, however, she reminded Molly that he had led the Roosevelt forces in San Francisco and was a loyal Democrat.[13]

During the 1938 midterm election, allegations arose that officials of the Works Progress Administration had coerced employees to work on behalf of Democratic candidates, had sought to influence the votes of WPA clients, and had used federal funds to fund local campaigns. In response, Republican members of Congress pushed through the Hatch Act of 1939. The act proscribed the use of public funds to support political campaigns, and it prohibited federal employees from soliciting votes with promises of jobs, contracts, or financial assistance. Concerned that the act would prohibit her campaign activities, Nellie sought a legal opinion from the attorney general, who informed her that she was indeed constrained by the act's restrictions.[14] Nellie was horrified. "I am impelled to express to you my feeling, akin to shock, that I shall be expected to sit silent and inert while our party a few months hence will be waging a mighty battle to keep control of the government," she wrote Eleanor Roosevelt. Nellie asked Treasury to request that the attorney general reconsider his interpretation because the act exempted individuals appointed by the president with the advice and consent of the Senate. A few months later, the attorney general reversed himself and agreed that Nellie was exempt.[15]

Secretary Morgenthau was annoyed when he learned that Nellie had gone over his head and had appealed directly to the attorney general for a ruling. When informed of Nellie's action in one of his morning staff meetings, Morgenthau complained, "Isn't there a penalty for going to the Attorney General without first giving my lawyers a cut?" He joked that his staff needed to do a better job of controlling Nellie, and then he descended to gossip. "Strictly in the room, you know what she does, don't you? She makes these talks and gets paid for them. . . . She won't make a political talk or any kind of a talk unless she gets paid."[16]

Secretary Morgenthau was correct that, with the exception of her campaign work, she had continued to earn money from her speeches. After the Redpath Bureau folded in the mid-1930s, Nellie had found a new booking agent, Alber and Wickes. Under her contract, Alber and Wickes agreed to find Nellie speaking engagements for a minimum fee of $350; Nellie and the speakers bureau split the fee and shared traveling expenses.[17] Nellie used Edness to field any speech requests that bypassed her booking agent and came to her directly. Edness was instructed to decline invitations that came without the promise of a hefty honorarium. "About the Delphians—I hate to disappoint them but I have only so much time," she wrote Edness about one 1933 request. "I don't want to spend the vitality unless there is some worth while compensation in it."[18]

Nellie simply could not resist the temptation to take advantage of the speechmaking requests. Neither her growing portfolio of stocks and real estate nor her steady income as Mint director prevented her from worrying about her economic security; the wolf seemed always to lurk just outside the door. She wrote her brother, "My fear of dependency in my old age has always been so acute as to keep me from thoroughly surrendering myself to the enjoyment of any but the most essential creature comforts. . . . If only we knew how long life would last and how to apportion our little resources to tide us over it would be simpler." George, the rational businessman, assured her that her fears were groundless. If she were not reappointed to a third term, George pointed out that she had accumulated enough capital to live comfortably on the income it produced. Even if her savings proved insufficient, he promised her that as long as either he or Alfred was alive, Nellie would never have to worry about money.[19]

Despite her protestations of strict economy, Nellie occasionally indulged in luxuries, although she did so with an eye for a bargain. Over her lunch hour, she would slip over to a nearby auction house to bid for fine furniture and oriental rugs at prices below market.[20] Using overwork and poor health as a frequent justification, she took several cruises and other trips, and she was tickled when her celebrity status resulted in complimentary upgrades of her accommodations. She bought herself a mink coat in 1935, and she even had her portrait painted the same year. "I must be crazy having this portrait painted," she wrote Edness. I can not well afford it; have no place, really, to hang it." She asked Edness not to mention the portrait project to anyone at the Mint. "There is something so immodest about the idea of spending so much for one's own portrait, and I think if I have it painted I shall probably make no display of it, but just keep it for one of the children."[21] The portrait would hang on her dining room wall at the Dresden until her death.

Another purchase that brought Nellie great happiness was a two-hundred-acre farm in rural Calvert County, Maryland. Nellie had always loved the country; she loved to wake to the sound of birds singing and to watch the countryside change with the seasons. From the moment she first saw La Trappe in April 1937, she adored it; she bought the property the next day. Nellie looked beyond the broken windows and rotting boards in the decrepit buildings and saw the promise of the abandoned house, the beautiful old trees, and the fallow fields. There was also a practical aspect to her purchase, as she noted in an article she wrote for the *Calvert County News:* "A farmhouse, however modest in importance, affords a considerable measure of security against want in event of economic disaster. . . . [A] woman . . . could raise chickens, grow a garden and probably manage a few pigs."[22] She intended the farm to be a money-making concern; Bradford would manage the farm, and together they would learn how to raise tobacco. Every weekend, Nellie, Bradford, and other young friends would escape to the farm, where they threw themselves into renovating the farmhouse and buildings, taking care of the farm animals, and cultivating their crops.[23]

Both of Nellie's sons launched legal careers during the 1930s. Bradford had moved back to Washington after graduating from the University of Virginia. He lived with Nellie while he worked on his law degree at George Washington University, and he stayed with her until 1938, practicing law and managing the farm. After George completed his Oxford studies, he joined a New York law firm and later became law secretary to a justice of the New York State

Supreme Court. In 1932, George became active in Roosevelt's presidential campaign, for which he was rewarded with an appointment as a deputy administrator at the National Recovery Administration. George and his first wife, Willard Tomlinson, presented Nellie with her second grandchild in 1937, a little girl they named Nellie Tayloe Ross.

Nellie was deeply distressed when George divorced Willard just two years after the birth of his daughter. He immediately entered into a second marriage to Mary Steele Shropshire, an executive in the Public Works Administration. "It's been very hard to take," she wrote Nelle in Memphis. "Somehow I can't keep my soul from rebelling—although I recognize that each person has a right, even one's child, to lead his own life as he will. Willard will always have a friend in me. Her letters to me nearly break my heart. Still as I've said before to you, these intimate marital affairs are something upon which no outside person can properly pass judgement."[24] Willard and her baby moved to Nashville, where Nellie visited them occasionally when she passed through Tennessee. It bothered Nellie a great deal that George was not involved in the rearing of his daughter and that he seldom saw her while she was growing up, although he supported her financially.[25]

In 1938, Bradford decided to move back to Cheyenne and practice law with John Loomis, the husband of Nellie's gubernatorial secretary, Ruth Harrington. Bradford had fallen deeply in love with Dorothy Hardy and was eager to establish a practice that would allow him to support a wife. It had not been an easy decision to leave Nellie and a potentially glamorous life in Washington. "I never would have left had I not fallen in love with Dorothy and realized that I was at a standstill in Washington," he wrote his mother. "Perhaps I shall never have the pleasure in life that [you and I] enjoyed together [in Washington], but I do hope so and believe I can attain a position of respect and make a home like you and father had—and that beats all the embassies and luxuries in the world."[26]

After Bradford left for Wyoming, Nellie rented his bedroom to their young friend, Kenneth Failor. Ken joined two other Treasury employees to whom Nellie already rented rooms in order to subsidize her rent: Dorothy Tomlinson, whose sister was George Ross's first wife, and Dr. Edward Dolan, who was the register at the U.S. Treasury.[27] "It sounds as if I were running an inn," she confessed to Nelle. "Of course I couldn't live in that big apartment alone & I hated to give it up, it is so lovely. The present arrangement is cheaper than was my living at the Mayflower & infinitely more comfortable & satisfactory. If I were utterly alone I would be very lonesome."[28]

Nellie and her new "family" fell into a comfortable routine in the Dresden apartment. Most mornings, the maid would set out a large breakfast for Nellie's housemates in the dining room and would carry in a breakfast tray to Nellie, who ate her breakfast in bed before starting to dress. If the maid was off, Nellie herself prepared breakfast for her boarders. Ken and Dorothy, who shared a bathroom with Nellie, got ready while Nellie was eating her breakfast. Dorothy left first, catching the streetcar to the office, while Ken drove his big Packard around to the front door of the Dresden to pick up Nellie. After work, Ken headed off to night classes at George Washington University. Nellie left the office around five o'clock; seldom did she take work home from the office. She rode the streetcar back up Connecticut Avenue and got off at Columbia Road. She walked up a steep hill to the stores in the Mt. Pleasant shopping district, where she purchased food and other items before walking home. Most evenings, Nellie and Dorothy ate a quiet dinner together. After dinner, Nellie usually spent a few hours reading; her favorite reading materials were the *Congressional Record, Reader's Digest,* and newsmagazines such as *Newsweek.* Nellie seldom slept more than four hours a night, so Ken would find her awake when he returned from class. Some evenings, Nellie had already retreated to her big sleigh bed to write her voluminous letters to family and friends; other evenings, Ken and Nellie would play Chinese checkers together.[29]

By the end of 1939, Bradford was earning enough income to support a wife. Bradford was coming east in time to celebrate Christmas at the Dresden with his mother and her housemates. Then he and his mother traveled to New York City, where Dorothy's uncle, an Episcopal minister, married the couple on January 12, 1940. Before the couple headed back to Cheyenne, Nellie hosted a large reception in their honor, which a society editor called the "gayest—and definitely the largest—party of the day." Nellie was thrilled to see how happy the young couple were together. Dorothy was "radiant with happiness. As for Bradford he looked the whole time as if he could eat her," Nellie reported to Nelle.[30]

Nellie visited the young couple in their Cheyenne apartment a few months later. It brought back a flood of memories to see her young lawyer son and his adoring wife, doing their best to get by on love and very little money, just as Nellie and William had done almost forty years earlier. "O, how [Dorothy] & Bradford are trying! She watches every detail of expense so carefully it made me feel a little sorry for her." Bradford mentioned to Nellie that the home she and William had built in 1907 had come on the market. The three of them made an appointment to view the house. They found to their surprise that it was in excellent shape, and the asking price was very low because the neighborhood was no longer fashionable. Bradford and Dorothy made an offer on the house, which was accepted. They had despaired of being able to afford a house, so they were thrilled that they would not only have a lovely home, but one with so many family memories.[31]

Determined to follow in his father's footsteps, Bradford ran for the state legislature and was elected in 1940 to represent Laramie County; he was the youngest member in the Twenty-sixth Legislature. The session ended on February 22, 1941, and two days later he was inducted into the U.S. Army and ordered to Fort Lewis, Washington.[32] Bradford had joined the Wyoming National Guard before his marriage to Dorothy to augment his meager legal income. However, the army had begun to prepare for the possible entry of the United States into World War II. Bradford wrote his nervous mother in late March that the most dangerous activity he had undertaken since reporting to Fort Lewis was three to four hours of daily marching. Despite the passage of the Lend-Lease Act earlier that month, Bradford assured Nellie that he did not think the army would ever engage in combat.[33]

Nellie was delighted that Bradford and Dorothy were expecting their first baby in June 1941. She combined a trip to the West Coast Mint installations with a few days of vacation in late June, and the baby obligingly waited to be born until his grandmother arrived. Bradford and Dorothy named him William Bradford Ross III and called him "Braddie" to distinguish him from his father. Late that year, Bradford received the good news that he was being transferred back to Washington, D.C., where he would serve in the office of the Judge Advocate General. He reported to his new assignment in December 1941, the same month that the Japanese bombed Pearl Harbor and the United States entered the war. Bradford and Dorothy moved into a small apartment near Nellie's. Nellie cherished the time she got to spend with Braddie, an opportunity that she had missed with Ambrose's son and George's daughter. "Frankly I'm just silly about him," Nellie reported to Nelle. "He has been nearer by than my other two grandchildren and has been such a joy."[34]

Nellie reported to Nelle that Bradford was showing the strain of working long hours and that he expected to be called for foreign duty at any time. Nelle's son Howard had also entered military service, and her daughters were involved in war work. Nellie worried constantly for the safety of her son and nephew, and she also worried whether the Allies would be strong enough to defeat both the Germans and the Japanese. "The way ahead looks dark to me," she wrote Nelle. "Often I wonder if it may take years & years & years (all that will be left of my life) before the war is over. . . . I fear that the America we have known & loved will be greatly changed in the end."[35]

During the war years, George and Mary Steele moved to New York City, where George had accepted an executive position in the aviation industry. Nellie had become fond of Mary Steele, and she was pleased that the couple seemed so happy, but she worried that George tended to jump from one job opportunity to another, just like his twin had done; fundamentally, he was still the same young man who had been counseled by his father in the 1920s for his impetuosity. George had already tried government service, lobbying, and a managerial position in Chicago with a manufacturing concern. The very characteristics that made him so good with people—his charm and his optimistic enthusiasm—made it difficult for him to stick with one career; there always seemed brighter possibilities just over the horizon. "I do hope that my George can & will stay put right where he is," Nellie wrote Nelle. However, in short order, George moved on to a position with the International Chamber of Commerce. In the 1950s, he accepted a State Department position in Washington and then an executive position with a trade group in Florida before moving to Virginia to go into real estate. George was already fifty-seven when Nellie wrote Nelle that "George hasn't gotten settled at anything yet which is a major concern of mine." To provide the couple a little steady income, Nellie established a trust for the period of their lifetimes. Before her death, she would name Bradford, who *had* established a successful career in law, as the executor of the trust.[36]

Bradford never was posted overseas during the war years, but he traveled frequently on various assignments around the country. He was in San Francisco when his second son, David, was born prematurely on August 15, 1943. When the war ended in May 1945, he was faced with the decision of whether to return to Wyoming. After more than four years of absence, he would have to start over again to establish a legal practice in Cheyenne, and now he had a family of four to support. He and Dorothy decided to remain in Washington. Early in January 1946, he was offered a position as general counsel of the Federal Power Commission. He would remain at the Federal Power Commission until 1953, when he would leave government and cofound the legal firm of Ross, Marsh and Foster. Nellie was elated at the prospect of having her son and two of her grandchildren nearby.

In April 1946, Nellie suffered a terrible blow when her brother George died. He remained conscious until the last, and Nellie, who had arrived about a week before, took turns with the other family members, spending a few moments by his side. George had seen Nellie through all the most difficult moments of her life, and she would miss him terribly. From now on, she would increasingly turn to Bradford to assume the supportive role that George had played for Nellie since her childhood.

Until the end of her life, Nellie expected and received a great deal of attention from Bradford, who adored his mother too much to begrudge her demands. Fortunately, her daughter-in-law got along well with Nellie; if she resented the fact that Bradford was at his mother's beck and call, she stifled her feelings for the sake of family harmony. Inevitably, Nellie was closer to her grandchildren by Bradford because they were nearby and they spent so much time with her. Nellie helped to rear Bradford's four sons, especially Braddie, who called his grandmother "Gah." Bradford had bought a farm in southern Maryland in the early 1950s, a few years after Nellie sold La Trappe, and the entire family spent most weekends there. Nellie took Braddie blackberry picking at dawn, she watched him play with his pony, Cocoa, and she read him to sleep in her big bed on hot summer nights.[37] When a rebellious Braddie reached an impasse with his parents around age thirteen, he even moved in with his grandmother for the summer.[38]

Two years before Nellie retired, she accepted an invitation from the Spanish government to present a collection of medals coined by the Mint at an international exhibition of medallic art in Madrid. Nellie and Dorothy Tomlinson, who accompanied Nellie on her ten-week trip, had a wonderful time. The State Department had instructed the embassies in London, Paris, Brussels, and Madrid to provide Nellie celebrity treatment and, as always, Nellie adored the receptions, cocktails, and dinner parties that were arranged in her honor within the diplomatic community. In Paris, she met General Eisenhower and lunched with his wife; in Madrid, she met a gracious Generalissimo Franco. As she and Dorothy crossed the French border, a delegation of Spanish officials was waiting, arms filled with flowers, to greet their train and to accompany them to Madrid. Nellie loved the Spanish capital; "I've never seen a place so enchanting," she wrote Nelle from the Hotel Ritz.[39] Nellie took advantage of the bargains to be had in Spanish furnishings, carpets, and clothes, and she even had an evening gown made to order in a heavy silk of soft blue.

Nellie was so taken with Spain that shortly after she retired, she returned to spend the winter of 1953–1954. She settled in Palma on the island of Mallorca, where she stayed in a small hotel overlooking the Mediterranean. Each day, she explored the narrow, winding streets of Palma, peeking through grillwork gates into patios filled with pots of blooming plants while she enjoyed the intoxicating fragrance of the flowering vines that spilled down from balconies above her. Sitting on her sunny balcony at the hotel, she wrote her family enthusiastic letters about the sights, sounds, and flavors of Palma. She returned for another extended stay in 1955. As long as she stayed in one place, she informed her family, she could live in relative luxury for very little money. She had many American friends who had settled in Palma for that reason, but Nellie could not bring herself to leave Bradford's family permanently.

In August 1956, Nellie took a fifteen-year-old Braddie to Europe with her for a grand tour through Great Britain and the continent, just as she had taken his father at about the same age. Her grandson was stunned when Nellie turned to him after boarding the ship in New York and said, "Braddie, here's the money, here's the passport, and you're in charge."[40] Braddie rose to the challenge, and Nellie wrote his father a few weeks later with satisfaction, "You'll never see again the same *little* boy you sent away with me. The way he has taken on grown-up ways amazes me."[41]

As she introduced Braddie to the history and sophistication of the Old World, Nellie became a combination of mentor and Auntie Mame. She introduced Braddie to the cathedrals and universities of the English countryside and to the sophistication of London, where she introduced him to the Queen. In Vienna, she dressed him in evening clothes and took him to the opera, where they took seats in the orchestra section, surrounded by glitter and elegance. In Brussels, he watched as Nellie swept out of a hotel she considered below her standard and called the American ambassador, who secured them the presidential suite at a luxury hotel.[42]

At a party in Paris, Nellie gave him a lesson in discretion that he never forgot. As Braddie began to voice his negative opinion of General Eisenhower, who had just been reelected president, he felt a sharp pain in his shins when his grandmother kicked him—hard—under the table. When they returned to the hotel, Nellie sat Braddie down and told him, "I'm not going to allow you to embarrass me. If you don't know your facts, don't speak. On *any* issue. Silence is a great virtue. And furthermore, we are Americans, and I don't care who's elected president, he's our president whether we support him or not. Don't you ever forget that and don't you ever, ever, do that again."[43]

Five years later, it was her grandson David's turn to accompany Nellie on her travels. This time, an eighty-five-year-old Nellie went around the world—Europe, Egypt, Israel, India, Thailand, Hong Kong, and Japan.[44] It was the experience of a lifetime for David, whose life was cut short just two years later. David had returned to Parsons College in Iowa, where he was majoring in business administration. He was driving a car filled with three of his classmates on a highway a few miles from New London, Iowa, when the car hit the rear of a truck filled with Christmas trees that had stalled on the road. The

Christmas trees were blocking the truck's lights, so David had no warning of the impending collision. "O, Nelle, I did so love that boy," Nellie mourned. "It was like living again through the tragedy that took my precious Ambrose."[45]

In 1968, George and Mary Steele took Nellie with them on a seven-day cruise through the Mediterranean. Two years later, when Nellie was ninety-four, the three of them spent two months in the Holy Land. Nellie confided to Bradford, "It's going to be quite a treat for me to get away on a trip. It's been a long time I've been confined in [my] house. [George and Mary Steele] are angels to take me on." Nellie did well on the trip; "she had us all worn out," George told a newspaper reporter after returning from the trip.[46] George had changed their original reservations to secure a ship that carried a doctor on board when Nellie's Washington doctor refused to let her travel across the ocean without medical care available.[47] He hired a car to take them to many of the sites important in the life of Jesus: to Jerusalem, where Nellie slowly walked the Garden of Gethsemane; to Galilee, where Jesus preached the Sermon on the Mount; to Capernum, where he turned water into wine and multiplied the loaves and fishes to feed a multitude.[48]

The older Nellie got, the more important her Christian faith had become to her. By the 1970s, Nellie had given up most of her social activities, and she was rarely seen out in public, but she remained an active member of St. Margaret's, an Episcopal parish on Connecticut Avenue, near the Dresden. She attended Bible classes and she revived her girlhood pastime of hand-sewing to help the Altar Guild ladies make vestments and altar cloths.

Nellie lost her last brother, Alfred, in 1968, and she lost her dear sister-in-law and correspondent, Nelle, in 1973. Nellie was the last member of her Tayloe generation to survive. Although her hearing was very poor and she had suffered from a bad knee since 1966, she remained in good health until almost the end of her life. Nellie's last boarder and friend, the Countess of Castellane, had left her in the 1950s, so after Nellie had a knee operation, Bradford arranged for a companion, Virginia Higgs, to come live with Nellie and look after her at the Dresden. Virginia kept an eye on Nellie during the night, and while she was gone to work during the day, Nellie still had the elderly maid, Mary Fountain, who had been with her for decades.

Nellie's last trip was in May 1972, when she traveled to Wyoming to be the guest of honor at the hundredth anniversary of the founding of Yellowstone, the nation's first national park. She and Braddie, who accompanied her, flew to Denver by plane, over the prairies that she had crossed by train as a bride exactly seventy years earlier. Two hundred people attended the centennial dinner at the high school gymnasium in Cody, Wyoming. Braddie, who had never heard his grandmother speak before a large crowd, remembered that she "delivered a very gracious speech about how glad she was to be back, and . . . that the people of Wyoming had bestowed on her a wonderful career, and . . . how deeply appreciative she was to the people of Wyoming."[49]

The women's movement was in full swing by 1972. Since Nellie had been a pioneer in the advancement of women, it was inevitable that the reporters who approached Nellie after the dinner for an interview would ask Nellie's opinion of the women's liberation movement. "I have no interest in women's lib," Nellie tartly replied to the managing editor of the *Casper Star-Tribune.*[50] In a response that again highlighted the contrast between her stated beliefs and her own long and distinguished career, she told a young female reporter from United Press International, "As far as I'm concerned, I've gone on record before as saying that the highest, the highest, fulfillment for a woman is motherhood and family. And that's just my perspective."[51]

The Victorian American culture from which Nellie had absorbed her life values and attitudes had vanished decades earlier. Nellie had been right when she had worried in the closing years of World War II that the world she had known might cease to exist. In 1963, Nellie wrote Nelle nostalgically, "looking back I feel as if I had lived about three lifetimes, so many changes have come into my life."[52] In the technological arena, Americans had dropped the first atomic bomb in 1945, resulting in a frightening escalation of the tensions between the Soviet Union and the West. The 1940s development of jet airplanes and rockets had culminated in the Soviets sending the first man to space, triggering the race to put the first man on the moon. Wartime medical advances had helped to usher in the widespread development and application of antibiotics, vaccines, X-rays, and radiotherapy. Watson and Crick had received a Nobel Prize in 1962 for their discovery of the structure of DNA, setting the stage for a revolution in genetic and microbiological research. The first crude computers, developed in the 1940s, were revolutionized as a result of the integrated circuit, introduced in 1959. On the consumer front, the introduction of the television, microwave, and a myriad of household appliances would transform the life of the American family—particularly that of the American wife and mother.

The technological developments were far easier for Nellie to accept than the changes in America's culture and values. Even though the "cult of domesticity" had enjoyed a resurgence in the 1950s—the rate of working women had declined, the divorce rate had dropped, the birthrate had boomed, and the Levittown suburbs had grown—a quiet insurgency was occurring that would transform relations between men and women. In 1963, Betty Friedan, herself a suburban wife from the upper middle class, wrote the *Feminine Mystique,* an indictment of the very values that Nellie claimed to hold most dear, even though she herself had transcended a purely domestic life twenty years earlier. Friedan pointed out the dissatisfaction in the mainstream woman's life: "As she made the beds, shopped for groceries, matched slipcover material, ate peanut butter sandwiches with her children, chauffeured Cub Scouts and Brownies, lay beside her husband at night—she was afraid to ask even of herself the silent question—'Is this all?' . . . The American housewife," who was admired by women throughout the world, was "freed by science and labor-saving appliances from the drudgery, the dangers of childbirth and the illnesses of her grandmother." She "had found true feminine fulfillment." But something was wrong: "Other women were satisfied with their lives, she thought. . . . She was so ashamed to admit her dissatisfaction that she never knew how many other women shared it." Friedan saw that the dissatisfaction was reaching a crisis point: "We can no longer ignore that voice within women that says: 'I want something more than my husband and my children and my home.' "[53]

The Baby Boom was over by 1957, and the American birthrate began to fall; by the late 1960s, it had fallen below the birthrate of the Great Depression, with no end in sight, and the use of birth control had become commonplace. By 1958, the divorce rate had begun to climb. By 1960, twice as many women were in the workforce than in 1940, and there were four times as many women entering the workforce as men; married women accounted for almost the entire growth in the numbers of working females. Families increasingly needed the wife's second income to maintain their standard of living, thanks to an increase in the expense of rearing and educating children and the rising demand for material goods—the newest cars and appliances, the latest fashions, and expensive but easy convenience foods. The Equal Pay Act of 1963 and the Civil Rights Act of 1964 made employment discrimination against women illegal, but nevertheless, women struggled for true equality in education, employment, and legal rights. The National Organization for Women (NOW), founded in 1966, fought for women's equal rights with their publications, lawsuits, and lobbying activities.[54]

On the civil rights front, blacks who had accepted discrimination in employment, housing, and citizenship before World War II were now determined to obtain their full rights as Americans. Nellie's fellow Missourian, Harry

Truman, provided unexpected support when he established the President's Committee on Civil Rights in 1947; the committee's report faulted the nation for its "failure of democracy" in the treatment of blacks.[55] That same year, the Supreme Court overturned a lower-court decision that had upheld restrictive housing covenants that prevented homeowners from selling their property to blacks or Jews. In 1948, President Truman issued two executive orders that prohibited discrimination in the armed forces and in civilian federal employment.

Nellie's adopted home of Washington, D.C., was a focus of the civil rights struggle. In 1951, citizens' groups in Washington began to picket chain stores and department stores that refused to serve blacks at their lunch counters. In 1953, the Supreme Court struck down another lower-court decision, effectively ending the official segregation of Washington's restaurants, theaters, playgrounds, swimming pools, and other public establishments. And with its *Brown v. Board of Education* decision in 1954, the Court rejected the separate-but-equal policy that had permitted the continued existence of two Washington school districts, one for blacks and one for whites, each with its own facilities, teachers, and administration.

In 1963, Nellie wrote a letter to Harry Truman, now a private citizen, after reading about an interview in which he had suggested that northern civil rights workers should concentrate on problems in their own backyards instead of agitating in the South.

> I write to say I glory in the boldness with which you declared your common-sense views. . . . There is so much fanatical concern that the Negro should have privileges far beyond his Civic rights. It seems to me the Civic rights of us white people are being threatened, even to the extent that we may be deprived of the right to sell our own private property to whom we please; to me a dismaying thought. And why doesn't somebody start a crusade against the hideous crimes, committed chiefly by Negroes, that make it unsafe for a woman in Washington to stick her head out of the door at night. I hear no out-cry against them![56]

During the 1965 debate of the Voting Rights bill, Nellie wrote her sister-in-law that she found the sit-ins and demonstrations during the 1965 debate of the Voting Rights bill to be "nerve wrecking. We all I'm sure want the Negroes to have the right to vote and all the other rights to which they are entitled. . . . But I do wish they would quiet down awhile. . . . Of course we had a lot of it here last Sunday, but I didn't go farther afield than down the street to church."[57] Nellie's comment to President Truman suggests her concern that civil rights activists had gone too far, and the Washington race riots, which occurred just a few short blocks from Nellie's home, were understandably frightening to a ninety-three-year-old woman. Nellie was grappling with a world that was far different from the Missouri plantation on which she had been born. Nevertheless, when her son Bradford resolved that his son should be bused across Washington to an integrated junior high, Nellie was supportive of his decision.[58]

In November 1976, Nellie celebrated her one hundredth birthday, and in honor of the occasion, Bradford hosted a birthday party for family and friends. Nellie, dressed in a gown of her signature blue color and adorned by an orchid, presided over the gathering with queenly dignity as her relatives and guests each greeted her in turn. John Snyder, the Treasury secretary during the last part of Nellie's tenure as Mint director, was there to honor her, as were the two directors who succeeded her in office. Her old friend Ken Failor was in attendance, full of stories from the Mint years. He reminded Nellie how embarrassed she would become when Secretary Snyder, on occasion, had startled her with a kiss on the cheek. Nancy Dussault, cohost of ABC's *Good Morning, America,* was there with a camera crew to interview her for television. From her family, all three of Bradford's sons were there, as were George, Mary Steele, and George's daughter, Tayloe. Braddie was accompanied by his wife and Nellie's two-and-a-half-year-old great-granddaughter, Aviza. Finally, Nellie's Memphis relatives were well represented; three of the four children of George and Nelle had traveled to Washington to honor their Aunt Nellie. Displayed around the room were dozens of birthday greetings sent to Nellie by schoolchildren in Wyoming.[59]

Nellie continued to live in her apartment, with the support of Virginia Higgs. It was no longer possible for her to travel out to Bradford's farm, and she longed for the countryside. One weekend during her last spring, the woman who had been so precise in her writing during her career sent a wistful note in shaky handwriting to Dorothy, who was out on the farm. "The flowers & plants must be beautiful ~~new~~ now—the dogwood ~~espectly~~ especially. Your ~~had~~ hedge is beautiful of dogwood. I always liked to see the ~~cattle~~ cattle in the field near by."[60]

Shortly after her 101st birthday, Nellie took a fall in her apartment. Unwilling to leave her home—probably fearing that she would never be able to return if she left—Nellie tried to recover on her own with the aid of round-the-clock nursing care, but the fall had weakened her too much. After a couple of difficult weeks, her family insisted that she move to a nursing home. George and Mary Steele were living in Spain, but Bradford kept them posted on Nellie's status with frequent letters. On December 7, he wrote George that "since my last letter to you nothing here has changed. We have been to see Mother daily, except last Sunday when Virginia went to see her, and while we are apparently recognized there is rarely any communication."[61] Nellie held on for two weeks at the nursing home, but on December 19, 1977, she passed away.

Nellie's body was returned to Wyoming, which had honored her and made her famous. At ten o'clock on December 21, Nellie's casket was carried into the Capitol Rotunda, where it lay in state for two hours, surrounded by a military honor guard. Governor Ed Herschler placed a wreath in front of the casket and then delivered a short eulogy to the small gathering. "There is no need to review her distinguished career in government, only to note that it was characterized by the same dignity and compassion that attended her whole life. She leaves to her family, and to all of us, a legacy of the best of Wyoming life, of dedication, patriotism and peace of mind."[62]

That afternoon, Nellie's funeral service was conducted at St. Mark's Episcopal Church, where she had held the funerals for her husband and two sons. Nellie's passing was honored by the state—one former state governor, two former first ladies, and the state treasurer and secretary of state attended the service. But aside from her family and the children of a few old acquaintances, only forty or so persons came to the funeral. She had outlived all of her generation, and she had been forgotten by the public at large.[63]

A string of cars fell in line behind the hearse on that sunny winter afternoon as it slowly drove the few blocks to Lakeview Cemetery through one of Cheyenne's oldest neighborhoods. The stark and dusty prairie streets that Nellie had remembered from her earliest days were gone; the stately trees that arched over the route of the funeral procession marked the passage of the many years since her arrival as a bride. The hearse stopped in front of the peaceful family plot, marked by venerable blue spruces. There, near the graves of her sons Alfred and Ambrose, Nellie Tayloe Ross was laid to rest next to her beloved husband, William.

Notes

Abbreviations

ADT	Alfred Duff Tayloe
AHC	American Heritage Center, University of Wyoming
EKW	Edness Kimball Wilkins
ER	Anna Eleanor Roosevelt
FDR	Franklin Delano Roosevelt
GGT	George Green Tayloe
GTR	George Tayloe Ross
JAR	James Ambrose Ross
JHR	John Hardy Ross
JTJ	Jane Tayloe Janus
KF	Kenneth Failor
KTC	Kaye Tayloe Collins
MD	Mary W. (Molly) Dewson
MMO	Mary Margaret O'Reilly
NKT	Nelle Kreider Tayloe
NTR	Nellie Tayloe Ross
RTR	Robert Tayloe Ross
SGT	Samuel Green Tayloe
SL	Schlesinger Library, Radcliffe
WBR I	William Bradford Ross I
WBR II	William Bradford Ross II
WBR III	William Bradford Ross III
WSA	Wyoming State Archives

Preface

1. *Coin World,* December 15, 1976, 3.
2. Phil McAuley, "First Woman Governor at Party," *Casper Star-Tribune,* May 31,

1972; "The Nation's First Woman Governor Has Really Come a Long Way—She's Now 100," *People Magazine,* November 29, 1976, 102.

3. *New York Times,* December 21, 1977.

4. Lillian Faderman, *To Believe in Women: What Lesbians Have Done for America—A History,* 79–81.

5. Emily Newell Blair, "A Who's Who of Women in Washington," 39.

6. Anne Firor Scott, *The Southern Lady: From Pedestal to Politics, 1830–1930,* x-xi, 4–9.

7. *Proceedings,* Democratic Convention 1928, 104–7, 236, 249–50.

8. NTR Papers, accession no. 10526-97-10-07, box 6, folder 12; Kaye Tayloe Collins phone interview, July 31, 2002; Ann Loomis Jesse interview, January 20, 2003, Denver, Colorado.

9. Paul A. Carter, *Another Part of the Twenties,* 104, 205. The ABC national news as well as *Time* and *Newsweek* magazines were cited for their error regarding Ella Grasso in a *Douglas Budget* article on November 14, 1974 (Wyoming State Archives, Acquisition H81-1, box 10). Recent (2005) Internet searches under "Ella Grasso" yield references to her being the first woman governor in the United States, though many qualify the statement with the phrase "elected in her own right."

10. "Capable and Clean," *Casper Star-Tribune,* November 30, 1976.

11. EKW Papers, OH-2242, EKW audiotape interview, December 20, 1977.

12. Marjorie Williams, "A Working Mom's Comedy," *Washington Post,* October 2, 2002, A17. See also Sheila M. Rothman, *Woman's Proper Place: A History of Changing Ideals and Practices, 1870 to the Present,* 229. By 1972, over half of American mothers with school-age children were in the workforce; by 1974, about one-third of mothers with preschool children were also working. See also Alan Roland and Barbara Harris, eds., *Career and Motherhood: Struggles for a New Identity.*

13. Sylvia Ann Hewlett, *Creating a Life: Professional Women and the Quest for Children,* 5–7.

14. NTR Papers, accession no. 948-97-10-07, box 3, "Speeches by Nellie Tayloe Ross, ca. 1920–1953, #2."

ONE ~ Missouri Roots

1. Nellie wrote down the story about the fire on the back of a photograph of the burial plot on the family farm; see NTR Papers, box 14, "Reid, Reed, and Ross Families, 1968–1977." She estimated that she was about six when the house burned, probably as the result of a defective flue. There was no mention of the fire in the Andrew County papers for the years 1882 through 1884. Based on a May 19, 2002, interview with the grandson of the man who purchased the farm from Nellie's parents, there was no house on the property when Henry Hoffelmeyer took possession on March 5, 1884. It is likely that the house burned down during the winter of 1883–1884, which was shortly after Nellie turned seven. In a 1925 interview, Nellie's first grade teacher recalled having spent a few nights in the house at the Tayloe farm, and the only year he taught Nellie was the school year of 1883–1884.

2. NTR to GGT, September 23–31, 1902, NTR Papers, box 1, "Family and Personal, 1902–1930."

3. Henry Hoffelmeyer interview, May 21, 2002, Andrew County, Missouri. Mr. Hoffelmeyer, the namesake of the man who bought the farm from the Tayloes, stated that his grandfather learned of the Tayloe farm when it was advertised in an upcoming sheriff's sale. However, the warranty deed that transferred the land from the Tayloes to Mr. Hoffelmeyer was a clear warranty deed, so James must have been able to effect the transfer before the sheriff seized the farm.

The story of Nellie's parents' generation is based on James Tayloe's reminiscences, written in his eightieth year (referred to hereinafter as JWT History). The outline of events that James created in his reminiscence has been supplemented using census data, court records, interviews, secondary sources, and several contemporary newspapers from Andrew County, St. Joseph, Miltonvale, and Omaha. Copies of the JWT History are available from the Andrew County Museum and in the NTR Papers, box 13, "Family History, 1912–1990."

4. Paul C. Nagle, *Missouri: A Bicentennial History,* 5–6.

5. Perry McCandless, *A History of Missouri: Volume II, 1820 to 1860,* 134.

6. For background information on the history of St. Joseph, see Mildred B. Grenier, *St. Joseph: A Pictorial History;* Hazel A. Faubion, *Tales of Old "St. Joe" and the Frontier Days;* Preston Filbert, *The Half Not Told: The Civil War in a Frontier Town,* 4–6; and "A Brief History of St. Joseph," from the St. Joseph city Web site, http://www.ci.st–joseph.mo.us/ briefhist.html., accessed May 5, 2001.

7. No connection could be found between James Tayloe's stepfather, William Bailey, and his business partner J. W. Bailey. William had no sons still living with him in 1850 other than James and his siblings, and earlier census records only record the names of heads of household. If the two had been related, James would probably have said so in his memoir.

8. McCandless, *History of Missouri: Volume II,* 37; Earl J. Nelson, "The Passing of Slavery in Missouri," 8; Filbert, *Half Not Told,* 3–4. See also R. Douglas Hurt, *Agriculture and Slavery in Missouri's Little Dixie,* xii–xiv, 6, 52–56. While the seven counties on which Hurt focused did not include Andrew County, his observations concerning the slave-owning culture brought to Missouri by Kentucky settlers are relevant to the story of the Green family.

9. *History of Andrew and DeKalb Counties, Missouri, from the Earliest Time to the Present,* 81–95. See also Christopher Phillips, *Missouri's Confederate: Claiborne Fox Jackson and the Creation of Southern Identity in the Border West,* 6–52. Like Samuel Green, Claiborne Jackson was born in Kentucky of Virginia parents and migrated to Missouri as a young man. Phillips's chronicle of frontier life in Kentucky and the mass migration of Kentuckians to Missouri illuminates Samuel Green's life.

10. Samuel Green's real estate valuation is from the 1850 census. Concerning the value of Samuel's slaves, R. Douglas Hurt stated that in the mid-1850s, "prime male field hands" sold for as much as $1,500; women with young children sold for $1,100 to $1,300; boys as young as three sold for $226; and girls around age nine sold for $600. These prices held for the entire Little Dixie region; see Hurt, *Agriculture and Slavery,* 224–25. See also Harrison A. Tresler [*sic*], "The Value and the Sale of the

Missouri Slave," which notes that James Shannon, president of the state university, declared in 1855 that "the average Missouri slave was worth $600, and that field hands 'will now readily sell for $1200" (71n8).

11. Samuel Green bought the eighty acres on which his plantation house sat on February 7, 1848. Andrew County Deed Book 3, p. 235.

12. Georgia Bryan Conrad, *Reminiscences of a Southern Woman,* 10.

13. Catherine Clinton, *The Plantation Mistress: Woman's World in the Old South,* 30; Hurt, *Agriculture and Slavery,* 267.

14. Clinton, *Plantation Mistress,* 20–31. See also Elizabeth Fox-Genovese, *Within the Plantation Household: Black and White Women of the Old South,* 103–4; Mary S. Hoffschwelle, "Women's Sphere and the Creation of Female Community in the Antebellum South: Three Tennessee Slaveholding Women," 83–85; Scott, *Southern Lady,* 29–31; and Diane Mutti Burke, "'May We as One Family Live in Peace and Harmony': Relations between Mistresses and Slave Women in Antebellum Missouri." Although Burke focuses not on the large slave-owning Missouri families but on the more typical situation of families with just a few slaves, her observations concerning the relationship between mistress and slaves and her discussion of the mistress's responsibilities are relevant to Amanda Green.

15. Clinton, *Plantation Mistress,* 50.

16. L. H. Sigourney, "Intellectual Bouquet," 179–80.

17. Clinton, *Plantation Mistress,* 19. See also Hoffschwelle, "Women's Sphere," 80–82; and Scott, *Southern Lady,* 27.

18. Hurt, *Agriculture and Slavery,* 200–203.

19. The 1852 Richmond city directory lists over twenty educational institutions for young women, including the Richmond Young Ladies Institute, St. Joseph's Female Institute, Rev. M. D. Hoge's Boarding and Day School for Young Ladies, and Mrs. Pellet's Boarding School. The references to Richmond female seminaries may all be found in the collection of the Virginia Historical Society, Richmond, Virginia.

20. Pamphlet for Hoge's School, 1849; Samuel B. Wilson to Rev. M. D. Hoge, November 30, 1848, in pamphlet for Southern Female Institute, 1858, Virginia Historical Society, Richmond.

21. William Alexander MacCorkle, *The White Sulphur Springs,* 395–397, quote from 397.

22. Robert S. Conte, "Romance at White Sulphur Springs."

23. Greenbrier County, Virginia, 1860 census, 368. (Greenbrier County became part of West Virginia when that state seceded as a result of the Civil War.)

24. The acreage total is taken from the probate inventory for Samuel Green's estate, dated 1864. The JWT History noted, "He was a very prominent man in Kansas and died before the Civil War. He had 100 slaves and fine lands." It was not possible to locate any Kansas land records for Samuel Green, who is also not mentioned in the 1864 probate of Samuel Green's estate. It was also not possible to verify James's estimate of 100 slaves; therefore, the size of the family slave holdings is based on data from the 1850 and 1860 censuses.

25. Samuel apparently never made a will. The original probate file is now owned by the Andrew County Historical Society. The Green probate papers listed the name,

age, and sex of each slave but did not include their market values. For information on the valuation of Missouri slaves, see note 10 of this chapter. Hiring out slaves was a common and lucrative practice. In 1857, the going rate for hiring out skilled slaves was two hundred dollars per year, yielding their owners a 12–15 percent return on their investment. See Hurt, *Agriculture and Slavery,* 240–41; and McCandless, *History of Missouri: Volume II,* 60–61.

26. Edwin C. McReynolds, *Missouri: A History of the Crossroads State,* 164–65.

27. Hurt, *Agriculture and Slavery,* 302.

28. Michael Fellman, *Inside War: The Guerrilla Conflict in Missouri during the American Civil War,* 8; McCandless, *History of Missouri: Volume II,* 270–88; William E. Parrish, *A History of Missouri: Volume III, 1860 to 1875,* 1–10; Phillips, *Missouri's Confederate,* 130–32.

29. Floyd Calvin Shoemaker, *Missouri and Missourians: Land of Contrasts and People of Achievements,* 918–19. For a discussion of the formation of the home guard units, see Parrish, *History of Missouri: Volume III,* 10–18. See also William E. Parrish, *Missouri under Radical Rule, 1865–1870,* 205; Jay Monaghan, *Civil War on the Western Border, 1854–1865;* and "The Civil War Letters of Colonel Bazel F. Lazear, Part I," 254–73. For a detailed discussion of the period between the passage of the Kansas-Nebraska Act and the death of Claiborne Jackson in December 1862, see Phillips, *Missouri's Confederate,* 196–273.

30. Parrish, *History of Missouri: Volume III,* 52–53.

31. *Reminiscences of the Women of Missouri during the Sixties,* 278–79.

32. Mrs. S. E. Ustick, "An Incident of the Civil War," 36–37. See also Parrish, *History of Missouri: Volume III,* 67–70.

33. JWT History.

34. Grenier, *St. Joseph,* 57.

35. Filbert, *Half Not Told,* 96–100.

36. *History of Andrew and DeKalb Counties,* 228.

37. Fellman, *Inside War,* v; Parrish, *History of Missouri: Volume III,* 70. For more detailed background on the skirmishes between Union sympathizers and secessionists and the random violence experienced by Missouri citizens, see Fellman, *Inside War;* Shoemaker, *Missouri and Missourians,* 893–94; *History of Andrew and DeKalb Counties,* 218–36; and Parrish, *History of Missouri: Volume III,* 59–80.

38. "More Houses Burned," *St. Joseph Morning Herald,* September 2, 1863.

39. *History of Andrew and DeKalb Counties,* 224.

40. James Tayloe placed the value of the home considerably higher, at more than $30,000. Whatever its value, it would have been worth about 30 percent more just two years earlier, based on a dollar conversion chart developed by Robert Sahr of Oregon State University.

41. JWT History. James's statement as written was inaccurate because Lizzie died twenty-six years after the mansion burned. James also indicated that Lizzie's health improved after the family's move to Kansas, which took place in 1884.

42. "Mrs. Ross Attended First School Here," *St. Joseph News-Press,* January 24, 1925, 3.

43. McReynolds, *Missouri,* 287–98; Eric Foner, *Reconstruction: America's Unfinished*

Revolution, 1863–1877, 22–23; John A. Garraty, *The American Nation: A History of the United States,* 523; Jean Strouse, *Morgan: American Financier,* 130, 151.

44. Foner, *Reconstruction,* 30–43.

45. NTR, Women's Division of the Democratic National Committee, "Foundation Stones of the Democratic Party," FDR Papers, DNC box 880. The pamphlet consisted of a collection of quotations from Thomas Jefferson that Nellie assembled to explain the fundamental principles of the party as she saw it. Two excerpts are "The states should be left to do whatever acts they can do as well as the General Government," and "It is not by the consolidation or concentration of powers, but by their distribution, that good government is effected."

46. *History of Andrew and DeKalb Counties,* 139–40.

47. Fox-Genovese, *Within the Plantation,* 113.

48. The 1870 census for the Tayloe family lists no servants or farm laborers on the property other than Samuel Green. The 1880 census lists one farm laborer and his wife or daughter living with the Tayloes.

49. Rothman, *Woman's Proper Place,* 15.

50. Jeffrey Ostler, *Prairie Populism: The Fate of Agrarian Radicalism in Kansas, Nebraska, and Iowa, 1880–1892,* 93; Sandra L. Myres, *Westering Women and the Frontier Experience, 1800–1915,* 146–66.

51. Deborah Fink, *Agrarian Women: Wives and Mothers in Rural Nebraska, 1880–1940,* 61.

52. WBR III telephone interview, October 14, 2002.

53. "Mrs. Ross Attended First School Here," *St. Joseph News-Press,* January 24, 1925, 3.

54. JWT History.

55. James E. Kirby, Russell E. Richey, and Kenneth E. Rowe, *The Methodists,* 168.

56. For a detailed discussion of the founding of Southern Methodism and of its impact during the years of Nellie's childhood, see Hunter Dickinson Farish, *The Circuit Rider Dismounts: A Social History of Southern Methodism, 1865–1900.*

57. Ibid., 204–6. See also Matthew Simpson, *A Hundred Years of Methodism,* 305–6; Paul Wesley Chilcote, *John Wesley and the Women Preachers of Early Methodism,* 24; McCandless, *History of Missouri: Volume II,* 206; and Henry Wheeler, *Methodism and the Temperance Reformation,* 246–47.

58. Caroline E. Merrick, *Old Times in Dixie Land: A Southern Matron's Memories,* 79–80.

59. Andrew County does not maintain tax records back to this period. It donated the surviving records on personal property assessments and back taxes to the Northwest Missouri Genealogical Society, St. Joseph, Missouri. Only the 1877 book has survived.

60. "Mrs. Ross Attended First School Here," *St. Joseph News-Press,* January 24, 1925, 3.

TWO ~ Prairie Girlhood

1. *Miltonvale News,* January 25, 1884.
2. Fannie S. Palmer and Kathryn P. Chilen, "Miltonvale—1982," 5.
3. Ibid., 6; *Miltonvale Record,* September 7, 1933.
4. *Miltonvale News,* December 2, 1882, March 23, 1883.
5. William Frank Zornow, *Kansas: A History of the Jayhawk State,* 165; Richard White, *"It's Your Misfortune and None of My Own": A History of the American West,* 227–31; E. F. Hollibaugh, *Biographical History of Cloud County, Kansas,* 112.
6. Hollibaugh, *Biographical History of Cloud County,* 112.
7. *Miltonvale News,* March 20, 1884. The arrival of the Davis family had been announced in the paper on November 9, 1883.
8. *Miltonvale News,* April 10, 1884. Fortunately for the biographer, no detail of daily life was too small for the *Miltonvale News,* including grades, gossip of every kind, town visitors, private parties, and even local pranks.
9. *Miltonvale News,* January 8, 1885.
10. The house was described in the December 23, 1886, and January 20, 1887, issues of the *Miltonvale News.* The landscaping was described in the March 17, 1887, issue. Some of the large old trees that currently surround the house may be survivors from this first planting. The horses and buggy are described in *Miltonvale News,* May 5, 1887, and August 11, 1887.
11. JWT History, NTR Papers, box 13, "Family History, 1912–1990."
12. *Miltonvale News,* February 3, 1887, April 24, 1890, September 29, 1887.
13. For an informative discussion of nineteenth-century child-rearing practices and philosophy, see Mary P. Ryan, *The Empire of the Mother: American Writing about Domesticity, 1830–1860,* 45–62.
14. The presence of a hired servant in the Tayloe household was documented in the Kansas State Census records of 1885. See also Susan Strasser, *Never Done: A History of American Housework:* "[D]omestic service by no means allowed women of the middle class to become 'managers' of a home. The more common situation was a division of labor" (91).
15. Robert M. Jackson, *Destined for Equality: The Inevitable Rise of Women's Status,* 6; Myres, *Westering Women,* 6–7; Glenda Riley, *The Female Frontier: A Comparative View of Women on the Prairie and the Plains,* 2. See also Fink, *Agrarian Women,* 6–9. Fink writes, "With men tending to the business of the world, women had a place of their own within the home, and white middle-class feminists in the nineteenth century generally supported the separation of male and female spheres. . . . If women could not participate as men's equals in the political world outside the home, they could aspire to equality with their husbands within the conjugal home. The position of mother was also elevated in the construction of this domestic domain" (7). Nevertheless, one should exercise caution in applying the dichotomy of public and domestic spheres. Women like Lizzie, who had functioned as an economic partner to her husband in Missouri, had attained a status within the marriage that gave them

power. Despite the four attributes of "true womanhood" identified by Mary P. Ryan—purity, piety, domesticity, and submissiveness—antebellum women "may have been pure, pious, and domestic, but they were seldom very docile." Ryan, *Empire of the Mother,* 2.

16. Strasser, *Never Done,* 64.

17. The November 20, 1886, issue of the *Miltonvale News* announced the opening of the reading room, sponsored by the editor of the newspaper.

18. WBR II interview, May 20, 1994, Maiden Point Farm, Maryland, 24, NTR Papers, box 14, "Biographical Information—Interview with WBR II, 1994."

19. KF interview, March 22–25, 2002, Scottsdale, Arizona.

20. *Miltonvale News,* October 1, 1886.

21. *Miltonvale: Record, Biography, Reminiscence.* See also Riley, *Female Frontier,* 97–101.

22. *Miltonvale News,* April 18 and October 24, 1889.

23. *Miltonvale News,* June 5, June 26, and July 17, 1891.

24. *Miltonvale News,* May 2, 1889.

25. Undated speech to the Girl Scouts of Rock Springs, Wyoming, NTR Papers, original accession set, box 4, "Speeches by NTR, ca. 1920–1953."

26. Ibid.

27. Monthly school attendance records from the *Miltonvale News* for the years that the Tayloes lived in Miltonvale, which regularly listed Nellie as having perfect attendance, would suggest that any periods of illness were relatively short. Nellie's niece, Jane Tayloe Janus, referred to Nellie's poor childhood health in a telephone interview, April 22, 2002. Nellie's son Bradford referred to Nellie's tendency to become easily exhausted, attributing it to low blood pressure; WBR II interview, May 20, 1994, 11.

28. Barbara Leslie Epstein, *The Politics of Domesticity: Women, Evangelism, and Temperance in Nineteenth-Century America,* 86. Coventry Patmore coined the phrase "angel in the house" in his 1856 book of the same name.

29. Scott, *Southern Lady,* 73. Scott quotes from the diary of Cornelia Phillips.

30. *Miltonvale News,* September 6 and 27, 1888.

31. For the demographics of the WCTU membership, see Ruth Bordin, *Woman and Temperance: The Quest for Power and Liberty, 1873–1900,* 165–70.

32. Jack S. Blocker Jr., *American Temperance Movements: Cycles of Reform,* 84–85.

33. Nancy G. Garner, "For God and Home and Native Land: The Kansas Woman's Christian Temperance Union, 1878–1938," 13. Garner dates the term *biblical feminism* to the 1974 writings of Letha Dawson Scanzoni and Nancy A. Hardesty. In describing the WCTU's impact on Lizzie's generation, Nancy M. Theriot (*Mothers and Daughters in Nineteenth-Century America: The Biosocial Construction of Femininity,* 134–36) writes that "late-nineteenth-century women replaced passive suffering and submission as the base of femininity with active, self-directive but altruistic public service," which "came to be the new standard for middle-class true womanhood." For a brief history of the WCTU, see Epstein, *Politics of Domesticity,* 115–46. Finally, Carolyn De Swarte Gifford has produced a scholarly editing of the journal of Frances Willard, the most important president of the WCTU: *Writing Out My Heart: Selections from the Journal of Frances E. Willard, 1855–96.*

34. Bordin, *Woman and Temperance,* 8–9. See also Foner, *Reconstruction,* 520; and Riley, *Female Frontier,* 178–81.

35. For background on the prohibition movement in Kansas, see Robert W. Richmond, *Kansas: A Land of Contrasts,* 183–88.

36. Garner, "God and Home," 193.

37. *Miltonvale News,* February 15, 1887.

38. *Miltonvale News,* April 7, 1887.

39. *Miltonvale News,* January 20 and August 11, 1887, and May 2, 1889.

40. JWT History.

41. *Miltonvale News,* December 27, 1888.

42. *Miltonvale News,* December 27, 1889.

43. WBR III interview, May 21, 1994, Maiden Point Farm, Maryland, 38, NTR Papers, box 15, "Biographical Information—Interview with WBR III, 1994."

44. JWT History.

45. "Such confidence and trust between brothers and sisters was common in middle-class families of the time," wrote E. Anthony Rotundo. "The authors of advice books held up the sibling tie as a shining example of chaste, Christian love between a male and a female. . . . [B]oys were required to play a protective role in their sisters' lives. . . . The duties of sororal service and fraternal protection created a reciprocal kindness in the relationship of sister and brother, but those same duties also emphasized the difference between the sexes" (*American Manhood: Transformations in Masculinity from the Revolution to the Modern Era,* 93–94).

46. In 1948, Nellie submitted this anecdote in response to a request from Press Features to submit a 250-word article as part of a series on "When I Was a Teenager"; see NTR Papers, original accession set, box 1, "Correspondence, Professional, 1935–1952." In "Notes to be kept about Gov. Ross incidents," handwritten notes by EKW about several anecdotes for speech inclusion, EKW names Sam as the brother who counseled Nellie about her vanity; see EKW Papers, box 10, "Ross, Nellie Tayloe—Information."

47. JWT History. See also Hollibaugh, *Biographical History of Cloud County,* 112–13; Ezra R. Morgan, "Miltonvale: The Western Terminus of the Narrow Gauge, to 1910," 46; and Kenneth S. Davis, *Kansas: A Bicentennial History,* 126–27, 148.

48. Palmer and Chilen, "Miltonvale—1982," 9.

49. Morgan, "Miltonvale," 44.

50. David M. Wrobel, *The End of American Exceptionalism: Frontier Anxiety from the Old West to the New Deal,* 23.

51. *Miltonvale News,* July 31, 1890.

52. Omaha City Directory, 1891.

53. *Miltonvale Record,* November 13, 1924. Following Nellie's election as governor, the newspaper interviewed Nellie's high school principal, A. J. Culp, about her high school years.

54. *Miltonvale News,* January 30, 1891, November 29, 1888, and January 3, 1889.

55. JTJ telephone interview, April 22, 2002.

56. Data on the family occupations and address changes throughout this chapter are from the Omaha city directories for the years 1891–1910.

57. For a detailed discussion of the impact of the closing frontier on American culture and thought, see Wrobel, *End of American Exceptionalism.*

58. Conrad Taeuber and Irene B. Taeuber, *The Changing Population of the United States,* 112–21.

59. The 1890 census lists Omaha's population as 140,000, but most researchers have concluded that Omaha's census returns were padded. See Edgar Z. Palmer, "The Correctness of the 1890 Census of Population for Nebraska Cities."

60. Mark Sullivan Jr., *Our Times: America at the Birth of the Twentieth Century,* 185.

61. Based on official census figures, Omaha actually lost thirty thousand during the 1890s. Recall, however, that the 1890 population total was probably padded.

62. David Bristow, *A Dirty, Wicked Town: Tales of 19th Century Omaha,* xiii.

63. Rudyard Kipling, "Omaha between Trains," quoted in Bristow, *Dirty, Wicked Town,* 228–29; see also Roger Daniels, *Not Like Us: Immigrants and Minorities in America, 1890–1924,* 42–46; Frank Van Nuys, *Americanizing the West: Race, Immigrants, and Citizenship, 1890–1930,* 12–19; and Wrobel, *End of American Exceptionalism,* 18–20 and 49–53.

64. Douglas County, Nebraska, Census of 1900, vol. 14, sheet 4, line 92. Although the practice of boarding had begun to lose its social acceptability in the middle class, it remained a common practice during the first decades of the twentieth century. W. R. and Harriet Davis were themselves boarding a young female teacher. In 1900, almost ninety thousand American households had boarders; a 1910 study estimated that between one-third and one-half of urban Americans were either providing for or were themselves boarders. See John Modell and Tamara K. Hareven, "Urbanization and the Malleable Household: An Examination of Boarding and Lodging in American Families," 467–79; and Thomas J. Schlereth, *Victorian America: Transformations in Everyday Life, 1876–1915,* 104.

65. Nellie referred to the Sidwells in her gossip about the wedding in a letter to her brother George; see NTR to GGTR, September 23–31, 1902, letter courtesy of KTC.

66. Lillian W. Betts, "The Principles of Housekeeping," 131.

67. Omaha City Schools, *Annual Report of the Board of Education,* 14–15. This report documents the existence of the Omaha teacher training program but provides no additional information about its requirements or structure. Nellie's short official biography referred to her completion of a teacher training program in Omaha, but it did not indicate what institution sponsored this program. If she had attended a college, it is likely she would have mentioned it in her biography. A review of the enrollment records from all the Omaha colleges and preparatory schools established that she did not attend any of them. Likewise, she did not matriculate at Plattsburg Normal School in Missouri, where her cousin Minnie graduated and where Nellie could have lived with family. The Tayloes did not have the funds to pay both tuition and housing in some other town. Likewise, she did not graduate from Omaha Central High School, and the Omaha High School of Commerce did not open until 1912. None of the contemporary private business schools offered teacher training. The most likely venue, therefore, was the Omaha city school program, which would have been convenient and low-cost. The Omaha city schools have not retained

records of the graduates from their teacher preparation program, so it is impossible to be sure that it is where Nellie received her training.

68. Rothman, *Woman's Proper Place,* 27. See also Riley, *Female Frontier,* 103–6.

69. Schlereth, *Victorian America,* 244–45.

70. Mary Hurlbut Cordier, *Schoolwomen of the Prairies and Plains: Personal Narratives from Iowa, Kansas, and Nebraska, 1860s–1920s,* 20.

71. Ibid., 27–28.

72. Ibid., 74, 2.

73. Sullivan, *Our Times,* 150.

74. As Joel M. Roitman described, "The school was seen as the prime institution which would be used to solve the social, political, and economic issues of the day as they affected the immigrant." Roitman, "The Progressive Movement: Education and Americanization," 18. See also Agnes Snyder, *Dauntless Women in Childhood Education, 1856–1931,* 174; Robert L. Church and Michael W. Sedlak, *Education in the United States: An Interpretive History,* 269; and Selma Berrol, "Immigrant Children at School, 1880–1940," 42–60.

75. Paula S. Fass, *Outside In: Minorities and the Transformation of American Education,* 13–35; Christina Hardyment, *Dream Babies: Child Care from Locke to Spock,* 147–49; Robert A. Carlson, *The Quest for Conformity: Americanization through Education,* 112–18.

76. Rothman, *Woman's Proper Place,* 99.

77. Lynn Sullivan telephone interview, System Reference Librarian, Omaha Public Library, October 24, 2002. Nellie taught at Castellar in Little Italy, Leavenworth in the Polish neighborhood, and Columbian, which was not in an immigrant area.

78. A 1948 biographical sketch of Nellie that was prepared for official government use during her tenure at the Mint states that "Mrs. Ross was born in St. Joseph, Missouri. She is descended on her mother's side from Samuel Ball Green whose mother, Patty Ball, was a cousin of George Washington." No mention is made of the Andrew County, Miltonvale, or Omaha years. *The National Cyclopedia of American Biography* notes that Nellie "was born at St. Joseph, Mo., daughter of James Wynne [*sic*] and Elizabeth Blair (Green) Tayloe, of Virginian ancestry. She was educated in public and private schools, specializing in literature." Again, there is no mention of Miltonvale or Omaha. The *American National Biography* observes that Nellie "was the daughter of James Wynns Tayloe, a merchant and farmer, and Elizabeth Blair Green. She attended public schools and was graduated from a two-year kindergarten teacher program in Omaha, Nebraska." An Associated Press biography, issued February 15, 1935, stated that Nellie "was of Virginia and Tennessee stock and spent her girlhood in the latter state. After education at private schools in Missouri, she was married September 11, 1902, and went immediately to Cheyenne." None of the four biographies mentions Nellie's teaching experience.

79. JTJ telephone interview, May 29, 2002.

80. It cannot be determined whether Nellie ever discussed Bailey with her sons, but her son Bradford did not mention him in existing interview transcripts. None of Bradford's three sons were aware of Bailey's existence.

81. Nellie told her son Bradford and all his sons about this early European trip,

and she always told them that her brothers had surprised her with the gift of the ticket. The family believed that George and Alfred had been the brothers who funded her trip; Bailey had died in 1899, and Nellie's descendants were unaware of his existence. Yet Alfred was still a child with no income when Nellie took her first European trip. It is far more likely that Bailey and George were her benefactors. It was not possible to identify exactly when Nellie made this trip; her grandson Robert believes that the trip occurred in 1893; however, Nellie would have been only sixteen that year, and it is difficult to imagine that a southern, Victorian family would have allowed a girl to travel to Europe unaccompanied at that age. Other than Duff and his wife, no other family members had the money to travel to Europe during the 1890s. Nellie was probably completing her teacher training in 1894, and she is listed in the Omaha City Directory for 1895 as a teacher. The only year in which she was unaccounted for is 1896. The fact that Nellie mentions wearing trains on her skirts during the trip also suggests a travel date of 1896 or later; according to Christina Walkley and Vanda Foster, *Crinolines and Crimping Irons: Victorian Clothes, How They Were Cleaned and Cared For,* trains on women's skirts reappeared around 1897.

82. Mary Suzanne Schriber, ed., *Telling Travels: Selected Writings by Nineteenth-Century American Women Abroad,* xii–xv.

83. Ibid., xvii. Schriber's quote is from Ida Tarbell, who was to become an important muckraking journalist.

84. Nellie's name could not be found on inbound passenger lists for any of the eastern or Gulf Coast ports, so it is not possible to reconstruct her cross-country journey from Omaha.

85. Louisa Stephens, *Golden Adventure: A Diary of Long Ago,* 51. Nellie was an indefatigable letter writer her entire life; her letters became her journal. Unfortunately, the family did not begin to save her correspondence until she married and moved to Cheyenne.

86. RTR telephone interview, October 13, 2002.

87. NTR Papers, original accession set, box 3, "Speeches by Nellie Tayloe Ross, ca. 1920–1953, #1."

88. Lucy Seaman Bainbridge, *Round the World Letters.*

THREE ~ Wife and Mother

1. Undated NTR narrative written ca. Coolidge inauguration, NTR Papers, original accession set, box 1, "Correspondence, 1922–1953."

2. Luzanne Wynns Tayloe to NTR, December 3, 1972, NTR Papers, box 13, "Family History, 1975–1986." In this letter, Luzanne answers questions from an earlier letter from NTR, in which NTR is reconfirming her memories of Paris.

3. NTR to WBR III, June 25, 1973, NTR Papers, box 13, "Family History, 1912–1990."

4. Undated NTR narrative written ca. Coolidge inauguration, NTR Papers, original accession set, box 1, "Correspondence, 1922–1953."

5. NTR, "The Governor Lady," pt. 1, 118.

6. Sherman Dorn, *A Brief History of Peabody College,* 9.

7. June 14, 2002 e-mail, Archives@LIBRARY.Vanderbilt.edu, Re: William Bradford Ross: "I have searched everywhere I can think of in our University of Nashville Collection but have not been able to find any mention of William Bradford Ross in the 1890's." See also *Alumni Directory of Peabody College, 1877–1909.*

8. WBR II to WBR III, December 15, 1986, NTR Papers, box 13, "Family History, 1912–1990": "Father had attended a small law school in Tennessee (Cumberland) working to save money for periods in between attending school so that he could finance his education." William is not listed as a Cumberland student in 1899 or in 1900, and he moved to Wyoming in 1901. However, the Cumberland student listing did not include summer and "irregular" students. The Cumberland summer school, which was introduced in 1896, "was avowedly a lecture course . . . over a period of eight weeks. [It] was not designed to take the place of any part of the regular course. . . . There was no credit or advancement placement derived from the course." David J. Langum and Howard P. Walthall, *From Maverick to Mainstream: Cumberland School of Law, 1847–1997,* 73–74, 110–11.

9. NTR to WBR III, June 25, 1973, NTR Papers, box 13, "Family History, 1912–1990."

10. "Governor Dies This Morning," *Laramie Republican-Boomerang,* undated clipping, Grace Raymond Hebard Papers, box 44, folder 5.

11. Small-town newspapers of this period invariably included the comings and goings of local residents and their visitors. No reference to visits between William and Nellie appeared in the Stewart County weekly paper nor in the *Cheyenne Daily Leader* during the years 1900 to 1902. The September 11, 1902, notice of the Omaha wedding in the *Cheyenne Daily Leader* stated that Nellie "comes from one of the best families of that place." Since this information would have come from William, it suggests that William based his knowledge of Nellie's Omaha social status on her written inferences rather than on firsthand observation of the Tayloe family's modest living circumstances.

12. WBR II interview, May 20, 1994, Maiden Point Farm, Maryland, 1, NTR Papers, box 14, "Biographical Information—Interview with WBR II, 1994."

13. According to a story told by his son George, William went into practice with a Judge Clark. Based on advertisements in the *Cheyenne Daily Leader,* however, it is clear that William practiced alone until around June 30, 1902, when he established a short-lived partnership with Clyde M. Watts. Nellie refers to Mr. Watts in her first letter home to her brother George after arriving in Cheyenne.

14. Richard Hofstadter, *The Age of Reform: From Bryan to F.D.R.,* 5.

15. Duane A. Smith, *Rocky Mountain West: Colorado, Wyoming, and Montana, 1859–1915,* 196. Robert C. McMath Jr., in *American Populism: A Social History, 1877–1898,* noted, "If the Populist crusade could not itself survive the tumultuous 1890s, what was its legacy? Early students of the People's Party . . . saw a continuity between populism and the two great currents of twentieth-century liberalism—progressivism and the New Deal. Populism was, in this telling of the story, the seedbed of liberal reform"

(209). See also Sean Dennis Cashman, *America in the Age of the Titans: The Progressive Era and World War I,* 48; Robert W. Cherny, *Populism, Progressivism, and the Transformation of Nebraska Politics, 1885–1915;* Michael E. McGerr, *A Fierce Discontent: The Rise and Fall of the Progressive Movement in America, 1870–1920;* Thomas C. Reeves, *Twentieth-Century America: A Brief History,* 21–29; and Alun Munslow, "The Progressive Era, 1900–1919," 14–45.

16. *Cheyenne Daily Leader,* August 9, 1902.

17. Undated news clipping from an unknown Omaha newspaper, NTR Papers, box 1, "Family and Personal, 1902–1930."

18. *Cheyenne Daily Leader,* September 11, 1902.

19. Nellie asked, "How late did [the wedding guests] stay at the house the other night after we went to the train?" NTR to GGT, September 23–31, 1902, letter courtesy of KTC. The arrival time for train no. 5 was listed in the *Cheyenne Daily Leader.*

20. NTR to GGT, September 23–31, 1902, letter courtesy of KTC.

21. Ibid.

22. Ibid.

23. Ibid.

24. NTR, "Governor Lady," pt. 1, 31.

25. NTR to GGT, September 23–31, 1902, letter courtesy of KTC.

26. Elizabeth Bowles Warbasse, *The Changing Legal Rights of Married Women, 1860–1861;* Joan Hoff, *Law, Gender, and Injustice: A Legal History of U.S. Women,* 80–90, 128–33; Jackson, *Destined for Equality,* 5–30; Bordin, *Woman and Temperance,* 7; T. A. Larson, *Wyoming: A Bicentennial History,* 76–92, 104.

27. NTR to NKT, September 4, 1908, letter courtesy of KTC; NTR, "Governor Lady," pt. 1, 118.

28. NTR, "Governor Lady," pt. 1, 118.

29. NTR to GGT, September 22, 1903, NTR Papers, box 1, "Family and Personal, 1902–1930"; NTR, "Governor Lady," pt. 1, 118.

30. NTR to NKT, December 22, 1905, letter courtesy of KTC; *Cheyenne Daily Leader,* August 19, 1905.

31. *Wyoming Tribune,* February 19, 1906.

32. NTR to WBR III, June 25, 1973, NTR Papers, box 13, "Family History, 1912–1990."

33. NTR, "The House Called Home," NTR Papers, original accession set, box 3, "Newspapers, Newspaper and Magazine Clippings, 1926–53"; WBR II interview, May 20, 1994, Maiden Point Farm, Maryland, 2, NTR Papers, box 14, "Biographical Information—Interview with WBR II," 1994.

34. NTR, "Governor Lady," pt. 1, 118.

35. Marti Bressler interview, July 19, 2001, Cheyenne, Wyoming. The Bresslers owned the Ross home at the time of the interview. Nellie's son Bradford told Marti this anecdote during one of his visits to Cheyenne.

36. NTR to WBR III, June 25, 1973, NTR Papers, box 13, "Family History, 1912–1990."

37. NTR to WBR II, June 25, 1973, NTR Papers, box 13, "Family History, 1912–1990."

38. WBR I to NTR, December 18, 1919, NTR Papers, box 1, "Family and Personal, 1902–1930."

39. NTR, "Governor Lady," pt. 1, 31.

40. WBR I to NTR, n.d., NTR Papers, box 1, "Family and Personal, 1902–1930."

41. NTR to WBR II, June 25, 1973, NTR Papers, box 13, "Family History, 1912–1990."

42. NTR, "Governor Lady," pt. 1, 122. Nellie's concern about the impact of William's political career on their finances continued after his election as governor, when she wrote to her sister-in-law, "[W]hile people frequently predict Will's running for the Senate, not for anything in the world would I have him do it. Even if he were elected we couldn't possibly sustain the position—it's too hard in this one." NTR to NKT, August 28, 1923, letter courtesy of KTC. The family's money problems were not merely unfounded worries; on at least two occasions, Nellie had to respond to her son George's requests for funds with explanations that there simply was no money in the bank and that she and William were struggling under a burden of debt; see NTR to GTR, September 4, 1923, and NTR to GTR, September 12, 1923, both in NTR Papers, box 1, folder 1.

43. Undated NTR narrative written ca. Coolidge inauguration, NTR Papers, original accession set, box 1, "Correspondence, 1922–1953."

44. Ernest Rutherford Groves and William Fielding Ogburn, *American Marriage and Family Relationships,* 31–33. See also Robert S. Lynd and Helen Merrell Lynd, *Middletown: A Study in Modern American Culture,* 114–18; and Sullivan, *Our Times,* 375–80.

45. Steven Mintz and Susan Kellogg, *Domestic Revolutions: A Social History of American Family Life,* 113–17.

46. Groves and Ogburn, *American Marriage,* 37. For a discussion of the nineteenth-century culture of manliness that shaped the development of William's generation, see Rotundo, *American Manhood.* Tom Pendergast, in *Creating the Modern Man: American Magazines and Consumer Culture, 1900–1950,* identifies two "major constellations" of masculine imagery—Victorian masculinity and modern masculinity. William was reared in the Victorian world but lived in the modern one. Pendergast focuses on the role of the media and the growing consumer economy in shaping the twentieth-century male. See also Paula S. Fass, *The Damned and the Beautiful: American Youth in the 1920's,* 71–78.

47. NTR to NKT, September 4, 1908, letter courtesy of KTC.

48. Margaret Deland, "The Change in the Feminine Ideal," 291–93.

49. Ibid., 291.

50. Women's clubs records, Wyoming State Archives.

51. Teva J. Scheer, "The 'Praxis' Side of the Equation: Club Women and American Public Administration," 520–21.

52. Edward Bok, "My Quarrel with Women's Clubs," 5; J. Cardinal Gibbons, "The Restless Woman," 6; Grover Cleveland, "Woman's Mission and Woman's Clubs," 4. See also Karen J. Blair, *The Clubwoman as Feminist: True Womanhood Redefined, 1868–1914.* In the preface to *Clubwoman as Feminist,* Annette K. Baxter wrote, "Men had barely sanctioned escape from the kitchen and nursery for the more compelling

reasons of missionary work, educational endeavors, and health care. How could they be expected to tolerate such desertion for a closer familiarity with the poetry of Robert Browning?" xi–xii.

53. NTR, "Governor Lady," pt. 1, 120.

54. "William B. Ross," *Wyoming Tribune,* November 18, 1907; "Gov. William B. Ross: State's First Citizen," *Casper Daily Tribune,* February 11, 1923; "Presbyterian Brotherhood Organized in Cheyenne," *Cheyenne Daily Leader,* November 17, 1906; St. Mark's Episcopal Church Records, Record H-24, Wyoming State Archives, Cheyenne, Wyoming.

55. "Gov. William B. Ross: State's First Citizen," *Casper Daily Tribune,* February 11, 1923.

56. "Ross-Stoll Contest," *Wyoming Tribune,* November 10, 1904.

57. "A Republican Speaks Out," *Cheyenne Daily Leader,* October 23, 1906; NTR, "Governor Lady," pt. 1, 122.

58. NTR, "Governor Lady," pt. 1, 122.

59. NTR to NKT, August 28, 1923, NTR Papers, box 1, "Miscellaneous Early, 1905–1938."

60. JAR to WBR I, March 19, 1923, NTR Papers, box 1, "To Governor William Bradford Ross, 1923–1925."

61. WBR I to GTR, July 7, 1923, NTR Papers, box 1, "Family and Personal, 1902–1930."

62. NTR to GGT, n.d., NTR Papers, box 1, "Family and Personal, 1902–1930."

63. Mary Cable, *The Little Darlings: A History of Child Rearing in America,* 173–76; Harvey J. Graff, *Conflicting Paths: Growing Up in America,* 302–27; Joseph M. Hawes, *Children between the Wars: American Childhood, 1920–1940;* Mintz and Kellogg, *Domestic Revolutions,* 118–19; Sullivan, *Our Times,* 375–76; Lynd and Lynd, *Middletown,* 123–49.

64. Lynd and Lynd, *Middletown,* 143.

65. "Now Facing the Common Enemy," *Wyoming State Tribune,* September 12, 1922.

66. Teapot Dome is a rock formation near Casper, Wyoming. It sits atop a tract of public land containing oil reserves that were intended for future use by the navy. Instead, shortly after he was appointed secretary of the Interior by President Harding, former senator Albert B. Fall convinced the secretary of the navy to allow the reserves to be leased secretly to private companies. A series of investigations and congressional hearings concluded that Fall had accepted gifts and loans from the oil companies in exchange for the leases. He eventually went to prison, and several other Harding administration officials were tainted by the scandal. The affair was a primary reason that the Harding administration acquired a reputation for corruption and malfeasance. For a discussion of the Wyoming repercussions of Teapot Dome, see Mike Mackey, *Black Gold: Patterns in the Development of Wyoming's Oil Industry,* 65–83; and Walter L. Samson Jr., "The Political Career of Senator Francis E. Warren, 1920–1929," 50–56. See also J. Leonard Bates, *The Origins of Teapot Dome: Progressives, Parties, and Petroleum, 1909–1921.*

67. NTR, "Governor Lady," pt. 1, 122.

68. William B. Ross campaign literature, NTR Papers, box 10, "WBR Political, 1907–1925"; "Ledger Won't Take Sides," *Wyoming State Ledger,* August 3, 1922.

69. "Ross Election Big Surprise," n.d., unidentified newspaper, NTR Papers, accession no. 948-97-10-07, box 7, folder 1.

70. William B. Ross inaugural address, NTR Papers, original accession set, box 3, "Speeches by NTR, 1920–53, #1."

71. "Ross Starts Well," *Douglas Budget,* January 5, 1922, NTR Papers, box 11, "WBR Political, 1924."

72. The proposed amendment was placed before Wyoming voters in November 1924. Although 39,109 voters voted affirmatively and 27,795 voted against, the amendment failed to garner a simple majority of the total number of voters—84,822. Despite an additional attempt to pass a severance tax in 1940, the state's voters waited until 1969 to approve a 1 percent severance tax.

73. Carter, *Another Part of the Twenties,* 105.

74. NTR to NKT, August 29, 1923, NTR Papers, box 1, "Family and Personal, 1902–1930."

75. Ibid.

76. NTR to GGT, September 18, 1923, NTR Papers, box 1, "George Ross, 1923."

77. Nellie wrote George in 1931 that she knew Alfred had come up with the idea of allowing her to purchase the stock after Nellie confided in him her distress about William's indebtedness. NTR to GGT, December 3, 1931, letter courtesy of KTC.

78. NTR to GGT, February 23, 1924, NTR Papers, box 1, "Miscellaneous Early, 1905–1938."

79. Douglas R. Craig, *After Wilson: The Struggle for the Democratic Party, 1920–1934,* 52–53.

80. The October 2, 1924, obituary from the *Wyoming State Tribune* stated that William's operation took place on Tuesday, but this date contradicted both a *Tribune* article dated September 29, 1924, and an unattributed article from the Grace Raymond Hebard Papers, box 44, folder 5: "Tax Talk Here Was Governor's Last Address."

81. NTR Papers, original accession set, box 6, "Estate Papers & Death Certificate of WBR I."

FOUR ~ Governor

1. GGT to NKT, October 6, 1924, letter courtesy of KTC.

2. This assessment is based on a discussion with Phil Roberts, professor of history, University of Wyoming, July 22, 2003. It is bolstered by a study of the recruitment of women candidates by the major parties, which concluded that women tend to be tapped when there are no strong male candidates, so the party risks nothing in appearing to be inclusive. "It would have made little difference to the final outcome if some voters were prejudiced against women, the candidate was destined to lose anyway. And party leaders might have felt that voters' image of women as uncorrupted,

honest, and trustworthy would work to the advantage of the party and lead to a better showing than with a male candidate." Susan J. Carroll, *Women as Candidates in American Politics,* 28.

3. NTR, "The Governor Lady," pt. 2, 37.

4. GGT to NKT, October 12, 1924, letter courtesy of KTC.

5. "Wyoming Officers in Quandary on How to Select Governor to Serve Out W. B. Ross' Term," *Denver Post,* October 7, 1924. The article listed the Wyoming governor's salary as five hundred dollars per month.

6. GGT to NKT, October 8, 1924, letter courtesy of KTC.

7. NTR, "Governor Lady," pt. 2, 206: "It is difficult to define the conscious and unconscious reasons that determined my decision in the final crucial moment. As nearly as I can understand it, I was influenced by the desire to carry on my husband's unfinished work, and to find for myself a compelling interest that would absorb me completely. Moreover, I believed that I better than any one else, understood [William's] ideals and program."

8. GGT to NKT, October 8, 1924, letter courtesy of KTC.

9. Ibid.

10. NTR, "Governor Lady," pt. 2, 37.

11. *Wyoming State Tribune,* October 11, 1924.

12. NTR to NKT, October 17, 1924, letter courtesy of KTC.

13. "Wyoming's Woman Governor Accepts Her Election as a Tribute to Her Dead Husband," *Kansas City Star,* November 9, 1924.

14. "Senator Kendrick Urges Election of Mrs. Ross," a statement to the voters of Wyoming, October 18, 1924, NTR Papers, box 1, "Governorship for Nellie Tayloe Ross, 1924."

15. NTR, "Governor Lady," pt. 2, 207.

16. "Wyoming's Woman Governor Accepts Her Election as a Tribute to Her Dead Husband," *Kansas City Star,* November 9, 1924.

17. NTR, "Governor Lady," pt. 2, 207.

18. "An Archive of Memorable Quotes by Women," http://www.wendy.com/women/quotations.html#f, accessed June 22, 2005.

19. "Mrs. Ferguson Wins 2 to 1 in Texas Race," *New York Times,* November 5, 1924.

20. Duncan Aikman, "Politics and Ma Ferguson in Texas"; "Texas Woman Governor-Elect Just 'Plain Folks' Who Halted Campaign to Save Fine Peaches," *Denver Post,* November 5, 1924; "State Capitol: Petticoat Junction?" *Tuscaloosa News,* May 2, 1956; "Ferguson, Miriam Amanda Wallace," *Handbook of Texas Online,* http://www.tsha.utexas.edu/handbook/online/articles/FF/ffe6.html, accessed June 22, 2005.

21. "Nellie T. Ross Sends Message to Neighbors," *Wyoming State Tribune,* November 3, 1924.

22. In deference for Nellie's period of mourning, Wyoming officials offered to let her stay in the Executive Mansion, irrespective of the election results, through December. She planned to move into the Cheyenne Apartments, not to return to the Ross home, if she were defeated.

23. Mabel E. Brown, "Nellie Tayloe Ross," 1.

24. "Wyoming Elects One of the Two First Women Governors in the United States," *Denver Post,* November 5, 1924.

25. "Wyoming's Woman Governor Accepts Her Election as a Tribute to Her Dead Husband," *Kansas City Star,* November 9, 1924.

26. NTR to GGT and ADT, November 5, 1924, telegram courtesy of KTC.

27. Although Nellie and Miriam Ferguson were elected the same day, Nellie earned the distinction of being the first woman governor because she was sworn in several days before Ferguson.

28. "'Governess' Would Never Do!" *New York Times,* November 7, 1924. All other newspaper quotes from "Woman's 'Bigger Dent in Politics,'" 17.

29. "Women in Government," *Wyoming State Tribune,* November 11, 1924. Nellie joined Katherine A. Morton, longtime state superintendent of public instruction, on the ex-officio boards.

30. Huie was appointed for a four-year term by William Ross on February 1, 1923; he resigned November 28, 1924, shortly after Nellie was elected, to go into banking.

31. NTR, November 6, 1924, November 7, 1924, and November 7, 1924, three telegrams courtesy of KTC.

32. Byron S. Huie to NTR, November 7, 1924, NTR Papers, original accession set, box 1, "Correspondence—Personal, 1922–1957."

33. NTR, "Governor Lady," pt. 2, 211.

34. White, *"Your Misfortune,"* 464.

35. T. A. Larson, *History of Wyoming,* 412.

36. Henry A. Wallace, *The American Choice,* 70–71, cited in Lloyd P. Jorgenson, "Agricultural Expansion into the Semiarid Lands of the West North Central States during the First World War," 30.

37. Larson, *History of Wyoming,* 414–15, 417. Larson summarizes filing data from the annual reports of the secretary of the Interior.

38. Milton L. Woods, *Sometimes the Books Froze: Wyoming's Economy and Its Banks,* 103.

39. Data extracted from Norris E. Hartwell, state bank examiner, and published in Larson, *History of Wyoming,* 413.

40. Woods, *Sometimes the Books Froze,* 102–5.

41. Robert Harold Brown, *Wyoming: A Geography,* 189; Mackey, *Black Gold,* iv, 54–59; Larson, *Wyoming: A Bicentennial History,* 154–56; and Larson, *History of Wyoming,* 422–23.

42. A. Dudley Gardner, *Forgotten Frontier: A History of Wyoming Coal Mining,* 133–59; White, *"Your Misfortune,"* 280–81; and Smith, *Rocky Mountain West,* 172–73.

43. NTR, "Governor Lady," pt. 2, 211.

44. "Nellie Tayloe Ross Becomes Wyoming's Governor at Noon Monday with Simple Ceremony," *Wyoming State Tribune,* January 5, 1925.

45. NTR, "Governor Lady," pt. 2, 211.

46. Notes from Grace Hebard Papers, quoted in Barbara Jean Aslakson, "Nellie Tayloe Ross: First Woman Governor."

47. In her account of the inauguration in the September 1927 issue of *Good*

Housekeeping, Nellie wrote of her vivid memory of signing the oath of office at William's desk following the swearing-in ceremony. A contemporary account, which states that she signed the oath before the public swearing-in, contradicts her account of events; see "Mrs. Ross Inaugurated Governor of Wyoming," *Gillette News,* January 7, 1925. However, it seems more likely that she would have been sworn in before, not after, signing the oath.

48. Larry Sabato, *Goodbye to Good-Time Charlie: The American Governorship Transformed,* 3; William H. Young, "The Development of the Governorship."

49. See Gregg Cawley et al., *The Equality State: Government and Politics in Wyoming,* 20: "The Wyoming Constitution is largely a stitching together of borrowings from other states."

50. Leslie Lipson, *The American Governor from Figurehead to Leader,* 41.

51. John C. Buechner, *State Government in the Twentieth Century,* 117.

52. For an overall survey of state practices concerning the position of governor, see Joseph E. Kallenbach and Jessamine S. Kallenbach, *American State Governors, 1776–1976,* 1:1–19.

53. "New Governor Executes Her First Routine," *Wyoming State Tribune,* January 6, 1925.

54. "Governor Names Roy Seney Budget Officer of Wyoming," *Wyoming Eagle,* August 30, 1925; NTR, "The Governor Lady," pt. 3, 184–85.

55. Cawley et al., *Equality State,* 78. See also Maggie Murdock, "Responding to Crises: Change in Wyoming's State Government," 16–22.

56. NTR, "Governor Lady," pt. 2, 212.

57. Neal R. Peirce, *The Mountain States of America: People, Politics, and Power in the Eight Rocky Mountain States,* 76–81.

58. Richard D. Lamm and Michael McCarthy, *The Angry West: A Vulnerable Land and Its Future,* 55–56.

59. "Wyoming's 18th Legislature Convenes Tuesday Noon with Organization Details Ahead," *Wyoming State Tribune,* January 12, 1925.

60. NTR, speech delivered before the Cheyenne Woman's Club, February 3, 1926, NTR Papers, original accession set, box 3, "Speeches by Nellie Tayloe Ross, 1920–1953, #3."

61. "Hall of Representatives at Capitol Packed When Woman Governor Delivers Message," *Wyoming State Tribune,* January 15, 1925.

62. "Message of Governor Nellie Tayloe Ross to the Eighteenth Wyoming Legislature," *Wyoming State Tribune,* January 15, 1925.

63. Ibid.

64. "Wyoming Senators Refuse to Pass Child Labor Amendment; Put Aside Governor's Advice," *Wyoming State Tribune,* January 20, 1925.

65. NTR, "Governor Lady," pt. 3, 188.

66. NTR, "Governor Lady," pt. 2, 217, 214–15.

67. Coleman B. Ransone Jr., *The American Governorship,* 158; see also Sabato, *Goodbye to Good-Time Charlie,* 76–78. Veto transmission memoranda, NTR to Secretary of State Lucas, February 28, 1925, NTR Papers, box 1, "Governorship for

Nellie Tayloe Ross, 1924"; see also two undated, unattributed news clippings from the Grace Raymond Hebard Papers, box 43, folder 22: "Gubernatorial Knife Applied to Two Bills" and "Governor Vetoes Seven Bills Passed by Eighteenth Session." Data on Wyoming bills passed and vetoed are from the indexes and appendixes to the legislative journals. The number of bills made law were 116 for the Seventeenth Legislature, 166 for the Eighteenth, and 135 for the Nineteenth. The indexes did not clearly distinguish between bills that were vetoed and those that met without gubernatorial approval; Nellie's vetoes, for example, were listed as not meeting gubernatorial approval. Data on general gubernatorial usage of the veto are from Ransone, *American Governorship,* 140. Ransone listed the ratio of bills vetoed to bills passed for the years 1945 and 1975 as about 5 percent for both years.

68. "Ross Vetoes Engineer Act," *Wyoming State Tribune,* February 19, 1925.

69. NTR to Secretary of State Frank E. Lucas, February 28, 1925, NTR Papers, box 1, "Governorship for Nellie Tayloe Ross, 1924."

70. NTR, "Governor Lady," pt. 2, 215.

71. "The Eighteenth Session," *Casper Daily Tribune,* February 27, 1925, cited from typewritten copy of editorial found in the Grace Raymond Hebard Papers, box 43, folder 20; "The Eighteenth Session," *Wyoming State Tribune,* February 24, 1925.

72. Anonymous governor's response, cited in National Governors' Association, *Governing the American States: A Handbook for New Governors,* 85.

FIVE ~ Wyoming Statesman

1. Thomas R. Dye, "State Legislative Politics," 196.

2. Eula W. Kendrick to NTR, January 18, 1925, NTR Papers, accession no. 948-97-10-07, box 1, "Correspondence, Professional, 1922–1926." For a discussion of the establishment and operation of the Woman's Democratic clubs, see Chapter 8.

3. NTR to NKT, February 8, 1925, NTR Papers, accession no. 10526-97-10-07, box 1, folder 1. See also Susan Almon to NKT, February 6, 1925, courtesy of KTC: "The Democratic Woman's Club Banquet will be postponed until 7th of March if she may go. That will give plenty of time to finish here & also prepare an address."

4. "Ross Given Hand at Inaugural Festival," a *Wyoming State Tribune* recount of the *Washington Post* article, NTR Papers, accession no. 10526-97-10-07, box 7, folder 3.

5. "Democrats Honor Woman Governor," *Washington Star,* undated clipping, NTR Papers, accession no. 10526-97-10-07, box 7, folder 3; Florence J. Harriman to NTR, April 18, 1925, NTR Papers, accession no. 10526-97-10-07, box 1, folder 1.

6. NTR, Coolidge inauguration reminiscence, NTR Papers, accession no. 948-97-10-07, box 1, "Correspondence, Professional, 1922–1926."

7. Ibid.

8. NTR, "Governor Lady," pt. 3, 72.

9. For a detailed explanation of her activities on these various boards, see the speech that Nellie delivered before the Cheyenne Woman's Club, February 3, 1926,

NTR Papers, accession no. 948-97-10-07, "Speeches by Nellie Tayloe Ross, 1920–1953, #3." Nellie discussed her concern about missing the board meetings in a letter to Nelle Tayloe, February 15, 1925, NTR Papers, accession no. 10526-97-10-07, box 1, folder 1.

10. Ross clipping file, Bureau of the Mint.

11. Joyce Clark to NTR, March 5, 1925, NTR Papers, accession no. 10526-97-10-07, box 1, folder 7.

12. Ruth Harrington to JAR, April 28, 1925, NTR Papers, accession no. 10526- 97-10-07, box 1, folder 1.

13. NTR speech for the Luncheon for Famous Women, April 23, 1925, NTR Papers, accession no. 948-97-10-07, box 3, "Speeches by NTR, 1920–1953, #3."

14. NTR to NKT, July 5, 1925, NTR Papers, accession no. 10526-97-10-07, box 1, folder 1.

15. Joseph P. Harris, "The Governors' Conference: Retrospect and Prospect."

16. Sabato, *Goodbye to Good-Time Charlie,* 171.

17. *Lewiston (Maine) Daily Sun* quoted in "Governor Nellie Ross Wins High Honor at Executive Meet," *Wyoming Eagle,* July 19, 1925; *New York World* quoted in Cecilia Hennel Hendricks, "When a Woman Governor Campaigns," 88. Hosting governor Ralph Owen Brewster's correspondence with Nellie concerning the conference consisted of polite exchanges concerning her travel arrangements and his invitation that she address the conference. There were no written exchanges between Governor Brewster and the other governors concerning Nellie's performance and participation.

18. Quoted in Kristi Anderson, *After Suffrage: Women in Partisan and Electoral Politics before the New Deal,* 134. See also Sophonisba P. Breckinridge, *Women in the Twentieth Century: A Study of Their Political, Social, and Economic Activities,* 330–32.

19. Elisabeth I. Perry, *Belle Moskowitz: Feminine Politics and the Exercise of Power,* 153; Susan Ware, *Partner and I: Molly Dewson, Feminism, and New Deal Politics,* 224; George Martin, *Madam Secretary, Frances Perkins,* 146.

20. Margaretta Newell, "Must Women Fight in Politics?" cited in Anderson, *After Suffrage,* 39.

21. Emily Newell Blair, "Men in Politics as a Woman Sees Them," cited in Anderson, *After Suffrage,* 38.

22. Ted Carlton Harris, "Jeannette Rankin: Suffragist, First Woman Elected to Congress, and Pacifist," 107, 117.

23. "Mrs. Ross Inaugurated Governor of Wyoming," *Gillette News,* January 5, 1925; "A Sure Enough Woman Governor," *Sunday Oregonian,* January 17, 1926; *New York Times* cited in Anderson, *After Suffrage,* 127.

24. Anderson, *After Suffrage,* 133.

25. Emily Newell Blair, *Bridging Two Eras: The Autobiography of Emily Newell Blair,* 214.

26. Undated clipping from Grace Raymond Hebard Papers, box 43, folder 5; "An Apology for Mrs. Ross," *Wyoming Eagle,* July 5, 1925.

27. Aslakson, "Nellie Tayloe Ross," 55.

28. NTR, "Governor Lady," pt. 3, 73, 180.

29. Ibid., 180.

30. The fourth state is New Mexico, whose governor was unable to attend the meeting. He subsequently added his signature to the document prepared at the Denver meeting.

31. The *Sunday Oregonian,* January 17, 1926, did a major spread on the water rights dispute, in which the paper declared that "Nellie is virtually the leader of the upper-basin states in the water-rights controversy." However, the *Wyoming Eagle,* which never missed an opportunity to promote Nellie, did not accord her a leadership role in its stories of September 6 and October 18, 1925. In her study of Nellie's administration, Barbara Aslakson concluded, "Whether Mrs. Ross was the leader of the upper basin states and whether or not she was solely responsible for the favorable decision of the Commission is doubtful." Aslakson, "Nellie Tayloe Ross," 49.

32. NTR to GGT, August 30, 1925, NTR Papers, accession no. 10526-97-10-07, box 1, folder 10.

33. NTR, "Governor Lady," pt. 3, 180.

34. Undated condolence letter from the Superintendent of Yellowstone Park, NTR Papers, accession no. 948-97-10-07, box 1, "Sympathy and Get Well Correspondence, 1924." The announcement of George's selection appeared in the *Denver Post,* December 25, 1925.

35. JAR to NTR, November 9, 1924, box 1, "Correspondence, 1924. Get Well & Sympathy (Death of W. B. Ross)"; JAR to NTR, November 29, 1924, box 1, "Sympathy and Get Well Correspondence, 1924," NTR Papers, accession no. 948-97- 10-07.

36. JAR to GGT, February 28, 1925, and NTR to JAR, April 19, 1925, both in NTR Papers, accession no. 10526-97-10-07, box 1, folder 1.

37. NTR to NKT, June 11, 1926, letter courtesy of KTC.

38. "Frank Emerson Endorsed by Republicans as Party Candidate for Governor," *Wyoming Eagle,* June 13, 1926.

39. "Contest of Auditor's Job Only Race Slated in Democratic Primary," *Wyoming Eagle,* July 16, 1926.

40. NTR, "To the Voters of Wyoming," NTR Papers, accession no. 948-97-10-07, box 3, "Speeches by NTR, ca. 1920–1953, #2." Her platform was also published in several Wyoming newspapers during the 1926 campaign.

41. *Wyoming State Tribune,* September 20–21, 1926, cited in Aslakson, "Nellie Tayloe Ross," 60.

42. Frank C. Emerson Papers, box 2, folder 7.

43. "Taliaferro Says Wyoming Women Are Facing Crisis," unattributed article, Grace Raymond Hebard Papers, box 44, folder 1; Therese A. Jenkins, "An Open Answer," Grace Raymond Hebard Papers, box 44, folder 2; Mrs. H. C. Chappell, October 22, 1926 letter to *Wyoming State Tribune* cited in Aslakson, "Nellie Tayloe Ross," 66.

44. "'Trail of Lies' is 'Nailed to Cross' by Charles Winter in Stirring Address Friday," *Wyoming State Tribune,* October 24, 1926; NTR, "Governor Lady," pt. 3, 185.

45. Letter from Phil Roberts, associate professor of history at the University of Wyoming, to Teva Scheer, July 25, 2003. There is also a useful analysis of Wyoming voting patterns in John B. Richard, *Government and Politics of Wyoming,* 19–27.

46. Hendricks, "Woman Governor."

47. NTR to GGT and ADT, October 26, 1926, letter courtesy of KTC.

48. "False Charges against Governor Illustrative of Desperate Tactics Opponents Now Employ," *Wyoming Eagle,* October 29, 1926; NTR to GGT and ADT, October 26, 1926, letter courtesy of KTC.

49. Aslakson, "Nellie Tayloe Ross," 69.

50. Phil Roberts to Teva Scheer, July 25, 2003.

51. *Wyoming Eagle* editorial, November 19, 1926. See also Tracy S. McCracken to ADT, GGT, and SGT, November 11, 1926, NTR Papers, accession no. 948-97-10-07, box 1, "Correspondence, Professional, 1924–26."

52. NTR to GGT and ADT, November 5, 1926, letter courtesy of KTC.

53. *Wyoming Eagle* editorial, November 5, 1926.

54. Ruth Harrington Loomis, interview with David Cookson, University of Wyoming, May 22, 1979, Cheyenne, Wyoming, audiotape courtesy of Ruth's daughter, Ann Loomis Jessee. When asked, "What do you feel the accomplishments were of Nellie Tayloe Ross as governor?" Ruth answered, "I really can't answer that question, except to [say,] I'm sure she did a good job, but if there were goals, then I've forgotten. . . . I don't think I've heard that asked about a great many governors, and I've never heard a very satisfactory reply. If you don't get the state in financial trouble and you go along, that's [chuckle] about all that you can hope for."

55. Cited in Aslakson, "Nellie Tayloe Ross," 85.

56. For more on these three basic gubernatorial responsibilities, see Ransone, *American Governorship,* 86–88.

57. Carey's legislative program espoused an improved workman's compensation program, establishment of a modern public health system, improved management of oil royalties, and passage of the executive budget act. For a detailed discussion of the early Wyoming governors' legislative programs and accomplishments, see Frances Birkhead Beard, ed., *Wyoming from Territorial Days to the Present.*

58. Joseph A. Schlesinger, *How They Became Governor: A Study of Comparative State Politics, 1870–1950,* 11–18.

59. Alfred E. Smith, *Up to Now: An Autobiography,* 136.

SIX ~ Chautauqua Speaker

1. NTR to NKT, December 22, 1926, letter courtesy of KTC.

2. Nellie sold a short article to *People's Popular Monthly,* "The House Called Home," in late 1925. The article was published in the February 1926 issue. The NTR Papers include correspondence with the McClure Newspaper Syndicate concerning a second 1926 article entitled "Marriage Problems"; it was not possible to locate a copy of this second article.

3. Based on Nellie's correspondence with her Mint secretary, O'Mahoney was still helping Nellie to prepare her tax returns in the 1940s. In later years, her son Bradford assumed responsibility for advising Nellie financially.

4. NTR Papers, original accession set, box 1, "Correspondence—Professional,

1922–1926." The folder also contains an article entitled "What I Like Best about My Home," written for the *People's Popular Monthly* in October 1926. The same folder contains a handwritten letter from O'Mahoney to Nellie, expressing his concern about her arrangements with Eula McClary.

5. NTR, "Mine Own People," 67, 204–9.

6. Jennifer Burek Pierce, "Portrait of a 'Governor Lady': An Examination of Nellie Tayloe Ross's Autobiographical Political Advocacy," 31–44.

7. Virginia Jeans Laas, introduction to Blair, *Bridging Two Eras,* xix.

8. NTR to GGT and NKT, December 4, 1926, letter courtesy of KTC; "Wyoming Federation's Most Distinguished Member Honored," *Wyoming Clubwoman* 7 (January 1927): 5.

9. "Wyoming Federation's Most Distinguished Member Honored," 6.

10. "Women Foresee New Honors for Governor Ross," undated and unattributed clipping, NTR Papers, box 12, "Miscellaneous Clippings, 1924–1925."

11. "Nellie T. Ross Is Favorably Mentioned by Nation's Press," *Wyoming Eagle,* July 30, 1926.

12. "Govern'r Ross Accepts 'Bryan Contract' on Leading Eastern Chautauqua Circuit," *Wyoming Eagle,* December 31, 1926; "Governor Ross Begins Lecture Tour East Next Week; Forced to Decline Many Invitations," *Wyoming Eagle,* undated clipping from Grace Raymond Hebard Papers, box 44, folder 3.

13. NTR to NKT, December 22, 1926.

14. Ruth Harrington Loomis interview, May 22, 1979, Cheyenne, Wyoming; EKW speech in honor of NTR's 100th birthday, November 29, 1976, Cheyenne, Wyoming, audiotape from the Oral History Collection, OH-2243, Wyoming State Archives. The speculating columnist was Drew Pearson, who wrote a column entitled *Washington Merry-Go-Round;* Nellie's reaction to Pearson's column is from an interview with WBR II, May 20, 1994, Maiden Point Farm, Maryland, 5, NTR Papers, box 14, "Biographical Information—Interview with WBR II, 1994."

15. KF interview, March 22–25, 2002, Scottsdale, Arizona. Mr. Failor first met Nellie when he was working as a stenographer before completing college. He described the process of working with her on her Chautauqua speech: "I remember her lying on a sofa, dictating, and she went over and over and over: 'Now, go back to here. . . . Go back to there.' And when I got through, I don't know how I ever typed that speech. . . . And later on, I asked her whether she memorized her speeches or how she prepared her speeches. And she said, 'I have the speech in my mind by the time I'm ready to give it. But I have it written down. And I have it in my pocketbook. And I figure if I ever get stage fright, I can open my pocketbook up and continue reading my speech!'"

16. EKW interview, December 20, 1977, undocumented Wyoming location, audiotape from the Oral History Collection, OH-2242, Wyoming State Archives.

17. NTR, "Mine Own People," 67.

18. Beginning in 1826, many New England communities founded "lyceums" that sponsored lectures for the public. Lyceums were usually winter programs, while the Chautauqua was always a summer event. In large cities such as Boston and New York,

existing literary societies took over sponsorship of lyceum programs. Eventually, lyceum societies spread across the nation, as did the Chautauquas. However, unlike the lyceums, Chautauqua remained a small-town phenomenon, generally scorned by the eastern urban intellectual community. As the popularity of the Chautauquas and lyceums faded in the late 1920s, their programs became interchangeable.

19. Gay MacLaren, *Morally We Roll Along,* 79.

20. Before World War I, radio enthusiasts were largely limited to amateurs with wireless sets. During the war, the government claimed control of the airwaves. Wartime technological advances led to the earliest commercial broadcasts after 1919, the year that the Radio Corporation of America (RCA) was formed. The first public showings of movies occurred in the late 1890s, but the cinema was a curiosity that was generally limited to large cities. D. W. Griffith's *Birth of a Nation* was released in 1915, when there were about three thousand cinemas in the United States. By the time that *The Jazz Singer,* complete with a sound track, was released in 1926, cinema had become the fourth largest industry in the United States.

21. Harry P. Harrison, *Culture under Canvas: The Story of Tent Chautauqua,* 17. The extensive records of the Redpath Chautauqua Bureau are part of the Special Collections Department at the University of Iowa. The voluminous file on Nellie documents her correspondence with the bureau, her speaking contracts and fees, and her promotional material.

22. MacLaren, *Morally We Roll Along,* 272–73.

23. John E. Tapia, *Circuit Chautauqua,* 12–17.

24. The description of Nellie's speech patterns and delivery is based on a few surviving audiotapes of her later radio speeches, from the audio/visual archive of the American Heritage Center, University of Wyoming.

25. NTR, "Mine Own People," 67.

26. Joseph C. O'Mahoney to Harry P. Harrison, December 28, 1927, NTR file, Redpath Chautauqua Collection.

27. Emily Child to Harry P. Harrison, December 14, 1927, NTR file, Redpath Chautauqua Collection.

28. Harrison, *Culture under Canvas,* 268.

29. NTR, "Mine Own People," 204.

30. The texts of several NTR speeches open with the Samuel Johnson story; for examples, see the NTR papers, original accession set, box 3, "Speeches by NTR," 1920–1953."

31. Ibid.

32. NTR to Harry P. Harrison, December 14, 1928, NTR file, Redpath Chautauqua Collection.

33. Karl Detzer, introduction to Harrison's *Culture under Canvas,* xvii.

34. Bruce Bliven, "How Radio Is Remaking Our World," 152. See also Tom Lewis, *Empire of the Air: The Men Who Made Radio,* 1–6.

35. Smith, *Up to Now,* 391.

36. "Houston's Keynote Speech Scheduled to Suit Radio Fans," *Washington Post,* June 27, 1928.

37. "Governors Meet at 'Mike,'" *Wyoming State Tribune,* clipping from NTR file, Grace Raymond Hebard Papers.

38. It does not appear that any Ross family members were present at Ambrose and Thelma's wedding, and they may not have been aware of the marriage until after the fact. No wedding announcement appeared in the Cheyenne or Laramie papers, nor was it possible to locate a birth certificate or birth announcement for their son, William. The scanty information about Ambrose and Thelma comes from the 1928–1929 Laramie city directory, the 1930 census, and a series of letters, following Ambrose's death, between Nellie and the bank that held the note on Ambrose's car. See NTR Papers, box 2, "Miscellaneous, 1930s." Although the correspondence referred to Ambrose's residence in Amarillo, one of Ambrose's obituaries stated that the couple had settled in New Mexico; see "Ambrose Ross Death Saddens State; Wife, Son Live Laramie," *Wyoming Eagle,* January 4, 1929. After Ambrose's death, Thelma returned to live with her parents and two sisters. When the family was enumerated for the 1930 census, they were living in Denver. The enumeration, which occurred in April 1930, stated that William A. Ross was born in Arizona and that he was two years and one month old.

39. NTR to GGT, March 3, 1928, letter courtesy of KTC; EKW, speech notes, EKW Papers, box 10, "Ross, Nellie Tayloe—Historical Information"; NTR to JAR, April 5, 1928. NTR papers, box 2, "Miscellaneous, 1924–1929."

40. The Grace Raymond Hebard Papers, box 44, folder 3, contain four articles or obituaries about Ambrose's death. The one obituary that describes the automobile accident does not state which man was driving the automobile; however, that Ambrose was the owner of the vehicle and was pinned while his friend was thrown clear suggests that Ambrose was likely the driver.

41. NTR to Harry P. Harrison, March 2, 1929, NTR file, Redpath Chautauqua Collection.

42. Nellie kept a journal of her impressions of this trip; see NTR Papers, original accession set, box 9, folder 7.

43. NTR Papers, original accession set, box 3, "Speeches by NTR, 1920–1953, #1." In Great Britain, women over thirty years of age gained the right to vote in 1918; in 1928, the voting age for women was lowered to twenty-one.

44. Ibid.

45. NTR to Harry P. Harrison, April 25, 1929, NTR file, Redpath Chautauqua Collection; NTR Papers, original accession set, box 3, "Speeches by NTR, 1920–1953, #1."

46. NTR Papers, original accession set, box 3, "Speeches by NTR, 1920–1953, #1."

47. In a February 9, 1929, telegram to Harry P. Harrison, Nellie inquired whether he had "MADE INQUIRY OF FRIEND REGARDING SECURITY OF RAILROAD MENTIONED IN CONVERSATION MONDAY. SEE NO QUOTATION, WONDERING IF DESIRABLE PURCHASE AT MARKET." She also learned to solicit stock tips from the businessmen she met in the club cars on her numerous train trips, according to her friend Kenneth Failor.

48. Until the passage of the Social Security Act in 1935, unemployment insurance was a function of state governments, whose relative generosity varied considerably.

49. Arthur S. Link, *American Epoch: A History of the United States since the 1890's*, 257. See also Ian Purchase, "Normalcy, Prosperity, and Depression, 1919–1933," 67–68; Charles F. Holt, "Who Benefited from the Prosperity of the Twenties?" and Frank Stricker, "Affluence for Whom? Another Look at Prosperity and the Working Classes in the 1920s," 5–33. Stricker cited four studies that calculated the percentage of all American families under the poverty level in 1929 at 42.3–56.5 percent (23). He concluded that "[f]or the majority of those below the median family income of $1700 in 1929, security rather than affluence or profligate expenditure lay at the core of the American dream" (32).

50. Dorothy Brown, *American Women in the 1920s: Setting a Course*, 7–16; Michael E. Parrish, *Anxious Decades: America in Prosperity and Depression, 1920–1941*, 82; Sullivan, *Our Times*, 588–89.

51. WBR II interview, May 20, 1994, Maiden Point Farm, Maryland, 20, NTR Papers, box 14, "Biographical Information—Interview with WBR II, 1994."

52. NTR to Harry P. Harrison, March 26, 1930, NTR file, Redpath Chautauqua Collection.

53. Ibid.

54. WBR II interview, May 20, 1994, Maiden Point Farm, Maryland, 5, NTR Papers, box 14, "Biographical Information—Interview with WBR II, 1994."

SEVEN ~ National Campaigner

1. Harry P. Harrison to Joseph C. O'Mahoney, May 19, 1928, NTR file, Redpath Chautauqua Collection.

2. Peter L. Peterson, quoted in Craig, *After Wilson*, 1. See also David Burner, *The Politics of Provincialism: The Democratic Party in Transition, 1918–1932*, xi–xii, 11–15; and Parrish, *Anxious Decades*, 7–8.

3. Parrish, *Anxious Decades*, 95–97. By 1914, more than one-fourth of the states had passed prohibition measures in response to the lobbying by the WCTU and other groups. In Wyoming, William Ross had been among the leaders of the prohibition movement; he campaigned actively for the state prohibition statute, which passed in 1916. In 1917, Congress passed the Lever Act, which prohibited the use of grain in alcoholic beverages, and it submitted the Eighteenth Amendment to the states for ratification. For good measure, in 1919 Congress passed the Volstead Act, which extended the wartime prohibition on the distillation, brewing, and sale of alcoholic beverages.

4. Thomas R. Pegram, *Battling Demon Rum: The Struggle for a Dry America, 1800–1933*, 88.

5. Edward Behr, *Prohibition: Thirteen Years That Changed America*, 3.

6. Pegram, *Battling Demon Rum*, 166–69.

7. NTR, "Progress, Prohibition, and the Democratic Party," 612–13.

8. Undated text of NTR telegram to Al Smith; his reply was dated March 3, 1928; see NTR Papers, box 1, "Miscellaneous Early, 1905–1938."

9. "Mrs. Ross Censured by W.C.T.U. When She Endorses Smith," *Lusk Herald*, February 9, 1928.

10. "Mrs. Ross Would Like Catholic President," Associated Press release, April 25, 1927, copy in NTR file, Douglas County Historical Society, Omaha, Nebraska.

11. Joseph C. O'Mahoney to Belle Moskowitz, March 7, 1928, and Belle Moskowitz to Joseph C. O'Mahoney, March 13, 1928, both in NTR Papers, box 1, "Miscellaneous Early, 1905–1938"; "California, Too, Suggests Gov. Ross for Vice-President," undated clipping, Grace Raymond Hebard Papers, box 44, folder 3. For more on the opposition to Nellie's speeches, see Glenda E. Morrison, "Women's Participation in the 1928 Presidential Campaign," 52–55.

12. Allan J. Lichtman, *Prejudice and the Old Politics: The Presidential Election of 1928*, 5.

13. Ibid., 5–15; see also Perry, *Belle Moskowitz*, 115.

14. Perry, *Belle Moskowitz*, 114, see also 154. For more on Moskowitz's role, see "Women's Participation," xii, 45–46.

15. Martin, *Madam Secretary*, 143, 205.

16. Anna E. Roosevelt, *This I Remember*, 42–43.

17. "Gov. Smith Repeats Stand for Amending Dry Laws," *Washington Post*, June 22, 1928.

18. "Houston in Gala Mood," *New York Times*, June 26, 1928. The first women to attend a national party convention were three who were seated as alternates at the 1892 Republican convention; however, few women attended national conventions until 1920, the year that the Nineteenth Amendment established national suffrage for women. See Marguerite J. Fisher and Betty Whitehead, "Women and National Party Organization"; and Breckinridge, *Women in the Twentieth Century*, 284–87.

19. Will Rogers, "Heat and Crowds Impress Rogers," *New York Times*, June 26, 1928.

20. "Women Add Voices to Universal Din as Convention Nears," *Washington Post*, June 25, 1928.

21. "Prohibition Forces Divided, Like Foes, on Plank Draft," *Washington Post*, June 27, 1928.

22. Democratic National Committee, *Official Report of the Proceedings of the Democratic National Convention, Held at Houston, Texas, June 26, 27, 28, and 29, 1928*, 98; "Roosevelt Names New York Governor," *New York Times*, June 28, 1928.

23. Democratic National Committee, *Official Report of the Proceedings at Houston*, 104–7.

24. Ibid., 106; "Smith in Accepting, Urges Modification of Dry Laws," *Washington Post*, June 30, 1928. As was customary for candidates before 1932, Smith did not attend the convention, instead tending to his gubernatorial duties in Albany.

25. Democratic National Committee, *Official Report of the Proceedings at Houston*, 236.

26. Ibid., 240–41, 246–52.

27. "Senator Robinson Gains in Strength for Second Place," *Washington Post*, June 26, 1928; see also "Western Nominee for Vice President Being Considered," *Washington*

Post, June 24, 1928. In 1984, the Democrats nominated Geraldine Ferraro as the running mate for Walter Mondale. Mondale and Ferraro lost the election to Ronald Reagan and George Bush.

28. Al Smith to NTR, July 6, 1928, NTR Papers, box 2, "Miscellaneous, 1924–1929."

29. Smith, *Up to Now,* 383.

30. Undated, unattributed news clipping from NTR file, Douglas County Historical Society, Omaha, Nebraska. Nellie is also listed as head of women's activities in the 1928 DNC organization chart; her two committee members are Eleanor Roosevelt and Caroline O'Day. A copy of the organization chart was found in the George Van Namee Papers.

31. Perry, *Belle Moskowitz,* 194–95.

32. Anna E. Roosevelt, "Women Must Learn to Play the Game as Men Do," 141–42.

33. Joseph P. Lash, *Eleanor and Franklin: The Story of Their Relationship Based on Eleanor Roosevelt's Private Papers,* 24–58.

34. Blanche Wiesen Cook, *Eleanor Roosevelt,* 339–40.

35. Ibid., 338.

36. Arthur M. Schlesinger Jr., foreword to Lash, *Eleanor and Franklin,* x–xi.

37. Cook, *Eleanor Roosevelt,* 342.

38. Roosevelt, *This I Remember,* 38–39.

39. See, for example, "Rival Political Machines Geared for Drives to Win Presidency," *New York Herald Tribune,* September 16, 1928. For ER's account of her role, see *This I Remember,* 38–39.

40. ER's report begins, "This is the report of work done under Mrs. Franklin D. Roosevelt whom Governor Taylor [*sic*] Ross as Vice Chairman of the National Democratic Committee appointed as chairman of the Women's Activities and Women's Advisory Committee," undated report by NTR, ER Papers, "General Correspondence, 1928–32; Politics—Democratic State Committee." A copy of the 1928 DNC organization chart was located in the papers of George Van Namee, vice chairman of the DNC Executive Committee.

41. The FDR quote is cited in Gloria Winden Newquist, "James A. Farley and the Politics of Victory, 1928–1936," 83–84. See also Perry, *Belle Moskowitz,* 106.

42. NTR, July 18, 1928, NTR Papers, box 7, "Speeches and Addresses, 1925–1930."

43. Elliott Roosevelt, ed., *F.D.R.: His Personal Letters,* 1:639–40.

44. ER to Elinor Morgenthau, August 9, 1928, ER Papers, "Elinor Morgenthau Correspondence—Eleanor Roosevelt, 1927–28."

45. Roosevelt, *This I Remember,* 41.

46. Mary W. Dewson, "An Aid to the End," 1:21.

47. Mary Teresa Norton to NTR, September 24, 1928, and Agnes O'Mahoney to NTR, undated telegram text, both in NTR Papers, box 1, "Correspondence, Professional, 1928–1952." For an example of the demand for Nellie as a speaker, see a petition from Raleigh, North Carolina, women, dated October 10, 1928, NTR Papers, accession no. 10526-97-10-07, box 1, folder 2.

48. Roosevelt, *This I Remember,* 42.

49. Ware, *Partner and I,* xi.

50. The quotation is from Dewson, "Aid to the End," 2:2. On June 15, 1937, Dewson delivered a speech in New London, Connecticut, in which she addressed how Democratic women could achieve more in politics. In her speech notes, she specifically excepted "individuals who are catapulted into power because they are widows of some Democratic leader about whom the men leaders feel sentimental. . . . I am talking about [i.e., interested in] Democratic women in general who have no short cut." Mary W. Dewson Papers, Schlesinger Library, Radcliffe College.

51. Emily Newell Blair, "Women in the Political Parties," 228.

52. Roosevelt, *This I Remember,* 41. See also Ware, *Partner and I,* 150–52.

53. Press quotes from "Views of Newspapers of All Sections on the National Result," *New York Times,* November 8, 1928.

54. Quoted in Brown, *American Women,* 222–23.

55. FDR to Emma Guffey Miller, November 22, 1928, Emma Guffey Miller Papers, box 39.

56. Joseph C. O'Mahoney to FDR, December 3, 1928, FDR Papers, DNC box 799.

57. NTR to FDR, December 8, 1928, and FDR to NTR, February 20, 1929, both in FDR Papers, Democratic National Committee, box 799.

58. Nellie mentioned this meeting with Roosevelt in the journal she kept during her 1930 trip to Europe. See NTR Papers, original accession set, box 9, "Diary and Daybook Information."

EIGHT ~ DNC Women's Director

1. Quoted in Burner, *Politics of Provincialism,* 144, 149–50. Another historian wrote, "[T]he party organization continued to be divided into factions after the debacle of 1924, and the party offices almost ceased to exist in 1926–27. The furniture and records were stored, and almost no continuing organizational activities were carried out. The Women's Division was in much the same condition. Emily Newell Blair was not enthusiastic about Smith's candidacy, and in the mid-1920's she devoted most of her time to the National Democratic Women's Club, an organization which had its headquarters in Washington, D.C. She became president of the club in 1928 and retired from the Women's Division and the vice-presidency of the national committee. Therefore, when Nellie Tayloe Ross took both of those positions, the Women's Division was a mere skeleton." Morrison, "Women's Participation," 109.

2. Burner, *Politics of Provincialism,* 149–50, 199–200; Paul C. Taylor, "The Entrance of Women into Party Politics: The 1920's," 371–72.

3. "Democrats to Give Mrs. Ross a Permanent Job," June 5, 1929, syndicated press article, Grace Raymond Hebard Papers, box 44, folder 3; "Southern Democrats 'Cut' Dinner for Raskob; Tribute Plans Are Declared 'Inopportune,'" *New York Times,* June 6, 1929; "Democrats Win Harmony in Dinner Tonight; Glass Lends Aid to Shouse-Raskob Affair," *New York Times,* June 10, 1929; "Democrats Cheer Raskob and Shouse as Party Builders," *New York Times,* June 11, 1929.

4. Jouett Shouse to NTR, June 27, 1929, and Jouett Shouse to John J. Raskob, August 29, 1929, both in John J. Raskob Papers, box 18, "Shouse, June–August 1929."

5. Jouett Shouse to NTR, August 31, 1929, John J. Raskob Papers, box 18, "Shouse, June–August 1929."

6. Alfred E. Smith to NTR, September 10, 1929, NTR Papers, original accession set, box 2, "Correspondence, Professional, 1924–1929."

7. Diana L. Bailey, *The Mayflower: Washington's Second Best Address;* Judith R. Cohen, *The Mayflower Hotel: Grande Dame of Washington, D.C.*

8. WBR II to NTR, May 13, 1930, NTR Papers, box 2, "Miscellaneous, 1930s."

9. WBR II to NTR, January 5, 1931, and November 27, 1931, both in NTR Papers, box 2, "Miscellaneous, 1930s."

10. Blair, *Bridging Two Eras;* Kathryn Kish Sklar, "Coming to Terms with Florence Kelley: The Tale of a Reluctant Biographer," 18; Dee Garrison, "Two Roads Taken: Writing the Biography of Mary Heaton Vorse," 66. Blair spent her childhood and her early married years in Carthage, Missouri; she and her husband moved a few miles away to Joplin in late 1919. In addition to the positions Blair held in the party and within the women's suffrage movement, she was a prolific writer for a variety of magazines, including *Woman Citizen, Woman's Journal, Harper's, Green Book, Ladies' Home Journal,* and *Good Housekeeping.*

11. Susan Ware, "Unlocking the Porter-Dewson Partnership: A Challenge for the Feminist Biographer," 61; Alice Wexler, "Emma Goldman and the Anxiety of Biography," 41; Sklar, "Coming to Terms," 18; Joyce Antler, "Having It All, Almost: Confronting the Legacy of Lucy Sprague Mitchell," 104–5.

12. Blair, *Bridging Two Eras,* 222, 224.

13. Ibid., 303.

14. Morrison, "Women's Participation," 109.

15. Taylor, "Entrance of Women," 250–54.

16. NTR, draft article for the *Democratic Digest,* April 1940, NTR Papers, original accession set, box 3, "Manuscripts by NTR, ca. 1940."

17. NTR, "Democratic Women's Work Valuable," 12–13. Examples of Nellie's organizing letters and literature may be found both in her papers and in Eleanor Roosevelt's. See also Taylor, "Entrance of Women," 371–72. In his dissertation, Taylor gave Sue Shelton White rather than Nellie the primary credit for the accomplishments of the Women's Division during the years 1930–1932, claiming that White possessed the "driving administrative ability and high intelligence which Mrs. Ross lacked" (368). When asked to explain the basis for his conclusion, Dr. Taylor responded, "As I look back, . . . I did not give Nellie T. Ross the space and consideration she deserved. . . . I was probably unduly influenced by the circle of unmarried social feminists around Dewson. I didn't fully appreciate the national stature Ross had among women who were interested in politics." Paul C. Taylor to the author, October 10, 2003. It seems likely that White dedicated herself more single-mindedly to her political career than Nellie, and it is also true that she eventually earned the respect of Eleanor Roosevelt's political circle, which Nellie did not. However, there is no basis for concluding that Nellie was not deeply involved in developing the Women's

Division strategy, for she worked exhaustively and effectively in the time-consuming effort of growing the field organization: between 1929 and 1932, she had visited thirty-six states and two hundred cities.

18. ER to NTR, March 28, 1930, Sue Shelton White Papers.

19. O'Neill, *Everyone Was Brave,* 276. For a discussion of the controversies between women's groups during the suffrage struggle, see Eleanor Flexner, *Century of Struggle: The Woman's Rights Movement in the United States,* 256–345; and Dorothy Schneider and Carl J. Schneider, *American Women in the Progressive Era, 1900–1920,* 179–89.

20. Lois Scharf, "'The Forgotten Woman': Working Women, the New Deal, and Women's Organizations," 243.

21. Nancy F. Cott argues that Domestic Feminism captured a natural bridge from the domesticity of the "separate spheres" period to women's emergence in the public arena; see Cott, *The Bonds of Womanhood: "Woman's Sphere" in New England, 1780–1835,* 205–6. See also Nancy F. Cott, "What's in a Name? The Limits of 'Social Feminism'; or, Expanding the Vocabulary of Women's History." William L. O'Neill coined the term "social feminism" to distinguish women who were municipal reformers, labor activists, or women's club members from "hard core feminists" such as Elizabeth Cady Stanton and Susan B. Anthony; see O'Neill, *Everyone Was Brave: The Rise and Fall of Feminism in America.*

22. Brown, *American Women,* 50–65; June Sochen, *Movers and Shakers: American Women Thinkers and Activists, 1900–1970,* 65–75.

23. William Henry Chafe, *The American Woman: Her Changing Social, Economic, and Political Roles, 1920–1970,* 113–14. Chafe cites both W. L. George and William L. O'Neill in his discussion.

24. For a discussion of Molly's relationship with Polly Porter, as well as some background on the "Boston marriage" arrangements so common among their generation, see Ware, *Partner and I,* 56–61. For a biography of Sue Shelton White and a portrait of Sue by Dr. Florence Armstrong, see the Sue Shelton White Papers, "Personal recollections of Sue Shelton White by friends, family, and associates, 1958–59."

25. Morrison, "Women's Participation," 124–25; Scott, *Southern Lady,* 205–6.

26. NTR, "Comments on Sue White," unpublished testimonial dated September 1958, Sue Shelton White Papers, "Personal recollections of Sue Shelton White by friends, family, and associates, 1958–59."

27. Sue Shelton White to MD, June 11, 1931, Mary W. Dewson Papers, container 4, "White, Sue S., 1931–1936."

28. Cook, *Eleanor Roosevelt,* 382–84.

29. Several letters between Nellie and the New York State Women's Division are contained in the ER Papers, "General Correspondence, 1928–32; Politics—Democratic State Committee." Nancy Cook, who helped to organize the Women's Division in New York in 1920, introduced Eleanor to politics. Nancy and her partner, Marion Dickerman, were intimate friends of Eleanor's for more than fifteen years. In 1925, Eleanor, Cook, and Dickerman formed Val-Kill Industries, which provided furniture- and other craft-making opportunities on the grounds of the Roosevelt estate in New

York. The three women shared Val-Kill cottage together until the 1936 dissolution of Val-Kill Industries.

30. "Nellie T. Ross May Be Senator," *Boston Herald,* November 27, 1929.

31. Joseph O'Mahoney to NTR, November 27, 1929, NTR Papers, box 2, "Miscellaneous, 1930s."

32. "Senator's Successor May Be Designated Following Funeral," *Denver Post,* November 26, 1929; "Pat Sullivan Offered Warren's Senate Seat," *Denver Post,* November 30, 1929; "Ambiguous Statute Causes Doubt as to Proper Action," *Denver Post,* December 1, 1929; "Patrick Sullivan Succeeds Warren in U.S. Senate," *Denver Post,* December 4, 1929; "Wyoming May Drop Plans for Special Senatorial Election," *Denver Post,* December 12, 1929.

33. "Joseph O'Mahoney Rumored as Successor to Sen. Kendrick," *Denver Post,* November 7, 1933.

34. "Mrs. Ross Says Time to Change Administration," October 18, 1930, unattributed news clipping in NTR file, Douglas County Historical Society, Omaha, Nebraska.

35. Cook, *Eleanor Roosevelt,* 485; James A. Farley, *Behind the Ballots: The Personal History of a Politician,* 64–73; Lash, *Eleanor and Franklin,* 338.

36. ER to MD, July 18, 1931, Mary W. Dewson Papers, container 3.

37. Farley, *Behind the Ballots,* 73–76. See also Craig, *After Wilson,* 3–6; and Burner, *Politics of Provincialism,* 246n.

38. Ruth Harrington Loomis interview with David Cookson, University of Wyoming, May 22, 1979, Cheyenne, Wyoming, interview tape courtesy of Ruth's daughter, Ann Loomis Jessee. Nellie later wrote, "We in the woman's end at headquarters underwent a painful struggle between our sense of good ethics and the urge within us to proclaim our preference [for] Governor Roosevelt." NTR, draft article for the *Democratic Digest,* April 1940, NTR Papers, original accession set, box 3, "Manuscripts by NTR, ca. 1940."

39. In *This I Remember,* ER wrote, "the regular machinery of the Democratic National Committee . . . was, of course, favorable to Smith" (70).

40. "Raskob Attacks Roosevelt Men for Insisting on Post for Walsh," *Washington Post,* June 22, 1932; Democratic National Committee, *Official Report of the Proceedings of the Democratic National Convention, Held at Chicago, Illinois, June 27–July 2, 1932;* Farley, *Behind the Ballots,* 141–54; "Raskob Given Warm Praise," *Washington Post,* July 3, 1932.

41. Newquist, "James A. Farley," 195; ER to MD, July 16, 1932, Mary W. Dewson Papers, container 14.

42. ER to MD, July 21, 1932, Mary W. Dewson Papers, container 13; NTR to MD, July 1932, and Florence Caspar Whitney to MD, July 22, 1932, both in Mary W. Dewson Papers, container 14.

43. Sue Shelton White to MD, August 4, 1932, Mary W. Dewson Papers, container 14.

44. Dewson, "Aid to the End," 1:69–70.

45. This excerpt from Hoover's speech at Madison Square Garden was quoted in "Revolution of 1933," *News-Week* 1 (12) (May 6, 1933): 3.

46. NTR to John J. Raskob, November 8, 1932, John J. Raskob Papers, file 602.

47. NTR to WBR II, October 9, 1932, NTR Papers, box 2, "NTR to Son, Bradford, 1930–1933."

48. NTR to MD, December 6, 1932, Mary W. Dewson Papers, container 14.

49. MD to NTR, December 8, 1932, Mary W. Dewson Papers, container 14.

50. Ware, *Partner and I,* 174.

51. The clipping, without headline, was attached to a letter endorsing O'Mahoney for a cabinet position. The clipping was undated, but based on the O'Mahoney letter, it was published some time before November 11. FDR Papers, folder 989, "Patronage Correspondence, 1932–33."

52. Dewson, "Aid to the End," 1:78.

53. E. R. Hardy to MD, November 29, 1932, Mary W. Dewson Papers, container 3, General Correspondence, "Frances Perkins 1924–1947."

54. Samuel Tayloe referred to the letter-writing campaign three years later in a letter to his sister: "I well recall [Sue Shelton White's] loyal and efficient aid rendered in your behalf when we were attempting to land you in a Cabinet position." SGT to NTR, July 2, 1936, NTR Papers, box 2, "Miscellaneous, 1930s."

55. Sue sanitized and summarized the exchange of letters for MD; see Mary W. Dewson Papers, container 3, General Correspondence, "Frances Perkins 1924–1947."

56. Emily Newell Blair to MD, December 6, 1932, and Emily Newell Blair to MD, December 8, 1932, both in Mary W. Dewson Papers, container 3, General Correspondence, "Frances Perkins, 1924–1947."

57. In comparison to Nellie's seventy endorsements, Frances Perkins received 357, some of which were petitions with from five to hundreds of signatures; see FDR Papers, DNC 989, "Patronage Correspondence," 1932–33."

58. Helen C. Donahue to FDR, December 28, 1932, FDR Papers, DNC 989, "Patronage Correspondence," 1932–33."

59. "Green Choice of Roosevelt in Labor Post," *Washington Post,* February 5, 1933.

60. "Tentative List of Roosevelt Cabinet Included Miss Perkins of New York, Ickes, Roper, Dern, and Wallace," *New York Times,* February 23, 1933. The *New York Times* listed Thomas J. Walsh as attorney general; the actual appointee was Homer S. Cummings.

61. "Mrs. Ross to Be Federal Treasurer; State Department Post for Ruth Bryan Owen," *New York Times,* March 23, 1933.

62. MD to ER, March 23, 1933, ER Papers, container 575. In one of her voluminous notebooks of clippings, next to a 1935 article entitled "Democratic Women in Washington for Second Annual Conference" that listed all the women appointed by Roosevelt, Dewson wrote, "Almost all of these women had been suggested by MWD for their appointments except . . ." thereupon she listed four names, none of which was Nellie's. See Mary W. Dewson Papers, "Clippings 1932–35."

63. "Jesse Jones Slated as R.F.C. Chairman," *New York Times,* April 12, 1933.

64. Emily Newell Blair to MD, undated letter, Mary W. Dewson Papers, container 16.

65. Judith Sealander, *As Minority Becomes Majority: Federal Reaction to the Phenomenon of Women in the Work Force, 1920–1963,* 134–37.

66. James Farley to NTR, undated draft letter by Eleanor Roosevelt, ER Papers, Series 100 Personal Letters, "Dewson, Mary W., Jan.–June 1933."

67. ER to NTR, May 2, 1933, ER Papers, Series 100 Personal Letters.

68. *Mayflower Log,* February 1934.

69. Ware, *Partner and I,* 200.

70. Dewson's autobiography mentions Nellie only six times in the 141 pages of the first part and twice in the 246 pages of the second part.

71. "Mrs. Ross Quits as Democratic Vice-Chairman," *New York Herald Tribune,* March 8, 1934.

72. NTR to James Farley, March 6, 1934, FDR Papers, Democratic National Committee, box 11, folder 15.

73. KF Interview, March 22–25, 2002, Phoenix, Arizona.

NINE ~ Bureau Chief

1. "Happy Birthday, Nellie Tayloe Ross," *Coin World,* October 27, 1976, NTR historical file, Bureau of the Mint, Washington, D.C.

2. Walter A. Ostronecki Jr., "Many Firsts for First Female Mint Director" [ca. 1983], historical files, Bureau of the Mint, Washington, D.C. The Mint's historian provided a clipping of this article, but unfortunately, the publication in which this article appeared was not noted on the Mint copy; the historian believes that the article either appeared in *Coin World* or *Numismatic News.*

3. Garraty, *American Nation,* 835–39; Parrish, *Anxious Decades,* 294–97.

4. Helen M. Burns, *The American Banking Community and New Deal Banking Reforms, 1933–1935;* Link, *American Epoch,* 391–96.

5. Executive Order 6102, "Forbidding the Hoarding of Gold Coin, Gold Bullion, and Gold Certificates." Individuals were reimbursed for their gold. The hundred-dollar gold-coin limit represented the equivalent of two to three months' wages for the average 1933 worker, so the executive order did not prohibit coin collectors from maintaining their collections.

6. Presidential Proclamation No. 2067, December 21, 1933; "President Hears Banking Experts," *New York Times* August 15, 1934. The Mint's silver regulations, issued on August 9, 1934, issued instructions on the delivery of silver to the Mint installations, and it clarified that silver coin, silver owned by central banks or foreign governments, and silver required for industrial or other legitimate purposes were excluded from the order.

7. See *Annual Report of the Director of the Mint,* 1933. When Nellie took over the Mint, it consisted of a tiny headquarters staff of thirteen in Washington; coinage mints at Philadelphia, San Francisco, and Philadelphia; an assay office in New York City, responsible for large sales of fine gold bars; mints at New Orleans and Carson City; and assay offices in Boise, Helena, Seattle, and Salt Lake City. The last six field installations functioned as bullion-purchasing agencies for the larger mints and also served the public by making assays of ores and bullion. The largest of these six offices was at Seattle, with nine employees; all six offices were closed at the end of Fiscal Year

1933. The assay function, which is the highly technical process of assessing the weight and purity of the precious metals used by the Mint, continues to be one of the bureau's most important statutory responsibilities.

8. *Annual Report of the Director of the Mint,* 1934.

9. The two women were Helen Hamilton Gardener, who served as Civil Service Commissioner from 1920 until her death in 1925, and Jessie Dell, who was subsequently appointed to what became, in effect, a woman's seat; Dell served from 1925 to 1933. She was succeeded by a Franklin Roosevelt appointee, Lucille Foster McMillin.

10. "Democratic Women in Washington for Second Annual Conference," *Washington Post,* March 29, 1935.

11. Bureau of the Census and Civil Service Commission data, from Women's Bureau Bulletin No. 230, *Women in the Federal Service, 1923–1947, Part I, Trends in Employment.*

12. Lucille Foster McMillin, *Women in the Federal Service,* 12–23.

13. Ibid., 3.

14. Women's Bureau Bulletin No. 182, *Employment of Women in the Federal Government, 1923 to 1939,* 50.

15. "Biographical Profile of Nellie Tayloe Ross, Director of the Mint," reproduced from a July 1948 State Department publication.

16. Henry Morgenthau III, *Mostly Morgenthaus: A Family History,* 263–64, 307; "One of Two of a Kind," 138; P. W. Ward, "Henry Morgenthau and His Friends."

17. In *Mostly Morgenthaus,* Henry Morgenthau Jr.'s son, Henry III, referred to his father's sexism when he wrote about the "male chauvinist jokes exchanged on chits of paper" with which Roosevelt and Morgenthau amused themselves during cabinet meetings. He included in his photograph section an example in which Roosevelt and Morgenthau were making fun of Frances Perkins.

18. Morgenthau was compulsive in his creation and collection of notes and documents; his "diaries" are located at the FDR Presidential Library.

19. Morgenthau diary 53, 204–5. The transcription of the discussion reads as follows:

> McReynolds [administrative assistant to Morgenthau]: There's another thing.
> Morgenthau (to Haas): Yes, wait a minute.
> McReynolds: Mrs. Ross . . .
> Morgenthau: That's different.
> (Hearty laughter)
> Bell [assistant to the secretary]: That is a headache.
> * * *
> Morgenthau: . . . Tell her she's welcome to go and see the President. All right, Mac?
> McReynolds: Well, she won't even come and see you about it. All she'll do is heckle me.
> Morgenthau: Well, if you had taken care of Mrs. Ross's interests, she wouldn't bother you so much.
> (Hearty laughter)

20. See the minutes of Morgenthau's weekly staff meetings, interspersed throughout the Morgenthau diaries.

21. Morgenthau Diary 134, July 15, 1938, 231–34. As of 1938, the salaries for the Mint director and the U.S. treasurer, the only positions to be held by women, were $8,000. The comptroller of the currency received $15,000; the directors of Internal Revenue, Customs, and the Federal Alcohol Administration, $10,000; and the directors of the Narcotics Bureau, the Public Debt Service, and the Bureau of Engraving and Printing, $9,000. The directors of the Coast Guard, the Public Health Service, and the Procurement Division all received military pay, so their salaries were not listed, but it is almost certain that they received more than Nellie in annual salary and allowances. See *Official Register of the United States,* 1938.

22. Arthur W. Macmahon and John D. Millett, *Federal Administrators: A Biographical Approach to the Problem of Departmental Management,* 307.

23. Fritz Morstein Marx, "The Departmental System," 189. See also J. Leiper Freeman, *The Political Process: Executive Bureau-Legislative Committee Relations,* 11.

24. The oversight of federal agencies has always presented a legal conundrum. The Constitution failed to grant supervisory powers to the president yet also failed to provide for the establishment of *any* federal agencies. Therefore, the legislature oversaw the departments, and Congress was understandably jealous of its prerogative for agency direction. When Congress created the first U.S. Mint in 1792, the legislation's only mention of the president was to require him to insure that the Mint had the buildings and equipment it needed. The Mint director was subject only to Congress and to his oath of office. In 1838, the Supreme Court affirmed the limited authority of the president to direct the affairs of the departments and, by extension, the authority of his cabinet secretaries to direct the affairs of the bureaus. In *Kendall v. United States,* 37 U.S. 524, the Court wrote, "It by no means follows that every officer in every branch of [a] department is under the direction of the President. . . . It would be an alarming doctrine that Congress cannot impose upon every executive officer any duty they may think proper . . . and, in such cases, the duty and responsibility grow out of and are subject to the control of the law, and not to the direction of the President."

In 1869, Secretary George S. Boutwell entered office with a goal of improving the organization of the Treasury Department. A prime goal was to reorganize the Mint, which had been placed under the general oversight of the Treasury secretary in 1835 by an act of Congress. Boutwell complained that "although the mints and assay offices are nominally under the charge of the Treasury Department, there is not, by authority of law, any person in the Department who, by virtue of his office, is supposed to be informed upon the subject, and none on whom the Secretary of the Treasury can officially rely for information as to the management of this important branch of the Government business." Boutwell spent the next four years studying Mint operations and drafting a bill to reorganize the agency. On February 12, 1873, after prolonged consultations with Boutwell and his staff, Congress passed the Mint Act, establishing the Mint as a bureau of Treasury, with a director in Washington (previously, the various Mint offices had reported to the director of the Philadelphia Mint). The director would still be appointed by the president, with the advice and consent of the Senate, for five-year terms. The director had to make an annual report to the secretary concerning Mint operations. The bulk of the legislation governing the Mint's responsibilities and internal organization was unaffected by the three brief paragraphs that made the Mint a bureau of the Treasury Department.

25. KF interview, March 22–25, 2002, Scottsdale, Arizona.

26. EKW, May 12, 1933, note to the file, EKW Papers, box 10, "U.S. Mint—Employment."

27. "Notes to be kept about Gov. Ross—Incidents," a handwritten summary of several anecdotes, EKW Papers, box 10, "Ross, Nellie Tayloe—Historical Information." The notes are undated, but some are from late in Nellie's Mint tenure. She related some of the same anecdotes in a November 1976 luncheon in honor of Nellie's hundredth birthday, and others in a December 1977 interview following Nellie's death.

28. Edness apparently saved every letter that Nellie sent her, from 1933 until Nellie's death. She also kept carbon copies of many of the letters she sent to Nellie, so together their correspondence serves as a weekly, and sometimes daily, journal of Nellie's work, activities, and personal life.

29. "Notes to be kept about Gov. Ross—Incidents," EKW Papers, box 10, "Ross, Nellie Tayloe—Historical Information." One of Edness's speech notes in her NTR historical folder reads, "New job as Director. Suspicion of employees."

30. Other than Nellie's immediate predecessor, the last Mint director who rose through the ranks was Robert E. Preston, director from 1893 to 1898. Biographies of the Mint directors through the late 1960s may be found in *Medals of the United States Mint,* a 1969 Bureau of the Mint publication.

31. The classic study of the relationship between political appointees and career civil servants is Hugh Heclo's *A Government of Strangers: Executive Politics in Washington.*

32. EKW Papers, "Notes to be kept about Gov. Ross—Incidents," box 10, "Ross, Nellie Tayloe—Historical Information."

33. KF interview, March 22–25, 2002, Scottsdale, Arizona.

34. Macmahon and Millett, *Federal Administrators,* 446. See also Rosamond E. Cole, "They Mint Money," a 1936 article on NTR and MMO from an unnamed publication, NTR Papers, box 12, "Political, 1934–1937."

35. WBR II interview, May 20, 1994, Maiden Point Farm, Maryland, 19, NTR Papers, box 14, "Biographical Information—Interview with WBR II, 1994."

36. MMO to NTR, October 9, 1933, and MMO to NTR, September 22, 1934, both in EKW Papers, box 10, "Mint, 1933–41." Box 10 of the EKW Papers includes numerous letters and telegrams between the two women, dating from 1933 until at least 1936.

37. KF telephone interview, August 18, 2001.

38. NTR to EKW, January 5, 1939, EKW Papers, box 9, "NTR Correspondence, 1936–1939."

39. EKW, official 1938 Mint biography of NTR, NTR historical file, Bureau of the Mint, Washington, D.C.

40. NTR to EKW, May 26, 1935, EKW Papers, box 9, "NTR Correspondence, 1933–1935."

41. *Annual Report of the Director of the Mint,* 1934; EKW, official 1938 Mint biography of NTR.

42. NTR to Henry Morgenthau Jr., March 8, 1934, file 243, Morgenthau Papers; Agent-in-Charge Wilson to William H. McReynolds, Administrative Assistant to the Secretary, January 28, 1938, General Records of the Department of the Treasury, RG 56, box 190, "Mint Bureau, 1933–1955," National Archives.

43. "'Sweetheart of Treasury' Quits at 73 after 33 Years," *New York Times,* October 30, 1938. File series 43-A, folder O, from the FDR Presidential Papers contain the correspondence relating to O'Reilly's three extensions of appointment.

44. Frederick Tate telephone interview, August 15, 2002, Washington, D.C.

45. NTR to KF, September 10, 1942, letter courtesy of KF.

46. KF interview, March 22–25, 2002, Scottsdale, Arizona.

47. KF telephone interview, July 9, 2001.

48. KF interview, March 22–25, 2002.

49. Ibid.; Frederick Tate telephone interview, August 15, 2002.

50. KF interview, March 22–25, 2002.

51. Ibid.

52. Ibid.

53. Henry Morgenthau Jr., to Franklin Delano Roosevelt, March 17, 1938, FDR Presidential Papers, file 21-F; U.S. Congress, *Congressional Record: Proceedings and Debates of the 3d Session of the 75th Congress,* 4143.

54. NTR to Franklin Delano Roosevelt, March 25, 1938, FDR Presidential Papers, file 21-F.

55. *Annual Reports of the Director of the Mint,* 1934 and 1941.

56. Memorandum, NTR to Treasury secretary John W. Snyder, November 28, 1952. In response to a request from Snyder, Nellie summarized the activities of the Mint during her tenure.

57. NTR to Arthur D. Eaton, August 4, 1945, EKW Papers, box 10, "Mint, 1942–1946."

58. "Mint Lacks Craftsmen," *New York Times,* August 20, 1941. On April 4, 1941, Nellie wrote to the department to request its support to secure the Civil Service Commission's agreement to include the Mint in the list of national defense agencies so that it would receive priority in government recruiting. The Civil Service Commission denied her request on June 6, 1941. Letters from General Records of the Department of the Treasury, RG 56, box 190, "Mint Bureau, 1933–1955," National Archives.

59. "Mrs. Moneybags," *Newsweek,* April 12, 1943, 41.

60. U.S. Congress, Senate, *Hearings before the Committee on Banking and Currency,* 3–12.

61. Treasury Department press releases, September 23, 1942, and October 13, 1942, General Records of the Department of the Treasury, RG 56, box 190, "Mint Bureau, 1933–1955," National Archives.

62. Morgenthau Diary 667, 72–78.

63. Treasury Department news release, October 22, 1943, General Records of the Department of the Treasury, RG 56, box 190, "Mint Bureau, 1933–1955," National Archives.

64. "End of a Bad Penny," *New York Times*, December 28, 1943.

65. Ross obituary, *New York Times*, December 21, 1977.

66. John Morton Blum, *Roosevelt and Morgenthau: A Revision and Condensation of "From the Morgenthau Diaries,"* 638–46; Morgenthau, *Mostly Morgenthaus*, 404–6.

67. "The Man Who Holds Our Economic Reins," *New York Times Magazine*, September 23, 1954, 13, 48; "Harry's Friend John," *Newsweek*, June 24, 1946, 33. Snyder attended Nellie's hundredth birthday party in 1977; see "Nellie Tayloe Ross Marks 100th Birthday with Party," *Coin World*, December 15, 1975.

68. NTR to John W. Snyder, April 18, 1950, John W. Snyder Papers, box 139. Nellie also discussed the Mint's accounting innovations in her November 28, 1952, memo to Snyder in which she summarized the activities of the Mint during her tenure.

69. *Annual Report of the Director of the Mint*, 1950, 250–51.

70. NTR to John W. Snyder, November 28, 1952, summary of Mint activities during Nellie's tenure.

71. *Annual Report of the Director of the Mint*, 1950, 10–11. See also the 1952 *Annual Report*, 8–11.

72. "Heretic in Skirts Heads Mint; Returns Money to Congress," North American Newspaper Alliance syndicated article, June 25, 1950, copy in the NTR file, Douglas County Historical Society, Omaha, Nebraska.

73. Frederick C. Othman, "Boss of the Mint Sends Out Plea: Needs Money to Make Pennies," unattributed syndicated column, March 11, 1952, copy in the NTR file, Douglas County Historical Society, Omaha, Nebraska.

On the accounting side of the Mint's fiscal management practices, it was among the first federal bureaus to establish, around 1940, an integrated system of accrual and obligation accounting; the Mint's financial system met private industry standards and also permitted it to develop performance-based budget estimates for Congress. Unlike the majority of federal agencies, whose funding derives from annual Congressional appropriations, the Mint was an income-producing, manufacturing operation. The Mint's sizable income derives principally from seigniorage, which is the difference between the cost of metals purchased and the lesser cost of turning them into coins. The Mint also earns income on its sale of commemorative and collection coins and the coinage services it provides to other nations. Given her lifelong emphasis on economy and efficiency, Nellie must have been particularly proud of this accomplishment. While accounting practices are anything but headline news, the Mint had achieved a professional standard that some federal bureaus are still struggling to achieve in the early twenty-first century.

74. "Many Firsts for First Female Mint Director," undated, unattributed news clipping, Historical files, Bureau of the Mint, Washington, D.C.

75. Both employee testimonials are from the NTR Papers, box 2, "Third Appointment as Head of Mint, 1943."

76. John W. Snyder Papers, box 266, "Oral History Interview."

77. NTR to NKT, undated note, NTR Papers, box 3, "NTR to George and Nelle Ross, 1943–1951."

78. U.S. Congress, House, *Hearings before the Subcommittee of the Committee on Appropriations*, 1950, 346–52.

TEN ~ The Washington Years

1. Bess Furman, *Washington By-Line: The Personal History of a Newspaperwoman,* 26–29; Federal Writers' Project, *The WPA Guide to Washington, D.C.;* Keith Melder, *City of Magnificent Intentions: A History of Washington, District of Columbia.*

2. Furman, *Washington By-Line,* 144–45.

3. KF to the author, January 6, 2004.

4. Furman, *Washington By-Line,* 158; Melder, *City of Magnificent Intentions,* 403–5, 428–36.

5. Furman, *Washington By-Line,* 30–31.

6. NTR Papers, original accession set, box 3, "Programs and Invitations: 3 folders"; "On Government," NTR speech text, NTR Papers, original accession set, box 3, "Speeches by NTR, ca. 1920–1953, #2."

7. *The Mayflower Log,* March 1930, 12; "Mrs. Ross Tea Hostess," *New York Times,* February 18, 1935; Invitation list, NTR Papers, original accession set, box 3, "Programs and Invitations: 3 folders."

8. "'Grandma' Ross Likes Home Life," unattributed 1937 newspaper article; clipping from NTR Papers; NTR to EKW, October 18, 1935, EKW Papers, "NTR Correspondence, 1936–1939."

9. Nellie continued to serve as a campaign speaker through the election of 1952. The 1952 convention was the first that she did not attend since her first in 1928. She wrote Edness on July 21, 1952, "Now that [the convention] is underway I'll confess that it seems very queer—not quite right—for me not to be there."

10. EKW to NTR, October 1, 1934, EKW Papers, box 10, "US Mint—Edness Kimball Wilkins, Sep 1933–Aug 1936"; NTR to EKW, October 6, 1934; EKW Papers, box 9, "NTR Correspondence—1933–1935."

11. NTR to MMO, October 24, 1934, EKW Papers, box 10, "Mint—1933–1941."

12. Mrs. James H. Wolfe to NTR, February 24, 1936, MD to NTR, August 12, 1936, MD to NTR, September 2, 1936, NTR to Mrs. James H. Wolfe, May 2, 1936, and NTR to Molly Dewson, August 10, 1936, all in FDR Papers, Democratic National Committee, box 11, folder 25.

13. NTR to MD, March 16, 1936, FDR Papers, Democratic National Committee, box 11, folder 25. Nellie's correspondence with Edness contains several examples of political referrals. Nellie also speaks to her disgust with the poor quality of applicants received off civil service registers and her frustration with the slow pace and the inflexibility of civil service rules.

14. Edward G. Kemp, Assistant to the Attorney General, to NTR, September 1, 1939: "Since the Director of the Mint does not appear to be an officer who determines policies . . . , it is the opinion of this Department that the provisions of the Hatch Act regarding the political activities of employees in the Executive Branch of the Federal Government apply to you." NTR Papers, box 3, "Hatch Act, 1939."

15. NTR to ER, September 25, 1939, NTR Papers, box 3, "Hatch Act, 1939"; Edward G. Kemp to NTR, December 19, 1939: "Upon request of representatives of the

General Counsel of the Treasury Department, we have given further study to the [applicability of the Hatch Act to NTR], and have reached a [different] conclusion. . . . [T]he prohibitions . . . do not apply to the Director of the Mint." NTR Papers, box 3, "Hatch Act, 1939."

16. Morgenthau Diary 215, 200–201.

17. See the correspondence between Nellie and Alber and Wickes in the NTR Papers, original accession set, box 1, "Correspondence, Professional, 1934–1937" and "Correspondence, Professional, 1935–1952."

18. NTR to EKW, October 10, 1933, EKW Papers, box 9, "NTR Correspondence—1933–1935."

19. NTR to GGT, November 15, 1938, and GGT to NTR, November 17, 1938, both in NTR Papers, box 3, "NTR to George Tayloe and his wife Nelle, 1925–1942."

20. KF interview, March 22–25, 2002, Scottsdale, Arizona.

21. NTR to EKW, December 11, 1935, EKW Papers, box 9, "NTR Correspondence—1933–1935"; NTR to EKW, December 6, 1935, EKW Papers, box 10, "U.S. Mint—Employment."

22. A copy of the draft article can be found in the NTR Papers, box 8, "Articles Written by NTR, 1926–1956."

23. Several news clippings on Nellie's farm can be found in the NTR Papers, box 12, "Miscellaneous Clippings, 1938–1940." Bradford became part-owner of the farm in 1944, but he and Nellie sold La Trappe in 1948. Between his career and his young family, Bradford could not find the time to devote to managing the farm, even with a tenant farmer.

24. "'Grandma' Ross Likes Home Life," unattributed 1937 newspaper article, clipping from NTR Papers; "Profile: George Ross," article in a Williamsburg community newsletter, box 1, "George Ross, 1923"; NTR to NKT, February 9, 1939, and March 22, 1939; box 3, "NTR to George and Nelle Tayloe, 1925–1942."

25. NTR to NKT, March 15, 1943, NTR Papers, box 3, "NTR to George and Nelle Tayloe, 1943–1951."

26. WBR II to NTR, November 20, 1938, NTR Papers, box 2, "Miscellaneous 1930s."

27. As register, Dr. Dolan's job was to oversee the retirement of Treasury obligations.

28. NTR to NKT, December 20, 1938, NTR Papers, box 3, "NTR to George and Nelle Tayloe, 1925–1942."

29. KF telephone interview, August 8, 2002.

30. "Mrs. Ross Entertains for Son and His Bride," January 15, 1940, unattributed clipping, NTR Papers, box 12, "Miscellaneous Clippings, 1938–1940"; NTR to NKT, January 27, 1940, NTR Papers, box 3, "NTR to George and Nelle Tayloe, 1925–1942."

31. NTR to NKT, April 18, 1940, NTR Papers, box 3, "NTR to George and Nelle Tayloe, 1925–1942."

32. Information on Bradford's election and induction courtesy of Carl Hallberg, Wyoming State Archives.

33. WBR II to NTR, written between March 29 and April 1, 1941, NTR Papers,

box 1, "Family and Personal, 1902–1930." Note that the letter was misfiled by date; it may have been moved during the 2003 reprocessing of the papers.

34. NTR to NKT, November 9, 1942, NTR Papers, box 3, "NTR to George and Nelle Tayloe, 1925–1942."

35. NTR to NKT, June 30, 1942, NTR Papers, box 3, "NTR to George and Nelle Tayloe, 1925–1942."

36. NTR to NKT, November 9, 1942, NTR Papers, box 3, "NTR to George and Nelle Tayloe, 1925–1942"; NTR Papers, box 9, "Correspondence, Indenture of Trust, NTR Will, 1958–1960"; NTR Papers, box 9, "Legal Correspondence, 1965–1971."

37. WBR III interview, February 15, 2002, Maiden Point Farm, Maryland:

> WBR III: But [Nellie] wouldn't hesitate to tell you the direction you were going to be going.
>
> Interviewer: Including her son?
>
> WBR III: Yes. Including my dad. My mother used to say, "I think Brad has two wives."
>
> Interviewer: How did [your mother] feel about that?
>
> WBR III: Well, she was, she felt, see, my father married my mother when she was nineteen. So my mother grew up with my grandmother.

38. WBR III interview, May 21, 1994, Maiden Point Farm, Maryland, NTR Papers, box 15, "Biographical Information—Interview with WBR III, 1994."

39. NTR to NKT, November 23, 1951, NTR Papers, box 3, "NTR to George and Nelle Ross, 1949–1954."

40. WBR III interview, May 21, 1994.

41. NTR to WBR II, August 20, 1956, NTR Papers, box 2, "Miscellaneous, 1940–1957."

42. WBR III interview, May 21, 1994; WBR III interview, February 15, 2002.

43. WBR II interview, May 21, 1994.

44. NTR to NKT, June 16, 1961, and January 3, 1962, NTR Papers, box 3, "NTR to George and Nelle Ross, 1960–1970."

45. NTR to NKT, February 5, 1964, NTR Papers, box 3, "NTR to George and Nelle Ross, 1960–1970"; "4 College Students Die in Car Crash in Iowa," *Washington Star,* December 9, 1963.

46. William E. Clayton, "Nellie Tayloe Ross Is 95," syndicated article for United Press International.

47. NTR to WBR II, undated letter from November or December 1968, NTR Papers, box 3, "NTR to WBR II while traveling, 1955, 1967–1978."

48. NTR to WBR II, December 6, 1970, NTR Papers, box 4, "Miscellaneous, 1970–1978."

49. "Yellowstone Birthday State's Biggest Bash," May 31, 1972, *Casper Star-Tribune;* WBR III interview, May 21, 1994.

50. "Yellowstone Birthday State's Biggest Bash."

51. WBR III interview, May 21, 1994.

52. NTR to NKT, January 1, 1963, NTR Papers, box 3, "NTR to George and Nelle Ross, 1960–1970."

53. Betty Friedan, *The Feminine Mystique,* 11, 13, 14, 27.

54. June Sochen, *Herstory: A Record of the American Woman's Past,* 355–63; William L. O'Neill, *Feminism in America: A History,* 307–15.

55. Constance McLaughlin Green, *The Secret City: A History of Race Relations in the Nation's Capitol,* 279.

56. NTR to Harry Truman, September 25, 1963, Harry S. Truman Papers, box PPGF-388, "General—'Ross J–Z.'"

57. NTR to NKT, March 19, 1965, NTR Papers, box 3, "NTR to George and Nelle Ross, 1960–1970."

58. RTR e-mail to author, July 22, 2005: "Our grandmother was a moderate on civil rights issues, and she favored equal treatment of all citizens under the law. I was bussed across Washington, D.C., to an integrated junior high school. I remember discussions with our grandmother and father during which they both approved of my participation in the bussing program."

59. "Nellie Tayloe Ross Marks 100th Birthday with Party," *Coin World,* December 15, 1976.

60. NTR to Dorothy Ross, undated partial letter, NTR Papers, original accession set, box 8, "Genealogy/Family History."

61. WBR II to GTR, December 7, 1977, NTR Papers, original accession set, box 8, "Genealogy/Family History."

62. Ed Herschler eulogy, NTR Papers, box 12, "Death of NTR, 1977."

63. "Mrs. Ross Buried beside Husband," December 22, 1977, *Casper Star-Tribune.* Wyoming State Archives, Acquisition HB81-1, box 10.

Bibliography

Manuscript Collections

Brewster, Ralph Owen, Papers. George J. Mitchell Department of Special Collections, Bowdoin College, Maine.

Democratic National Committee Papers. FDR Presidential Library, Hyde Park, New York.

Department of the Treasury General Records. RG 56, National Archives and Records Administration, Washington, D.C.

Dewson, Mary W. "An Aid to the End." Vols. 1 and 2. Unpublished, undated autobiography. Copies available at the FDR Library and the Schlesinger Library.

Dewson, Mary W., Papers. FDR Presidential Library, Hyde Park, New York.

Emerson, Frank C., Papers. Accession Number 43, American Heritage Center, University of Wyoming, Laramie.

Haist, Sharon Ann. "Miltonvale, Kansas, Home of Nellie Tayloe Ross." Copy available at the Cloud County, Kansas, Historical Museum, Miltonvale, Kans.

Hebard, Grace Raymond, Papers. 1829–1947, Accession Number 4000008, American Heritage Center, University of Wyoming, Laramie.

Loomis, Ruth, Papers. Accession Number 95-05-31, American Heritage Center, University of Wyoming, Laramie.

Miller, Emma Guffey, Papers. Schlesinger Library, Radcliffe Institute for Advanced Study, Boston, Massachusetts.

"Mint Bureau, 1933–1955." Department of the Treasury, RG 56. National Archives, Washington, D.C.

Morgenthau, Elinor, Papers. FDR Presidential Library, Hyde Park, New York.

Morgenthau, Henry J., Jr., Diaries. FDR Presidential Library, Hyde Park, New York.

Morgenthau, Henry J., Jr., Papers. FDR Presidential Library, Hyde Park, New York.

O'Mahoney, Joseph C., Papers. Accession Number 275-53-06-00, American Heritage Center, University of Wyoming, Laramie.

Palmer, Fannie Smith, and Kathryn Palmer Chilen. "Miltonvale—1982." Copy in archives of Kansas State Historical Society, Topeka. [1981.]

Pinchot, Cornelia Bryce, Papers. Library of Congress, Washington, D.C.

Raskob, John J., Papers. Accession Number 473, Hagley Museum and Library, Greenville, Delaware.

Redpath Chautauqua Collection. Special Collections Department, University of Iowa Libraries, Iowa City, Iowa.

Roosevelt, Anna Eleanor, Papers. FDR Presidential Library, Hyde Park, New York.

Roosevelt, Franklin Delano, Papers. (President's Personal Files and Official Files.) FDR Presidential Library, Hyde Park, New York.

Ross, Nellie Tayloe, Gubernatorial Papers. RG 0001.24, Wyoming State Archives, Cheyenne.

Ross, Nellie Tayloe, Papers. Ca. 1880s–1994, Accession Number 948-97-10-07, American Heritage Center (AHC), University of Wyoming, Laramie. *[Note: When this biography was prepared, the NTR Papers consisted of two separate but overlapping sets of boxes and folders: one comprised copies from letters and other items loaned to the AHC by the Ross family; the other contained the original documents that the family subsequently donated. As of early 2004, these papers have been reorganized and reindexed. Every effort has been made to translate citations into the new organizational scheme; however, if an item cited in the present volume does not appear to have been incorporated into the newly indexed material, the citation refers to the box and file number in the "original accession set."]*

Ross, William Bradford, Gubernatorial Papers. RG 0001.22, Wyoming State Archives, Cheyenne.

Snyder, John W., Papers. Harry S. Truman Presidential Library, Independence, Missouri.

Truman, Harry S., Papers. Harry S. Truman Presidential Library, Independence, Missouri.

Van Namee, George, Papers. Catholic Diocese of Fresno, Fresno, California.

Virginia Historical Society. General Collection. Richmond, Virginia.

White, Sue Shelton, Papers. Schlesinger Library, Radcliffe Institute for Advanced Study, Boston, Massachusetts.

Wilkins, Edness Kimball, Papers. Accession Number H81-1, Wyoming State Archives, Cheyenne.

Interviews

Bressler, Marti. Interview with author. Cheyenne, Wyoming, July 19, 2001.

Failor, Kenneth. Interviews with author. Scottsdale, Arizona, March 22–25, 2002.

Failor, Kenneth. Telephone interviews with author. July 9, 2001; August 8, 2002.

Hoffelmeyer, Henry. Interview with author. Andrew County, Missouri, May 19, 2002.

Janus, Jane Tayloe. Telephone interviews with author. April 22, May 29, 2002.

Loomis, Ruth Harrington. Interview with David Cookson. Cheyenne, Wyoming, May 22, 1979.

Ross, Robert Tayloe. Telephone interview with author. October 13, 2002.

Ross, William Bradford, II. Interview. Maiden Point Farm, Maryland, May 20, 1994. Nellie Tayloe Ross Papers, American Heritage Center, University of Wyoming, Laramie.

Ross, William Bradford, III. Interviews. Maiden Point Farm, Maryland, May 21, 1994; February 15, 2002. Nellie Tayloe Ross Papers, American Heritage Center, University of Wyoming, Laramie.

Ross, William Bradford, III. Telephone interview with author. October 14, 2002.

Sullivan, Lynn (system reference librarian, Omaha Public Library). Telephone interview with author. October 24, 2002.

Tate, Frederick. Telephone interview with author. August 15, 2002.

Articles by Nellie Tayloe Ross

"Democratic Women's Work Valuable." *Democratic Bulletin* 7 (June 1932): 12–13.

"The Governor Lady." Pt. 1. *Good Housekeeping* 85, no. 2 (August 1927): 30–31, 118–23.

"The Governor Lady." Pt. 2. *Good Housekeeping* 85, no. 3 (September 1927): 36–37, 206–18.

"The Governor Lady." Pt. 3. *Good Housekeeping* 85, no. 4 (October 1927): 72–73, 180–95.

"The House Called Home." *People's Popular Monthly* 31, no. 2 (February 1926): 7–8.
"Mine Own People." *Good Housekeeping* 86 (July 1928): 67, 204–9.
"Progress, Prohibition, and the Democratic Party." *Scribner's* 82 (May 1928): 608–13.
"Two Platforms." *Woman's Journal* 13, no. 8 (August 1928): 15.
"Why a Woman 'Dry' Supports Governor Smith." *Woman's Journal* 13, no. 9 (September 1928): 18.

Secondary Sources

Aikman, Duncan. "Politics and Ma Ferguson in Texas." *Independent* 115 (December 19, 1925): 703–4, 720.
Alpern, Sara, Joyce Antler, Elisabeth Israels Perry, and Ingrid Winther Scobie, eds. *The Challenge of Feminist Biography: Writing the Lives of Modern American Women.* Urbana: University of Illinois Press, 1992.
Alumni Directory of Peabody College, 1877–1909. Nashville: Alumni Association of Peabody College, [1909].
Ambrose, Stephen E. *Nothing Like It in the World: The Men Who Built the Transcontinental Railroad, 1863–1869.* New York: Simon and Schuster, 2000.
Anderson, Kristi. *After Suffrage: Women in Partisan and Electoral Politics before the New Deal.* Chicago: University of Chicago Press, 1996.
Antler, Joyce. "Having It All, Almost: Confronting the Legacy of Lucy Sprague Mitchell." In Alpern et al., *Challenge of Feminist Biography,* 97–115.
Arnold, Peri E. "The First Hoover Commission and the Managerial Presidency." *Journal of Politics* 38, no. 1 (February 1976): 46–70.
Aron, Cindy S. *Ladies and Gentlemen of the Civil Service: Middle-Class Workers in Victorian America.* New York: Oxford University Press, 1987.
Aslakson, Barbara Jean. "Nellie Tayloe Ross: First Woman Governor." Master's thesis, University of Wyoming, 1960.
Bader, Robert Smith. *Prohibition in Kansas: A History.* Lawrence: University Press of Kansas, 1986.
Bailey, Diana L. *The Mayflower: Washington's Second Best Address.* Virginia Beach: Donning, 2001.
Bainbridge, Lucy Seaman. *Round the World Letters.* Boston: D. Lothrop, 1882.
Bane, Frank. "The Job of Being a Governor." *State Government* 31 (summer 1958): 184–89.

Barclay, Thomas S. "The Publicity Division of the Democratic Party, 1929–1930." *American Political Science Review* 25 (1931): 68–72.

Bates, J. Leonard. *The Origins of Teapot Dome: Progressives, Parties, and Petroleum, 1909–1921.* Westport, Conn.: Greenwood Press, 1963.

———. "The Teapot Dome Scandal and the Election of 1924." *American Historical Review* 60 (January 1951): 303–22.

Beach, Cora M. "Governor Nellie Tayloe Ross." In *Women of Wyoming,* 32–39. Casper, Wyo.: S. E. Boyer, 1927.

Beard, Frances Birkhead, ed. *Wyoming from Territorial Days to the Present.* Chicago: American Historical Society, 1933.

Beecher, Catharine E., and Harriet B. Stowe. *The American Woman's Home; or, Principles of Domestic Science.* New York: J. B. Ford, 1869. Reprint, New York: Arno Press, 1971.

Behr, Edward. *Prohibition: Thirteen Years That Changed America.* New York: Arcade Publishing, 1996.

Bernstein, Marver H. *The Job of the Federal Executive.* Washington, D.C.: Brookings Institution Press, 1958.

Berrol, Selma. "Immigrant Children at School, 1880–1940." In *Small Worlds: Children and Adolescents in America, 1850–1950,* ed. Elliott West and Paula Petrik, 42–60. Lawrence: University Press of Kansas, 1992.

Betts, Lillian W. "The Principles of Housekeeping." In *The Woman's Book: Dealing Practically with the Modern Conditions of Home-Life, Self-Support, Education, Opportunities, and Every-Day Problems,* vol. 1. New York: Charles Scribner's Sons, 1894.

Beyle, Thad L. "Governors' Views on Being Governor." *State Government* 52 (summer 1979): 103–9.

Blair, Emily Newell. *Bridging Two Eras: The Autobiography of Emily Newell Blair,* ed. Virginia Jeans Laas. Columbia: University of Missouri Press, 1999.

———. "May the Best Man Win." *Good Housekeeping* 87 (September 1928): 26–27.

———. "Men in Politics as a Woman Sees Them." *Harpers Magazine* 152 (May 1926): 703–9.

———. "A Who's Who of Women in Washington." *Good Housekeeping* 102, no. 1 (January 1936): 38–39, 166–68.

———. "Women in the Political Parties." *Annals of the American Academy of Political and Social Science* 143 (May 1929): 217–29.

Blair, Karen J. *The Clubwoman as Feminist: True Womanhood Redefined, 1868–1914.* New York: Holmes and Meier Publishers, 1980.

Bliven, Bruce. "How Radio Is Remaking Our World." *Century Magazine* 108, no. 2 (June 1924): 147–54.

Block, M., ed. *Current Biography.* Vol. 1. New York: H. W. Wilson, 1940.

Blocker, Jack S., Jr. *American Temperance Movements: Cycles of Reform.* Boston: Tawyne Publishers, 1989.

Blum, John Morton. *Roosevelt and Morgenthau: A Revision and Condensation of "From the Morgenthau Diaries."* Boston: Houghton Mifflin, 1970.

Bok, Edward. "My Quarrel with Women's Clubs." *Ladies' Home Journal* 27, no. 2 (January 1910): 5–6.

Boorstin, Daniel J. *The Americans: The Democratic Experience.* New York: Random House, 1973.

Bordin, Ruth. *Woman and Temperance: The Quest for Power and Liberty, 1873–1900.* Philadelphia: Temple University Press, 1981.

Breckinridge, Sophonisba P. *Women in the Twentieth Century: A Study of Their Political, Social, and Economic Activities.* New York: McGraw-Hill, 1933.

Bristow, David. *A Dirty, Wicked Town: Tales of 19th Century Omaha.* Caldwell, Idaho: Caxton Press, 2000.

Brown, Dorothy. *American Women in the 1920s: Setting a Course.* Boston: Twayne Publishers, 1987.

Brown, Mabel E. "Nellie Tayloe Ross." In *First Ladies of Wyoming, 1869–1990,* ed. Mabel E. Brown, 1–9. Cheyenne: Wyoming Commission for Women, 1990.

Brown, Robert Harold. *Wyoming: A Geography.* Boulder, Colo.: Westview Press, 1980.

Buechner, John C. *State Government in the Twentieth Century.* Boston: Houghton Mifflin, 1967.

Burke, Diane Mutti. "'May We as One Family Live in Peace and Harmony': Relations between Mistresses and Slave Women in Antebellum Missouri." In *Women in Missouri History: In Search of Power and Influence,* ed. LeeAnn Whites, Mary C. Neth, and Gary R. Kremer, 64–81. Columbia: University of Missouri Press, 2004.

Burner, David. *The Politics of Provincialism: The Democratic Party in Transition, 1918–1932.* New York: Norton, 1967.

Burns, Helen M. *The American Banking Community and New Deal Banking Reforms, 1933–1935.* Westport, Conn.: Greenwood Press, 1974.

Cable, Mary. *The Little Darlings: A History of Child Rearing in America.* New York: Charles Scribner's Sons, 1975.

Carlson, Robert A. *The Quest for Conformity: Americanization through Education.* New York: John Wiley and Sons, 1975.

Carroll, Susan J. *Women as Candidates in American Politics.* 2d ed. Bloomington: Indiana University Press, 1994.

Carter, Paul A. *Another Part of the Twenties.* New York: Columbia University Press, 1977.

Case, Victoria, and Robert Ormond Case. *We Called It Culture: The Story of Chautauqua.* Garden City, N.Y.: Doubleday, 1948.

Cashman, Sean Dennis. *America in the Age of the Titans: The Progressive Era and World War I.* New York: New York University Press, 1998.

Cawley, Gregg, Michael Horan, Larry Hubbell, James King, and Robert Schuhmann. *The Equality State: Government and Politics in Wyoming.* 4th ed. Dubuque, Iowa: Eddie Bowers Publishing, 2000.

Chafe, William Henry. *The American Woman: Her Changing Social, Economic, and Political Roles, 1920–1970.* New York: Oxford University Press, 1972.

Cherny, Robert W. *Populism, Progressivism, and the Transformation of Nebraska Politics, 1885–1915.* Lincoln: University of Nebraska Press, 1981.

Chilcote, Paul Wesley. *John Wesley and the Women Preachers of Early Methodism.* Metuchen, N.J.: American Theological Library Association and Scarecrow Press, 1991.

Chittenden, Hiram Martin. *History of Early Steamboat Navigation on the Missouri River.* New York: F. P. Harper, 1903.

Church, Robert L., and Michael W. Sedlak. *Education in the United States: An Interpretive History.* New York: Free Press, 1976.

Clarke, Edward H. *Sex in Education; or, A Fair Chance for the Girls.* Boston: James R. Osgood, 1873.

Cleveland, Grover. "Woman's Mission and Woman's Clubs." *Ladies' Home Journal* 22, no. 6 (May 1905): 3–4.

Clinton, Catherine. *The Plantation Mistress: Woman's World in the Old South.* New York: Pantheon Books, 1982.

Cohen, Judith R. *The Mayflower Hotel: Grande Dame of Washington, D.C.* New York: Balance House, 1987.

"Coinage: The Mints Grind Out Millions of Shiny New Pieces." *Newsweek* 4 (December 15, 1934): 31–32.

Conrad, Georgia Bryan. *Reminiscences of a Southern Woman.* Hampton, Va.: Hampton Institute Press, 1902.

Conte, Robert S. "Romance at White Sulphur Springs." *Virginia Country,* July/Aug. 1984, 21–23.

Cook, Blanche Wiesen. *Eleanor Roosevelt.* London: Bloomsbury Publishing, 1993.

Cooke, John Esten. "The White Sulphur Springs." *Harpers* 57 (1878): 337–56.

Cordier, Mary Hurlbut. *Schoolwomen of the Prairies and Plains: Personal*

Narratives from Iowa, Kansas, and Nebraska, 1860s–1920s. Albuquerque: University of New Mexico Press, 1992.

Costin, Lela B. *Two Sisters for Social Justice: A Biography of Grace and Edith Abbott.* Urbana: University of Illinois Press, 1983.

Cott, Nancy F. *The Bonds of Womanhood: "Woman's Sphere" in New England, 1780–1835.* New Haven: Yale University Press, 1977.

———. "What's in a Name? The Limits of 'Social Feminism'; or, Expanding the Vocabulary of Women's History." *Journal of American History* 76, no. 3 (December 1989): 809–19.

Craig, Douglas R. *After Wilson: The Struggle for the Democratic Party, 1920–1934.* Chapel Hill: University of North Carolina Press, 1992.

Croly, Mrs. J. C. *The History of the Woman's Club Movement in America.* New York: H. G. Allen, 1898.

Dahlgren, Mary B. "Fifty Years of Service: History of the Wyoming Federation of Women's Clubs, 1904 to 1954." Master's thesis, University of Wyoming, 1956.

Daniels, Roger. *Not Like Us: Immigrants and Minorities in America, 1890–1924.* Chicago: Ivan R. Dee, 1997.

Davis, Kenneth S. *Kansas: A Bicentennial History.* New York: Norton, 1976.

Deland, Margaret. "The Change in the Feminine Ideal." *Atlantic Monthly* 105, no. 3 (March 1910): 289–302.

Democratic National Committee. *Official Report of the Proceedings of the Democratic National Convention, Held at Chicago, Illinois, June 27–July 2, 1932.* Chicago: n.p., 1932.

———. *Official Report of the Proceedings of the Democratic National Convention, Held at Houston, Texas, June 26, 27, 28, and 29, 1928.* Indianapolis: Bookwalter-Ball-Greathouse Printing, 1928.

Donnelly, Thomas C., ed. *Rocky Mountain Politics.* Albuquerque: University of New Mexico Press, 1940.

Dorn, Sherman. *A Brief History of Peabody College.* Nashville: Peabody College of Vanderbilt University, 1996.

Dye, Thomas R. "State Legislative Politics." In *Politics in the American States: A Comparative Analysis,* ed. Jacob Herbert and Kenneth N. Vines, 151–256. Boston: Little, Brown, 1965.

Easton, Carol. "Honorable Nellie." *Westways,* November 1976, 23–25, 70.

Eggar, Rowland. "The Period of Crisis: 1933 to 1945." In *American Public Administration: Past, Present, Future,* ed. Frederick C. Mosher, 49–96. University, Ala.: University of Alabama Press, 1975.

Epstein, Barbara Leslie. *The Politics of Domesticity: Women, Evangelism, and*

Temperance in Nineteenth-Century America. Middletown, Conn.: Wesleyan University Press, 1981.

"Ex-Governor Nellie Ross—We Need a Conscience." *World's Work* 55 (February 1928): 370–72.

Faderman, Lillian. *To Believe in Women: What Lesbians Have Done for America—A History.* New York: Houghton Mifflin, 1999.

Farish, Hunter Dickinson. *The Circuit Rider Dismounts: A Social History of Southern Methodism, 1865–1900.* New York: Da Capo Press, 1969.

Farley, James A. *Behind the Ballots: The Personal History of a Politician.* New York: Harcourt, Brace, 1938.

Fass, Paula S. *The Damned and the Beautiful: American Youth in the 1920's.* New York: Oxford University Press, 1977.

———. *Outside In: Minorities and the Transformation of American Education.* New York: Oxford University Press, 1989.

Faubion, Hazel A. *Tales of Old "St. Joe" and the Frontier Days.* St. Joseph. Mo.: National League of American Pen Women, St. Joseph Branch, 1977.

Federal Writers' Project. *The WPA Guide to Washington, D.C.* Washington, D.C.: U.S. Government Printing Office, 1937. Reprint, New York: Pantheon Books, 1983.

Fellman, Michael. *Inside War: The Guerrilla Conflict in Missouri during the American Civil War.* New York: Oxford University Press, 1989.

Filbert, Preston. *The Half Not Told: The Civil War in a Frontier Town.* Mechanicsburg, Pa.: Stackpole Books, 2001.

Fink, Deborah. *Agrarian Women: Wives and Mothers in Rural Nebraska, 1880–1940.* Chapel Hill: University of North Carolina Press, 1992.

Fisher, Marguerite J., and Betty Whitehead. "Women and National Party Organization." *American Political Science Review* 38 (October 1944): 895–903.

Flexner, Eleanor. *Century of Struggle: The Woman's Rights Movement in the United States.* Cambridge: Belknap Press of Harvard University Press, 1975.

Flynn, Shirley E. *Our Heritage: 100 Years at St. Mark's Episcopal Church, Cheyenne, Wyoming.* Cheyenne: Pioneer Printing, 1968.

Foner, Eric. *Reconstruction: America's Unfinished Revolution, 1863–1877.* New York: Harper and Row, 1988.

"Fooling the Women in Politics." *Ladies' Home Journal* 40 (September 1923): 29, 159–60.

Fox-Genovese, Elizabeth. *Within the Plantation Household: Black and White Women of the Old South.* Chapel Hill: University of North Carolina Press, 1988.

Frazer, Elizabeth. "Here We Are—Use Us." *Good Housekeeping* 71 (September 1920): 161.

Freeman, J. Leiper. *The Political Process: Executive Bureau-Legislative Committee Relations.* Garden City, N.Y.: Doubleday, 1955.

Friedan, Betty. *The Feminine Mystique.* New York: Dell, 1963.

Furman, Bess. *Washington By-Line: The Personal History of a Newspaperwoman.* New York: Alfred A. Knopf, 1949.

Gale, Zona. "Katytown in the Eighties." *Harper's* 157 (August 1928): 288–94.

Gardner, A. Dudley. *Forgotten Frontier: A History of Wyoming Coal Mining.* Boulder, Colo.: Westview Press, 1989.

Garner, Nancy G. "For God and Home and Native Land: The Kansas Woman's Christian Temperance Union, 1878–1938." Ph.D. diss., University of Kansas, 1994.

Garraty, John A. *The American Nation: A History of the United States.* 2d ed. New York: Harper and Row, 1971.

Garrison, Dee. "Two Roads Taken: Writing the Biography of Mary Heaton Vorse." In Alpern et al., *Challenge of Feminist Biography,* 65–78.

Gawthrop, Louis C. *Bureaucratic Behavior in the Executive Branch: An Analysis of Organizational Change.* New York: Free Press, 1969.

George, Elsie L. "The Women Appointees of the Roosevelt and Truman Administrations: A Study of Their Impact and Effectiveness." Ph.D. diss., American University, 1972.

Gibbons, J. Cardinal. "The Restless Woman." *Ladies' Home Journal* 19, no. 2 (January 1902): 6.

Gifford, Carolyn De Swarte. *Writing Out My Heart: Selections from the Journal of Frances E. Willard, 1855–96.* Urbana: University of Illinois Press, 1995.

Graff, Harvey J. *Conflicting Paths: Growing Up in America.* Cambridge: Harvard University Press, 1995.

Green, Constance McLaughlin. *The Secret City: A History of Race Relations in the Nation's Capitol.* Princeton: Princeton University Press, 1967.

Grenier, Mildred B. *St. Joseph: A Pictorial History.* Virginia Beach: Donning, 1981.

Groves, Ernest Rutherford, and William Fielding Ogburn. *American Marriage and Family Relationships.* New York: Henry Holt, 1928.

Gulick, Luther, and Lyndall Urwich, eds. *Papers on the Science of Administration.* New York: Institute of Public Administration, 1937.

Hardyment, Christina. *Dream Babies: Child Care from Locke to Spock.* London: Jonathan Cape, 1983.

Harris, Joseph P. "The Governors' Conference: Retrospect and Prospect." *State Government* 31 (summer 1958): 190–96.

Harris, Ted Carlton. "Jeannette Rankin: Suffragist, First Woman Elected to Congress, and Pacifist." Ph.D. diss., University of Georgia, 1972.

Harrison, Harry P. *Culture under Canvas: The Story of Tent Chautauqua.* New York: Hastings House, 1958.

"Harry's Friend John." *Newsweek* 27 (June 24, 1946): 33.

Harvey, Donald R. *The Civil Service Commission.* New York: Praeger Publishers, 1970.

Hatch, Nathan O., ed. *The Professions in American History.* Notre Dame, Ind.: University of Notre Dame Press, 1988.

Hawes, Joseph M. *Children between the Wars: American Childhood, 1920–1940.* New York: Twayne Publishers, 1997.

Hebard, Grace Raymond. *The Government of Wyoming: The History, Constitution, and Administration of Affairs.* 7th ed. San Francisco: C. F. Weber, 1917.

Heclo, Hugh. *A Government of Strangers: Executive Politics in Washington.* Washington, D.C.: Brookings Institution Press, 1977.

Heller, Trudy. *Women and Men as Leaders: In Business, Educational, and Social Service Organizations.* New York: Praeger Publishers, 1982.

Hendricks, Cecilia Hennel. "When a Woman Governor Campaigns." *Scribners* 81 (July 1928): 81–91.

Herbert, Jacob, and Kenneth N. Vines, eds. *Politics in the American States: A Comparative Analysis.* Boston: Little, Brown, 1965.

Hewlett, Sylvia Ann. *Creating a Life: Professional Women and the Quest for Children.* New York: Talk Miramax Books, 2002.

History of Andrew and DeKalb Counties, Missouri, from the Earliest Time to the Present. [Reprint of *Godspeed's 1888 History of Andrew and DeKalb Counties.*] Greenville, S.C.: Southern Historical Press, 1998.

Hoff, Joan. *Law, Gender, and Injustice: A Legal History of U.S. Women.* New York: New York University, 1991.

Hoffschwelle, Mary S. "Women's Sphere and the Creation of Female Community in the Antebellum South: Three Tennessee Slaveholding Women." *Tennessee Historical Quarterly* 50, no. 2 (1991): 80–89.

Hofstadter, Richard. *The Age of Reform: From Bryan to F.D.R.* New York: Vintage Books, 1955.

Hollibaugh, E. F. *Biographical History of Cloud County, Kansas.* N.p., 1903.

Holt, Charles F. "Who Benefited from the Prosperity of the Twenties?" *Explorations in Economic History* 14, no. 3 (July 1977): 277–89.

Hunter, Louis C. *Steamboats on the Western Rivers.* New York: Octagon Books, 1969.

Hurt, R. Douglas. *Agriculture and Slavery in Missouri's Little Dixie.* Columbia: University of Missouri Press, 1992.

Ickes, Harold L. *The Secret Diary of Harold L. Ickes: The First Thousand Days, 1933–1936.* New York: Simon and Schuster, 1953.

Jackson, Robert M. *Destined for Equality: The Inevitable Rise of Women's Status.* Cambridge: Harvard University Press, 1998.

Jacob, Herbert. *Politics in the American States: A Comparative Analysis.* Boston: Little, Brown, 1965.

Jorgenson, Lloyd P. "Agricultural Expansion into the Semiarid Lands of the West North Central States during the First World War." *Agricultural History* 23 (January 1949): 30–41.

Kahn, Jonathan. *Budgeting Democracy: State Building and Citizenship in America, 1890–1928.* Ithaca: Cornell University Press, 1997.

Kallenbach, Joseph E., and Jessamine S. Kallenbach. *American State Governors, 1776–1976.* Vol. 1. Dobbs Ferry, N.Y.: Oceana Publications, 1977.

Kane, Joseph N. *Famous First Facts: A Record of First Happenings, Discoveries, and Inventions in American History.* New York : H. W. Wilson, 1981.

Kaufman, Herbert. *The Administrative Behavior of Federal Bureau Chiefs.* Washington, D.C.: U.S. Government Printing Office, 1981.

Kennedy, Susan Estabrook. "Frances Perkins." In *American National Biography,* ed. John A. Garraty and Mark C. Carnes, 339–41. New York: Oxford University Press, 1999.

Kirby, James E., Russell E. Richey, and Kenneth E. Rowe. *The Methodists.* Westport, Conn.: Praeger, 1998.

Lamm, Richard D., and Michael McCarthy. *The Angry West: A Vulnerable Land and Its Future.* Boston: Houghton Mifflin, 1982.

Langum, David J., and Howard P. Walthall. *From Maverick to Mainstream: Cumberland School of Law, 1847–1997.* Athens: University of Georgia Press, 1997.

Larson, T. A. *History of Wyoming.* 2d ed., revised. Lincoln: University of Nebraska Press, 1978.

———. *Wyoming: A Bicentennial History.* New York: Norton, 1977.

Lash, Joseph P. *Eleanor and Franklin: The Story of Their Relationship Based on Eleanor Roosevelt's Private Papers.* New York: Norton, 1971.

Lewis, Tom. *Empire of the Air: The Men Who Made Radio.* New York: Edward Burlingame Books, 1991.

Lichtman, Allan J. *Prejudice and the Old Politics: The Presidential Election of 1928.* Chapel Hill: University of North Carolina Press, 1979.

Lindeman, Eduard C. "After Lyceum and Chautauqua, What?" *Bookman* 65 (May 1927): 246–50.

Link, Arthur S. *American Epoch: A History of the United States since the 1890's.* 2d ed. New York: Alfred A. Knopf, 1963.

Lipson, Leslie. *The American Governor from Figurehead to Leader.* New York: Greenwood Press, 1939.

Lynd, Robert S., and Helen Merrell Lynd. *Middletown: A Study in Modern American Culture.* New York: Harcourt, Brace and World, 1929.

MacCorkle, William Alexander. *The White Sulphur Springs.* New York: Neale Publishing, 1916.

Mackey, Mike. *Black Gold: Patterns in the Development of Wyoming's Oil Industry.* Casper, Wyo.: Western History Publications, 1997.

MacLaren, Gay. *Morally We Roll Along.* Boston: Little, Brown, 1938.

Macmahon, Arthur W., and John D. Millett. *Federal Administrators: A Biographical Approach to the Problem of Departmental Management.* New York: Columbia University Press, 1939. Reprint, New York: AMS Press, 1967.

Macy, John. "Equality of Woman with Man: A Myth." *Harper's* 153 (November 1926): 705–13.

Maranto, Robert, and David Schultz. *A Short History of the United States Civil Service.* Lanham, Md.: University Press of America, 1991.

Marshall, Brenda DeVore, and Molly A. Mayhead, eds. *Navigating Boundaries: The Rhetoric of Women Governors.* Westport, Conn.: Prager Publishers, 2000.

Martin, Anne. "Women and 'Their' Magazines." *New Republic* 20 (September 20, 1922): 91–93.

Martin, George. *Madam Secretary, Frances Perkins.* Boston: Houghton Mifflin, 1976.

Marx, Fritz Morstein. "The Departmental System." In *Elements of Public Administration,* 2d ed., 169–90. Englewood Cliffs, N.J.: Prentice-Hall, 1959.

McCandless, Perry. *A History of Missouri: Volume II, 1820 to 1860.* Columbia: University of Missouri Press, 1971.

McGerr, Michael E. *A Fierce Discontent: The Rise and Fall of the Progressive Movement in America, 1870–1920.* New York: Free Press, 2003.

McKinley, Charles. "Federal Administrative Pathology and thc Separation of Powers." *Public Administration Review* 11, no. 1 (winter 1951): 17–25.

McMath, Robert C., Jr. *American Populism: A Social History, 1877–1898.* New York: Hill and Wang, 1993.

McMillin, Lucille Foster. *Women in the Federal Service.* 3d ed. [Civil Service

Commission booklet.] Washington, D.C.: U.S. Government Printing Office, 1941.

McReynolds, Edwin C. *Missouri: A History of the Crossroads State.* Norman: University of Oklahoma Press, 1962.

Melder, Keith. *City of Magnificent Intentions: A History of Washington, District of Columbia.* 2d ed. Washington, D.C.: Intac, 1977.

Merrick, Caroline E. *Old Times in Dixie Land: A Southern Matron's Memories.* New York: Grafton Press, 1901.

Miltonvale: Record, Biography, Reminiscence. Compiled by Fannie Palmer. Copy in Frank Carlson Library, Condordia, Kans. N.p., 1959.

Mintz, Steven, and Susan Kellogg. *Domestic Revolutions: A Social History of American Family Life.* New York: Free Press, 1988.

Modell, John, and Tamara K. Hareven. "Urbanization and the Malleable Household: An Examination of Boarding and Lodging in American Families." *Journal of Marriage and the Family* 35, no. 3 (August 1973): 467–79.

Monaghan, Jay. *Civil War on the Western Border, 1854–1865.* Boston, Little, Brown, 1955. Reprint, Lincoln: University of Nebraska Press, 1985.

Morgan, Ezra R. "Miltonvale: The Western Terminus of the Narrow Gauge, to 1910." Master's thesis, Kansas State College of Agriculture and Applied Science, 1956.

Morgenthau, Henry, III. *Mostly Morgenthaus: A Family History.* New York: Ticknor and Fields, 1991.

Morrison, Glenda E. "Women's Participation in the 1928 Presidential Campaign." Ph.D. diss., University of Kansas, 1978.

"Mrs. Moneybags." *Newsweek* 21 (April 12, 1945), 41–44.

Munslow, Alun. "The Progressive Era, 1900–1919." In *America's Century: Perspectives on U.S. History since 1900,* ed. Iwan W. Morgan and Neil A. Wynn, 14–45. New York: Holmes and Meier, 1993.

Murdock, Maggie. "Responding to Crises: Change in Wyoming's State Government." In *Wyoming Blue Book,* vol. 4, ed. Loren Jost, 16–22. Cheyenne: Wyoming State Archives, 1991.

Myres, Sandra L. *Westering Women and the Frontier Experience, 1800–1915.* Albuquerque: University of New Mexico Press, 1982.

Nagel, Paul C. *Missouri: A Bicentennial History.* New York: Norton, 1977.

National Governors' Association. "A Day in the Life of a Governor." [Excerpted from *Governing the American States—A Handbook for New Governors.*] *State Government* 52 (summer 1979): 110–16.

———. *Governing the American States: A Handbook for New Governors.*

Washington, D.C.: National Governors' Association Center for Policy Research, 1978.

Nelson, Earl J. "The Passing of Slavery in Missouri." Master's thesis, University of Missouri, 1932.

Nelson, Michael. "A Short, Ironic History of American National Bureaucracy." *Journal of Politics* 44 (2): 747–78.

Neustadt, Richard E. "Presidency and Legislation: Planning the President's Program." *Political Science Review* 49, no. 4 (December 1955): 980–1021.

———. "Presidency and Legislation: The Growth of Central Clearance." *Political Science Review* 48, no. 3 (September 1954): 641–71.

Newell, Margaretta. "Must Women Fight in Politics?" *Woman's Journal* (January 1930): 10–11, 34–35.

Newquist, Gloria Winden. "James A. Farley and the Politics of Victory, 1928–1936." Ph.D. diss., University of Southern California, 1966.

Noggle, Burl. *Teapot Dome: Oil and Politics in the 1920s.* Westport, Conn.: Greenwood Press, 1962.

O'Neill, William L. *Everyone Was Brave: The Rise and Fall of Feminism in America.* Chicago: Quadrangle Books, 1971.

———. *Feminism in America: A History.* 2d ed. New Brunswick, N.J.: Transaction Publishers, 1989.

"One of Two of a Kind." *Fortune* 9, no. 5 (May 1934): 60–64, 131–38.

Ostler, Jeffrey. *Prairie Populism: The Fate of Agrarian Radicalism in Kansas, Nebraska, and Iowa, 1880–1892.* Lawrence: University Press of Kansas, 1993.

Painter, Nell I. *Standing at Armageddon: The United States, 1877–1919.* New York: Norton, 1987.

Palmer, Edgar Z. "The Correctness of the 1890 Census of Population for Nebraska Cities." *Nebraska History* 32, no. 4 (December 1951): 259–67.

Parrish, Michael E. *Anxious Decades: America in Prosperity and Depression, 1920–1941.* New York: Norton, 1992.

Parrish, William E. *A History of Missouri: Volume III, 1860 to 1875.* Columbia: University of Missouri Press, 1973.

———. *Missouri under Radical Rule, 1865–1870.* Columbia: University of Missouri Press, 1965.

Pegram, Thomas R. *Battling Demon Rum: The Struggle for a Dry America, 1800–1933.* Chicago: Ivan R. Dee, 1998.

Peirce, Neal R. *The Mountain States of America: People, Politics, and Power in the Eight Rocky Mountain States.* New York: Norton, 1972.

Pendergast, Tom. *Creating the Modern Man: American Magazines and Consumer Culture, 1900–1950.* Columbia: University of Missouri Press, 2000.

Perkins, Frances. *The Roosevelt I Knew.* New York: Viking Press, 1946.

Perry, Elisabeth I. *Belle Moskowitz: Feminine Politics and the Exercise of Power.* New York: Oxford University Press, 1987.

Peterson, Henry J. "Wyoming: A Cattle Kingdom." In *Rocky Mountain Politics,* ed. Thomas C. Donnelly, 115–49. Albuquerque: University of New Mexico Press, 1940.

Phillips, Christopher. *Missouri's Confederate: Claiborne Fox Jackson and the Creation of Southern Identity in the Border West.* Columbia: University of Missouri Press, 2000.

Pierce, Jennifer Burek. "Portrait of a 'Governor Lady': An Examination of Nellie Tayloe Ross's Autobiographical Political Advocacy." In *Navigating Boundaries: The Rhetoric of Women Governors,* ed. M. Mayhead and B. DeVore Marshall, 31–44. Westport, Conn.: Praeger, 2000.

Portrait and Biographical Record of Buchanan and Clinton Counties, Missouri. Chicago: Chapman Bros., 1893.

Pratt, Ruth Baker. "The Lady or the Tiger." *Ladies' Home Journal* 45 (May 1928): 8, 119.

President's Committee on Administrative Management. *Administrative Management in the Government of the United States.* Washington, D.C.: U.S. Government Printing Office, 1937.

———. *Fiscal Management in the National Government.* Washington, D.C.: U.S. Government Printing Office, 1937.

———. *Problems of Administrative Management.* Washington, D.C.: U.S. Government Printing Office, 1937.

Purchase, Ian. "Normalcy, Prosperity, and Depression, 1919–1933." In *America's Century: Perspectives on U.S. History since 1900,* ed. Iwan W. Morgan and Neil A. Wynn, 46–79. New York: Holmes and Meier, 1993.

Ransone, Coleman B., Jr. *The American Governorship.* Westport, Conn.: Greenwood Press, 1982.

Read, Phyllis J. *The Book of Women's Firsts.* New York: Random House, 1992.

Reeves, Thomas C. *Twentieth-Century America: A Brief History.* New York: Oxford University Press, 2000.

Reminiscences of the Women of Missouri during the Sixties. Ed. United Daughters of the Confederacy, Missouri Division. Jefferson City, Mo.: Hugh Stephens Printing, 1913.

"Revolution of 1933." *Newsweek* 1 (May 6, 1933), 3–5.

Rice, Stuart A., and Malcolm M. Wiley. "American Women's Ineffective Use of the Vote." *Current History* 20 (July 1924): 641–47.

Richard, John B. *Government and Politics of Wyoming.* 3d ed. Dubuque, Iowa: Kendall/Hunt, 1974.

Richmond, Robert W. *Kansas: A Land of Contrasts.* 3d ed. Arlington Heights, Ill.: Forum Press, 1989.

Rigby, Cora. "The Democrats at Houston." *Woman's Journal* 13, no. 8 (August 1928): 10–12, 29–30.

Riley, Glenda. *The Female Frontier: A Comparative View of Women on the Prairie and the Plains.* Lawrence: University Press of Kansas, 1988.

Roitman, Joel M. "The Progressive Movement: Education and Americanization." Ph.D. diss., University of Cincinnati, 1981.

Roland, Alan, and Barbara Harris, eds. *Career and Motherhood: Struggles for a New Identity.* New York: Human Sciences Press, 1979.

Roosevelt, Anna E. *This I Remember.* New York: Harper and Row, 1949.

———. "Women Must Learn to Play the Game as Men Do." *Red Book Magazine* 50 (April 1928): 78–79, 141–42.

Roosevelt, Elliott, ed. *F.D.R.: His Personal Letters.* Vol. 1. New York: Duell, Sloan and Pearce, 1948.

Roosevelt, Theodore. *An Autobiography.* New York: Charles Scribner's Sons, 1924.

Ross, Ishbel. *Grace Coolidge and Her Era.* New York: Dodd, Mead, 1962.

Ross, James. *The Life and Times of Elder Reuben Ross.* Philadelphia: Grant, Faires and Rodgers, 1882.

Rothman, Sheila M. *Woman's Proper Place: A History of Changing Ideals and Practices, 1870 to the Present.* New York: Basic Books, 1978.

Rotundo, E. Anthony. *American Manhood: Transformations in Masculinity from the Revolution to the Modern Era.* New York: Basic Books, 1993.

Ryan, Mary P. *The Empire of the Mother: American Writing about Domesticity, 1830–1860.* New York: Harrington Park Press, 1985.

Sabato, Larry. *Goodbye to Good-Time Charlie: The American Governorship Transformed.* 2d ed. Washington, D.C.: CQ Press, 1983.

Samson, Walter L., Jr. "The Political Career of Senator Francis E. Warren, 1920–1929." M.A. thesis, University of Wyoming, 1951.

Scharf, Lois. "'The Forgotten Woman': Working Women, the New Deal, and Women's Organizations." In *Decades of Discontent: The Women's Movement, 1920–1940,* ed. Lois Scharf and Joan M. Jenson, 243–59. Westport, Conn.: Greenwood Press, 1983.

Scheer, Teva J. "Feminine Pioneer: Nellie Tayloe Ross, First Woman Governor."

In *Outstanding Women in Public Administration: Leaders, Mentors, and Pioneers,* ed. Claire L. Felbinger and Wendy A. Haynes, 65–80. Armonk, N.Y.: M. E. Sharpe, 2004.

———. "The 'Praxis' Side of the Equation: Club Women and American Public Administration." *Administrative Theory and Praxis* 24, no. 3 (September 2002): 519–36.

Schiesl, Martin. *The Politics of Efficiency: Municipal Administration and Reform in America, 1800–1920.* Berkeley: University of California Press, 1977.

Schlereth, Thomas J. *Victorian America: Transformations in Everyday Life, 1876–1915.* New York: HarperCollins, 1991.

Schlesinger, Joseph A. *How They Became Governor: A Study of Comparative State Politics, 1870–1950.* East Lansing: Governmental Research Bureau, Michigan State University, 1957.

Schneider, Dorothy, and Carl J. Schneider. *American Women in the Progressive Era, 1900–1920.* New York: Facts on File Books, 1993.

Schneider, Miriam, ed. *Feminism in Our Time: The Essential Writings, World War II to the Present.* New York: Vintage Books, 1994.

Schriber, Mary Suzanne, ed. *Telling Travels: Selected Writings by Nineteenth-Century American Women Abroad.* DeKalb: Northern Illinois University Press, 1995.

Schuler, Loring A. "The Moral Issue." *Ladies' Home Journal* 45 (November 1928): 32.

Scott, Anne Firor. *The Southern Lady: From Pedestal to Politics, 1830–1930.* Chicago: University of Chicago Press, 1970.

Sealander, Judith. *As Minority Becomes Majority: Federal Reaction to the Phenomenon of Women in the Work Force, 1920–1963.* Westport, Conn.: Greenwood Press, 1983.

Shapiro, Laura. *Perfection Salad: Women and Cooking at the Turn of the Century.* New York: Farrar, Straus and Giroux, 1986.

Shoemaker, Floyd Calvin. *Missouri and Missourians: Land of Contrasts and People of Achievements.* Chicago: Lewis Publishing, 1943.

Sigourney, L. H. "Intellectual Bouquet." *Patriarch* 1, no. 4 (1841): 177–80.

Silverberg, Helene, ed. *Gender and American Social Science: The Formative Years.* Princeton: Princeton University Press, 1998.

Simpson, Jeffrey. *Chautauqua: An American Utopia.* New York: Harry N. Abrams, 1999.

Simpson, Matthew. *A Hundred Years of Methodism.* New York: Phillips and Hunt, 1881.

Sklar, Kathryn Kish. "Coming to Terms with Florence Kelley: The Tale of a Reluctant Biographer." In Alpern et al., *Challenge of Feminist Biography,* 17–33.

Smith, Alfred E. *Up to Now: An Autobiography.* Garden City, N.Y.: Garden City Publishing, 1929.

Smith, Duane A. *Rocky Mountain West: Colorado, Wyoming, and Montana, 1859–1915.* Albuquerque: University of New Mexico Press, 1992.

Smith, Michael E. "Bureau Chiefs in the Federal Government, 1958." In *Public Policy, 1960,* 62–91. Cambridge: Harvard University, Graduate School of Public Administration, 1960.

Snyder, Agnes. *Dauntless Women in Childhood Education, 1856–1931.* Washington, D.C.: Association for Childhood Education International, 1972.

Sochen, June. *Herstory: A Record of the American Woman's Past.* 2d ed. Palo Alto: Mayfield Publishing, 1982.

———. *Movers and Shakers: American Women Thinkers and Activists, 1900–1970.* New York: Quadrangle/New York Times, 1973.

Springen, Donald K. *William Jennings Bryan: Orator of Small-Town America.* New York: Greenwood Press, 1991.

Stephens, Louisa. *Golden Adventure: A Diary of Long Ago.* Pasadena, Calif.: San Pascual Books, 1941.

Stewart, Eliza D. *Memories of the Crusade.* Columbus, Ohio: William G. Hubbard, 1889.

Strasser, Susan. *Never Done: A History of American Housework.* New York: Pantheon Books, 1982.

Stratton, Joanna L. *Pioneer Women: Voices from the Kansas Frontier.* New York: Simon and Schuster, 1981.

Stricker, Frank. "Affluence for Whom? Another Look at Prosperity and the Working Classes in the 1920s." *Labor History* 24, no. 1 (winter 1983): 5–33.

Strouse, Jean. *Alice James: A Biography.* New York: Bantam Books, 1980.

———. *Morgan: An American Financier.* New York: Random House, 1999.

Sullivan, Mark, Jr. *Our Times: America at the Birth of the Twentieth Century.* Ed. Dan Rather. New York: Scribner, 1996.

Taeuber, Conrad, and Irene B. Taeuber. *The Changing Population of the United States.* New York: John Wiley and Sons, 1958.

Tapia, John E. *Circuit Chautauqua.* Jefferson, N.C.: McFarland, 1997.

Taxay, Don. *The U.S. Mint and Coinage: An Illustrated History from 1776 to the Present.* New York: Arco, 1966.

Taylor, Marie. *Proud Early American Settlers.* Baltimore: Gateway Press, 1976.

Taylor, Paul C. "The Entrance of Women into Party Politics: The 1920's." Ph.D. diss., Harvard University, 1966.

Theriot, Nancy M. *Mothers and Daughters in Nineteenth-Century America: The Biosocial Construction of Femininity.* Lexington: University of Kentucky Press, 1996.

Trenholm, Virginia Cole, ed. *Wyoming Blue Book.* Vols. 2 and 4. Cheyenne: Wyoming State Archives and Historical Department, 1974.

Tresler [*sic*], Harrison A. "The Value and the Sale of the Missouri Slave." *Missouri Historical Review* 8 (January 1914): 69–85.

Trimble, Sarah Ridley, ed. "Behind the Lines in Middle Tennessee, 1863–1865: The Journal of Bettie Ridley Blackmore." *Tennessee Historical Quarterly* 12 (1953): 48–80.

U.S. Bureau of the Census. *Compendium of the Eleventh Census: 1890.* Pt. 1, Population.

———. *Compendium of the Tenth Census.* 1880, pt. 1.

———. *Population of the United States in 1860, Compiled from the Original Returns of the Eighth Census.*

———. *The Statistics of the Population of the United States, Embracing the Tables of Race, Nationality, Sex, Selected Ages, and Occupations.* 9th census, 1870, vol. 1.

———. *Statistics of the Population of the United States at the Tenth Census.* 1880.

———. *The Statistics of the Wealth and Industry of the United States.* 9th census, 1870, vol. 3.

———. *Twelfth Census of the United States, 1900.* Vol. 1, Population.

U.S. Bureau of the Mint. *Annual Report[s] of the Director of the Mint, 1933–1952.* Washington, D.C.: U.S. Government Printing Office.

U.S. Congress. *Congressional Record: Proceedings and Debates of the 78th Congress, 1st Session.* Washington, D.C.: U.S. Government Printing Office, 1943.

U.S. Congress. *Congressional Record: Proceedings and Debates of the 3d Session of the 75th Congress.* Washington, D.C.: U.S. Government Printing Office, 1938.

U.S. Congress. House. *Hearings before a Subcommittee of the Committee on Appropriations.* (1938 Appropriations) 75th Cong., 1st sess., 1937.

———. *Hearings before a Subcommittee of the Committee on Appropriations.* (1939 Appropriations) 75th Cong., 3d sess., 1938.

———. *Hearings before a Subcommittee of the Committee on Appropriations.* (1950 Appropriations) 81st Cong., 2d sess., 1949.

———. *Hearings before a Subcommittee of the Committee on Appropriations.* (1951 Appropriations) 81st Cong., 2d sess., 1950.

———. *Hearings before a Subcommittee of the Committee on Appropriations.* (1952 Appropriations) 82d Cong., 1st sess., 1951.

U.S. Congress. Senate. *Hearings before the Committee on Banking and Currency.* 77th Cong., 2d sess., 1942. S. 2889.

U.S. Department of Labor, Women's Bureau. "Employment of Women in the Federal Government, 1923 to 1929." Bulletin #182. 1941.

———. "The Status of Women in Government Service in 1925." Bulletin #53. 1926.

———. "Women in the Federal Service, 1923–1947: Trends in Employment." Bulletin #230-I. 1949.

———. "Women in the Federal Service: Occupational Information." Bulletin #230-II. 1950.

———. "Women's Occupation through Seven Decades." Bulletin #218. 1947.

Ustick, Mrs. S. E. "An Incident of the Civil War." In *Reminiscences of the Women of Missouri during the Sixties,* ed. United Daughters of the Confederacy, Missouri Division, 35–42. Jefferson City, Mo.: Hugh Stephens Printing, 1913.

Van Nuys, Frank. *Americanizing the West: Race, Immigrants, and Citizenship, 1890–1930.* Lawrence: University Press of Kansas, 2002.

Van Riper, Paul P. *History of the United States Civil Service.* Evanston, Ill.: Row, Peterson, 1958.

Walkley, Christina, and Vanda Foster. *Crinolines and Crimping Irons: Victorian Clothes, How They Were Cleaned and Cared For.* London: Peter Owen Limited, 1978.

Warbasse, Elizabeth Bowles. *The Changing Legal Rights of Married Women, 1860–1861.* New York: Garland, 1987.

Ward, Paul W. "Henry Morgenthau and His Friends." *Nation* 141 (August 14, 1935): 182–84.

Ware, Susan. *Beyond Suffrage: Women in the New Deal.* Cambridge: Harvard University Press, 1981.

———. *Partner and I: Molly Dewson, Feminism, and New Deal Politics.* New Haven: Yale University Press, 1987.

———. "Unlocking the Porter-Dewson Partnership: A Challenge for the Feminist Biographer." In Alpern et al., *Challenge of Feminist Biography,* 51–64.

Watts, Wellington. "Mrs. Money." *Family Circle,* July 1950, 21, 70–74.

Welter, Barbara. "The Cult of True Womanhood: 1820–1860." *American Quarterly* 18 (summer 1966): 151–74.

Wexler, Alice. "Emma Goldman and the Anxiety of Biography." In Alpern et al., *Challenge of Feminist Biography*, 34–50.

Wheeler, Henry. *Methodism and the Temperance Reformation.* New York: Phillips and Hunt, 1882.

White, Leonard Dupree. *Introduction to the Study of Public Administration.* 4th ed. New York: Macmillan, 1954.

———. *Trends in Public Administration.* New York: McGraw-Hill, 1933.

White, Richard. *"It's Your Misfortune and None of My Own": A History of the American West.* Norman: University of Oklahoma Press, 1991.

Wiggam, Albert E. "Is the Chautauqua Worthwhile?" *Bookman* 65 (June 1927): 399–406.

"Woman's 'Bigger Dent in Politics.'" *Literary Digest* 83, no. 3 (November 22, 1924): 17.

Woods, Milton L. *Sometimes the Books Froze: Wyoming's Economy and Its Banks.* Boulder: Colorado Associated University Press, 1985.

Wrobel, David M. *The End of American Exceptionalism: Frontier Anxiety from the Old West to the New Deal.* Lawrence: University Press of Kansas, 1993.

"Yes, That Gold Hoard Exists, and It's Scattered over U.S." *Newsweek* 15 (March 11, 1940): 50–51.

Young, William H. "The Development of the Governorship." *State Government* 31 (summer 1958): 181–83.

Zornow, William Frank. *Kansas: A History of the Jayhawk State.* Norman: University of Oklahoma Press, 1957.

Index

About the Author

Teva Scheer earned a Ph.D. from the University of Colorado in 2000. *Governor Lady* was nominated for best biography in 2001 by the Colorado Book Awards (Colorado Endowment for the Humanities). Teva and her husband live outside Victoria, British Columbia, where she writes, teaches, and gardens.